THE
PRESIDENT'S
HOUSE

Also by Margaret Truman

First Ladies
Bess W. Truman
Souvenir
Women of Courage
Harry S Truman
Letters from Father:
The Truman Family's Personal Correspondences
Where the Buck Stops
White House Pets

IN THE CAPITAL CRIMES SERIES
Murder at the Watergate
Murder in the House
Murder at the National Gallery
Murder on the Potomac
Murder at the Pentagon
Murder in the Smithsonian
Murder at the National Cathedral
Murder at the Kennedy Center
Murder in the CIA
Murder in Georgetown
Murder at the FBI
Murder on Embassy Row
Murder in the Supreme Court
Murder in the White House
Murder on Capitol Hill
Murder at the Library of Congress
Murder in Foggy Bottom
Murder in Havana
Murder at Ford's Theatre

THE
PRESIDENT'S
HOUSE

*A First Daughter Shares
the History and Secrets
of the World's
Most Famous Home*

Margaret Truman

BALLANTINE BOOKS • NEW YORK

975.3

A Ballantine Book
Published by The Random House Publishing Group
Copyright © 2003 by Margaret Truman

All rights reserved under International and Pan-American Copyright Conventions.
Published in the United States by The Random House Publishing Group, a division of
Random House, Inc., New York, and simultaneously in Canada by Random House
of Canada Limited, Toronto.

www.ballantinebooks.com

Library of Congress Cataloging-in-Publication Data

Truman, Margaret, 1924–
    The president's house : a first daughter shares the history and secrets of the world's
most famous home / Margaret Truman.—1st ed.
        p. cm.
    ISBN 0-345-44452-3
    1. White House (Washington, D.C.)—History. 2. White House (Washington,
D.C.)—History—Anecdotes. 3. Presidents—United States—History—Anecdotes.
4. Presidents—United States—Biography—Anecdotes. 5. Washington (D.C.)—
Buildings, structures, etc. I. Title.

F204.W5T76 2003
973'.09'9—dc21   2003045345

Book design by Susan Turner

Manufactured in the United States of America

First Edition: November 2003

10 9 8 7 6 5 4 3 2 1

In memory of my mother and father

***

Contents

1	*Magic and Mystery in a Unique Place*	*1*
2	*From Palace to Mansion to Powerhouse*	*21*
3	*The President's Park*	*47*
4	*History Happened Here*	*71*
5	*Working the House*	*93*
6	*Womanpower*	*123*
7	*The West Wing*	*151*
8	*Frontstairs, Backstairs*	*183*
9	*Bed, Breakfast and Beyond*	*211*
10	*Growing Up Under Glass*	*233*
11	*Here Come the Brides*	*261*
12	*Talking Dogs and Other Unnatural Curiosities*	*291*
13	*Minding the Media*	*319*
14	*Keeping Killers and Kooks at Bay*	*345*
15	*The People's White House*	*371*
16	*The White House Forever*	*395*
	Presidents and Their Wives	*397*
	Index	*400*

***

Acknowledgments

A book like this can only come to life with the help of many people. I hope no one thinks I learned all these fascinating facts and stories about the White House simply by hanging around the place in my twenties! High on my gratitude list is Scott Roley, assistant director of the Harry S Truman Presidential Library, who shared with me oral histories of several of the leading players in my father's administration. At least as much appreciation goes to my old friend Pauline Testerman, the Truman Library's audiovisual archivist, who supplied me with many of the pictures that appear in these pages. An equally warm thank you to the White House Historical Association, in particular Bill Bushong, Maria Downs, and photo archivist Harmony Haskins. Barbara McMillan of the White House Curator's Office and Candace Shyreman, assistant curator of Blair House, were always generous and enthusiastic. The John F. Kennedy and Franklin D. Roosevelt presidential libraries were also notably cooperative, as was the dedicated staff of the Library of Congress. Of crucial importance was—and is—my editor, Samuel S. Vaughan, whose wise counsel and knowledge of American history kept me on the right track in matters both small and large. Finally, I would like to thank Tom and Alice Fleming for their advice and insights during the research and organization of this book.

The South Portico at twilight. I've always thought that the White House looks particularly magical in the glow of early evening. Credit: White House Historical Association

1

★★★

Magic and Mystery
in a Unique Place

The last time I was in Washington, D.C., I walked by the White House on the way to dinner at a nearby restaurant. Hidden floodlights made the historic building glow like a mansion in a vision or a dream. Suddenly I thought: *I am not the woman who lived in that house more than fifty years ago. She is a completely different person. I barely know her.*

The words whispered in my mind like a voice from another world. I was remembering, or trying to remember, what it meant to be the daughter of the president of the United States, living in that shining shimmering house. The one inescapable thing I recalled was the difference. I have lived in several houses and apartments, and spent some time in splendid establishments, including a few royal palaces. But not one of them—or all of them together—can compare to the feeling I recalled from my White House days.

That was when I resolved to write this book about one of the most mysterious, terrifying, exalting, dangerous, fascinating houses in the world. It is a house that has changed people in amazing, unexpected ways. It is a house that has broken hearts and minds. It is a house that has made some people weep when they walked out the door for the last time—and others feel like escapees from a maximum security prison. Some marriages have been saved within those pristine white walls. Others have been irrevocably ruined.

Children have played marvelously clever games inside and outside this unique piece of architecture. Other children have twisted and turned in their death throes while their weeping parents, arguably the most powerful persons on the North American continent, clutched them in their impotent arms. In those same second-floor bedrooms, radiant brides have dressed in virginal white and descended to meet loving husbands as the world applauded.

Once, one of these brides married a president. I am speaking of Frances Folsom and Grover Cleveland. A century or so ago, when I was a twenty-something, I had the pleasure of meeting Mrs. Cleveland, who told me the reason she was married in the White House instead of in her family home: Nowhere else could she and the president have their privacy guaranteed.

The old house is, to put it mildly, a paradoxical place. People who think in straight lines have a very difficult time adjusting to it. And as history has shown again and again, many of them never do. Even so, I think everyone who has ever lived in the White House would agree that it's a special experience—a unique combination of history, tragedy, comedy, melodrama, and the ups and downs of ordinary living all under one roof.

II
***

Men bearing that unique title, president of the United States, the office my father called "the greatest in the history of the world," have paced the White House's darkened halls in periods of national crisis, gazing at portraits of their predecessors on the walls, seeking communion with their triumphs—or shuddering at their blunders. Women reached out to these men, trying to offer them guidance, or at the very least solace for their awesome burdens. My mother managed to play both roles in my father's presidency—a feat too many obtuse historians and biographers have failed to recognize.

In the basement and attic rooms are the memories of the hundreds of other people who lived a large part of their working lives in this unique house, and experienced its aura of power and history. Their stories belong in this book, too. Some, I regret to say, were slaves. But the house, paradoxical as always, gradually became a place where free African-Americans demonstrated their right to equality.

Maggie Rogers began working as a White House maid when William Howard Taft became president in 1909. Her daughter, Lillian Rogers Parks, was hired as a seamstress at the White House in 1929 and worked until the end of the Eisenhower administration in 1961. Growing up, Lillian once asked her mother if she would be happier (and better paid) at some millionaire's mansion elsewhere in the capital. Maggie Rogers scorned the idea. "Heavens no, child! Be it ever so elegant, there's no place like the White House. Why, I'm living history!" There was black pride and White House pride achieving a magical fusion.

Also worth commemorating are the efforts of the dedicated, courageous, amazingly patient men who have struggled to keep presidents and their families alive in the often malevolent glare of public criticism and spasms of national hatred. We know them now as members of the Secret Service. But their predecessors are equally memorable, standing guard at the White House's doors in suits that were a size too large for them—to conceal their pistols. Most people, including some of the presidents they guarded, were unaware of those hidden weapons.

There is a side to these protectors that few people know about, much less appreciate—the many acts of kindness and thoughtfulness they perform for presidents and first ladies. Perhaps the most touching story comes from the sad days of President Woodrow Wilson's decline. Felled by a stroke, he sank into near despair as

Congress rejected his dream of world peace embodied in the League of Nations.

When the crippled president went for a ride in the afternoon, the Secret Service used to round up a small crowd of government employees and strolling tourists, who waited at the White House gate to cheer him when he returned. It was a pathetic illusion, but a testament to how much these men cared about the president.

III
★★★

Perhaps the most intriguing White House denizens are the men and women who have worked beside presidents as their spokespersons or confidential advisers. More than anyone, they often shared the reflected glow of White House power. Not all of them were able to deal with it rationally or responsibly, though the vast majority have managed it. For many of them, the experience was more than a little harrowing—and in a few cases, fatal.

I am thinking of one of my most heartbreaking White House memories—the death of my father's boyhood friend and press secretary, Charlie Ross. Charlie went through high school with Harry Truman and went on to become a top-ranked Washington, D.C., reporter for the *St. Louis Post-Dispatch*. When my father turned to him for help in 1945, Charlie gave up a comfortable salary and rational hours for the ordeal of a White House in which clocks and sensible schedules ceased to exist. Five exhausting years later, during the frantic early months of the Korean War, when newsmen besieged the White House twenty-four hours a day, Charlie Ross collapsed and died of a heart attack at his desk. A weeping Harry Truman said the country had lost a great public servant—and he had lost his best friend.

IV

★★★

That memory leads us to another cadre of White House inhabitants, although many presidents and their families might be reluctant to bestow that title on them: the men and women of the media. They, too, participate in the aura of the White House—to the point where they sometimes act as if they run the place. I had a vivid reminder of this mind-set when I came to the White House to talk with Hillary Clinton in 1994 about my book in progress, *First Ladies*.

A badly misinformed White House policeman told me to enter the mansion through the press briefing room in the West Wing. The minute I stepped through the doorway, a half dozen reporters surrounded me. Why was I there? To advise Hillary on how to improve her performance as First Lady? What did I think of Hillary's latest hairstyle? Should she hold more press conferences à la Eleanor Roosevelt, or fewer à la Bess Truman (who held none at all)? I smiled sweetly and said "No comment" to these attempts to get me to put my foot in my mouth.

My favorite White House media story comes from my friend President Gerald Ford. Gerry says he and veteran newswoman Helen Thomas were strolling on a street near the White House when he saw one of those old-fashioned scales that gave you your fortune and weight for a penny. Gerry read the little fortune card aloud: "You are a marvelous orator and leader of men. Your future in your chosen career could not be brighter."

Helen, looking over his shoulder, said: "It's got your weight wrong, too."

As the wife (now widow) of a newspaperman, I recognize the necessity for such irreverence. As the daughter of a president, I don't have to like it. But I am prepared to include it, somewhat ruefully, in the White House's story.

V
✦✦✦

The White House is far more than the place where presidents and hundreds of staffers work and presidential families live. It is also the place where America's pride and dignity as a sovereign nation are displayed. At official dinners and receptions, when the president enters the room to the U.S. Marine Band's resounding "Hail to the Chief," people recognize not only a powerful man but the nation, the United States of America. The immense amount of time and effort that presidents and first ladies and the White House staff devote to entertaining visitors from around the country and the world is a fascinating and important story. It, too, is part of the White House aura.

What a roster these visitors constitute! They range from the king and queen of England, whose snobbish servants started an uncivil war with the White House staff, to Russian grand dukes and Japanese noblemen, from world renowned politicians such as Winston Churchill, who gave himself a mild heart attack trying to open his bedroom window, to Cherokee and Creek and Sioux Indian chiefs, who did war dances on the lawn. Marvelous musicians such as pianist Vladimir Horowitz, soprano Jessye Norman, and cellist Pablo Casals (who performed for the Theodore Roosevelts in 1901 and for the John F. Kennedys sixty years later) have filled presidential ears with beautiful music. Entertainers such as Frank Sinatra and Barbra Streisand have made the place sound, for a few hours, like Broadway. Thick-necked political bosses have more than once converted the president's second-floor study or the Oval Office in the West Wing into smoke-filled rooms, where political careers were empowered—or destroyed.

VI
✦✦✦

Admission to the White House has never been restricted solely to the elite. From the earliest days, presidents recognized its symbolic

importance as a place where they greeted anyone and everyone who
wanted to come in the door. Some of these early receptions make
picturesque reading. Several turned into mob scenes that threatened to ruin the rugs and wreck the furniture—and even made one
or two chief executives fear for their lives.

Presidents and their staffs soon learned they had to set limits to
White House access if they wanted to have time to conduct the nation's business. Doorkeepers and appointments secretaries began
screening scheduled visitors. But the tradition of the White House
as the people's house lived on—and is alive and well in contemporary Washington.

You used to be able to stroll by 1600 Pennsylvania Avenue any
day you chose, rain or shine, and see a long line of tourists—part
of the million and a half Americans who streamed through the
first-floor public rooms each year. As a small *d* as well as a large *D*
democrat, that statistic has always gladdened my heart. Visiting the
White House in person is a little like meeting a celebrity face-
to-face. You get impressions and feelings that a newspaper or TV
show—or even this book—can't communicate. After the terrorist attacks of September 11, 2001, and during the war with Iraq in
the spring of 2003, tours were temporarily suspended because of
concerns about security. Group tours, which have to be arranged
in advance, were eventually reinstated. I hope it won't be too
much longer before the tours for the general public will also be
resumed.

VII
★★★

The idea that the White House is the people's house has caused
fierce quarrels every time a president or first lady tried to change
the building in any significant way. There are squadrons of unofficial custodians, and not a few official guardians, who mount the
media ramparts to hurl vituperation at the hapless first couple. John

Quincy Adams was pilloried for buying a billiard table. Millard Fillmore was attacked for putting in a bathtub.

Grace Coolidge caused an uproar when she tried to redecorate the family quarters with furniture in the style of the period in which the White House was built. Ironically, Jacqueline Kennedy did the same thing for the public rooms some thirty-eight years later and was wildly acclaimed for her efforts. When my father added a balcony to the South Portico, you would have sworn from the screams that impeachment was just around the corner.

Then there are the media and congressional snipers who are ready to open fire if they detect the slightest hint of snobbery or pretentiousness in the president's lifestyle. This has caused chief executives and first ladies no end of grief, and was largely responsible for depriving at least one president, Martin Van Buren, of a second term in the White House.

Van Buren had served as Andrew Jackson's vice president, which all by itself made him a ripe target for the Whigs (forerunners of the Republicans) who were against anyone or anything connected with Jackson. On top of that, Van Buren liked to live, dress, and entertain in style, which made it easy to cast him as a decadent aristocrat.

The opening salvo was fired at a dinner at the President's House when a Whig congressman picked up a gold spoon and announced that if he could show it to his constituents in Kentucky, they would rush to vote Van Buren out of office. The gold spoons, like most of the other furnishings, had been in the White House before Van Buren moved in, but that didn't stop another Whig congressman, Charles Ogle of Pennsylvania.

In the spring of 1840, a few months before Van Buren began his campaign for reelection, the House of Representatives was considering a bill to allot $3,665 for landscaping the grounds and repairing the furniture in the President's House. Ogle took advantage of the occasion to launch a passionate diatribe against Van Buren.

Taking his listeners on an imaginary tour of the "Presidential Palace," Ogle commented on its "regal splendor," which far exceeded "the grand saloons at Buckingham Palace. . . ." He condemned the president's bonbon stands and green glass finger bowls and assailed him for serving fancy French food instead of such old-fashioned favorites as "hog and hominy" or "fried meat and gravy."

Ogle's harangue went on for three days. In the midst of castigating Van Buren for living like a king at public expense, he managed to inject more than a few comments about the down-home virtues of the Whig presidential candidate, William Henry Harrison. The congressman's oration kicked off one of the most vitriolic campaigns in American history, and sent Martin Van Buren home to New York.

Van Buren's ordeal may have been on Franklin D. Roosevelt's mind when he was planning a state dinner for the king and queen of England during their visit to the United States in 1939. FDR wanted to serve a typical American dish, terrapin à la Maryland, as the first course, but maître d'hôtel Alonzo Fields informed him that the White House had no terrapin dishes.

Fields took advantage of the opportunity to mention that the gold flatware that was used for these occasions was missing some crucial pieces. There were no soup spoons or fish knives, and the salad forks had to be washed between courses so they could double as dessert forks.

FDR was sympathetic. "But you know," he told Fields, "if we were to ask for all those things you say we need, the politicians would make headlines out of the gold tableware being bought for the White House."

Although Roosevelt was too astute a politician to go for the gold, he did manage to squeeze a set of terrapin dishes into the White House budget.

When the Clintons left the White House, they were accused of pirating half the furniture, and became the target of some blistering attacks in the media. They were not the first first family to undergo this little auto-da-fé. No less a supposedly beloved first lady than Edith Roosevelt, wife of Teddy, filed an official request to move a small, inexpensive sofa from a second-floor hall to the Roosevelt home in Oyster Bay. This modest proposal landed on the desk of the tightwad Republican Speaker of the House, "Uncle Joe" Cannon who hated Teddy Roosevelt. Uncle Joe released it to the press. The result was public embarrassment for the first lady and a great deal of private anger, I'm sure.

VIII
★★★

The history of the White House has much more to offer than its memorable quarrels or a cram course in rhetorical outrage. If you look at the building as a structure, you begin to think it has nine lives. It has survived several fires, including the total inferno set by invading British troops in 1814. Even more amazing is how close it has come to being demolished by presidents, first ladies, and assorted know-it-alls who declared the place too large or too small or too public or too old. The one first family who might have gotten away with it was the Trumans, who inherited a house that was threatening to fall down around our ears. Fortunately, my father was a president with a profound sense of history. By the time he left the Big White Jail, as he called it in his wryer moments, the White House had enough steel in its bones to last two more centuries, at least.

IX
★★★

For anyone living or working in the White House, or visiting it, or merely touring the place, everything seems larger than life, a kind of waking dream, outside time, yet paradoxically immersed in time. One reason for this effect is factual: The house *is* ten times larger than your ordinary dwelling and considerably larger than most mansions. George Washington, the man who saw the future greatness of America when it was a mere collection of quarrelsome former colonies, insisted on building it that way. At the same time, it is much smaller than Buckingham Palace or Louis XIV's Versailles, where the goal was the magnification of royal power and the reduction of the people to awed submission. The White House is the architectural equivalent of the American spirit of compromise that created the Constitution—neither too large to be undemocratic nor too small to project meaningful presidential power.

History is another reason for the White House's aura: It virtually oozes from the walls, the furnishings, the paintings. You find it impossible to forget you are walking halls and climbing stairs where Thomas Jefferson and Abraham Lincoln and Theodore Roosevelt trod before you. You may try to ignore it or deny it. In the solitude of your bedroom, you may remind yourself fiercely that you are a private person, living in your own slice of time, with hopes, dreams, and desires that are separate and distinct from this house. But the White House continues to envelop you the way history surrounds nations, a huge silent presence that is inescapable.

No one put the mystical side of the White House more succinctly than President Grover Cleveland. A big bulky blunt-talking lawyer from Buffalo, New York, he seemed the last man in the world to notice auras, either personal or architectural. But after a few months in the White House, he told a friend: "Sometimes I wake at night . . . and rub my eyes and wonder if it is not all a dream." If someone as fiercely commonsensical as Cleveland could be spooked, what chance do ordinary mortals have in the grip of this special atmosphere?

Don't get me wrong, the mystical side of the White House is by no means a bad thing. Presidents and others have found it often enlarges their courage, their vision, their patience—probably the three most important things in a chief executive's spiritual portfolio. "Occasionally," Gerald Ford recalled, "I'd step into the second-floor room where Lincoln used to hold cabinet meetings. History permeates the room. I would sit alone and gaze at the paintings and photographs of another time, and I could almost hear the voices of 110 years before. When I left the room, I always felt revived."

At night, Ronald Reagan liked to stand in the window of the Yellow Oval Room on the second floor and gaze south at the dark figure outlined beneath the floodlit dome of the memorial beside the Tidal Basin. "Thomas Jefferson," he sometimes said. "I look at him from here and he looks at me."

Another impulse to mysticism is the White House's setting. Even in contemporary Washington, D.C., with its automobile-jammed streets and looming government buildings, the mansion manages to stand alone on its eighteen acres of green grass and trees. It was even more splendidly isolated in its early years. One of my favorite descriptions of the place comes from a letter written by First Lady Sarah Polk's niece, Joanna Rucker, who arrived in Washington from Tennessee in 1846 to help her aunt cope with presidential entertaining. Like most people, she had seen illustrations of the White House in magazines and newspapers. But she was unprepared for her first sight of it—drenched in the light of a full moon. Not even in her imagination, she told her mother, had she dreamt it was "as beautiful as it is." For Joanna it was love at first sight.

One of my favorite first ladies, Grace Coolidge, summed up the White House better than anyone else. She called it "a home rich in tradition, mellow with years, hallowed with memories."

X
***

There are few White House families who are not aware of the mansion's history and traditions. Occasionally they hark back to them in a lighthearted way. Part of the lore, for instance, is how Abigail

Adams, the first first lady to inhabit the place, hung her wash in the unfinished East Room. In 1930, First Lady Lou Hoover gave a linen shower for one of her secretaries who was leaving to be married. While the guests were having lunch, Mrs. Hoover had the White House staff string a clothesline across the East Room and drape the shower gifts from it. After lunch, everyone adjourned to the big room to see the bride open her gifts and there it was: Abigail Adams's washday re-created, sort of. The White House staffer who told the story said: "It really looked like a typical washline, full of clothes on Monday morning. It *was* Monday, by the way."

When Grandmother Truman came to visit us, not long after my father became president, Dad decided to tease her with another tradition. On the way from the airport, he told Mamma Truman, as we all called her, that she was going to sleep in Abraham Lincoln's bed. Mamma was an unreconstructed Confederate, who never got over Union guerrillas from Kansas robbing and burning farms in Missouri during the Civil War. She said she would sleep on the floor before she did any such thing. She got so worked up, Dad had to confess he was just kidding.

XI
***

This aura of a living house goes beyond artifacts. My father was convinced that the old house was haunted. Let me give you a verbatim excerpt from a letter he wrote to my mother.

> *Night before last I went to bed at nine o'clock after shutting my doors. At four o'clock I was awakened by three distinct knocks on my bedroom door. I jumped up and put on my bathrobe, opened the door, and no one was there. Went out and looked up and down the hall, looked into your room and Margie's. Still no one there. Went back to bed after locking the doors and there were footsteps*

in your room whose door I'd left open. Jumped up and looked and no one there! Damn place is haunted sure as shootin'. Secret Service said not even a watchman was up here at that hour.

I told Dad, "You better lock your door and prop up some chairs and next time you hear knocks, don't answer. It may be Andrew Jackson in person!"

Lillian Rogers Parks, working in the small room in the northwest corner of the house (later my bedroom), next to a larger room where Lincoln's bed and other furniture were at that time, heard footsteps approaching the door between the two rooms. Every time she opened it, there was no one there. She asked the houseman on duty why he was walking back and forth in that room without coming in the door.

"I just came on duty," he informed her. "That was Abe you heard."

He was "perfectly serious," Mrs. Parks added.

XII
★★★

It may seem absurd to say that the White House, overrun with politicians, job seekers (often one and the same), VIP visitors, and tourists, is also one of the loneliest places on the face of the earth. But that is nothing less than the truth. Moreover, the loneliest person in this lonely place is often the president.

The White House becomes especially lonely at night. Somehow darkness seems to enlarge the place. When you go down the long, high-ceilinged second-floor hall and hear the wind sighing in the trees, you can easily imagine you are the last person left on earth, and any moment you, too, may disappear into the shadows.

For presidents, the midnight loneliness is more political. The pressures of the impossible job do not go away. They murmur at the windows and doors, they gnaw at the mind, intrude upon sleep.

Throw in a few personal problems and between midnight and dawn you have a very lonely man.

I have occasionally composed a list of lonely presidents. At its head are the bachelors, James Buchanan, who also had to cope with the looming secession of the South, and Grover Cleveland, who eased his loneliness by marrying a little more than a year after his first election. Next are the widowers, Thomas Jefferson, Andrew Jackson, Martin Van Buren, John Tyler, and Chester A. Arthur. (Tyler solved his problem by marrying one of my favorite first ladies, lively and spectacularly beautiful Julia Tyler.) Then comes a sadder group, presidents whose marriages were in name only. At the head of this subdivision is Franklin D. Roosevelt, then Warren Harding, and saddest of all, in my opinion, Bill Clinton.

Almost as lonely because of his total inability to deal with the press was Herbert Hoover. In a species of loneliness unto itself is Richard Nixon during his second term, as the jaws of impeachment widened with every passing day. One winces at the hours of midnight torment this driven, desperate man endured.

XIII
✯✯✯

Another reason for the disorienting effect of the White House is the incredible power it emanates. That alone can induce strange behavior in men and women. The day after my father became president, he summoned his old friend, business executive Eddie McKim, to the Oval Office to discuss the possibility of a job in his administration. Dad and Eddie had been in the army together during World War I. They had been close friends for twenty-five or thirty years. Yet when Eddie stepped into the Oval Office, a kind of mental and emotional paralysis seized him. He kept calling Dad "Mr. President" and stood at virtual attention before the big desk.

In words that may well have been colorful, Dad told Eddie to call him "Harry"—and sit down. "I can't do that Har . . . Mr. President,"

Eddie said. Reluctantly, Dad decided it might be better if Eddie supported the Truman administration as a private citizen, a job he undertook with unflagging enthusiasm for the next eight years.

Lyndon Johnson described this side of the presidency best when he told one of his aides: "It's so different now. There's a wall around me that nobody gets through—people I've known for years, worked with side by side [in the Senate] . . . they come in here and they don't see me. They see the President. I'm now 'Mr. President' to my oldest friends!"

An opposite variation on the effect of power on personality is a syndrome my father christened "Potomac fever." Its main symptom is a ballooning self-importance that runs roughshod over anyone and anything in its way. PF can and does afflict almost everyone in the Washington, D.C., power structure, but it is especially prevalent in the White House. The mere ability to get on the telephone and say "This is the White House calling" is enough to make anyone's judgment go squishy.

There are outbreaks of Potomac fever in every president's White House. Dad had a classic case in Jake Vardaman, a St. Louis banker who had done some good work for him in his Senate races before serving in the navy during World War II. Appointed the White House naval aide, Jake started telling half of Washington how to operate. Complaints cascaded into the Oval Office while President Truman struggled to cope with Joe Stalin, Congress, greedy American labor leaders, and even greedier corporate CEOs.

Then Jake made a fatal mistake. He started telling my mother how to run her end of the White House. He was on his way out the door faster than you can say Independence, Missouri.

Another classic case was Sherman Adams, President Eisenhower's chief of staff. A New England Yankee with all the charm of a chip of frozen granite, he made enemies by the dozen during his White House days. Worse yet, he forgot Ben Franklin's great adage, "There is no such thing as a little enemy." One day Sherman's scores of little enemies gathered their forces to reveal that he was accepting free hotel rooms, a vicuña coat, and an oriental rug from a textile magnate friend. The resultant media explosion blew Mr. Adams all the way back to New Hampshire.

A page from the memoir of Bill Clinton's secretary of labor, Robert Reich, who was regularly on the receiving end of the White House calling line, illustrates what I mean. It opens with Reich's secretary telling him:

"The White House wants you to go to Cleveland."

"Houses don't make phone calls. Who called?"

"I don't know. Someone from cabinet affairs. Steve somebody. I'll schedule it."

"How *old* is Steve?"

"What difference does it make? They want you to go to Cleveland. You're going to Cleveland."

"I'll bet he's under thirty. Some twerp in the White House who has no clue what I'm doing in this job. Screw him. I won't go."

Reich went on to vent his rage about White House arrogance in the Clinton era. "From the point of view of the White House staff, cabinet officials are provincial governors presiding over alien, primitive territories. Anything of any importance occurs in the imperial palace, within the capital city."

Guess what: Secretary Reich went to Cleveland.

The White House as a power center is by no means all bad. I am not one of those who fear power so much I don't want anyone to have it or use it. Presidents need power to get things done and the White House is one of their strongest assets. My favorite story in this department is a little soirée Lyndon Johnson hosted at 1600 Pennsylvania Avenue for a group of congressmen who had been voting against him much too often. "Nice place, isn't it?" LBJ said. "Take a good look around. If you guys don't change your votin' habits, it's the last time you'll see it while I'm president."

XIV
★★★

I've compiled another list: first ladies who loved the White House. They include the irrepressible Dolley Madison, iron-willed Helen Taft, and politically astute Lady Bird Johnson. The prize for the most acute case of White House affection probably belongs to Julia Grant, the diminutive wife of Ulysses S., the general who saved the Union's neck in the Civil War and accepted eight years in the White House (1869–77) as a well-deserved tribute from the grateful voters.

The Grants, being army folk, had never owned a house of their own. Julia, already a general's lady, was conditioned to relish the pomp and ceremony of the White House. She also loved the social side and became the queen of Washington society, ignoring snide journalists (they were around even then) who described her as "fair, fat and forty."

When it came time to leave the White House, Julia showed signs of refusing to go. On inauguration day, she gave an elaborate lunch for Lucy Webb Hayes, the incoming first lady, which included a seven-foot azalea tree behind Mrs. Hayes's chair and a table drenched in every flower the White House greenhouses had in bloom. As Julia said good-bye at the door, she could only think: "How pretty the house looked, flowers on the tables, the sunlight falling through the lace curtains." She retained her self-control until she reached the train that was to take her and the ex-president to New York. Then, "in an abandon of grief, [I] flung myself on the lounge and wept, wept oh so bitterly."

I remember telling this story to my mother a decade after her own White House years. She expressed amazement that any first lady could feel anything but relief at escaping such tasks as shaking hands with a few thousand people at official receptions, and poring over guest lists with social secretaries and chiefs of protocol to make sure no VIP nose would be out of joint if its owner was seated in the wrong place or—heaven forbid—left off the list.

"Do you miss anything about the White House?" I asked in my suspicious way. Although Mother loved to complain about the Secret Service and the nosy reporters and the carping congresspersons, I could remember more than a few good laughs shared in the privacy of the family quarters on the second floor.

The light of other days came into Bess Truman's eyes. "One thing," she admitted. "One thing that any woman would miss. All that wonderful help."

So even the most reluctant first ladies—Mother is definitely high on that list—can find some White House memories to cherish. One can only conclude, once again, that 1600 Pennsylvania Avenue is a veritable palace of paradoxes.

XV
★★★

That same conclusion applies to presidents. More than one has told me that on his last day in the White House, he walked through all the rooms on the first floor, from the East Room to the State Dining Room, remembering moments of pride and pleasure. The harrowing memories—Dad once wrote to his mother that he barely had time to eat his meals as he raced from crisis to crisis—fade away. What remains is the central meaning of the White House and the unique satisfaction of winning a place in its history.

If I had to put that meaning into one word, I would choose glory. I don't think even the most cynical newspaper or TV reporter, who knows the worst failings of presidents and first ladies, would deny that in the long run, glory is what the White House is all about. Everyone who has ever lived or worked there has a piece of the glory of this vanguard nation, the United States of America. Even for those who found more unhappiness than happiness in the White House, the glory is still there—a consolation and a reward.

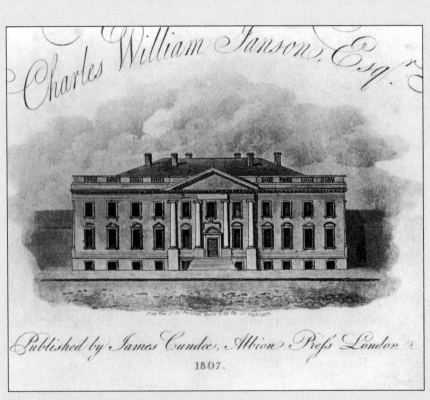

This 1807 print is the earliest known picture of the White House. You have to study it closely to realize it's the same building.
Credit: White House Historical Association (The White House Collection)

2

From Palace to Mansion to Powerhouse

T he White House has 132 rooms, 32 bathrooms, 5 full-time chefs, a tennis court, a jogging track, a movie theater, a billiard room, infrared electric sensors that can detect any movement on the grounds, a SWAT team standing by on the roof every time the president enters or leaves the building, a digitalized locator box that tracks each member of the first family anywhere in the world, and a Situation Room that can monitor troop movements by satellite, retrieve reports electronically from key government agencies, and otherwise deal with almost every conceivable crisis in our terror-ridden modern world.

Two centuries separate this high-tech house from the building that Pierre Charles L'Enfant, the French engineer and architect, designed in 1791 while simultaneously laying out the plans for Washington, D.C. L'Enfant envisioned a Versailles-like palace about five times the size of today's White House. It was to stand in the middle of an eighty-acre President's Park with terraces, fountains, and formal gardens stretching all the way down to the Potomac River.

This lavish vision must have been hard for Americans to share. At the time, the Federal City, as Washington was called in its infancy, was nothing but a collection of fields, swamps, and farms, and the United States was a pipsqueak republic that had yet to find its place in the world.

II
★★★

President George Washington heartily endorsed L'Enfant's plans for a presidential palace. He believed that a certain amount of pomp and ceremony was essential to lend dignity and importance to the new government. Not everyone in his administration agreed. Early in his first term, his cabinet members had split into two parties—the Federalists, led by Alexander Hamilton, and the Anti-Federalists or Republicans, led by Thomas Jefferson. Don't be confused by the names. The Republicans were actually the more liberal party, the political ancestors of today's Democrats. Many historians call them Democratic-Republicans, a term that better reflects their politics.

The Democratic-Republicans were quick to condemn L'Enfant's design as a Federalist monstrosity whose occupants might view themselves as royalty and behave accordingly. L'Enfant's concept of a palace proved to be short-lived for reasons more personal than political. The volatile Frenchman managed to alienate everyone he worked with, including George Washington, and he soon found himself unemployed.

A competition was held to find a new architect for what was now being called the President's House. Nine proposals were submitted and the winner was a Charleston, South Carolina, man, Irish-born James Hoban. Among the losers was a gifted amateur architect, Thomas Jefferson, who had submitted his design under the pseudonym A.Z.

Hoban's building was considerably smaller and plainer than L'Enfant's planned palace. Washington requested that it be made larger and grander. One feature of Hoban's design that he particularly liked, and may even have suggested, was an eighty-foot-long audience room, today's East Room, for presidential receptions.

Washington had wanted the President's House built entirely of stone but the cost was prohibitive, so the inner walls were made of brick. The stone was cut from a quarry in Virginia and shipped up the Potomac by boat. It was sandstone, which tended to be porous, so whitewash was applied to keep out the moisture.

Additional money could have been saved by reducing the size of the building. Washington agreed to two stories rather than three, but he refused to change any other dimensions. The President's House would be enormous by the standards of the era in which it was built, but Washington confidently predicted that one day it would be too small—and was he ever right.

III
★★★

Building the Federal City was slow work. Meanwhile, the Democratic-Republicans were on the attack again. Many of them saw no need to build such a magnificent house for the president. One Democratic-Republican congressman introduced a bill to convert the presidential palace, as they persisted in calling it, into a hall for Congress; another brightlight wanted to use it for the Supreme Court.

As George Washington's second term drew to a close in 1796, both the President's House and the Capitol remained unfinished. The new government was required by law to transfer to Washington, D.C., in 1800. There was a good chance that the nation's political leaders would abandon the civilized comforts of Philadelphia to find themselves homeless in the so-called "federal village."

Neither the White House, as it was already starting to be called, nor the Capitol was finished on schedule, but the government moved anyway. On November 1 of that tumultuous year, with France and England at each other's throats in a war that raged around the globe, President John Adams became the first occupant of the President's House. The day after his arrival, he wrote to his wife, Abigail: "I pray Heaven to bestow the best of blessings on this house, and on all that shall hereafter inhabit it. May none but honest and wise men ever rule under this roof."

Abigail Adams, who arrived two weeks after her husband, may have shared his lofty sentiments, but she was not oblivious to the shortcomings of their official home. About half of the thirty-six rooms were still unplastered and only six were fit to live in; the main staircase existed only on paper; the grounds were nothing but weeds dotted with piles of rubble. Abigail found the house cold and dark and so large, it would take thirty servants to run it. In a letter to her daughter, she wrote: "the great unfinished audience-room, I make a drying-room of, to hang up the clothes in."

John and Abigail Adams made the best of their makeshift mansion during the four months that were left in his term. They held a number of receptions and dinners but getting to them could be a challenge. Visitors to the President's House often found the roads muddy and impassable, and there was a constant danger of getting lost in the woods that covered most of the acres of the largely unpopulated federal village.

IV

***

As a Democratic-Republican, John Adams's successor, Thomas Jefferson, might have been expected to refuse to live in the President's House. Even in its unfinished state, it seemed the epitome of Federalist ostentation. Although Jefferson described the house as "big enough for two emperors, one pope and the grand lama," he not only moved in, he set to work to make the place more habitable.

The grounds were still cluttered with workmen's shanties along with brick kilns and stagnant pools of water used for mixing mortar. On a dark night, wrote one congressman, "instead of finding your way to the house, you were likely to fall into a pit or stumble over a pile of rubbish." Jefferson's first order of business was removing the wooden privy that stood beside the house in full view of passersby. It was replaced by two water closets (toilets) installed at each end of the second floor.

Jefferson also commissioned the construction of wings on the east and west sides of the mansion to house the coach house, tack room, servants' quarters, and other important but not necessarily attractive areas. The wings were unobtrusive one-story extensions connected by colonnades to the basement of the White House, which was at ground level. The roofs of the wings abutted the first floor and could be used as terraces or outdoor promenades.

James Hoban's original design for the White House placed the main entrance on the North Portico as it is today. Abigail Adams had commented on the beautiful view from the south windows, so Hoban decided to move the entrance there. Jefferson asked the architect to move it back. For the time being it made very little difference. Both porticos remained unfinished for lack of funds.

Despite his commitment to Democratic-Republican simplicity, Jefferson expended not a few government dollars to sink a sixteen-foot-deep wine cellar, which he stocked with his favorite vintages. His much-publicized dedication to frugality in government was also belied by the fact that he added extensive ornamentation to the interior of the house, including new glass doors, chair rails, baseboards, and enough architectural details to require a whole new paint job.

The President's House took another step closer to becoming the elegant residence George Washington wanted it to be when James and Dolley Madison arrived in 1809. The Madisons liked to entertain, and they set about turning the mansion into a suitable setting for their parties. With a budget of $5,000 (about $72,000 in modern dollars), which Dolley extracted from Congress by inviting some of the leaders over to see how dreary the place looked, she focused her attention on three rooms along the south side of the house. Her goal was to make them the handsomest rooms in Washington.

Jefferson's former office became—and still is—the State Dining Room. A sitting room next to it was converted into Mrs. Madison's parlor. (It is now the Red Room, although Dolley decorated it in sunflower yellow.) The oval-shaped Elliptical Saloon, the present Blue Room, became the main drawing room.

The splendid rooms provided a superb backdrop for the Madisons' dinners and receptions. Their parties were the most glittering in Washington. Nothing short of a grave illness kept people away from their Wednesday drawing rooms.

V
★★★

James Madison's first term marked the high point of the President's House thus far. His second term, which coincided with the War of 1812, marked the low point of both the mansion and the American presidency. In the summer of 1814, a British army burned the Capitol, the President's House, and several other government buildings.

Rebuilding the President's House became a matter of national pride. Congress appropriated the necessary funds without a murmur and the original architect, James Hoban, was invited to reconstruct his mansion and to finish its north and south porticos as well.

The damage to the President's House was even worse than it had first appeared. The heat of the blaze had split the outside walls, and many of them had to be replaced. The work was still not finished when Madison's successor, James Monroe, arrived in 1817. Monroe ordered the work speeded up and was particularly insistent that the East Room be ready for the large receptions he planned.

Anyone who has ever been involved with a building contractor will not be surprised to hear that the workmen did not meet the eight-month deadline Monroe imposed on them. They had gotten as far as replacing the whitewash on the outside walls with white lead paint (which made the White House an even more popular name), but the north and south porticos were still under construction and the inside was a mess. The walls were unpapered, the floors were unfinished, and twenty-one marble mantels that had been ordered from Italy had yet to arrive.

Nevertheless, the Monroes moved in and Elizabeth Monroe set about decorating the house with furniture they had ordered from France and some additional items bought with a congressional appropriation. If the workmen's materials were removed, the President's House would at least be fit to entertain in. James Monroe gave the order, the materials were stashed away, and on New Year's Day, 1818, the president and first lady threw open the doors and invited the public to a gala reception. When it was over, the materials were replaced and work on the house resumed.

The Monroes continued this practice whenever they entertained, which meant the work took even longer. It stopped completely when the country was hit by the Panic of 1819 and did not resume until the economy improved. Five years later the South Portico was in place, and in 1829 the seventy-year-old Hoban was called back to build the North Portico. The whole job was finally completed in 1830, not long after Andrew Jackson moved in, a year before Hoban's death, and thirty-eight years after it was started.

VI
***

It should hardly be news that buildings don't last forever unless they receive very good care. Although a great deal of care was taken in

constructing—and reconstructing—the White House, once finished, it was pretty much neglected. Thirty-four years later, when
the commissioner of public buildings inspected it, he was so appalled by its condition that he pronounced it unfit for occupancy.
The Civil War was raging at the time and both the president and
the nation had other things on their minds. As frequently happens
in Washington, the report was put in a file and forgotten.

Three years passed and the next commissioner of buildings,
equally appalled, went so far as to select several sites for a new presidential mansion. All of them were in secluded areas several miles
from downtown Washington. By then, Ulysses S. Grant was in the
White House. He and his wife were fond of the historic building
and had no desire to live elsewhere. The plans to replace it were
quietly scrapped.

Chester A. Arthur, who took office in 1881 after the assassination
of President James A. Garfield, was one of those fussy New Yorkers
who had to have the latest and best of everything. During his initial
inspection of the Executive Mansion, he was so turned off by its
Victorian clutter and run-down appearance that he told the official
who was showing him around, "I will not live in a house like this."

Arthur undertook major redecorating to bring the place up to his
standards. Then he discovered that the house had even more serious problems. An engineer who inspected the building while the
decorators were at work found, just for starters, that the septic system was antiquated, the basement was crumbling, the servants'
quarters were not fit for human habitation, and the whitewash on
the kitchen ceiling was flaking off and falling into the food.

After totting up how much it would cost to cure all these ills,
Arthur concluded that it would make more sense to demolish the
building and replace it with a new one. The designs for a suburban
residence that had been drawn up in 1867 were trotted out, but
there was very little support for the plan.

As an alternative, Arthur proposed tearing down the White

House and building an exact replica on the same site. The new building would contain offices for the president and his staff, and an identical building erected next to it would provide a modern, comfortable residence for the president.

Although Arthur's plan met with no opposition, there was also very little enthusiasm for it. The White House had won a place in the hearts of the American people, and destroying it would have been an act of political folly.

Realizing that his hopes for a new house were doomed, the president embarked on another round of redecorating. He hired the gifted artist and designer Louis Comfort Tiffany to make the state rooms more stylish. Tiffany tossed out the profusion of velvet, fringes, and floral patterns that had been so popular in the past and opted for a more restrained style with an emphasis on rich colors and unusual fabrics and patterns. He worked with American motifs such as eagles and stars. His most striking contribution was a ten-foot-high mosaic of red, white, and blue glass that served as a screen between the entrance hall and the main corridor.

All told, Arthur spent $110,000—a princely sum in those days—to make the White House conform to his idea of how the nation's leader should live. It was the largest amount that had been expended on the President's House since it was rebuilt after the War of 1812.

VII
★★★

Ever since Andrew Jackson's day, the president's office had competed for space on the second floor with the chief executive's family. This meant that visitors to the mansion were constantly trekking up and down the stairs and halls, allowing first families little privacy. As the responsibilities of the president increased, particularly during the Civil War, additional secretaries and clerks were hired and more work space was needed, impinging still further on the first families' living arrangements.

Chester A. Arthur had made a stab at providing separate quarters for the president and his staff without success. The idea was revived—and rejected—during Grover Cleveland's first administration. Cleveland, who had gotten married during his presidency but had yet to have a family, did not press the issue.

With President Benjamin Harrison's arrival, however, additional space became crucial. The Harrison household included their daughter, her husband, and their two-year-old son and baby daughter; Mrs. Harrison's ninety-year-old father; and a widowed niece. A daughter-in-law and her daughter were frequent visitors. With so many people in residence, there was very little room and even less privacy. Caroline Harrison made several attempts to free up space, including trying to use the state rooms as family sitting rooms, but it soon became apparent that the only solution was expanding the building itself.

Mrs. Harrison consulted an architect who drew up a plan that would add large wings at either end of the mansion. The one on the west would provide office space for the president, leaving the entire second floor available for his family.

The plan got a warm welcome in the Senate but it came to a dead stop in the House. The Speaker, brooding about the fact that President Harrison had failed to appoint one of his friends to a federal job, refused to bring it to the floor.

VIII

★★★

In 1900, as part of the program celebrating the centennial of Washington, D.C., the American Institute of Architects held a symposium to discuss the need for improving the city's appearance. There was no question that a makeover was needed. The capital had evolved in a way that would have grievously offended the artistic

sensibilities of its original designer, Pierre L'Enfant. Public buildings had been put up in a variety of architectural styles. Vacant land
was overgrown with ratty-looking patches of grass and fouled by
grazing livestock. Railroads ran up and down the streets and criss-
crossed the Mall, and there were a half-dozen different terminals
scattered around the city.

Prompted by the architects' symposium, Senator James McMillan, a member of the Committee on the District of Columbia, appointed a commission to develop and improve the city's parks. Its
members, architects David Burnham and Charles McKim, landscape architect Frederick Law Olmstead, Jr., and sculptor Augustus
Saint-Gaudens, were among the leading tastemakers of the day, and
they quickly recognized that a lack of parks was only the beginning
of the city's problems.

The commission drew up the McMillan Plan, based on Pierre
L'Enfant's original design for Washington, which called for a city of
stately buildings, beautiful vistas, and manicured lawns and parks.
L'Enfant, who had been booted out in disgrace a little more than a
hundred years earlier, would have been delighted to learn that he
had suddenly become a hero and that his vision of the nation's capital would finally be realized.

Essentially, the McMillan Plan created the Washington of today,
with federal buildings clustered around the Capitol and on either
side of the Mall, and Union Station replacing the street-level railroad tracks and individual terminals. The Arlington Memorial
Bridge was designed to line up with the Custis-Lee Mansion on the
other side of the Potomac, and the yet to be built Lincoln Memorial was to be situated in a direct line with the Washington Monument and the Capitol.

It was hardly surprising that the White House, possibly the most
prominent building in Washington, was high on the McMillan
Commission's list of items that needed attention. One suggestion,
resurrecting the plans drawn up by Caroline Harrison's architect,
had already been vetoed, and with good reason. The projected east

and west wings were almost as large as the White House itself, and although they echoed James Hoban's original design, they were capped by glass domes, adapted from the French style that was popular at the time.

Another suggestion, also tabled, was to convert the White House into an executive office building and build a new presidential home on the grounds of the U.S. Naval Observatory, where the official residence of the vice president now stands.

While the insiders were mulling these options, an outsider suddenly stepped into the picture. Mrs. John B. Henderson, a wealthy and colorful Washingtonian who was the wife of one senator and the niece of another, decided to make the White House her pet project. Mrs. Henderson's uncle had been one of the supporters of the 1867 plan for a suburban President's House, and she was determined to fulfill his dream.

She purchased land on the site her uncle had favored, Meridian Hill. The neighborhood, a little over a mile north of the White House, was largely undeveloped except for a few large estates, one of which had been leased by John Quincy Adams after he left the White House in 1829.

Although Mrs. Henderson hired an architect and made a public announcement of her plan, she was unable to win government approval. Unfazed, she developed the area on her own, persuading the government to lay out a twelve-acre park and building a palatial home for herself and her husband, which became known as Henderson's Castle. Ever the shrewd businesswoman, she also erected a group of similarly imposing houses that she sold at a hefty profit.

IX
***

The McMillan Commission's activities were suspended after President William McKinley's assassination in 1901. His successor,

Theodore Roosevelt, had no immediate interest in revamping his new home except to issue an order changing its official name from the Executive Mansion to the White House.

The president's indifference to his living quarters was short-lived. With six children and an assortment of pets, the Roosevelts were squeezed into a home that had too few bedrooms, bathrooms, and closets. The kitchen was old-fashioned and grimy, the State Dining Room was too small, and the floor had to be propped up with ten-by-ten-inch timbers whenever there was a large party in the East Room.

Something had to be done. The president asked Congress to appropriate $16,000 for repairs and redecorating and Edith Roosevelt sought the advice of Charles McKim, a member of the McMillan Commission and a partner in the renowned New York architectural firm of McKim, Mead and White.

After a careful inspection of the building, McKim reported that the $16,000 appropriation would not even come close to covering the cost of everything that needed to be done. With Senator James McMillan as his advocate, McKim persuaded Congress to vote a staggering $475,000 to remodel the White House and build a separate executive office building for the president and his staff. The total might have been higher if Edith Roosevelt hadn't insisted on cutting back on several of McKim's decorating ideas. The fact that neither Congress nor the country complained about the expense was a tribute to the nation's affection for the White House and their dedication to preserving it.

Charles McKim's 1902 renovation altered the external appearance of the building and produced the look that characterizes the present-day White House. A wrought-iron fence that ran along the driveway on the North Portico was taken down because it interfered with the view of the house. The remains of Thomas Jefferson's east and west wings were rebuilt and enlarged, and a complex of greenhouses on the west side of the White House was also removed, but only after lengthy negotiations with Edith Roosevelt, who, like so many first ladies before her, found them a convenient and inexpensive source of fresh flowers. The greenhouses were replaced by a "temporary" Executive Office Building—today's West Wing—a plain one-story structure with long windows that was set back from the White House but connected to it by a colonnade.

McKim's work on the inside of the house was even more extensive. He transformed the basement from a gloomy and forbidding collection of utility areas into a series of rooms that could be used for social functions. Additional space was achieved by converting the attic into servants' quarters and workrooms.

McKim took a dim view of most of the furnishings purchased during previous administrations and had them carted off to be sold at auction. Among the discards was Chester A. Arthur's Tiffany screen, which was snapped up by a real estate developer for $275. It is believed to have ended its days at the Belvedere Hotel in Chesapeake Beach, Maryland, which burned down in 1923.

If McKim had had his way, the Victorian furniture that is now in the Lincoln Bedroom would have been hauled away as well. But Edith Roosevelt liked its elaborate carving and her husband respected its historical significance. Thus, the old-fashioned rosewood bed was saved, along with a dresser, wardrobe, and circular table.

Charles McKim wanted the house to reflect the period in which it was built. To that end he purchased eighteenth- and early-nineteenth-century furniture, including reproductions of some of the pieces the Monroes had ordered from France. In another bow to history, he had the cab of the new White House elevator decorated with wood from the beams of Boston's Old South Meeting House, where the Boston Tea Party was organized.

For the Roosevelts, the most welcome result of McKim's renovation was the reconfiguration of the family quarters. The remodeled second floor now boasted seven bedrooms, each with its own bath, plus a library and private sitting rooms.

Charles McKim was under orders from the president to complete his renovations of the White House in six months. Amazingly, and not without some offstage grumbling, he did. Unfortunately, he had to cut a few corners in the process, but it was some time before anyone realized this fact.

Theodore Roosevelt, with his strong sense of history, continued to work in the White House, as presidents had been doing since John Adams's day, and used McKim's temporary Executive Office Building as headquarters for his staff, summoning them to his White House study whenever they were needed.

William Howard Taft would have preferred to continue this tradition, but he recognized the value of having the entire executive branch in a single location. Shortly after he took office in 1909, Taft hired an architect to enlarge McKim's Executive Office Building—a tacit acknowledgment that the addition could no longer be considered temporary. A key part of the architect's plans for remodeling that first Executive Office Building was an Oval Office for the president, its shape chosen in homage to James Hoban's design for the Blue Room.

In the course of the next few decades, McKim's Executive Office Building became known as the West Wing. If nothing else, the designation eliminated any confusion when a new Executive Office Building was created during the Truman administration, almost fifty years later.

Recognizing the need for additional office space, my father originally proposed building an addition to the West Wing. Congress declined to put up the money and Dad and his staff continued to work in cramped quarters. In 1949, the State Department moved to a new building and their former headquarters, the French Second Empire–style building at 17th Street and Pennsylvania Avenue, became available.

This marvelous old heap, which was completed in 1888 and originally housed the Departments of War and Navy, became the Executive Office Building. The E.O.B. seemed to offer more than enough space for the president's staff, but during the Kennedy administration, Vice President Lyndon B. Johnson became the first in a succession of vice presidents to have offices there. With the vice president's staff growing almost as fast as the president's, it soon became apparent that yet another Executive Office Building was needed.

In 1967, Federal Office Building #7 was erected on 17th Street, a block or so from the White House. The structure was immediately dubbed the New Executive Office Building, leaving the former State Department headquarters with the label Old Executive Office Building. Although most people still call it that, the building's official name is the Eisenhower Executive Office Building. The new name was approved by President Bill Clinton in 1999, and the building was rededicated and formally renamed by President George W. Bush in 2002. In Washington, D.C., this snail's-pace way of getting things done is known as progress.

X
★★★

When Calvin Coolidge moved into the White House in 1923, he was informed by the officer in charge of public buildings that the roof needed to be repaired. After hearing that the work would cost half a million dollars, Coolidge, a thrifty New Englander, decided against it. But a year or so later, when cracks appeared in the ceiling on the second floor and debris started raining down from the attic, the president was forced to change his mind.

The wooden framing that had been in place since the White House was rebuilt after the War of 1812 was sagging under the weight of additional bathrooms, new appliances, and similar conveniences that had been installed in the interim. The engineers recommended rebuilding the roof and the second-floor ceiling and replacing the decaying timbers that were holding up the third floor with concrete and steel beams.

The Coolidges moved out while the work was done. They returned to a sturdier White House with a completely redesigned third floor. It added eighteen rooms to the family quarters, including bedrooms and bathrooms, a solarium, and space for housekeeping and other services.

The roof did fall in on Herbert Hoover, figuratively at least, when the stock market crashed seven months after he took office in 1929. Hoover had already done some major remodeling of the West Wing. He found the space much too small for his staff, which numbered almost forty people. At the president's behest, the size of the lobby was doubled, several new offices were added, the basement was remodeled to provide office space for secretaries and file clerks, and central air-conditioning was installed.

A little more than six months after the renovations were completed, a fire on Christmas Eve 1929 destroyed almost the entire West Wing. It must have been a horrifying sight, with flames shooting up in all directions and teams of firemen struggling to control the blaze. Fortunately, most of the president's papers were saved, as was a puppy that one of his secretaries had left in the office. The man had planned to pick it up later that evening and surprise his son on Christmas morning, but in the panic and confusion of the fire he completely forgot it. To his immense relief, the president remembered the animal and sent one of the firefighters to the rescue.

When the West Wing was rebuilt, Hoover was tempted to enlarge it still further, but he knew better than to request the necessary funds. The Great Depression had started and belt-tightening was the order of the day.

XI

★★★

Franklin D. Roosevelt's plans for the West Wing were even more ambitious than his predecessor's. With a staff more than twice the size of Hoover's, FDR's need for additional space was even more acute. He proposed to tear down the existing building and replace it with a larger structure that he himself had designed.

The Commission of Fine Arts, which had been formed to uphold the principles of the McMillan Plan, was horrified at the thought of tearing down the building, much less replacing it with a design by an amateur architect. Eric Gugler, a highly respected architect who was a disciple of Charles McKim and a personal friend of the Roosevelts, was asked to intervene. Gugler managed—though not without considerable effort—to talk the president out of the idea and instead presented his own plan, which FDR grudgingly accepted.

The architect doubled the size of the West Wing but managed to keep it from overpowering the White House by making the additions so unobtrusive that they were all but invisible. For example, a second story was added but it was set back from the first, making it difficult to see from the ground. Additional square footage was achieved by extending the basement southward and concealing its roof with grass and shrubbery. As part of the renovation, the Oval Office was moved from the center of the West Wing to the southeast corner where it looked out on the Rose Garden that had been planted by Woodrow Wilson's first wife, Ellen, in 1913.

XII

★ ★ ★

With each new administration, the White House could expect a certain amount of redecorating and occasionally some renovation, but unless there were serious signs of trouble, like the near-disaster with the Coolidges' ceiling, nobody gave much thought to the building's underpinnings. My father was the rare exception.

In 1945, soon after we moved into the Big White Jail, Dad asked the commissioner of public buildings to give the place a thorough going over. He knew that any building as old as the White House needed to be inspected at regular intervals to make sure it was structurally sound.

A year went by and nothing happened, until the evening of an official reception in the East Room. Mother and Dad made their entrance down the Grand Staircase from the second floor, preceded, as usual, by a color guard of four servicemen carrying the American and the presidential flags. As the Four Horsemen (their White House nickname) came marching across the room, Dad looked up and saw the huge chandelier above his head swaying. He lost no time in reporting it to the commissioner of public buildings, but it was several weeks before anyone got back to him. When they did, they didn't exactly pick the best time.

Dad was hosting the last official reception of the 1946–47 season and the guests were being treated to a concert by pianist Eugene List. Howell Crim, the chief usher, and Jim Rowley, the Secret Service agent in charge of the White House detail, quietly informed Dad that the inspection team had found that the chain holding up the center chandelier was on the verge of giving way.

Crim and Rowley probably thought Dad would interrupt the concert and ask his guests to leave—after all, the chandelier weighs twelve hundred pounds—but Dad decided that if the chain hadn't broken yet, it would probably hold up for a little while longer. Nevertheless, his first order of business the next day was to have the chandelier taken down. Not long after this near disaster, one of the White House butlers came into Dad's study with his breakfast tray and the entire floor began to sway. The commissioner of public buildings was ordered to bring in a team of engineers to check it out.

Meanwhile, Dad had set off a few vibrations of his own. In the summer of 1947, he decided it would be a good idea to add a second-floor balcony to the South Portico. He had always liked porches and he knew enough about architecture to realize that an upstairs porch wouldn't detract from—and might actually enhance—the original design. In his view, the columns on the South Portico were out of proportion to the size of the house; a balcony would tone down their massive appearance.

I won't deny that Dad was thinking of the comfort of the first family. An upstairs balcony would provide us with a pleasant and private outdoor sitting room. But Dad's interest in the balcony had a strong practical side. In warm weather, the South Portico was protected from the sun by awnings hanging between the columns, about twelve feet above the floor. The effect was not particularly attractive, especially when you add in the fact that the awnings got covered with mildew during the humid Washington summers. The balcony would eliminate the need for these cumbersome unsightly things.

Dad presented his idea to the Commission of Fine Arts, which had to be consulted about any changes to the White House. The commissioners voted unanimously to reject it. Dad fired off a letter to the chairman saying, among other things, "I can't understand your viewpoint when those dirty awnings are a perfect eyesore with regard to that south portico. I have had them painted; I have had them washed and they have been renewed every year and still they look like hell when they are on the porch."

Since the commission did not have the power to block Dad's plan and Congress had already voted a general appropriation that would cover the cost, Dad went ahead with the balcony. You should have heard the uproar! He was condemned for meddling with a historic monument, accused of being an ignoramus about architecture, and called an assortment of names that are not worth repeating.

As usual, Dad ignored the fuss. The Truman balcony was built and the baggy awnings were replaced by a set of good-looking blinds that rolled up and down like window shades. Before long, the Truman balcony began to look as if it had always been there. Several experts on historical architecture have praised its design, and more than one presidential family has told me how much they enjoyed it.

XIII

★★★

As so often happens in Washington, the balcony quickly became old news as a new problem loomed on the horizon. The engineers who had been ordered to "check things out" when Dad felt the floor swaying had come back with a gloomy report. The second floor, where we lived and where Dad had his study, was about to fall and the ceiling in the State Dining Room would come crashing down with it. Dad insisted that the floor be shored up at once and vowed to have a concrete and steel floor put in before we moved out.

Shoring up the second floor was no small job. It resulted in a forest of steel pipes running through the private rooms. To get in and out of Dad's study, my sitting room, and mother's bedroom you had to wend your way through a metal maze.

Spurred on by the threat of a cave-in, Dad appointed another committee of engineers and architects to inspect the entire White House and tell him what needed to be done. Their report was not reassuring. The foundation was sinking into the swampy ground and the ceiling in the Green Room was held up by only a few rusty nails. If any further evidence was needed that the White House was falling apart, it came in the summer of 1948 when the piano in my sitting room broke through the floor. One of its legs wound up jutting into the family dining room below.

That did it. Dad was banished from his bedroom and forbidden to use his bathroom lest it collapse and land in the Red Room. Mother and I spent most of that summer in Independence, and in the fall we joined Dad on the whistle-stop tour that led to his upset victory in the 1948 presidential election.

By the time we returned to the White House in November, the engineers and architects had concluded that it would be dangerous for us to live there. The third floor was fine, thanks to the repairs that had been made during the Coolidge administration, but the first and second floors were in a precarious state. They were supported (so to speak) by the same wooden beams that James Hoban had installed when the White House was rebuilt after the War of 1812.

Not only were the beams rotting with age, they were riddled with gashes made by several generations of workmen sawing into the wood to install new plumbing and wiring. Worse yet, the wooden beams were interspersed with steel beams, which Charles McKim, in his haste to complete the 1902 renovations, had socketed into the inner brick walls. Apparently nobody tested the decaying brick to see if it would be strong enough to support their weight.

A swarm of construction workers had already put up scaffolds in the East Room and propped up most of the second floor. After further inspection the experts determined that the entire house would have to be gutted and rebuilt from the ground up. The only thing that could be saved was the outside walls. Shades of 1814—and this time we couldn't even blame the British!

The Trumans moved across the street to Blair House, a lovely 1824 mansion once owned by the family of Washington power brokers who first came to Washington in Andrew Jackson's administration. In 1942, the house became the president's official guest house. In preparation for our arrival, Blair House was enlarged by creating an opening to the Lee House next door, giving us a total of thirty-four rooms. The second house had been built for one of the Blair daughters, who married a man named Lee, a third cousin of the famous Robert E.

With the White House vacant, the construction crews took over. Dad occasionally looked in on their efforts but I never did. Although I knew it was necessary, the thought of the White House being "gutted" stirred distress in the pit of my stomach.

By the time they were finished in 1952, a new White House had risen out of the shell of the old one. The improvements included a concrete and steel frame, a deeper foundation that allowed room for two sub-basements for service areas and utilities, with additional room under the North Portico for workshops and air-conditioning equipment.

Still more space was acquired by adding mezzanines at each end of the building, providing room for new pantries, rest rooms, and the like. One of the improvements Dad was particularly happy about was the new Grand Staircase. It was not as steep as the old one and it had a couple of landings so he and Mother didn't have to keep looking down at their feet to avoid tripping as they descended.

Dad was always proud of the fact that his administration had overseen the construction of a White House that would last for ages to come. Mother and I agreed with him. But I have to confess that we would have been happier if another first family got stuck with the disruptions.

XIV
✩ ✩ ✩

Furnishing the rebuilt White House was the responsibility of the building commission, which chose the highly respected and now defunct Fifth Avenue department store B. Altman & Co. to do the job. Altman's did amazingly well on a limited budget, but their decorating efforts couldn't compare to those of Jacqueline Kennedy, who set out to make the White House not just a well-furnished mansion but a repository of American history.

Jackie concentrated on acquiring original or period furnishings that she incorporated into the State Rooms with her inimitable style. She deserves additional credit for persuading private citizens to donate most of the items, thus saving the taxpayers quite a bit of money.

In addition to redoing the historic rooms on the main floor, Jackie converted the oval room on the second floor into a formal drawing room that is gradually acquiring a history of its own. During previous administrations, the space had sometimes been used as a family sitting room. Millard Fillmore had bookcases designed to fit the curving walls and his wife, Abigail, set up the first White House library, paid for with a $2,000 appropriation from Congress. Franklin D. Roosevelt and Harry S Truman made the room their private study. Dwight Eisenhower turned it into a trophy room.

Jackie redecorated the space using a yellow color scheme and furnishings in the Louis XVI style of late-eighteenth-century France, still popular when the White House was built. Now known as the Yellow Oval Room, it is available for the first family's personal use and also provides a gracious and intimate setting for the president and first lady to receive foreign chiefs of state and heads of government before state luncheons and dinners. These days, the room is so closely identified with the White House that it has become as famous as the Blue Room below it.

To ensure that Jacqueline Kennedy's valuable acquisitions would not be jettisoned in some future redecorating project, Congress passed a special act making all the items belonging to the White House part of a permanent collection and stipulating that the museum character of the State Rooms would be preserved in perpetuity.

Although it is not generally known, President Richard M. Nixon sponsored an even more ambitious acquisition of antiques, again paid for by private donors. His wife, Pat, had the State Rooms redesigned to showcase the pieces, using wallpaper, draperies, and decorative items in the style of the period the rooms represented. Together, the Nixons assembled the beautiful and historically accurate State Rooms that exist today. Jackie Kennedy, after an off-the-record visit, wrote Pat a touching tribute: "I have never seen the White House look so perfect. There is no hidden corner of it that is not beautiful now."

XV
★ ★ ★

Every time I visit the White House, I am reminded of all the people at every level who have contributed to its grandeur. If I had to name names, I would single out for their extraordinary contributions George Washington, who had the foresight to realize how important the nation and its president would become; James Hoban, who created such an enduringly elegant design; and Harry S Truman, who made sure the White House will still be standing long after the rest of us are gone.

We have Lady Bird Johnson to thank for the handprints of presidential grandchildren set in the paths of the Children's Garden. Credit: White House Historical Association

3
***

The President's Park

I seldom visit the White House without pausing for a moment to contemplate a venerable tree that graces the south front. Known as the Jackson magnolia after the president who planted it, those gnarled old limbs provided shade on the August day in 1944 when Harry S Truman had lunch with Franklin D. Roosevelt not long after Dad had been nominated to run with FDR in 1944.

It did not take my father long to realize the rumors about Mr. Roosevelt's declining health were all too true. The president's hand shook so violently, he could not spoon sugar into his coffee. On his face was the pallor of death. FDR asked Dad how he was going to campaign. When Dad said he was thinking of using a plane, the president shook his head. "One of us has to stay alive," he said. That was the day Harry S Truman realized he might become president of the United States.

That meeting is a good example of why no story of the White House can be complete without an exploration of the acres of grass and gardens and trees that surround it. The grounds are an essential part of the mansion's ambience, and their history is as full of unexpected twists and turns as the history of the house itself.

In the summer of 1800, several months before he moved into the

Executive Mansion, John Adams ordered the ground prepared for a small "kitchen garden" on the northeast side of the house. It was intended to produce vegetables and herbs, which were grown at home in that era. But when planting time came around the following spring, poor old John Yankee, defeated in his run for a second term, was back in New England, where he spent the next twenty-five years grousing about his humiliation.

The first president to take a serious interest in the White House's potential for natural beauty was Thomas Jefferson, a man who loved plants and flowers. On paper he planned a landscaped park with picturesque romantic touches, such as small groves of trees and clumps of rhododendron and other shrubs. He marked off one area as the "garden" where vegetables and decorative flowers would grow, fenced off about eight acres of the land set aside for a "President's Park," and made plans to build a high stone wall at the south end of the property.

Although he never got around to doing much about this imagined landscape, Jefferson planted scores of seedling trees including oaks, sycamores, and chestnuts. Sadly, most of the park was trampled by British troops and the army of workmen who arrived to rebuild the mansion. Many of his trees were chopped down by this same combination of marauders and used as firewood.

II

★★★

The next president to take a serious interest in the grounds was John Quincy Adams. He might have been impelled by want of anything better to do. He and Congress were barely on speaking terms for most of his presidency. To be fair, this very intelligent man had a lifelong interest in horticulture. He planted and tended gardens in every house he inhabited, and the White House grounds presented a major challenge to his talents.

Soon after John Quincy took office, he fired Charles Bizet, whom

James Monroe had hired as "Gardener to the President of the U. States." The impressively titled Bizet was kept busy grading the grounds and otherwise repairing the scars inflicted by the years of heavy work it took to rebuild the house after its destruction by the British.

Adams replaced Bizet with John Ousley, who became almost as permanent a part of the mansion's landscape as the trees and flowers he planted. Under President Adams's guidance, Ousley devised a park that would be a pocket tour of America's forests and plants. Seedlings were gathered from all parts of the country, and soon walnut, persimmon, willow, oak, and other trees were growing on the White House grounds. Near the south entrance gate, Ousley planted a two-acre garden in which Adams took an intense interest. His diary is filled with comments about the success and failure of various plants.

The president often arose at dawn to do some digging of his own. One morning he wrote of planting "eighteen whole red-cherries" and noted with pleasure that the "casual poppies" were flowering, the mustard and anthemis were in full bloom, and the currants were ripening nicely. By the summer of 1827, a delighted Adams was bragging to his diary that the two acres contained over a thousand different trees, shrubs, hedges, flowers, and vegetables.

III
★★★

John Quincy's successor, Andrew Jackson, had more ambitious plans for the White House grounds, and another phase of the exterior history of the mansion began. Jackson called in the public gardener of the city of Washington, an Irishman named Jemmy Maher, to help him plant trees and plan an overhaul of the President's Park. Soon there were over sixty laborers, most of them Irish, laying out garden paths and spreading gravel.

At some point in the course of this work, the White House's most famous tree, the Jackson magnolia, was supposedly planted. There is no written record of its arrival, and William Seale, the leading authority on the White House's architecture and landscaping, has his doubts about the tree's origin.

I share his skepticism but I am inclined to follow the advice I once got from a veteran reporter: "Never check an interesting fact." This venerable tree has been called the Jackson magnolia for well over a hundred years, and I see no reason to rename it now.

One thing we know for certain is that Jemmy Maher and his men not only planted dozens of trees, but did a tremendous amount of drinking in the process. Their sometimes riotous behavior led to complaints to the president, our first Irish-American chief executive. But Jackson liked Maher, who hated the British as much as he did, so Jemmy stayed on.

Boozing aside, Maher knew his business. He replaced Jefferson's plantings with maples, sycamores, lindens, and other trees that he ordered from the finest nurseries in the country. Among Maher's best selections were horse chestnuts, which produced beautiful white blossoms that added an exotic dimension to the White House grounds.

Another clever purchase, warmly approved by Jackson, was a miniature fire engine, which could be trundled around the grounds, spraying water on the grass and plants along its way. Between the "watering machine" and a hand-pushed roller, the White House lawn became a marvel—a perfect shade of green and so smooth it looked sculpted.

It always amuses me that Andrew Jackson, the supposedly uncouth westerner, was the first president to make sure the White House grounds were worthy of the house that stood on them. Does this opinion having anything to do with my Missouri roots? Of course not!

In the gardens, Maher purchased "vine-trainers" for rose arbors—the first mention of the flower that has become a White House standby. Other flowers and shrubs included altheas, dwarf rose trees, and boxwood. Soon the gardens began attracting visitors. Years later, Jessie Benton Fremont, the daughter of Senator Thomas Hart Benton of Missouri, recalled "stands of camellias and laurestina banked row upon row, the glossy dark green leaves bringing into full relief their lovely wax-like flowers."

In 1835, President Jackson supervised the installation of an orangery—a hothouse where plants could be cultivated year-round so that residents of the White House could enjoy fruit and flowers during the winter months. A woodstove and oil heaters burned during cold weather, keeping the temperature tropical.

Jackson's orangery went up just in time to save a Malayan palm tree that had been cultivated from seed in the orangery at Mount Vernon by another enthusiastic horticulturist, George Washington. Old Hickory, who was an admirer of the first president, took great satisfaction in rescuing the tree after the Mount Vernon orangery burned down. The exotic creature survived until 1867, when it was destroyed in a second fire, this one in the White House orangery.

IV
***

John Ousley retained his job through the next four administrations, although it wasn't always easy. With the election of William Henry Harrison in 1840, the Whigs were in control of Congress. They lost much of their clout when Harrison died a month after his inauguration. Vice President John Tyler, who stepped into the job, was nominally a Whig, but he proved to be less than a party stalwart.

Tyler was regularly embroiled in feuds with the Whig-controlled Congress. When he vetoed their pet projects, they retaliated by withholding funds for the White House. Without the frugal hardworking Ousley, the gardens might have vanished.

Ousley developed an ingenious scheme for cutting the grass at no cost. When it got knee-high, he let a local livery stable owner scythe it and feed it to his horses as hay. Then he called in a farmer, who pastured a herd of sheep there for a few days and reduced the grass by another few inches. By then the lawn was ready for Ousley and his roller to flatten it into a smooth green carpet.

The periodic arrival of the sheep was not without its perils. Ousley had to fence in his shrubbery lest the omnivorous creatures consume that, too. Another worry was visitors' horses, who were equally eager to snack on the plantings along the driveway.

A modern visitor would barely recognize Ousley's grounds. There were fewer trees and those that existed were still rather spindly. Instead of a unified plan, there was a collection of small groves and gardens. The plot that received the most attention was the vegetable garden on the southwest side of the mansion. In a good year, it provided enough produce to feed the entire White House, saving cash-strapped chief executives more than a few dollars.

On the east side of the house, Ousley maintained a colorful flower garden. Among his favorite plants were roses, which he trained to climb along a white wooden arbor. Records reveal that Ousley planted over a hundred different varieties of this popular flower. They did not resemble our modern multipetaled roses but had flat, single blossoms, much like dogwood. Their fragrance undoubtedly contributed not a little to presidential pleasure, especially if you consider the other less lovely odors that swirled in and around the house from the swamps of the Potomac Flats to the south.

Oddly, the presidents and first ladies of Ousley's tenure seldom brought cut flowers into the house. The quacks who passed for doctors in that era had convinced the public that fresh flowers would poison the air indoors. It may surprise you to learn (it did me) that until the 1850s most of the flowers in the White House were wax. But women visitors were often given bouquets as favors, and little girls received nosegays.

V

★★★

President James Polk, hoping to launch a trend, decorated the north lawn with an impressive statue of Thomas Jefferson, suggesting that the Democrats were in the White House to stay. Alas, they lost the next election to the Whig candidate, Zachary Taylor, who did little for the lawn but park his warhorse, Whitey, on it.

Taylor's death in 1850 brought the White House its next amateur horticulturist of note—handsome silver-haired Millard Fillmore, otherwise considered a nonentity by most historians. President Fillmore hired Andrew Jackson Downing, the most famous landscape designer of his day. Downing's books, *The Theory and Practice of Landscape Gardening* and *The Architecture of Country Houses*, were in the library of anyone who lived on a plot large enough to landscape. Something of a prima donna, the thirty-three-year-old Downing bristled when Washington officials referred to him as a "public gardener" and insisted that his title be changed to "rural architect." When he arrived in Washington to confer with President Fillmore, Downing issued an ultimatum: "If I am interfered with, I will throw up the matter at once."

Everyone thought Downing was an original thinker in his profession, but in fact he stole most of his ideas from English landscape designers. No one, including Fillmore, knew the difference, and the self-styled genius got the authority to relandscape the public grounds, including the President's Park, Capitol Hill, and the Mall that stretched between the two.

The Mall was to be planted with groves of trees interspersed with winding footpaths and carriage drives. For the White House grounds, Downing proposed a new design, again using plenty of trees. Whether John Ousley, by now somewhat long in the tooth, protested is not clear. At any rate, he was abruptly informed that his services were terminated and he was ordered out of the wooden cottage to which he and his wife had moved after residing for many years in the east wing of the White House. Governments, as more than one politician has pointed out, are not big on gratitude.

Ousley was replaced by a young Scotsman named John Watt, who would later display a fondness for combining gardening and politics. But for the moment, the focus was on Downing. The rural architect boarded the Hudson River steamboat *Henry Clay* at his home town of Newburgh, New York, about fifty miles north of New York City, with drawings of his final plans for the Mall, the Capitol, and the White House. The *Henry Clay* caught fire and Downing died in the flames. With him perished his precious drawings. In Washington, the president and his aides were too stunned to do anything but lament. No one had the confidence or the ability to step into Downing's shoes.

In any case, Millard Fillmore participated in one White House beautification project. He presided at the unveiling of the equestrian statue of Andrew Jackson in Lafayette Square, just across Pennsylvania Avenue from the White House. The square is on land that was originally set aside for the President's Park and it is still considered part of the grounds despite the fact that it was cut off from the main property when Pennsylvania Avenue was extended in 1822. For much of the nineteenth century, Lafayette Square was the home of Washington's elite. Its park also became known as "the lobby of the White House" because it was a popular hangout for office seekers.

One of the things that made the Jackson statue remarkable was the way the sculptor, Clark Mills, poised the horse on its hind legs—a major feat of engineering in that era. I like the statue because it makes Old Hickory's legacy of a strong presidency, and a strong America, a permanent part of the White House's collective memory.

VI

★★★

The introduction of Andrew Jackson's statue inspired Washington's city fathers to put gas lamps in Lafayette Park and enclose it with an iron fence. As part of the beautification project, trees were planted along the city streets. Meanwhile, John Watt was revealing his talent for getting things done. He persuaded the new president, Franklin Pierce, to let him expand Jackson's rebuilt orangery into a greenhouse.

Four years later, Watt's greenhouse had to be demolished to make room for a wing of the Treasury Building, but not before plans were made for a replacement. It was to occupy the White House's western terrace and would be connected to the mansion itself to make it easily accessible to presidential families and their guests.

President Pierce was enthusiastic about the plans for the greenhouse, which was now being referred to as a conservatory, and looked forward to enjoying it during his second term. Alas, the Democrats informed the chagrined president that he was not getting the nomination. As a result, another Democrat, James Buchanan, became the first president to use this pleasant patch of indoor greenery when it was completed in 1857. Boasting lemon and orange trees plus dozens of different plants and flowers, the conservatory was furnished with chairs and benches and was gaslit for evening visits.

By this time, fears of being poisoned by having flowers indoors were beginning to wane. They all but vanished after Harriet Lane, James Buchanan's niece and official hostess, discovered that vases full of fresh flowers were all the rage in England. She immediately introduced them at the White House, with the conservatory providing a steady supply.

Among John Watt's prize specimens were several different varieties of japonicas, more familiarly known as camellias. In the late

1850s, they were the flower of choice at White House social events and were immediately adopted by every other hostess in the capital.

VII
★★★

Under the Lincolns, John Watt became more than a gardener. Mary Lincoln, unsure of the ways of official Washington, turned to him for advice. She was also a fan of his flowers, and he made sure she was constantly supplied with the finest specimens money could produce. Mrs. Lincoln filled almost every vase in the White House with camellias, hydrangeas, and other blossoms. At dinners and receptions, she often wore garlands of flowers on her dresses or entwined a few in her hair.

For a while, John Watt also made it a point to give her a daily bouquet. She found these floral gifts so beautiful, she mentioned them in letters and passed them along to friends in Washington. Mrs. Lincoln soon became a regular visitor to the conservatory, but she had more on her mind than flowers. Mary had run up horrendous bills on shopping trips to New York and was afraid to tell her husband about them. When she confided this news to Watt, he assured her that such things were easily handled, Washington-style. If she charged the expenses to several different accounts, the government auditors would be too confused to figure out where the money had gone.

In return for this advice, Watt solicited Mrs. Lincoln's aid in dealing with some sharper than expected government auditors who were on his trail for performing his own "hide the money" tricks. She wrote indignant letters in his defense to the secretary of the interior, Watt's putative boss. Some historians believe that Watt was siphoning off cash from his gardening budget to help Mary pay her shopping bills.

The first lady grew even more indignant when someone accused

Watt of being a Confederate sympathizer. He talked his way out of it, and Mary's faith in her covert benefactor became even more fervent. Before long, Watt expanded his job description. Besides being the first lady's favorite florist and tutor in the fine art of embezzling, he was also her self-appointed snoop. Talk about Potomac fever!

Watt reported on minor infractions by members of the staff and undoubtedly escalated some of them into more serious offenses. Several servants were fired on his say-so including the White House steward, who was replaced by Watt's twenty-one-year-old wife, Jane, giving the gardener even more power.

Almost predictably, Watt overreached himself. Now that he had the run of the White House, he wandered into the president's second-floor office one day and spotted a draft of the 1862 State of the Union address on the desk. Watt memorized a fair amount of it and recited it to another friend of Mary Lincoln's, a dashing man-about-town named Henry Wikoff, who promptly sold it to the virulently anti-Lincoln New York *Herald*.

Watt actually may have been a Confederate sympathizer. More probably, Wikoff paid him for the information. The speech was soon in the *Herald*, with an editorial criticizing Lincoln in sneering terms. After an investigation led to Wikoff's arrest, he confessed that he had gotten the information from Watt, and the gardener corroborated his statement under oath.

Lincoln was appalled to learn that his wife had befriended two such questionable characters. Some friends gave him even worse news. Wikoff had been overheard boasting that his main purpose in coming to Washington was to help the *Herald* undermine Lincoln's presidency.

In the midst of this conversation, Lincoln suddenly remembered that the first lady was entertaining Wikoff and a group of other friends in one of the White House parlors. He stormed downstairs and ordered the man out of the house. Mr. and Mrs. Watt soon followed.

VIII

White House gardening languished for a decade and a half after John Watt's departure. His replacement, James Nokes, did little but maintain the status quo, producing flowers by the dozen for the first ladies of the Johnson and Grant administrations. Julia Grant was especially grateful for his handiwork. He not only provided arrangements for White House parties, he also created bouquets that could be dropped off by a White House footman in lieu of the long, tedious social calls she would otherwise have had to make on her own.

Ulysses S. Grant made two notable additions to the Executive Mansion's grounds. He had a pool installed on the south lawn with a water spray powered by steam, and, in a symbolic gesture signaling a long Republican reign, he had the statue of Thomas Jefferson, the founder of the Democratic Party, moved from the north lawn and installed in the Statuary Hall at the Capitol. The statue was replaced by a magnificent circular flower bed designed by the Army Corps of Engineers. At its center was a pool with a jet of water that made no political statement whatsoever.

With the arrival of Rutherford B. Hayes in 1876, the White House had a first couple who were seriously interested in landscaping. Hayes replaced James Nokes with a Cincinnatian named Henry Pfister and put him to work improving the grounds.

One of the president's main concerns was the land to the south of the mansion. In the early days, this was a vast meadow that culminated in a swampy marsh along the banks of the Tiber Creek, one of the tributaries of the Potomac River. Eventually a section of the meadow was fenced off to create the south lawn, but a large swath of land remained.

During the Civil War, cattle-feeding pens and a slaughterhouse had occupied much of this terrain. When they vanished, a barren patch of scraggly shrubs and trees was left. Meanwhile, the Tiber Creek and its marshes had been drained and the land filled in.

Andrew Jackson Downing had hoped to plant trees and grass and turn the area into a large circular "parade" where public celebrations and military reviews could be held.

Hayes, drawing on Downing's plan, decided to create a seventeen-acre park called the Ellipse, which became a popular spot for Sunday and holiday outings. Separated from the White House by a curving road, the Ellipse still provides a splendid vista from the South Portico with unobstructed views of the Washington Monument and the Jefferson Memorial.

The main object of this presidential gift, however, was to allow Rutherford B. Hayes to close the White House grounds to the public. He had become president on the electoral votes of southern states that were almost certainly purchased by Republican operators (one of them a future president, James Garfield). His daily mail contained not a few death threats.

Unlike the Grants and other presidential families, the Hayeses never sat on the South Portico or spent much time on the grounds lest an unseen sniper be lurking nearby. They preferred the conservatory because they could gather there with friends and family without being seen by the public.

During Hayes's administration, the conservatory was expanded. A separate Rose House was added, the walks were broadened, and iron benches were installed. Mrs. Hayes regularly invited guests to stroll through the indoor gardens after dinner. There was strategy as well as graciousness in this custom—Lucy had banned alcohol from the White House to set a national example of temperance, and she hoped the flowers and greenery would console those who longed for an after-dinner whiskey or liqueur.

IX
***

The conservatory continued to be popular during the Cleveland and Harrison administrations. It was still a ready source of floral ar-

rangements for every occasion and supplied the flowers that decorated the Blue Room for Grover Cleveland's wedding. Mrs. Cleveland loved flowers of all kinds but her particular favorites were
orchids, which you can be sure were grown in abundance during
both of her husband's terms.

Orchids were eclipsed by roses during William McKinley's presidency. His wife, Ida, adored them and the now-aging Henry Pfister
wore himself out making rose arrangements for her. Her husband
was equally fond of red carnations and started a national craze for
that flower. He considered them his good-luck charm and never
went anywhere without one in his buttonhole.

Edith Roosevelt's appetite for roses put all her predecessors in the
shade. She may have been influenced by her husband. Both he and
his father had a special fondness for roses, and Teddy had them put
on the crest that was used on the Roosevelt family's china. Alice
Roosevelt, with her usual irreverence, pooh-poohed this flirtation
with aristocracy. "Our ancestors were gardeners," she claimed.

Edith Roosevelt enlisted the new White House gardener, George
H. Brown, to design the centerpieces for her dinners. Roses invariably predominated. At one diplomatic dinner in 1903, six hundred
red roses and over three thousand other plants were used. The
White House conservatories could not possibly provide this many
blooms. Poor Brown had to depopulate half the commercial greenhouses in Washington to keep up with the demand.

By 1901, when the Roosevelts moved into the White House, the
conservatory had spawned so many annexes that they covered more
space than the main floor of the mansion. The west terrace was a
veritable village of glass houses, each in a different size, shape, and
style. When architect Charles McKim was called in to renovate the
White House a year later, the village's days became numbered.

McKim considered the greenhouses an excrescence on the White
House's formal beauty and would happily have smashed them all
into shards. It is hard to quarrel with the architect's aesthetic judgment, but when I read about how much pleasure the greenhouses

gave presidential families and what an abundance of fresh flowers they produced, I found myself wishing we had had one during our White House days.

Irwin Hood "Ike" Hoover, who began his forty-two years on the White House staff a few years before the greenhouses vanished, wrote a sort of elegy for them in his memoirs.

> *The dear old conservatory where the couples would roam during parties and be lost among the tall ferns! Here too would be stationed the Marine Band with their scarlet coats standing out against the green foliage. Here were all the funny kinds of plants and the tropical fruit trees whose dwarf fruit we were all so proud of. There were bananas, oranges, lemons, figs and nuts of various kinds; the artillery plant, whose blossoms would burst and send forth a sort of vapor like a cannon-blast; the fly catching plant, whose tender leaves would curl up when tickled in the center.*

You can see why First Lady Edith Roosevelt hated to see the greenhouses go. Her resolve was stiffened by a letter from the now retired Henry Pfister, who had cultivated many of the rare plants and flowers so many years before. He begged her not to let them be destroyed. Charles McKim made a special trip to Oyster Bay to plead his own case to the first lady. She finally relented, but only on condition that a few of the most attractive greenhouses be moved elsewhere and the most exotic plants be used as the nucleus of a botanical garden for the city of Washington.

X
✯✯✯

Edith Roosevelt called on Henry Pfister to help her design a colonial garden on the west side of the White House where the Rose House had stood. She eventually put in a similar garden on the east side and proudly displayed them both at spring garden parties. The two gardens were formally laid out, the flower beds outlined in box-wood and privet hedges, with gravel paths for visitors to stroll along.

Helen Taft put Edith Roosevelt's gardens to even greater use. In the tropical Philippines, where her husband, William Howard Taft, had been U.S. High Commissioner, outdoor entertaining was al-most de rigueur. Mrs. Taft continued the tradition at the White House, with a taste for more dazzling effects than those favored by her reserved, aristocratic predecessor. At Helen's first party, for in-stance, her guests advanced down a lane of flowers to the shade of some blooming pear trees, where the first lady received them.

Woodrow Wilson's wife, Ellen Axson Wilson, was another first lady with a passion for plants and a good eye for garden design. Edith Roosevelt's west wing colonial garden was just below Ellen Wilson's bedroom window. As she gazed down on it on Inaugura-tion Day in 1913, an alternative plan entered her mind. She told her daughters it would be "our rose garden with a high hedge around it." A subsequent study of the garden on the east side of the White House marked that one for a facelift, too.

Mrs. Wilson hired two professional landscape designers, George Burnap and Beatrice Farrand. After consulting with Burnap, Mrs. Wilson decided not only to change Edith Roosevelt's colonial gar-den into a Rose Garden but to add a tree-lined walkway for the president to use when he went to and from the Oval Office. Prior to that, the nation's chief executive reached his office via the White House basement, trudging past servants' rooms, the laundry, and assorted other utilitarian spaces.

After a great deal of jockeying over the costs, a lane of less costly hedges was substituted for the trees. The garden ran parallel to this path. True to Mrs. Wilson's plan, roses were the dominant plant-ings, but masses of smaller flowers were set along the borders.

At one end of the garden was a marble bench covered by an awning. Here Mrs. Wilson had a telephone installed so the president could continue to conduct business while he was enjoying her company. (I suspect this was more of a joke than a serious attempt to keep him in touch with the job.) Overlooking the garden was a statue of a little boy. The White House staff suspected it was the son Ellen wished she could have given the president to carry on his name.

To avoid the forlorn look of a flower garden in winter, the east wing plot was almost exclusively green. Evergreens and ivy predominated. Gone was Andrew Jackson Downing's emphasis on the rustic; the design was formal in the style of the time. In the center of the garden stood a rectangular lily pool, a tranquil sight for anyone looking out the east windows.

XI
★★★

Mrs. Wilson's gardens flourished and were praised and beloved by the next two decades of White House residents. But when Franklin D. Roosevelt arrived in 1933, he decided it was time to redo not only the White House (especially the West Wing) but also the grounds. He hired the most distinguished landscape architect of the day, Frederick Law Olmstead, Jr., son of the man who had designed New York's Central Park.

Olmstead approached the task cautiously, with great respect for the old house's traditions. He found many aspects of the existing landscape had "great dignity and appropriateness." But there were also a few items that cried out for removal. Along the edge of the driveway, for instance, Olmstead noticed a rusted iron fence covered with rambler roses. No one could tell him where it had come from or why it was there.

Olmstead's main criticism of the south lawn was that it had far too many trees. He favored removing the ones in the center to allow for a broad sweep of lawn, about two hundred feet wide. The thick screen of trees and shrubbery along the sides would remain. Olmstead also urged a substantial revision of the gardens to achieve a super-formal look. Their appearance struck him as "makeshift"—a description that would have irked Ellen Wilson but can probably be blamed on less than diligent tending during the previous twenty years.

XII

Most of Olmstead's ideas were gradually introduced, giving the White House grounds the overall appearance they retain to this day. While the property boasts several very colorful gardens, trees have always predominated. Some of these leafy creatures are quite old. One of the oldest, an American elm planted by John Quincy Adams, lasted until 1991, when time and disease caught up to it. The White House gardeners, who, like everyone else connected to the mansion, have acquired a sense of history, foresaw its demise and propagated a new tree from it—so John Quincy's planting continues to flourish not far from where it originally grew.

Rutherford B. Hayes had hoped to see every president honored with a tree representing his native state. The Ohio-born Hayes started the ball rolling by planting a small forest of Ohio buckeyes, better known to Jemmy Maher and the rest of us as horse chestnuts. Other presidents, both before and since, have planted trees, but until recently it was a haphazard business.

At last count there were forty-one presidential trees, but some first families, such as the Bushes and the Clintons, have more than one to their credit. During their two terms in the White House, Bill and Hillary Clinton planted a number of white dogwoods, a willow oak, a littleleaf linden, and an American elm.

Among the trees planted by Jimmy Carter is a cedar of Lebanon, eminently suitable for a Bible-quoting man. Herbert Hoover has a willow oak down near the south fence. Gerry Ford planted an American elm along the north driveway to celebrate the country's bicentennial in 1976, and George H. W. Bush and Queen Elizabeth II planted a littleleaf linden to commemorate her visit to the White House in 1991.

I'm happy to say that Harry Truman has not gone unrepresented. He is responsible for the sturdy and perennially green English and American boxwood that graces the North Portico. In addition, Dad participated in the preservation of the celebrated Jackson magnolia. When the White House was reconstructed under his auspices, Dad watched with approval while the gardeners dug the old tree from the ground near the South Portico and replanted it in a safe place. It was moved during the winter when it was least likely to suffer damage.

When the restored White House opened for business on March 27, 1952, the venerable creature was returned to more or less the same spot. During our last spring in the White House, we enjoyed its lovely cream-colored blossoms beside our windows. For Dad it stirred memories of that unforgettable lunch with Franklin D. Roosevelt. For me it was a reminder of how often fate has played a part in making a man president.

There are now more than five hundred different kinds of trees on the White House grounds, all of them magnificent specimens, thanks to the tender, loving care they receive from the gardening staff year-round. William Seale, the chronicler of the mansion's architectural and landscape history, calls them the White House's "unsung glory." You can't improve on that.

XIII
★★★

In 1961, John F. Kennedy, perhaps inspired by his wife's determination to overhaul the White House's interior, decided the Rose Garden needed a new look. It was substantially unchanged since Ellen Wilson's day, so he may well have been right. Kennedy put two talented landscape designers, Rachel Lambert Mellon and Perry Wheeler, to work on the project, and the new superintendent of the grounds, Irvin M. Williams, executed their joint brainchild with something close to perfection.

The gardening staff had a few adventures in the course of their digging and planting. When they replaced the old sod with new dirt, they went down four inches and found themselves in an archaeological treasure trove—pieces of pots from the old greenhouses, Civil War horseshoes, and uniform buttons.

In one corner of the plot, their sharp-edged shovels inadvertently cut the cable for the hot line the president used to put the armed forces on full alert. Within seconds, the gardeners were surrounded by White House police, ready to charge them with sabotaging the nation's security. The cable had originally been laid during World War II, and no one had bothered to note its exact location.

JFK, with his instinct for media politics, had more than mere beautification in mind when he ordered the Rose Garden remodeled. The finished product had a lawn large enough to hold a thousand spectators. Limestone steps at the western end can be converted into a presidential podium in a matter of minutes. On the edges of the lawn are tasteful flower beds divided by boxwood hedges and flanked by a mix of magnolia and crab apple trees. The garden is a beautiful space and in between speeches and photo ops, it is the essence of tranquillity. Like the modern White House, the Rose Garden is a superb compromise between utility and history in the making.

Ellen Wilson's east wing garden remained pretty much intact until the Kennedy administration. Then JFK, inspired by the transformation of the Rose Garden, decided that its counterpart on the east side of the mansion needed some sprucing up as well. Plans were drawn up but the sad day in Dallas put an end to that dream, along with so many others. Fortunately, Lady Bird Johnson, a first lady with a green thumb and then some, took charge of the garden and saw it to fruition under Rachel Lambert Mellon's stewardship.

While Mrs. Mellon retained the Wilsonian idea of a mostly green garden, she added seasonal flowers and ornamental hedges, and balanced the lily pond with a pergola on the opposite side. This enchanted spot is often referred to as the First Ladies' Garden but it was officially dedicated by Lady Bird Johnson in honor of Jacqueline Kennedy—a fitting tribute to a first lady whose love for the White House will be remembered for a long time.

President Jimmy Carter encouraged the cultivation of an herb garden, which has been a godsend to the White House chef. He or one of his assistants can often be found snipping some cilantro or sage for one of their signature dishes. Old John Adams, the planter of that long ago kitchen garden, would no doubt approve this mix of beauty and utility.

XIV
★★★

The White House also has two very special gardens designed for the exclusive use of the first family and their guests. One is the Children's Garden, created by Lady Bird Johnson in a secluded section of the south lawn. Mrs. Johnson made the beautification of Washington, D.C., and much of the rest of the country the major project of her White House years. A logical extension of Lady Bird's joy in the beauties of nature, the Children's Garden was a Christmas present from the Johnsons to the White House.

This tiny treasure has a small waterlily pond in the center, and the names, footprints, and handprints of White House grandchildren set in bronze in the flagstones. George and Barbara Bush are way ahead in this department, with no less than fourteen "grands" recorded for posterity.

Lady Bird gave a lovely description of the garden in a letter she wrote not long after it was finished:

> *I've just walked down to see the tiny little garden which we want to leave for White House children and grandchildren of days to come.*
>
> *I like the way it's tucked away, and you're almost surprised to come upon flagstones leading through a "secret tunnel" lined by the holly trees. The apple tree will be lovely, with blossoms in spring, and fruit in Autumn and it's almost irresistibly "climbable." Wouldn't a small swing be nice there? I hope there will be some crocus among the flagstones for early Spring bloomings.*
>
> *I think of the spot as the sort of place a First Lady who is a grandmother might wheel a baby carriage and sit in the shade and enjoy her own backyard, in a quiet secluded spot. And very especially it would be a grand place for four-year-olds to have a "tea party," or watch the goldfish in the little pool—or for their mother or grandmother to read about Peter Rabbit or Winnie the Pooh.*
>
> *I shall think back affectionately about this dear House and these grounds we've loved these five years.*

The second garden, even more secluded than the Children's Garden, is outside the Oval Office, and is for the president's private use. It was created during the Reagan years and remains a closely guarded little preserve—a true secret garden. Presidents occasionally use it on a pleasant day for a lunch or informal meeting with one of the many VIPs who visit the White House.

XV
★★★

The gardens and grounds of 1600 Pennsylvania Avenue have become so popular, recent chief executives have been persuaded to open them for tours, drawing oohs and aahs of admiration from thousands. The tours are held in April and October and there is always a long line of people waiting to admire the carefully tended blossoms and critique the first family's taste in flowers. Maybe on garden tour days the president ought to have a sign on his desk that says: THE BUD STOPS HERE.

After Richard Nixon's decision to resign as president, he embraced his daughter Julie in one of the most poignant moments in White House history.
Credit: Oliver Atkins Collection, Special Collections and Archives, George Mason University Libraries

4

★★★

History Happened Here

On September 11, 2001, there was serious concern that the White House might become the target of a terrorist attack. Minutes after an American Airlines jet crashed into the Pentagon on that horrifying morning, a squadron of F-16s armed with missiles was airborne over Washington. The pilots had just confirmed the explosion at the Pentagon when the grim voice of a Secret Service agent was heard on their headsets: "I want you to protect the White House at all costs."

As we all know, the White House was spared. If it hadn't been, I hate to think of the toll in human lives and national morale, not to mention the loss of irreplaceable antiques and works of art. It would have been far worse than the previous attack on the President's House that occurred when it was a relatively new and still unfinished building.

In 1812, when America launched a "second War of independence" against England, no one ever imagined the White House would be in harm's way. To say that the politicians did not know what they were doing in this war would be a masterpiece of understatement. It never seemed to occur to them that they were taking on a country that had the most powerful navy in the world. Add to this fact British expertise in amphibious warfare and you have a recipe for a White House in peril.

In the summer of 1814, while most of the American army was up on the northern border trying to make Canada a part of the United States, a British fleet appeared off the Maryland coast. Soon, an army of 4,500 men landed without a shot being fired at them. President James Madison called out the militia—part-time soldiers with little or no training. They met the British professionals at Bladensburg, Maryland, on August 24, 1814, in one of the shortest battles in American history. Although they outnumbered the British, the amateurs ran for their lives at the first volley. President Madison and members of his cabinet, who had ridden out to watch the fight, were swept away in the human maelstrom.

In the White House, First Lady Dolley Madison was trying to go about her normal routine. She had instructed the mansion's steward to prepare the usual midafternoon dinner, and set extra places for any guests who might appear.

When hours passed with no news from her husband, she went upstairs and scoured the landscape with a telescope. "I am determined not to go until I see Mr. Madison safe," she told her sister in a letter that she wrote intermittently while waiting for news. For a while a detachment of militia was camped on the lawn with orders to protect the house. But when news of Bladensburg seeped into the capital, these heroes, too, ran away.

In the early afternoon, two hard-riding, dust-covered messengers came pounding up to the White House. "Get out!" they cried. "The British are on their way!"

Somehow Dolley procured a wagon, and with the help of the White House steward, loaded it with silver and other valuables. She filled trunks with government papers, leaving behind her own and the president's personal possessions. But she still refused to retreat, declaring that only a personal command from the president could persuade her to leave.

This finally arrived in the person of Jim Smith, a free man of color who came galloping up the lawn shouting: "Clear out! Clear out!" The president's friend Charles Carroll also appeared to escort Dolley to safety. Dolley refused to be hurried. As she later recalled it, Carroll was soon "in a very bad humor because I insisted on waiting while a large picture of General Washington was secured and it required to be unscrewed from the wall."

When the frantic White House servants were unable to take down the picture, Dolley ordered the frame broken and the canvas taken out. She was determined not to leave the Father of the Country to the mercy of his old enemies. But time was growing short. Two gentlemen from New York stopped by to see if they could help and Dolley entrusted the canvas, still on its stretcher, to them for safekeeping. On the way out, the first lady stopped to snatch up another precious relic—a framed copy of the Declaration of Independence.

Even now, Dolley was reluctant to abandon the house. She later told a friend she would have staged a fight to the finish if she had a few cannon to fire from the windows. "Alas, those who should have placed them [the cannon] fled before me," she said. The gallant first lady retreated only three miles, to the house of a friend on the outskirts of the capital.

At eight o'clock that evening, the scarlet-coated British army arrived in Washington. At their head were General Robert Ross and Admiral Sir George Cockburn. Without bothering to knock, they burst into the dark silent White House. To their vast amusement, they found the table set for Dolley's dinner guests. "Several kinds of wine in handsome glass decanters were cooling on the sideboard," one British officer wrote. "In the kitchen, spits loaded with joints [of meat] of various sorts turned before the fire." I have my doubts about the fire. Surely the flames would have been banked before the house was abandoned. Soldiers like to embellish the tales they tell.

But there is little doubt that the general and the admiral enjoyed a glass of wine courtesy of Dolley. Then they went to work on the White House. Under Admiral Cockburn's personal direction, 150 sailors from his fleet, professionals at starting fires, smashed out all the windows and piled the furniture in the various rooms in heaps. Retreating outside, fifty of these seaman seized long poles with oil-soaked rags on their ends and surrounded the house. At a signal from the admiral, a man with a torch ignited the rags and the poles were hurled through the smashed windows. An "instantaneous conflagration" sent flames gushing into the night sky.

The British thought the Americans had this fiery treatment coming to them because they had burned the public buildings in York, Canada, the previous year. But torching the White House proved to be the worst mistake the king's men made in the War of 1812. The United States had been badly divided over "Mr. Madison's War," as they called it in New England. Now a Baltimore orator cried: "The Spirit of the Nation is aroused!" Fort McHenry, defending Baltimore, withstood a nightlong bombardment from Admiral Cockburn's fleet. In the dawn, a Washingtonian named Francis Scott Key saw the flag still flying and scribbled some verses that became "The Star-Spangled Banner." In New York, huge numbers of volunteers rushed to complete coastal forts. A few months later General Andrew Jackson scored a decisive victory against the British at New Orleans. Confronted by a united, determined nation, London was more than willing to ratify a treaty of peace.

II

★★★

On October 7, 2001, a little more than three weeks after the terrorist assaults on the Pentagon and the World Trade Center, President George W. Bush addressed the nation from the Treaty Room of the White House. His announcement was brief and to the point: The United States was launching air strikes against the Taliban government of Afghanistan, the start of a campaign to destroy al-Qaeda, the terrorist network responsible for the attacks.

President Bush's speech added a new page to the history of this venerable room. For most of the mansion's early years it was a private meeting room. During Abraham Lincoln's administration it was the waiting room for the president's office next door.

In 1866, President Andrew Johnson turned the space into his Cabinet Room and the cabinet continued to meet there until 1902, when the West Wing was built. Twentieth-century presidents have used the room as an office or sitting room and sometimes both. Lou Henry Hoover furnished it with reproductions of the furniture James Monroe had bought for the White House and it became known as the Monroe Room.

It went by that name through the Roosevelt and Truman administrations and became the Treaty Room only after the Kennedys moved in. The name was chosen to commemorate President William McKinley's signing of the treaty of peace that ended the Spanish-American War in 1898.

A number of other memorable events have also occurred in this room. On March 1, 1845, four days before the end of his term, President John Tyler signed a controversial bill annexing the Republic of Texas to the United States. He gave the gold pen he used to his wife, Julia, whose magnificent White House parties had charmed key congressmen and senators into voting for the measure. Julia wore the pen around her neck for the rest of her life.

The Trumans have always had a special fondness for John Tyler. Dad's grandfather, Anderson Shippe Truman, married a direct descendent of President Tyler's brother. In addition, John Tyler was the first vice president to become chief executive after the death of a president. Dad regarded this as another bond between them.

III

☆☆☆

Theodore Roosevelt used the former Cabinet Room as his office and made it the scene of an extraordinary confrontation between himself and one of the most powerful men in America.

When Roosevelt became president after William McKinley's assassination in 1901, the United States was, in the opinion of many well-informed people, on the brink of a revolution. At the top of the economic pyramid, giants such as J. P. Morgan and Henry Clay Frick wielded fantastic power. While Morgan and his fellow tycoons enjoyed a world of mansions and yachts, factory workers toiled twelve hours a day, seven days a week, for less than ten dollars a week. Almost two million children between the ages of ten and fifteen worked twelve-hour days in New England textile mills.

Despairing of justice, working people talked of violent solutions. Union leaders such as Big Bill Haywood, hero of the western miners, advocated dynamite as the best answer to union-busting police and federal troops. Nobody had much hope that the forty-two-year-old accidental president would do anything to change things. He had been born rich, gone to Harvard, and appeared to be a typical member of the ruling class.

Only a few months after Roosevelt took office, the financiers pulled their worst stunt yet. J. P. Morgan and his friends organized the Northern Securities Company, a monopoly that put all the railroads in the Northwest under the same management and gave them complete control over the prices they charged.

Northern Securities was a clear violation of the Sherman Anti-Trust Act, but it was created on the cool assumption that the government would never attack big business. When scarcely a voice was raised in Congress, Theodore Roosevelt realized he would have to act alone. Without consulting his cabinet or anyone else, he ordered his attorney general, Philander C. Knox, to prosecute Northern Securities.

The suit was filed on February 18, 1902, and the news hit Wall Street like a cyclone. Stocks plummeted. J. P. Morgan exploded with rage, sputtering, among other things, that Roosevelt was "no gentleman."

Morgan was formidable. According to photographer Edward Steichen, looking into his eyes when he was angry was like confronting an onrushing express train. The infuriated financier boarded his private railroad car and headed for Washington, D.C.

Roosevelt and Attorney General Knox saw him in the president's second-floor office, the present Treaty Room. The conversation was tense. "If we have done anything wrong," Morgan growled to the president, "send your man [the attorney general] to my man [naming one of his lawyers] and they can fix it up."

"We don't want to fix it up," Attorney General Knox said. "We want to stop it."

"Are you going to attack my other interests?" the stunned Morgan asked.

"Certainly not," Roosevelt said. "Unless we find out they've done something we regard as wrong."

The victory was historic. By taking on the king of the financiers, and two years later winning the case in the U.S. Supreme Court, President Theodore Roosevelt made it clear to the whole country that "the biggest corporations, like the humblest private citizen, must be held to strict compliance with the will of the people." For the first time in decades the average man felt there was a president in the White House capable of taking his side in the struggle for a better life.

IV

***

The most famous room in the White House is unquestionably the Lincoln Bedroom—although Abraham Lincoln never slept in it. He used the room as his office. It was here, on January 1, 1863, that Lincoln emancipated the slaves of the eleven seceded southern states.

During the first year of the Civil War, the president had been savagely attacked by the radical members of his own party, the Republicans, for refusing to turn the war into a crusade to free the slaves. An astute politician, Lincoln knew that most Americans were not ready for such a move. At the same time, he detested slavery. From his youth, he had vowed to strike a blow at the awful institution if he ever got the chance.

One day, the president saw a way to do it—by giving the seceded states one last chance to return to the Union. If they refused, emancipation could be called a "war measure," a means to subdue the rebellion.

In the summer of 1862, Lincoln read to his cabinet a draft of a proclamation warning the Confederacy that if they did not make peace by the end of the year, all their slaves would be freed. The cabinet members did not object to the proclamation, but Secretary of State William Seward urged the president not to release it until the Union army had won a victory. Otherwise the move would seem like "the last shriek" of the expiring federal government.

Lincoln agreed and the proclamation was put aside until the Union army repulsed Robert E. Lee's invasion of Maryland in the bloody battle of Antietam. On September 22, five days after this tremendous clash, Lincoln announced his intention to issue the proclamation.

The news sent a wave of renewed hope through the city of Washington. That night a crowd marched up Pennsylvania Avenue to the music of the Marine Band. John Hay, Lincoln's secretary, described the scene at the White House. "The white columns of the Executive Mansion [stood] lucid and diaphanous . . . like the architecture of a dream. The crowd flowed in and filled every nook and cranny of the grand entrance . . . the band burst into stirring and triumphant harmony and . . . the tall President appeared at the window. He said only a half dozen words, but his voice was full of an earnest solemnity, and there was something of unusual dignity in his manner."

The Confederacy remained defiant and on January 1, 1863, Lincoln, true to his word, issued the proclamation. Messengers rushed it to the State Department where calligraphers would inscribe it on official parchment. Meanwhile the White House staff prepared for the annual New Year's Day reception. Around eleven A.M., the president and Mrs. Lincoln descended to the Blue Room to greet the diplomats and generals who had the place of honor at the head of the visitors' line. After shaking hands for an hour, Lincoln felt blisters swelling on his hand and retreated to his upstairs office to wait for the proclamation's return from the State Department.

Secretary of State Seward and his son Frederick brought the document over around three P.M. and found Lincoln alone in his office. They spread the proclamation on a table before the fire. Picking up a silvery steel pen, Lincoln gazed ruefully at his blistered hand. "I never in my life felt more certain I was doing right, than I do in signing this paper," he said. "But . . . my arm is stiff and numb. This signature will be closely examined. If they find my hand trembled, they will say 'he had some complications.' But anyway, it is going to be done."

Lincoln signed in one unhesitating flourish and three million slaves were freed. There is some evidence of a tremor in the signature. But the great deed was done.

Lincoln sat back and smiled at the two witnesses. Secretary of State Seward signed below Lincoln's name and Fred Seward put the seal of the United States on the document. Seward wanted to send the pen to the state of Massachusetts, the headquarters of the abolition movement, and Lincoln gave it to him. After a few more friendly words, the Sewards left the president alone in his office. It was all so low-keyed, even Lincoln found it hard to believe that he had just executed, as he later told an artist friend, "the central act of my administration and the great event of the nineteenth century."

V

★★★

At the start of the Civil War, the enemy was alarmingly close to the White House gates. Looking south from the upstairs windows,

President Lincoln could see Confederate flags on the other side of the Potomac. At night, Rebel campfires dotted the hills of Arlington. For a while, the executive mansion was guarded by Union soldiers who camped in the East Room and cadged food from the cooks. When the war widened, they left for the battlefront.

Whenever the Union won a victory, Lincoln ordered the White House illuminated. One of the doormen, Thomas Pendel, fixed small pieces of tallow candles to strips of wood inside all the windows on the north front. He later described "tiers and tiers of them lighting the entire front of the White House."

Unfortunately, for the first two years of the war, there were not many victories. The telegrams that were rushed from the War Department to the president's office on the second floor of the White House brought mostly bad news. Then, on July 4, 1863, there was a stunning turnaround. The Union army in the east had won a tremendous victory at Gettysburg. Another Union army in the west had captured Vicksburg, giving Lincoln's government control of the Mississippi River.

The White House was soon aglow, and a crowd of several hundred people gathered on Pennsylvania Avenue to serenade the president. Lincoln appeared in a window over the North Portico. Nearby was Tommy Pendel, holding a candle aloft so everyone could see the president. These "serenade speeches," as Lincoln called them, were always brief but often eloquent and full of emotion.

Two years later, on April 9, 1865, General Robert E. Lee surrendered at Appomattox Court House. As soon as the news became public, thousands of people poured onto the White House grounds, accompanied by a band. Lincoln came to the same north window and startled everyone by asking the band to play "Dixie." He said it was one of his favorite songs.

The next night Lincoln spoke to another crowd. This time he read from a speech outlining his plans to reconstruct the devastated South. Standing among the listeners on the lawn was the actor John

Wilkes Booth, who turned to a companion and snarled: "That's the last speech he'll ever make."

VI
⭐⭐⭐

Four days later, on Good Friday, Booth committed his terrible crime. The White House was plunged into unparalleled mourning by this first assassination of an American president. Mary Lincoln retreated to an upstairs bedroom and stayed there.

The president's body was taken to a bedroom on the northwest corner of the second floor, where six doctors performed an autopsy. The room was known as the Prince of Wales Room because the future King Edward VII had stayed there when he visited during James Buchanan's administration. It was also the room in which the Lincolns' son Willie had died a few years before.

After the autopsy, the body was embalmed and left in a coffin while Benjamin Brown French, the commissioner of public buildings, designed a huge catafalque in the East Room. It towered so high, the central chandelier had to be taken down to accommodate it.

Meanwhile the mansion was draped in black. Even the columns of the north and south porticos were wrapped in crape. On Monday night the body was carried to the East Room and the next day thousands of mourners filed past it. That night, carpenters hammered planks together to provide seats for six hundred people, while upstairs, poor Mary Lincoln screamed hysterically about hearing gunshots. On Wednesday, the carefully selected guests filed in for the funeral service.

The East Room was dim to the point of darkness, its curtains drawn, candles the only light. General Grant sat alone at the head of the catafalque in full uniform, tears streaming down his face. Reverend Phineas T. Gurley's sermon praised Lincoln as an American Moses who had led a captive people to the promised land of freedom. Afterward, the coffin was carried beneath the North Portico for a solemn procession to the Capitol, while thousands of mourners lined Pennsylvania Avenue. A dazed, sobbing Mary Lincoln remained in the White House. She would not leave for another six weeks. The mansion remained draped in its mourning garments until she departed.

VII
★★★

It's amazing how often the Fourth of July figures in the country's momentous events. In 1803, when the White House was barely three years old, Thomas Jefferson received some astounding news: Napoleon Bonaparte had agreed to sell the vast territory of Louisiana to the United States for about two cents an acre. By a happy coincidence, the news arrived the evening before the president's annual Independence Day reception, when the White House and the President's Park were open to all comers.

At daybreak on that unique July 4, vendors began putting up tents and booths to sell food and drink. At noon the crowds came swarming onto the grounds for what was essentially a country fair. Local artisans hawked baskets, rugs, and other wares. There were horse races and wrestling matches, cockfights and dogfights, along with displays of marches and drills by the Washington Militia and similar companies in resplendent dress uniforms.

The biggest excitement came not from all this hurly-burly but from the capital's favorite newspaper, the *National Intelligencer.* On the front page was the news of the Louisiana Purchase, which doubled the size of the United States in one stroke and was, without question, the biggest real estate deal in history.

No one was sure of the exact boundaries of this staggering chunk of the continent, but it was generally understood that the territory extended from the Mississippi River to the Rocky Mountains and from the Canadian border to the Gulf of Mexico. As part of the deal, the United States also acquired New Orleans, the thriving city at the mouth of the Mississippi that would provide a port for shipping cotton from the south and grain and corn from what was then considered the west.

Cheers exploded when a bareheaded President Thomas Jefferson and his five-member cabinet appeared on the White House steps to greet the crowd. For the better part of the preceding year, most Americans thought that even a small slice of this vast French possession could be obtained only by going to war with Napoleon Bonaparte, at that point the most powerful man on the globe.

Jefferson and his secretary of state, James Madison, had waged a masterful diplomatic war of nerves to prevent that dangerous development. Their diplomacy paid off when Napoleon abruptly decided to get some much-needed cash by selling the whole territory for $15 million.

This serendipitous timing went hand in hand with another historic event that occurred on this same Fourth of July. Early that morning, Thomas Jefferson's twenty-seven-year-old secretary, Captain Meriwether Lewis, departed to rendezvous with a Kentucky soldier named William Clark and begin their exploration of the West. The two men had orders to travel all the way to the Pacific Ocean and return with maps that would enable the War Department to plan forts to defend future settlers. The explorers were also charged with collecting plant and mineral specimens and reporting on the Indians they met along their line of march.

The news of the Louisiana Purchase so electrified Lewis that he left his wallet behind in the White House and had to rush back to retrieve it. This gave the youthful explorer a chance to exchange a second farewell with the exultant Jefferson, who was experiencing one of those rare presidential moments when everything seemed to be going right.

VIII

★★★

Franklin D. Roosevelt lived in the White House for twelve years—longer than any other president. When he arrived on March 4, 1933, the country was an economic and social basket case. For three years the Great Depression had resisted every attempt to break its grip on the American economy. A third of the workforce was unemployed and a staggering 9,106 banks had failed, taking with them the life savings of millions.

Two days after his inauguration, FDR closed all the banks in the country to prevent frantic depositors from withdrawing their cash and triggering total economic collapse. On Sunday, March 12, a solemn president announced that he would reopen the banks the next day. He also said he would give a radio address to the nation that evening to explain the legislation he had pushed through Congress, aimed at restoring financial stability.

The speech was a historic marriage of the 133-year-old White House and twentieth century technology. Broadcasting equipment was rushed into the Diplomatic Reception Room, the oval room facing the south grounds that Charles McKim had created out of a former boiler and furnace room.

At ten P.M., CBS radio announcer Robert Trout told some sixty million people sitting in front of an estimated twenty million radios: "The president wants to come into your homes and sit at your firesides for a little fireside chat."

That perfect name for FDR's talk was coined by the manager of the CBS Washington bureau, Harry Butcher. He got the idea from Roosevelt's press secretary Steve Early, who told Butcher that FDR liked to think of his audience as "a few people around his fireside."

A moment later, FDR began: "I want to talk for a few minutes with the people of the United States about banking. . . ." For fifteen minutes, that marvelous, mellifluous voice coursed across the airwaves to the American people, telling them that the banking system had been fixed and there was no need to withdraw any more money from their local banks. In fact, the president went on, it would be safer and smarter to put money into a sound bank rather than keep it under a mattress. "You must not be stampeded by rumors or guesses," FDR said in closing. "Let us unite in banishing fear. . . . Together we cannot fail."

The next day, even rock-ribbed Republican newspapers like the *Wall Street Journal* reported in near bewilderment that the banking crisis was over. Instead of runs on banks, people were actually depositing money. Speech experts attributed not a little of this magical transformation to FDR's voice. One said: "If Herbert Hoover had spoken the same words into the microphone, the stock market would have fallen another notch." They piled on adjectives like "fresh," "rich," "melodious," to explain the magic of that voice. I prefer the rueful words of journalist and author John T. Flynn, one of FDR's fiercest critics. He called the voice "golden," "seductive," and "challenging." It was unquestionably all three. I also think that knowing the voice was coming from the White House, the symbol of presidential power, had not a little to do with the incredible effect of that dramatic speech.

IX
☆☆☆

In 1962 another president found himself dealing with a serious crisis. This White House drama began on October 16 in President John F. Kennedy's second-floor bedroom. At 8:45 A.M., McGeorge Bundy, his special assistant for national security affairs, found the president sitting on the edge of his bed, still in his pajamas and bathrobe.

"Mr. President," Bundy said, "there is now hard photographic evidence that the Russians have nuclear missiles in Cuba."

So began the most harrowing two weeks in the White House's history. Seldom had a president and his administration been so badly surprised. Bundy and others had made public statements pooh-poohing the possibility that Moscow's alliance with Cuban premier Fidel Castro might lead to nuclear weapons on that controversial island only ninety miles off the coast of Florida. Now they were confronted with enough firepower to destroy every major American city except Seattle.

At 11:45 A.M., cabinet members and advisers poured into the West Wing for the first of many marathon conferences on how to meet this Russian power play. Communist boss Nikita Khrushchev was betting he could intimidate the young president, who had already faltered under pressure when an anti-Communist invasion of Cuba during the first days of his administration ended in a humiliating defeat at the Bay of Pigs.

In the Cabinet Room, the advisers quickly divided into two camps: those in favor of an immediate air strike to destroy the missile launchers and those in favor of an embargo on all military shipments to Cuba until the missiles were removed. The embargoists warned the air strikers that their route led straight to nuclear war. Voices grew angry and tempers frayed as the debate raged.

President Kennedy, meanwhile, tried to maintain an appearance of calm. He went about the business of the presidency. He spent a half hour in the Oval Office with the crown prince of Libya. He talked European politics with the foreign minister of Germany. He took astronaut Walter Schirra and his family to the south lawn for a visit with first daughter Caroline's ponies. In between these routine activities he would slip into the Cabinet Room to see how the debate was going. Each time, he found the two groups irreconcilable.

On the third day of the crisis, President Kennedy left the White House to attend a luncheon at the Libyan embassy. On the way he suddenly told his driver to take him to St. Matthew's Cathedral. He hurried into the green-domed red-brick church and knelt in one of the front pews for ten minutes. It was one of the most extraordinary moments in presidential history. Jack Kennedy was not a very religious man. A friend told me that soon after he was inaugurated, JFK remarked wryly to an aide: "I just realized now I'll have to go to church every Sunday for the next eight years."

But JFK had been raised a Catholic and his mother was a deeply devout woman. I think the staggering dimensions of the crisis he was facing lay behind this impromptu visit. He had discovered that there are moments when presidents talk to God because no one else can give them the kind of support they need. Lincoln testified to this experience, as did Gerald Ford.

A few days later, while the debaters in the Cabinet Room remained at odds, JFK asked his wife, Jackie, to return from their Virginia country house, Glen Ora, and bring their children, Caroline and John, with her. Soon the president was walking around the south lawn with Jackie, telling her what he confronted. He asked her if she wanted to return to Glen Ora. Jackie's answer was no. She would stay in the White House even though they both knew the mansion would be a primary target if nuclear missiles started to fly.

At the end of this harrowing week, John F. Kennedy told his still quarreling advisers in the Cabinet Room what he had decided. The United States would not make a surprise air strike on the Russian missile launchers. Instead, they would blockade Cuba and demand the swift withdrawal of the weapons of mass destruction—or the United States would remove them by force.

This astute combination of toughness and diplomacy proved to be the answer to the crisis. (If it had failed, I would not be writing this book and you would not be reading it.) Faced with a ring of American steel around blockaded Cuba and staggered by condemnations in the United Nations and almost every capital in the civilized world, Nikita Khrushchev backed down and withdrew his missiles.

In the Oval Office and the Cabinet Room, the White House returned to the everyday routines of ceremony and politics. But in those harrowing days in October 1962, Jack and Jackie Kennedy had added a new chapter to its glory.

X

★★★

The Lincoln Sitting Room is a small room next to the Lincoln Bedroom. It had no significant place in the history of the White House until August 6, 1974, when President Richard M. Nixon stayed there until about two A.M. writing his resignation speech.

The speech marked the end of the Nixon presidency in the welter of lies and half-truths and snarling vindictiveness of the Watergate scandal. Looking back on it from the distance of almost three decades, it becomes more and more apparent that this explosion of anger and anguish could only have happened to Richard Nixon, a politician who had made a career of taunting and triumphing over his enemies and then, by his own admission, "gave them a sword and they stuck it in and twisted it with relish."

The dark night of President Nixon's soul began during the 1972 election campaign, when overzealous subordinates burglarized the offices of the Democratic National Committee in Washington's Watergate apartment complex. For almost two years, Nixon stonewalled and evaded and lied to judges, Congress, and the American people to defend these men. His game plan began to unravel when Congress learned from an aide that Nixon had taped almost every conversation in the Oval Office.

In late July 1974, on one of these tapes, his lawyers heard Nixon telling his top aide, H. R. Haldeman, to use the CIA to restrain the FBI investigation of the break-in. It was incontrovertible proof that Nixon had obstructed justice—a doubly serious crime when it was committed by a president who has taken a solemn oath to uphold the law. Meanwhile, the Supreme Court had rejected the president's plea of executive privilege and ruled that the tapes had to be turned over to the special prosecutor investigating Watergate.

On July 30, 1974, this most isolated of presidents could not sleep. At 3:50 A.M. he sat up in bed and began listing the pros and cons of resigning. As dawn grayed the windows and the first sounds of life stirred in the President's House, he decided against resignation. The following day, however, his top aides, including his chief of staff General Alexander Haig and Secretary of State Henry Kissinger, listened to the damning tape. One by one, they came to the conclusion that resignation was the only option. On Thursday, August 1, Nixon did a 180-degree turn and told Haig he was going to resign.

Emotional scenes between Nixon and his family consumed much of the next two days. His daughters, Julie and Tricia, and their husbands, David Eisenhower and Edward Cox, begged him not to resign. First Lady Pat Nixon was especially adamant. She insisted he fight on.

While the president wavered back toward gambling against the odds, his staff continued to push for resignation. If he would not admit that he had lied to them and others about the tape, they, too, would face prosecution for making public statements about his innocence.

"The hell with it," Nixon said, and collapsed once and for all. Soon, whatever he decided or failed to decide became irrelevant. The transcript of the tape destroyed the loyalty of the last holdouts in Congress. Republican leaders told Nixon there was not the slightest doubt that the Senate would muster the two-thirds vote necessary for impeachment. Henry Kissinger warned that a prolonged trial would "paralyze" the nation's foreign policy and would be "demeaning to the presidency."

When Nixon finally sought sleep in his bedroom, he found a note on the pillow from his daughter Julie. She begged him to delay the resignation for a week or ten days. "Go through fire for a little bit longer," she wrote. "Millions support you."

Nixon later wrote that if anything could have changed his mind, that loving plea might have done it. But he had already decided to accept Henry Kissinger's argument that his resignation was best for the country. At nine P.M. on August 6, Nixon called Kissinger to the White House. They talked for a while about their foreign policy triumphs, particularly their decision to recognize the Communist regime in China, and their trip to Peking to formalize the new relationship.

The talk abruptly shifted to the possibility that Nixon would be prosecuted as a criminal after he left office. The president writhed in torment at the idea. Kissinger vowed to resign as secretary of state and defend him everywhere and anywhere. Deeply moved, Nixon led Kissinger to the Lincoln Bedroom and asked his secretary of state to join him in prayer. The two men knelt for several minutes, a scene that, for me, is one of the most painful—and also one of the most moving—moments in the history of the White House.

On August 8, Nixon told a stunned nation: "I shall resign the presidency, effective at noon tomorrow." After breakfast the next morning, the president and first lady said good-bye to the White House staff, gathered in the West Hall. "This house has a great heart which comes from you who serve," he said, shaking hands with each of them.

A weeping Pat Nixon and daughter Julie followed the president to the elevator and they walked to the East Room, jammed with aides and staffers. The Marine Band burst into "Hail to the Chief" one last time. Nixon gave a rambling, disjointed speech; many of the listeners thought he was about to break down. At the close, he blurted out an amazingly accurate summation of what had happened to him. "Always remember, others may hate you—but those who hate you don't win unless you hate them, and then you destroy yourself."

The Nixon family went downstairs to the Diplomatic Reception Room, where the new president, Gerald Ford, and his wife, Betty, were waiting. What irony that this was the last room in the White House that Richard Nixon visited, the room where Franklin D. Roosevelt had achieved his almost mystic bond with the American people with his fireside chats—a feat tragically beyond Richard Nixon.

On the south lawn, an army helicopter waited for the Nixons. The Fords accompanied them down a red carpet, past a military guard of honor. At the steps of the helicopter, the ex-president shook hands with Gerald Ford and ascended the steep ladder. At the top he turned and to everyone's amazement, managed to summon a smile. He raised both arms and made his trademark V-for-Victory sign. The door closed and the helicopter thundered into the blue sky.

XI
✯✯✯

Almost every part of the White House and its grounds is permeated with memories of important moments in American history. I can never look at the north lawn without remembering August 14, 1945—the day the Japanese surrendered and World War II finally ended. Dad announced the glorious news and then he and my mother went out on the lawn to wave to a huge cheering crowd. Dad flashed the V-for-Victory sign and the celebrators went wild. For a few minutes the Trumans and the people of Washington and the people of the entire country were united in a magical unforgettable way.

Everyone who has ever lived or worked in the White House has similar associations and memories. We have all had the privilege, and sometimes the pain, of being eyewitnesses to history. In truth, the house itself is history, which is why I and millions of other Americans pray that it will always be protected at all costs.

The State Dining Room in 1873. Back then, dinners lasted four or five hours and had at least six courses. A new wine with each course helped to ease the strain.
Credit: Library of Congress

5

Working the House

The White House is not only a shrine, a symbol, and a piece of living American history, it is also a political tool. In every administration, White House social events—coffees, luncheons, teas, receptions, dinners—have given the president an opportunity to strengthen his relationships with foreign leaders, members of Congress, the diplomatic corps, the party faithful and not so faithful, the opposition, and just about anyone else who can help him accomplish his programs and goals.

Even crusty, standoffish John Adams saw this potential when he moved into the White House in 1800. He did not yet know that he had narrowly lost his bid for reelection to Thomas Jefferson. Adams held his first formal reception on November 11, 1800, ten days after he arrived in Washington. A week or so later, he and Abigail continued the custom, established in Philadelphia, of inviting Congress to call on them. On January 1, 1801, the Adamses entertained the public at a New Year's Day reception and started a tradition that was to last for over a hundred years.

This revelry ended on a very sad note. By this time Adams knew he had lost and screamed in his ex-friend Jefferson's face: "You have turned me out! You have turned me out!" But that bitter denouement did not in the least diminish the White House as a political force majeure in Washington. Jefferson and succeeding presidents continued to use the house with politics uppermost in mind.

II
★★★

Two days before Christmas in 1963, less than a month after Lyndon and Lady Bird Johnson moved into the White House after the assassination of President John F. Kennedy, and the day the official mourning for President Kennedy ended, Lyndon said to a startled Lady Bird, "Let's have Congress over tonight."

Lady Bird agreed—it was hard to disagree with Lyndon—and the White House butlers hastily whipped up gallons of fruit and spiked punch, the kitchen staff set to work making tea sandwiches while other household staffers ransacked every store in Washington for enough cookies to serve to some five hundred congressmen and their spouses, the president's staff and his cabinet members—well over a thousand people in all.

Meanwhile, the White House carpenters and electricians took down the mourning crape and the florists replaced it with holly and poinsettias. A Christmas tree was set up in the traditional spot in the Blue Room and the lights and decorations were hauled out of storage.

It was the biggest short-notice party the White House had ever seen and it was a spectacular success. After the gloom following the Kennedy assassination, everyone was ready for something upbeat and, more to the point, LBJ schmoozed with key congressmen and convinced them that he would continue the policies of his predecessor.

III

★★★

One of the most seductive things about a White House event is the sheer perfection of it all. Then again, why shouldn't it be perfect?

The White House has a staff of almost a hundred people, including calligraphers, floral designers, chefs, butlers, ushers, and social secretaries. There's a chief of protocol, on loan from the State Department, to advise on seating and similar matters; the U.S. Marine Band to supply music; a bevy of military aides, resplendent in their dress uniforms, to keep things moving at the proper pace; and, perhaps the biggest perk of all, a contingent of servants to take care of the cleanup.

When we lived in the White House, I often used to slip downstairs before an important dinner just to take a look at the State Dining Room. It was a truly magnificent sight—the paneled walls and Corinthian pilasters, the marble mantel, the gilded wall sconces, the dining table set with gold flatware and gleaming crystal and china.

The room is also a mini-museum of American history. Inscribed on the mantel is John Adams's famous prayer invoking blessings on the White House. Hanging above it is George P. A. Healy's portrait of Abraham Lincoln. The mantel was originally designed with lions' heads carved on either side, but they became bisons' heads after Theodore Roosevelt decided a native American animal would be more appropriate. The mantel was replaced during the Truman renovation but Jacqueline Kennedy replaced the replacement with a reproduction of the original. The furnishings also include two rococo-revival candelabra, purchased during Rutherford B. Hayes's administration, and one of my favorite White House treasures: the Monroe plateau.

The plateau—the French call it a *surtour de table*—is a mirrored platform set in an ornate gilded bronze frame. It is about two and a half feet wide and, when all seven sections of it are put together, over thirteen and a half feet long. The frame is adorned with sixteen graceful nymphs—Bacchus and Bacchantes—bearing tiny wreaths that double as candleholders. They can also be mounted with small baskets for holding flowers or fruit.

The plateau includes a pair of urns and three baskets that can be used to hold fruit or flowers. The baskets create an especially dramatic effect when they are reflected in the mirror. The matched set is one of several items James and Elizabeth Monroe ordered from France to furnish the rebuilt White House.

There's also a small, and fortunately invisible, piece of Truman history in the State Dining Room. Way back in the dark ages—1946—I had a dinner dance at the White House for some of my friends. The party was held in the East Room, but in the course of the evening, one couple (who shall be nameless) wandered down the hall to the State Dining Room.

The young woman was intrigued by the massive chandelier that hangs above the mahogany dining table and she asked her escort to lift her up so she could touch it. When he did, she grabbed the metal arms to steady herself. Whereupon he decided to walk away and leave her dangling high above the floor. Fortunately, one of the butlers heard her screams and helped her down.

The young woman and I were the only people who didn't find this prank amusing. Even my father, who I expected to be as indignant as I was when I told him about it the next day, burst into laughter. Men!

IV

★★★

White House social events are scripted down to the minutest detail. When a foreign leader is expected, the chief of protocol checks out the guest's preferences in food and entertainment. When Jimmy and Rosalynn Carter were anticipating a visit from Prime Minister

Masayoshi Ohira of Japan, knowing that he liked American cooking and popular music made it easier to plan a dinner for him. Having been warned by the prime minister's daughter that classical music put him to sleep, the Carters invited pianist Bobby Short to play show tunes and other popular favorites.

It's also important to know whether or not foreign guests drink alcohol and if, as is the case in some Muslim countries, they are forbidden to have it served in their presence. Colors must also be considered. White is never used for Chinese visitors because in their country it is the color of mourning.

Heads of state are welcomed with an arrival ceremony on the south lawn. To make sure the rules of protocol are followed to the letter, toe cards are placed on the ground to indicate where everyone should stand. Toe cards are also used at state dinners so the president and first lady and their guests of honor are in the proper order on the receiving line.

Planning for a White House formal dinner is no easy matter. The guest list, menu, table settings, and floral arrangements are chosen weeks in advance, and the White House kitchen swings into action early in the morning of the appointed day. The events usually start with a reception at 7:30 P.M. and dinner is served about an hour later.

Most first ladies have their own ideas about how dinners should go. A notable exception was Barbara Bush, who told the staff "Just do what she did," referring to her predecessor, Nancy Reagan. Although the pendulum has swung back and forth between French food and American and the number of courses has varied from ten or twelve to four or five, there are a few rituals that are always the same.

One is the entrance ceremony for the president, which is enough to inspire respect in even the most die-hard political foe. It consists of a mini-parade led by the Presidential Color Team. In my day, they were called the Four Horsemen but now there are five of them, one for each branch of the armed services—army, navy, marines, air force, and coast guard. Back then, the air force was part of the army.

It is the Color Team's job to go to the president, who is usually waiting for them in the living quarters upstairs, and request permission to secure the colors. This means removing the American and presidential flags and carrying them down the Grand Staircase to the room in which the president will be receiving his guests. As the president and first lady follow the Color Team downstairs, the Marine Band announces their arrival with a fanfare, "Ruffles and Flourishes," followed by "Hail to the Chief."

At a dinner Jack and Jacqueline Kennedy gave in honor of my father in 1962, my parents and my husband, Clifton Daniel, and I had a private pre-dinner visit with the Kennedys, so we were part of the march down the Grand Staircase. For my parents, it must have seemed like old times, but I had not taken part in the ceremony that often and Clifton was a complete novice. He scolded me for forgetting to tell him that the line of march comes to a halt during the brief pause between "Ruffles and Flourishes" and "Hail to the Chief." As a result, he kept on walking and almost rear-ended Jackie.

By the way, if you've ever wondered where "Hail to the Chief" came from, it's an old Scottish air that was introduced by Sarah Polk for a supremely practical reason. Her husband, James, was not a particularly imposing man and she was afraid he might be overlooked when he entered the room at a large gathering.

Sarah also initiated another custom that has remained a White House ritual, the dinner march. Horrified at the way people swarmed into the State Dining Room and rushed to find their places at the table, she decreed that guests would file in two by two to the tune of "The President's March," better known to most of us as "Hail Columbia."

V

***

President William Howard Taft once remarked to his chief military aide, Major Archibald Butt: "The White House is a big political asset when used wisely."

Unfortunately, toward the end of his single term, Taft used the White House unwisely. When he and his wife celebrated their silver wedding anniversary, they made no secret of the fact that gifts would be welcome. As a result, they received more than a million dollars' worth of silver trays, teapots, tureens, and the like, many of them from total strangers who simply wanted to curry favor with the president.

I am hardly the first to question Taft's judgment in using his position for personal gain. It was a five-star scandal at the time. They'd probably call it Silvergate today. But in spite of my misgivings about that aspect of the event, I have to concede that the Taft's twenty-fifth anniversary celebration ranks as the most spectacular White House party of all time.

Since their anniversary fell in early June, one of the nicest times of the year in Washington, the Tafts decided to have a garden party. It was to be held on the south lawn in the evening and the guest list was to include just about everyone they had ever met. The lawn was to be decorated with hundreds of strands of multicolored lights and paper lanterns. The illuminated White House would provide the backdrop.

The preparations for the event were coordinated by Major Butt, a personable and debonair southerner whose military exploits consisted mainly of doing battle with caterers, florists, and social climbers. As chief military aide, Butt took on the role of party planner and social arbiter, two jobs for which he was extremely well-suited. His attention to detail was such that he kept meticulous records of the plans for every official party, thus saving untold amounts of work for the social secretaries who came later.

It took a team of electricians four days to cover all the trees and shrubbery in the President's Park with lights. When they were finished, Taft requested still more lights, including spotlights to showcase the fountain on the south lawn and the American flag on the White House roof. The flag was to be kept waving by a battery of electric fans concealed behind the chimneys. The U.S. Marine Band provided music for dancing and buffet suppers were set out in the State Dining Room and the East Room and in tents around the lawn. While the guests were dining, they were serenaded by a choral group concealed behind the magnolia trees.

Some four thousand people attended the party and shook hands with the Tafts beneath an arch with "1886–1911" spelled out in lights. Another fifteen thousand gathered outside the fence and cheered the president and his wife as they entered from the South Portico to the tune of the Bridal Chorus from Richard Wagner's *Lohengrin.*

The band, which had been scheduled to stop playing at one A.M., continued until two on orders from the president. Before retiring for the night, Taft gave instructions for the lights to remain in place and the musicians to return the next evening. The south lawn would be open to the public from eight to eleven P.M. so they, too, could enjoy the spectacle.

VI
★★★

If William Howard Taft deserves first prize for the most enchanting party ever given at the White House, Andrew Jackson deserves the booby prize for a pair of wingdings that he hosted. A frontiersman born into humble surroundings and elected by a larger popular vote than any of his predecessors, Jackson was "the People's President" and the people descended on Washington in droves to see him sworn in.

After taking his oath of office at the Capitol on March 4, 1829, the sixty-one-year-old chief executive rode to the White House on horseback, making his way slowly because of the hordes of admirers surging around him. Jackson had about an hour to greet his more important guests before the crowd of some twenty thousand people that had followed him from the Capitol surged past the doorkeepers and swarmed into the President's House.

Many of Jackson's fans climbed on chairs or tables to get a better look at him. Others elbowed and shoved their way to the tables in the East Room, where refreshments were being served. In the crush, china and crystal were smashed, fistfights broke out, and women screamed and fainted. The president found himself pressed against a wall, gasping for air. He finally escaped through the rear door and headed back to his hotel while the White House steward brewed up a washtub full of whiskey punch and set it on the lawn to lure the revelers outdoors.

You might think Jackson would have learned a lesson from this debacle, but things weren't that much better at his last public reception in 1837—maybe he wanted to go out the same way he came in. In any case, one of his supporters, a dairy farmer in Oswego County, New York, sent him a giant wheel of cheddar cheese. It was four feet across, two feet thick, and weighed fourteen hundred pounds. It arrived wrapped in bunting and draped with Jackson banners in a wagon drawn by twenty-four horses.

Jackson let the cheese age in the White House entrance hall for two years. He finally invited the public to enjoy it at the annual Washington's birthday reception. The city marshal and his deputies were posted at the door to maintain order, but the crowds outwitted them. They poured across the lawn and through the gardens and climbed in the windows of the East Room.

Diplomats, congressmen, and cabinet members were shoved aside as the interlopers scrambled to help themselves to chunks of cheese. Two hours later, the cheese was gone and the mob with it. The floors and rugs were littered with crumbs of cheddar, and the White House reeked of cheese for weeks.

VII
✫✫✫

What Andrew Jackson needed, aside from a little common sense, was the small army of military aides who later became a fixture at White House functions. During Theodore Roosevelt's administration, the aides replaced the servants and Secret Servicemen who had formerly assisted, directed, and, if necessary, evicted guests at official events.

The military aides, who are chosen for their smart appearance, are an attractive addition to White House parties, but their duties go beyond being merely decorative. They are what you might call social traffic cops, charged with seeing that schedules are adhered to, receiving lines keep moving, and ceremonies begin and end on time. At large dinners, they may also be called upon to introduce dinner partners, break the conversational ice, or fill out the table if there are more women than men or vice versa. In my day, the aides were all male. Nowadays, the list includes women.

The White House social office keeps a list of about twenty aides from various branches of the military. They have to be unmarried, stationed in the Washington area, and have the social smarts to talk to a wide variety of people, preferably in a couple of languages besides English. For a large reception, the entire roster of aides might be summoned to duty; for a dinner party, four or five will usually do.

It is considered something of an honor to be selected as a White House aide. John Horton, an army colonel who served in Europe during World War II and who later married my close friend Drucie Snyder, was a military aide during my father's administration. Former U.S. Senator Charles Robb was a marine corps officer who was selected to be a military aide during Lyndon Johnson's administration. Chuck ended up marrying the boss's daughter, Lynda Bird Johnson.

Except for John Horton, I never paid that much attention to the aides, unless I happened to be dating one of them. I later found out that they have a whole list of ploys to prevent White House guests from overstaying their welcome.

State dinners are rarely a problem because they end at an hour when most guests are ready to go home. Lingering is more common at late afternoon and evening receptions. That's when the military aides execute a maneuver they refer to as the turkey trot. It consists of forming a line, apparently by sheer accident, and gently but firmly moving the lingerers toward the door, much like herding turkeys into a pen. In no time at all, the guests are collecting their coats and heading home.

The turkey trot is an improvement over the technique Rutherford B. Hayes's son Webb devised. Webb, who served as his father's secretary, was also responsible for locking up the White House. It was, and still is, customary for the president and first lady to leave before their guests. When the guests stayed too long, Webb would arrange to have a heavy object dropped on the floor above. The startled guests would stop conversing and, in the interim, someone would look at his watch and see that it was time to go home.

VIII
★★★

The use of military aides at White House social functions is considered part of their duty to serve their commander in chief. This is also true of the U.S. Marine Band, a group of extremely talented musicians in scarlet uniforms who provide the music for state dinners and receptions and perform on the south lawn for the arrival ceremonies for foreign leaders.

The Marine Band is the country's oldest professional musical organization. It was established by an Act of Congress in 1798 and charged with providing music for the president of the United States and the commandant of the marine corps. Its first White House performance was for President John Adams's New Year's Day reception in 1801. A few months later, the band played for Thomas

Jefferson's inaugural, and it has performed at every presidential inauguration since. Jefferson, a lover of music and an accomplished musician himself, affirmed the unique status of the band by naming them "The President's Own."

During the administration of John Tyler, the Marine Band played on the South Portico of the White House on Saturday evenings in the summer and the public was invited to wander the grounds. The custom continued through the administrations of James Polk, Zachary Taylor, Millard Fillmore, and Franklin Pierce, although Mrs. Pierce, a deeply religious woman, requested that the day be changed to Wednesday because so much hubbub on Saturday evening interfered with her preparations for the Sabbath.

The members of the Marine Band are graduates of the country's most prestigious music schools. They audition for places just as they would for a major symphony orchestra. Since their enlistments are "for duty with the U.S. Marine Band only" they do not have to undergo basic training but instead report directly to Washington to prepare for their various musical assignments.

The Marine Band, in whole or in part, appears at the White House over three hundred times a year. They may be called upon to provide strolling violinists, a harp solo, a string quartet, or a dance band and they can probably play "Hail to the Chief" with their eyes closed.

I have danced to the music of the Marine Band at many a White House party and I can assure you they can play my favorites—Cole Porter and Rodgers and Hart—with the best of them. I can also assure you that their repertoire doesn't stop there. They can handle almost any number that will get people out on the dance floor. At a 1998 state dinner for President Václav Havel of the Czech Republic, they swung into the 1960s hit "Runaround Sue" just as the Clintons and the Havels were leaving. Unable to resist the beat, Havel did an about-face and took a few more spins on the dance floor.

In addition to their White House performances, the U.S. Marine Band appears at various events in and around Washington, and makes a concert tour to a different part of the country each fall. The tour was started by the band's seventeenth and most famous director, John Philip Sousa, who served from 1880 to 1892. His gold-tipped baton continues to be used by the band's conductor. Incidentally, Sousa was a second-generation Marine Band member. His father, a Portuguese trombonist, had played for President James Buchanan.

Most people know John Philip Sousa as the composer of such familiar marches as "Stars and Stripes Forever" and "Semper Fidelis." Few people are aware that he also composed a presidential polonaise. It was written at the request of President Chester A. Arthur, that fussy New Yorker, who didn't think "Hail to the Chief" was sufficiently dignified. Apparently no one agreed with Arthur. "Hail to the Chief" was revived after he left office and "The Presidential Polonaise" became just one of the many marches on Sousa's concert programs after he retired from the marines and formed his own band.

IX

★★★

As I mentioned earlier, seating is a big deal in Washington. Official White House gatherings are carefully choreographed and there are rules covering the order in which guests go through the receiving line and are seated at dinner. The operative word in the whole setup is rank.

On the surface, this may seem a bit ridiculous in a supposedly democratic country, but it makes quite a bit of sense. Presidential guests come from different parts of the country and the world and they are not always familiar with White House etiquette. There is less chance of making a mistake or committing a social blunder when everyone follows the same rules. There is also less chance of getting involved in the kind of social cold wars that can erupt when they don't.

Thomas Jefferson's egalitarian principles made him indifferent to the point of being hostile to the idea that one guest might be more important than another. In 1803, newly appointed British minister Anthony Merry arrived at the White House to meet the president. Merry was attired in full diplomatic dress, complete with plumed hat and sword, while Jefferson appeared in rumpled clothes and battered carpet slippers. Worse yet, as the two men sat talking, the president flipped one of the slippers up in the air and caught it with his big toe.

Jefferson's manners were no better when Anthony Merry and his wife attended a dinner at the White House a few days later. According to the diplomatic etiquette that prevailed in Europe, the president should have escorted Mrs. Merry in to dinner, and Mr. Merry should have followed with Dolley Madison, who, because Jefferson was a widower, served as his hostess at these events.

When dinner was announced, Jefferson ignored the Merrys and gave Dolley Madison his arm. Secretary of State James Madison rescued Mrs. Merry but her husband was left to walk in by himself and find his own place at the table, which turned out to be considerably below the salt.

Jefferson called this new style of etiquette "pêle mêle," a French play on words that means "to mix." The English translation is pell-mell, which comes closer to describing the disorder it produced.

In the aftermath of the evening, the president came in for some strong criticism in the diplomatic community, so much so that he felt constrained to defend himself by drawing up a set of rules to correct the impression that White House dinners were disorganized. The main one was that all guests were to be treated equally "whether foreign or domestic, titled or untitled, in or out of office."

It sounded good on paper, but in reality, someone would get a place near the head of the table and someone else would end up at the foot, a position a Supreme Court justice, say, might take exception to, particularly if one of his clerks got the choicer spot. As time went on, Jefferson slowly relented and pell-mell etiquette eventually disappeared.

There were still no hard-and-fast rules, however, until 1834, when Andrew Jackson's State Department drew up the Rules of Protocol that remain in effect today. They established a pecking order that includes just about everyone with a government title—king, prime minister, foreign secretary, sultan, ambassador, chief justice, general, or admiral—no matter which government the titlist comes from.

The Rules of Protocol were adopted to settle any and all arguments about rank. The theory was that once everyone knew where they stood—or sat—there would be no further problems. But when you're dealing with the kind of monumental egos that abound in Washington, somebody will inevitably feel slighted.

Supreme Court justices are especially touchy. The Constitution says they are a separate branch of the government, but they are few in number. That makes them all the more determined to get respect. If one of them is seated too far down the table, watch out.

During President McKinley's administration, Chief Justice Melville W. Fuller was placed below an ambassador. The Big Judge stamped out of the White House before the coffee was served, roaring that in the future he would demand a plan of the table before he came anywhere near the place. Another time, when word got out that the diplomatic corps would be received ahead of the Supremes at a reception for the high court, all nine justices boycotted their own party.

The navy has always been a little bit cross because the Rules of Protocol rank them below the army. They were particularly miffed after Admiral George Dewey won his decisive victory at Manila Bay during the Spanish-American War and became the hero of the moment. Egged on by his fellow naval officers and his famously ambitious wife, Dewey suggested to Secretary of War Elihu Root that he let the admirals precede the generals in the receiving line at President William McKinley's next reception on New Year's Day, 1900. Root's response was an unequivocal *no*.

Mrs. Dewey, however, proved to be a more skillful strategist than her husband. The wives of government bigwigs went through the receiving line separately, but, like their husbands, they were expected to line up in accordance with the Rules of Protocol. Mrs. Dewey sweet-talked one of McKinley's cabinet members into letting her get ahead of the generals' wives by claiming she and the admiral had to leave the reception early.

The army wives were outraged, which only added to the navy's wrath at being denied what they saw as their rightful place in line. The episode triggered a full-scale war between the two services with the White House caught in the middle. President McKinley tried to make amends by issuing a personal invitation to his annual army and navy reception to every navy officer in Washington. Although only a few deigned to accept, things did eventually calm down and the army-navy rivalry was relegated to the football field.

During Theodore Roosevelt's administration, the White House social season included three formal dinners: a cabinet dinner, a diplomatic dinner, and a dinner for the Supreme Court. A fourth— a Speaker's dinner—had to be added because the Speaker of the House of Representatives, imperious Joseph "Uncle Joe" Cannon, refused to attend the other three. He knew he would be seated below the cabinet and the Supreme Court and in his view, he outranked them all. To keep him happy, no one of higher rank was invited to the Speaker's dinner.

There was another flap over seating arrangements that made national headlines during Herbert Hoover's administration. Hoover's vice president, Charles Curtis, a widower, informed the secretary of state that at official dinners he expected his half-sister, Dolly Gann, who had served as his hostess when he was in the Senate, to be accorded the same courtesy that was traditionally given to the vice president's wife.

Secretary of State Frank B. Kellogg thought otherwise. Dolly

Gann was *not* the vice president's wife. Therefore she should not be seated in a position of honor near the head of the table. She would be listed as his guest and assigned to a lesser place.

Both Curtis and his half-sister, who, as the wife of a successful attorney, was already a power in Washington society, made no secret of their annoyance at Kellogg's ruling. They were vastly relieved when Kellogg resigned and was replaced by Henry L. Stimson. Instead of making the decision on his own, the new secretary solicited opinions from the diplomatic corps, who came back with the answer that they would welcome Mrs. Gann "with great pleasure." The matter was settled and Dolly was seated in a place of honor at a dinner given by the Chilean ambassador a few weeks later.

Putting out a fire in one spot doesn't mean it won't erupt someplace else. Mrs. Eugene Meyer, the wife of the owner of the *Washington Post*, let it be known that she would follow the State Department's rule at her next dinner party to which Alice Roosevelt Longworth was also being invited. This was unacceptable to Mrs. Longworth. Her father had been president and her husband, Nicholas, was Speaker of the House. She, a princess, should take precedence over Dolly Gann, a mere commoner. The Longworths declined to attend Mrs. Meyer's dinner and a number of other guests joined their boycott.

Fortunately, it was close to Memorial Day and the Washington social season was about to be put in mothballs for the summer. It resumed in the fall when Herbert Hoover hosted a state dinner for the prime minister of Great Britain and followed the usual custom of inviting both the vice president and the Speaker of the House. Knowing that Hoover would abide by the State Department's ruling, the Longworths sent their regrets.

By this time, every newspaper in the country was following the feud between Alice and Dolly. Washington hostesses were petrified to put together a guest list lest they offend one or the other. The social deadlock threatened to go on and on, until Mrs. Hoover finally come up with a solution. The White House would have a separate dinner for the vice president, just as they did for the Speaker of the House, and nobody who outranked him would be invited.

This left Washington hostesses on their own, but in *Dolly Gann's Book*, an account of her experiences in the capital, Dolly maintained that they all knew when rank was an issue, the simplest solution was not to invite the rivals to the same dinner party.

Dolly also insisted that she was a great admirer of Alice Roosevelt Longworth and the stories of their conflict were nothing but ugly rumors. In her later years, Alice Roosevelt Longworth joined Dolly in denying that there had ever been a feud and insisted that the whole thing had been overblown by the press, which may be true. She also said that her husband, Nick, was the one who objected to going to Mrs. Meyer's dinner because she never served liquor. That may be true, too. Nick did like to drink.

X
★★★

As you can see, entertaining at 1600 Pennsylvania Avenue involves complications and potential pitfalls that are unlikely to bedevil the average host or hostess.

Some of the thorniest problems involve visiting royalty. When Princess (now Queen) Elizabeth and her husband, the duke of Edinburgh (now Prince Philip), visited the United States in 1951, my father decided to meet them at the airport. The State Department had a conniption. According to protocol, the president only shows up at the airport to greet heads of state. Dad, being Dad, went anyway.

Theodore Roosevelt had a somewhat different and more confusing problem when Prince Henry of Prussia, the brother of Kaiser Wilhelm of Germany, visited the United States in 1902. The announced purpose of the visit was to launch the kaiser's racing schooner, the *Meteor*, which had been built in a New Jersey shipyard, but there was not much doubt that he also hoped to encourage a warmer relationship between the two nations.

Some members of the press hinted that there could be still another reason for the royal visit: The prince might be hoping to kindle a romance with Alice Roosevelt. Alice christened the *Meteor* and the prince presented her with a diamond bracelet as a gift from the kaiser, but apparently no sparks flew. Undeterred, the gossip columnists started to call her Princess Alice and the name stuck, probably because everyone, including Alice, felt it suited her.

Royal visits were, and still are, a rare phenomenon, and the State Department was sorely taxed trying to figure out the protocol. Although Roosevelt received the prince at the White House, for example, the two men could not be formally introduced because there was no American official of high enough rank to do the honors.

Another problem arose when the Roosevelts were planning a White House dinner for the prince. It was customary for the president to escort the wife of the guest of honor into dinner, but Prince Henry was a bachelor. "Will the prince take Mrs. R. while I walk in solemn state by myself?" Roosevelt wanted to know. Even the protocol experts had to think about that one. The solution they came up with was to have a reception for the ladies followed by a stag dinner for the men. It was held in the East Room and one hundred males attended, the first time that many guests at a White House dinner were seated at the same table and an indication of why the Roosevelts were eager to have Charles McKim enlarge the State Dining Room.

XI

***

Still another diplomatic crisis arose when Rutherford B. Hayes and his wife, Lucy, arrived in the White House in 1877. Strong supporters of the temperance movement, they never served wine or liquor in their home in Ohio, and there were rumors that they would continue this practice when they got to Washington. They wanted to set an example for the rest of the country, which showed signs of being on a permanent binge.

More than a few of the city's elite must have blanched at the possibility, but in the halls of the State Department, it threatened to provoke an international incident. The White House guest list regularly included diplomats and other representatives of foreign countries. They were used to having wine with their meals and would be noticeably unhappy if it were omitted.

The first test came in 1877, soon after Hayes was sworn in. Two emissaries of the czar of Russia, Grand Duke Constantine and Grand Duke Alexis, were planning to visit the United States and protocol required that they be given a formal dinner at the White House. Secretary of State William Evarts and his staff went on red alert. It would be unthinkable to subject the two young men to a "cold water" meal. To forestall such a dreadful possibility, Evarts enlisted the aid of Stanley Matthews, an old friend of the president's and one of his closest advisers.

A distinguished attorney who was later appointed to the U.S. Supreme Court, Matthews presented his case with lawyerly logic. In view of what they were accustomed to in their own country, "a dinner without wine would be an annoyance, if not an affront" to the grand dukes and, by extension, an affront to Russia, a longtime ally of the United States. To Secretary Evarts's enormous relief, Hayes was persuaded.

The dinner was a splendid affair. The state dining room was bedecked with flowers, the U.S. Marine Band played a Russian march as the guests filed in to dinner, the food was magnificent, and there were no less than seven glasses at each place, one for water and the rest for each of the six wines that were served. The grand dukes could hardly complain about being annoyed or affronted, although they may have groaned about being hungover the next morning.

According to some historians, that was the first and last time alcohol was served in the Hayes White House. But Secretary of State Evarts knew better than to subject the diplomatic corps to "cold water" meals. With the aid of a White House steward, he found a way to evade the rule.

It was customary to serve a sherbet course as a palate cleanser midway through the meal. Evarts quietly informed the hard-stuff crowd that the sherbet (in those days a beverage) would henceforth be a mixture of sugar, lemon juice, and beaten egg whites laced with a healthy shot of rum. The rum would be omitted from the president's and first lady's portions; they would not know that their rule was being violated. The concoction became known to state dinner regulars as the life-saving station.

Of course the president knew what was going on. In fact, he knew a lot more than the journalists, one of whom gloated that he seemed to be "wholly ignorant" of the operation. Six years after he left the White House, Hayes had the last laugh on the imbibers. On January 10, 1887, he wrote in his diary: "My orders were to flavor the punch rather strongly with the same flavor that is found in Jamaican rum. This took! There was not a drop of spirits in it!"

XII

★★★

In addition to the various dinners that take place at the White House each year, there is also a full schedule of receptions. The president may hold a reception for just about anyone he pleases— political leaders, the media, his favorite organizations—but there are several obligatory receptions in every social season. Traditionally these have been the diplomatic, judicial, congressional, departmental, and the army and navy. The diplomatic gets my vote for the most colorful. The ambassadors and their retinues wear either uniforms or full evening dress and they are rarely without decorations—sometimes sashes, more often medals, either on brilliant ribbons around their necks or marching across the chests of their tailcoats. Many of the wives wear evening gowns and sparkling jewelry but quite a few come in native dress.

Some of the receptions start at 5:30 P.M. but the more formal ones usually begin at eight. The guest list numbers about fifteen hundred and everyone has a chance to shake hands with the president. On a number of occasions, I was invited to join Mother and Dad in the receiving line. I didn't mind greeting their guests, most of them were quite pleasant, but I did mind shaking fifteen hundred hands. You can—and I did—incur serious damage to your fingers from pressing that much flesh.

At the height of the White House social season, Mother often averaged 2,500 shakes a week. By the time she left the White House, the glove size of her right hand had gone from 6 to 6½. My hand, too, had gone up half a size. I cannot claim to have shaken nearly as many hands as she did. But I had obviously passed some sort of boundary, after which the hand says: "I can't take it anymore."

XIII
★★★

Handshakitis is a common complaint among White House residents. Is there anything that can be done to avoid it? I've made a little study of the issue, with some help from several presidents. Early in his career Harry Truman examined the problem with the thoroughness that he brought to all aspects of any job he tackled. Dad decided that the essence of survival handshaking was timing. You should seize the other person's hand before he or she grabbed yours. You should always slide your thumb between the other person's thumb and index finger, so that you, not he or she, did the squeezing.

Another president who gave some thought to shaking hands was Woodrow Wilson. As a college president who went into politics late in life, he had to demonstrate a special eagerness to shake any hand that came his way, lest average folks think he was a snob. After several mashing marathons left his hand in an all-but-pulpy state, he devised his own survival formula.

Wilson's technique called for folding his middle finger down against the base of his thumb and crossing, or at least closing, the index finger and ring finger above it. That way, people could not get a grip and Wilson's welcoming hand slid through the guest's hand almost untouched.

Another president who studied the art of the handshake was James Polk of Tennessee. In his White House diary, Polk told of shaking hands with "several thousand persons" at the New Year's Day reception on January 1, 1849. Toward the close of this ordeal, friends asked if his arm was sore. Polk smiled and told them that he could shake hands from sunrise to sundown "without suffering any bad effects from it." His formula was almost exactly the same as the one Harry Truman devised. Shake and not be shaken, grip and not be gripped.

Some presidents and first ladies have devised alternatives to the handshake. Edith Roosevelt held a bouquet of flowers in both hands, exempting her from the need to endure mashing from all and sundry. Instead of extending his large Arkansas paw and letting it get crushed, Bill Clinton often grabbed outstretched hands and arms with both hands, delivering a friendly democratic squeeze— without getting squeezed in return.

XIV
★★★

Once White House guests have gone through the receiving line, they continue on to the State Dining Room where sandwiches, cakes, tea, coffee, wine, and punch are served, except at diplomatic receptions where liquor is omitted.

It may be hard to believe, but the president used to hold receptions on New Year's Day and the Fourth of July to which everyone in Washington was invited. I should hasten to add that they didn't all come. The social elite were almost always on hand but the working classes, realizing that neither their clothes nor their manners were suitable, mostly stayed home.

In James Monroe's era, New Year's Day receptions attracted about a thousand people, but as Washington grew into a full-fledged city, the crowds grew progressively larger. In 1857, President Franklin Pierce's New Year's Day reception started at eleven in the morning and ended at two that afternoon. In the course of those three hours, Pierce shook hands with some five thousand people.

By Grover Cleveland's day, the number had risen to six thousand, putting an inordinate amount of stress on both the president and the White House floors. Calvin Coolidge, already on his way out of office, dispensed with the 1929 event and spent the holidays in Florida instead. I can readily identify with his excuse: He and his wife were sick of getting bruises from shaking so many hands.

Herbert Hoover revived the tradition and between noon and 3:30 P.M. on New Year's Day, 1930, he shook hands with an incredible 6,348 people. That has to be a record of some sort. Hoover repeated his performance in 1931 and 1932, but that was the last New Year's Day reception at the White House. In 1933 the lame duck president followed Coolidge's example and decamped to Florida for the holidays. Between the Great Depression, World War II, and the burgeoning population of Washington, the receptions were never revived.

Still, you can't say they didn't have a good run. One hundred and thirty-one years is pretty impressive. The Fourth of July receptions, on the other hand, never even came close. They were started by Thomas Jefferson in 1803 and ended by Martin Van Buren in 1839.

Van Buren hated the crowds that poured into the White House for his New Year's Day and Fourth of July receptions and his guests usually came away hating him. To keep them from staying any longer than was absolutely necessary, he refused to serve refreshments, which was the main reason most of them came.

Van Buren was particularly impatient with the Fourth of July receptions, which interfered with his summer escape to New York. Determined to find a way out, he let it be known that the president would be out of town on July 4, 1839, and the White House would not be open for callers. Presumably his successors were equally anxious to escape Washington's beastly summer heat and humidity. Never again was there a reception on the Fourth of July. The Stars and Stripes were cheered elsewhere, but not at the White House.

XV
★★★

About fifty thousand people attend White House dinners and receptions each year. I am convinced that the White House catering staff deserves most of the credit for their success. Usually, they have a little more lead time than Lyndon Johnson gave them in 1963. But they are used to working miracles on short notice.

When former prime minister Ehud Barak of Israel visited the White House in 1999, Bill and Hillary Clinton planned an official working visit that included meetings with the president and his cabinet and a luncheon for eighteen people. When word of Barak's arrival got out, so many people wanted to meet him that on five days' notice the luncheon for eighteen turned into a dinner for five hundred.

Eleanor Roosevelt, who could never be called a social butterfly, was nevertheless a demon hostess. She was forever inviting supporters of the many causes she espoused to the White House for tea. There were so many of these gatherings that she frequently had two a day. One of my favorite White House staff members, Alonzo Fields, used to call them "doubleheader teas."

As Fields (the White House maître d'hôtel and butlers are always called by their last names) tells it, Mrs. Roosevelt would invite two different groups of women to tea, the first at four P.M. and the second at five P.M. There would be about four or five hundred people in each group. This meant that Fields and his staff of butlers had about thirty minutes between the two affairs to reset the table with clean tablecloths, china, and silver; replenish the platters of food; and put out fresh cups of tea and coffee.

The old-timers on the White House staff assured Fields it couldn't be done. Fields, who had a mathematical mind—which he may have picked up from his previous employer, the president of MIT—found a way. He put six waiters to work passing trays of tea and coffee as the guests entered the dining room. The trays could hold ten cups each, which meant that sixty guests could be served at a time. Fields calculated that the waiters could make the trip back and forth to the serving pantry in two minutes. In twelve minutes they could serve 360 guests. That left only a few guests to be taken care of at the stations set up at either end of the serving tables.

In another time-and-motion-saving move, Fields had the White House carpenters build a forty-foot table that was placed in front of the fireplace in the State Dining Room. This gave him additional room for the platters of sandwiches, cakes, and cookies, and shortened the wait to reach them. Fields's plan worked remarkably well. The guests had time to eat, but as soon as they took their last sip of tea, the military aides and staff ushers moved them along, with the excuse that another party was waiting.

Lou Henry Hoover gave Eleanor Roosevelt a run for her money when it came to inviting people to the White House. In one year alone, 1932, she presided at forty teas and held receptions for eighty different organizations. She and the president were also quick to extend luncheon and dinner invitations, often on very short notice. Once, after ordering food for a one o'clock luncheon for six people, Ava Long, the White House housekeeper, was informed a half hour before the guests were due to sit down that the number had changed to forty.

Mrs. Long instructed the cook to grind up every morsel of food she could find in the refrigerator and mix up a batch of croquettes.

This is what the White House looked like after the British paid a visit in 1814. A severe thunderstorm saved it from being completely destroyed. Credit: Library of Congress

Andrew Jackson's inaugural reception in 1829 was a study in total chaos. The president had to retreat through a back door to escape from the mob. Credit: White House Historical Association

Above: *My father had a memorable lunch with FDR in the shade of this famous Jackson magnolia tree. My mother had a beautiful view of it from her sitting room window.* Credit: *White House Historical Association*

Right: *Isn't this a striking portrait of Angelica Singleton Van Buren? The marble bust beside her is a likeness of her father-in-law.* Credit: *White House Historical Association (The White House Collection)*

George P. A. Healy painted this portrait of President John Tyler, one of my Truman ancestors. I'm afraid I inherited his nose. Credit: White House Historical Association (The White House Collection)

From all accounts, Grace Goodhue Coolidge was just as lovely as she looks in this painting. The White House staff gave her a secret nickname, "Sunshine." Credit: White House Historical Association (The White House Collection)

★ ★ ★

I realize the Lincoln Bedroom reeks of history, but I'm not a fan of Victorian furniture. The one time I slept in Abe's bed, I was happy to get back to my own.
Credit: White House Historical Association

The Queens' Bedroom is not off-limits to commoners. Among those who have stayed there: Winston Churchill, Russian foreign minister Vyacheslav Molotov, and me.
Credit: White House Historical Association

WASHINGTON, D. C.—AN UNIQUE FESTIVAL—EGG-ROLLING IN THE WHITE HOUSE GROUNDS ON EASTER MONDAY.
FROM A SKETCH BY A STAFF ARTIST.—SEE PAGE 132.

★ ★ ★

Above: *The decor of the Oval Office changes with each administration. President George W. Bush opted for warm colors and paintings of his native Texas. Credit: White House Historical Association*

Facing page, top: *This handsome plateau is one of a number of White House furnishings purchased by James and Elizabeth Monroe when he was serving as ambassador to France.*
Credit: White House Historical Association (photo by Bruce White)

Facing page, bottom: Frank Leslie's Illustrated Weekly *ran this picture of the White House Easter egg roll in 1887. Security was obviously not an issue in those days. Credit: Library of Congress*

★ ★ ★

The ceremonies welcoming Emperor Akihito of Japan in 1994 included a twenty-one-gun salute and a rendition of "Yankee Doodle" by the Old Guard Fife and Drum Corps.
Credit: White House Historical Association

Top: *This cutaway view of the White House as seen from the South Portico provides a good picture of its interior. The East Room is on the right.*
Credit: White House Historical Association

Bottom: *Here is an overview of the President's Park. Its eighteen acres of trees and gardens provide a taste of the country right in the middle of Washington,* D.C. Credit: White House Historical Association

Top: *The Rose Garden has been the scene of press conferences, presidential announcements, state dinners, and VIP receptions, but only one wedding.*
Credit: *White House Historical Association (photo by Donald J. Crump)*

Bottom: *Abigail Adams, shown here in a portrait by Gilbert Stuart, was the first mistress of the White House. The building was still under construction when she moved in.*
Credit: *Courtesy of the National Gallery of Art*

★ ★ ★

Jacqueline Kennedy created the Yellow Oval Room as a place where the president can receive important guests. I remember it as my father's study. Credit: White House Historical Association

Top: *The East Room was
designed for presidential
receptions, but Theodore
Roosevelt held boxing
matches there and Susan
Ford used it for her high
school prom.*
Credit: *White House
Historical Association
(photo by Bruce White)*

Bottom: *President John F.
Kennedy seems delighted to
have a pair of Halloween
visitors in the Oval Office.
Somehow I think he recog-
nized them even with those
masks on.*
Credit: *Cecil Stoughton,
White House/John
Fitzgerald Kennedy Library,
Boston*

President Lyndon Johnson and his guests follow the Color Guard down the Grand Staircase. The ceremony is a prelude to White House social events. Credit: LBJ Library, Photo by Yoichi Okamoto

★★★

Above: *Presidents often plant trees to commemorate important events. The Clintons planted this one to honor the victims of the Oklahoma City bombing in 1995.*
Credit: Clinton Presidential Materials Project

Facing page, top: *Among her many talents, Louisa Catherine Adams was an expert party-giver. Her social skills played a major role in helping John Quincy Adams win the presidency.*
Credit: Smithsonian American Art Museum, Adams-Clement Collection, gift of Mary Louisa Adams (Clement) in memory of her mother, Louisa Catherine Adams Clement

Facing page, bottom: *The Marine Band has a roster of 143 musicians and support personnel. Its members perform at the White House at least three hundred times a year.*
Credit: "The President's Own" U.S. Marine Band (photo by Andrew Linden)

The Center Hall on the second floor used to be a dark and dreary space. The Truman renovations transformed it into this pleasant sitting room. Credit: White House Historical Association

The crescent-shaped table is my favorite seating arrangement for White House dinners. This one, held in the East Room, celebrated the fiftieth anniversary of NATO.
Credit: Clinton Presidential Materials Project

The end product was served with a mushroom sauce and several guests actually raved about it. When one woman asked what the dish was called, Mrs. Long replied tartly, "White House Surprise Supreme." The housekeeper pulled off another surprise supreme when she handed in her resignation not long afterward.

XVI
★★★

My favorite example of staff inventiveness was told by my friend Fields some years after he left the White House. Fields had a secret recipe for the punch that was served at White House receptions during the Franklin Roosevelt administration. It never failed to be a big hit, and when you hear what was in it, you'll understand why.

When the Twenty-first Amendment repealing Prohibition was ratified in 1933, FDR was deluged with gifts from wineries all over the world. They were delivered to the White House by the case— claret, sauterne, muscatel, applejack, blackberry wine, every variety of sherry, even sake. Little of it was good enough to serve at the table, but FDR was too much of a penny-pincher to throw it away, so Fields was instructed to find a way to use it up.

Punch is one of the standard drinks at White House receptions. For a crowd of 1,200 people, Fields and his staff would prepare about 45 gallons of fruit punch for the nondrinkers and 110 gallons of spiked punch for those who liked stronger stuff, obviously the majority. Fields uncorked a few of the gift wines and went to work experimenting with various combinations until he came up with several recipes that passed his taste test. One of the most lethal contained muscatel, sauterne, applejack, and scuppernong. Another, only slightly less dangerous, combined blackberry wine, claret, sake, and sherry.

It didn't take long for the wines to disappear, but Fields occasionally had twinges of anxiety. "I could always see the headline," he said. "President's party has tragic end. Guests go berserk after drinking spiked punch at the White House. Chief Butler being held for investigation."

XVII
★★★

The inventiveness of the White House chefs is put to the test at state dinners where the menu must in some way acknowledge the guest of honor's nationality. For Prime Minister Tony Blair of the United Kingdom, the dessert was a concoction called Strawberries and Cream with a Devonshire sauce. When Premier Jiang Zemin of China was a guest, a fusion of Asian and American cuisine was served. The first course was lobster poached in lime leaves and lemongrass and the dessert was an elaborate orange and chocolate creation that included marzipan panda bears.

At a dinner for Italian prime minister Romano Prodi in 1980, pastry chef Roland Mesnier, who has worked at the White House since the Carter administration, created a special dessert in honor of the prime minister's hometown of Bologna. He made a replica of one of the twelfth-century towers that are among the city's most famous landmarks, sculpting it out of peach cake and chestnut ice cream parfait with chocolate caramel sauce on top. The dessert was a special challenge because the tower not only had to look authentic and taste divine, it also had to stand up straight. As Mesnier said, "We don't want dessert falling in anyone's lap."

On September 5, 2001, George and Laura Bush hosted their first state dinner for President Vicente Fox of Mexico. The mixture of American and Mexican cuisines included a soup that combined Maryland crab and Mexican sausage, followed by American bison and potatoes whipped with poblano chiles. Dessert was a mango and coconut ice cream dome with peaches served with a red chile pepper sauce and tequila sabayon. Those last two sound weird, I know, but I've tasted some of Roland Mesnier's desserts and I feel certain this one was absolutely delicious. In keeping with the American-Mexican theme, after dinner Metropolitan Opera soprano Dawn Upshaw performed works by Leonard Bernstein and the Spanish composer Manuel de Falla.

It sounds like a wonderful evening. Most White House dinners are wonderful, not only because of the fine food and fabulous entertainment, but because they allow the president of the United States to welcome guests from all over the world to the warmth and dignity of America's most famous home.

Dolley Madison personified the wise use of womanpower. Her warmth and wit won several political battles for her brilliant but reserved husband.
Credit: White House Historical Association (The White House Collection)

6

★★★

Womanpower

I find it amusing that the East Wing, which was built by Charles McKim in 1902 to provide a visitors' entrance and coatrooms, and rebuilt by Franklin D. Roosevelt to add extra office space during World War II, stands on the site of Thomas Jefferson's henhouse. I wonder what Jefferson would say if he could see the flock of females who are hanging out there now—the first lady's staff and sometimes the first lady herself, plus the predominately female White House social office.

There is irony at work here. Our third president did everything in his power to keep women, except for scullery maids and laundresses, out of the President's House.

Thomas Jefferson was undoubtedly a great man but he had some odd ideas along with his many good ones. Among the oddest was his conviction that women should have nothing to do with politics. A widower, Jefferson hoped to inspire a tradition whereby all the social events in the White House were relentlessly male. This, he averred, was the key to political peace and stability. Women's "omnipotent influence" should be kept behind the "domestic line."

The president's attitude was based on his experience in France, where he served as American ambassador for three years. In Paris, *salonnieres,* wealthy women who were more than mere hostesses, played politics with not a little ferocity and occasional genius. At Versailles, the king's mistress often had more influence than his chief minister. To Jefferson, this was decadent and—in his vocabulary, an even more damning adjective—aristocratic. He blamed the French Revolution on poor beheaded Marie Antoinette, declaring: "I have ever believed that had there been no queen there would have been no revolution."

When I read that I was tempted to say: "Now, Mr. Jefferson, that is just plain silly!" In the Washington, D.C., of his era, Jefferson's attitude was worse than silly. It all but paralyzed the government of the United States. Politics is not an art form that can be confined to legislative halls. It includes a vast amount of personal give and take in other venues, such as parties and dinners, where women can smooth the rough edges of abrasive and quarrelsome males.

Aside from all this, the president's deliberate exclusion of women infuriated them. One of my favorite White House scenes is the day a group of fashionably dressed Washington wives descended on the mansion en masse to greet the startled chief executive. Although Jefferson showed up in his riding clothes, he proved he was no slouch in the charm department. He went around the circle and chatted with each of the ladies, leaving them all somewhat nonplussed.

The women went away frustrated but still determined to partake of the political game. They found their opportunity for revenge when President Jefferson's view of women's place got entangled with his reception of the new British minister, Anthony Merry and his wife, Elizabeth. She was infuriated by Jefferson's "pêle-mêle" democratic etiquette, and had not a little to do with her husband's refusal to accept any further invitations to the White House.

The agitated Jefferson called Mrs. Merry a virago and blamed her for the contretemps. But he soon discovered that the women of Washington took Elizabeth Merry's side. They admired her intelligence and flair—their letters vibrated with admiration for her taste in clothes. Without quite saying so, they admired even more her refusal to let the "Democratic Emperor," as some of Jefferson's enemies called him, push her around. Prominent among the covert sympathizers was none other than Dolley Madison, the wife of the secretary of state.

Jefferson worked himself into a near frenzy defending his behavior, even writing an anonymous newspaper column. But the ladies of Washington flocked to Mrs. Merry's dinners, and the president slowly realized he had lost his battle to keep women out of politics.

II

★★★

If Jefferson had any doubts about his defeat, they vanished when James Madison was elected in 1808 and Dolley became the first lady. Already well known as a hostess, she swiftly made it clear that ignoring the rules of etiquette and men-only dinners in the White House were as dead as the dinosaur bones ex-president Jefferson liked to collect.

For openers, Dolley staged the first inaugural ball at nearby Long's Hotel. Attended by over four hundred people, it was heralded as "a handsome display of female fashion and beauty." Next, Dolley redecorated the first-floor rooms and turned the White House into a political and social power center, with the two ideas so intertwined that no one could tell the difference.

Womanpower. The term did not exist in the nineteenth century, but the White House came to personify it. The State Dining Room became the scene of weekly formal dinners for as many as thirty men and women, with Dolley at the head of the table, presiding over the conversation. At Dolley's Wednesday evening receptions in the Elliptical Saloon, today's Blue Room, she performed like an actress on a beautifully designed stage set. Dressed in stylish gowns of buff or yellow satin, she greeted other equally well-gowned women and their gentlemen escorts and engaged in conversation that was often highly political but simultaneously amusing and informative.

Soon visiting Frenchmen were calling Dolley "one of America's most valuable assets." Her cool detachment was among her greatest gifts. She often sat in the House gallery listening to some congressman, such as viper-tongued John Randolph of Virginia, eviscerate her husband. That night, in her drawing room, Dolley would cheerfully report: "It was as good as a play," shrinking Randolph's fangs to the vanishing point.

Few doubt that Dolley was responsible for her husband winning a second term in 1812. The warm atmosphere at her parties and her ability to make each guest feel important worked wonders on the congressmen and senators who could have blocked his nomination. By that time, if Dolley were mean-spirited (she wasn't), she might well have asked: "By the way, whatever became of that guy with the silly ideas about women—Tom Jefferson?"

III
✯✯✯

Dolley Madison singlehandedly transformed the White House into a public platform for womanpower. The next first lady to take advantage of this breakthrough was Louisa Catherine Adams, the wife of John Quincy Adams. Beautiful, charming, a gifted musician and writer, Louisa had only one problem: her husband. John Quincy had political ambitions, intense ones, but no political abilities whatsoever.

When Adams became secretary of state under James Monroe, Louisa decided she was his only hope of winning the White House. By 1817, when the Adamses arrived in Washington, congressional and senatorial wives were used to participating in Washington society. One rueful congressman wrote to his absent wife that he regularly had to apologize for not bringing his "better half" to the capital.

His better half may well have wished she were there. Thanks to Dolley, Washington had become a place where women could have front-row seats—and sometimes even play a role—in the ongoing drama of national and international politics. "I came here for the express purpose of seeing and being seen," one congressional wife told her sister.

Dolley established the custom of women attending the debates in Congress and the arguments before the Supreme Court. The most authoritative Washington watcher of them all, Margaret Bayard Smith, wife of the editor of the city's premier newspaper, the *National Intelligencer*, said: "The women here are taking a station in society that is not known elsewhere" in America.

Louisa Catherine Adams took that station and headed for the White House with it. At an Executive Mansion reception after President Monroe's reelection in 1820, friends teased her about the possibility of being in charge of a similar reception four years hence. Mrs. Adams only smiled enigmatically, suggesting that the idea may have already occurred to her.

Louisa plunged boldly into the swirling social stream. "There is a party for every night of the week," one congressman told his wife. Guest lists were frequently a statement of political fealty. Margaret Bayard Smith spoke of a "right down Crawford party" on behalf of another contender for the White House, Georgian William Crawford. In this milieu, Louisa Catherine Adams emerged as her husband's campaign manager, or perhaps a better term would be party chairman. She was certainly the mastermind of John Quincy's parties—and what a job she did.

In one morning, Louisa returned no less than twenty-five social calls, leaving cards for her soirées. She once spent two hours visiting eight or ten congressional boardinghouses trying to catch up to an important quarry. Simultaneously, she enlarged the Adamses' F

Street house, adding a spacious "entertainment room," while her gloomy husband predicted that they were going to end up in the poorhouse.

Louisa began giving a weekly dinner party, usually for about two dozen guests. For a while she experimented with inviting only men to multiply contacts with important congressmen, but a friend warned that she was flirting with social disaster. Regrouping, she launched "Mrs. Adams's Tuesday nights" in which men and women mingled in a convivial atmosphere reminiscent of Dolley Madison's drawing rooms.

Sensing momentum, Louisa announced there would be a party every Tuesday for the entire winter, upstaging competing hosts and hostesses, including President and Mrs. Monroe. As an added attraction, she provided entertainment in the form of musical performances and dancing. Louisa herself played the piano and harp beautifully and had a lovely voice. Talk about a triple threat campaign manager! Can any modern political maven compare to her? Even her unsociable husband begged Louisa to continue her "Tuesday campaigns."

In 1822, Louisa topped everyone including herself with a New Year's Eve party for five hundred. "The eye of the public is already on me," she triumphantly wrote to one friend. That meant, of course, said eye was also on her husband.

With the election of 1824 less than a year away, John Quincy finally got into the spirit of the race. By that time Senator Andrew Jackson of Tennessee, the hero of the 1815 battle of New Orleans, had emerged as his chief rival. John Quincy suggested they give a ball in Jackson's honor on January 8, the anniversary of the battle. It was a stroke of genius. Socially, it seemed to place the Adamses in a superior position, while simultaneously letting them savor a slice of Old Hickory's huge popularity with the voters. Louisa gleefully wrote out invitations to every member of the House, the Senate, the Supreme Court, and all the other capital VIPs she could find.

The affair was a magnificent success, inspiring one newspaperman to poetry:

Wend you with the world tonight?
Sixty gray and giddy twenty
Flirts that court and prudes that slight
Stale coquettes and spinsters plenty . . .
Belles and matrons, maids and madams
All are gone to Mrs. Adams.

Thanks to Louisa, John Quincy Adams won the presidency. I wish I could say the result was four years of triumphant happiness. Alas, the opposite was the case. John Quincy proved to be a poor president. A lot of his problems arose from the close election, which was decided in the House of Representatives. Louisa's partying paid dividends there, but Jackson, who won the popular vote, accused Adams of making a "corrupt bargain" with another contender, Kentuckian Henry Clay, to win his votes by making him secretary of state. The accusation wrecked Adams's relations with Congress.

Like a typical husband, John Quincy blamed Louisa for his presidential misery, and by the time their four years of torture ended, they were barely speaking to each other. Still, no one could take away Louisa's triumph; to this day she remains the only female campaign manager to put her candidate in the White House.

IV
★★★

There was a somewhat different example of womanpower in Andrew Jackson's administration. A woman ousted the entire cabinet and arguably changed the course of American history. The woman's name was Margaret O'Neale and her father ran one of the best hotels in Washington, D.C. Peggy was a beauty and Washington was full of lonely, often handsome, men. Before she was twenty, Peggy had a reputation that prompted First Lady Elizabeth Monroe to bar her from the White House.

Peggy married John Timberlake, a ship's purser who was away at sea for years at a time. During one of these voyages, Peggy became more than friendly with John Henry Eaton, a wealthy young senator from Tennessee who was close to Andrew Jackson. Shortly before Jackson's election, Peggy's husband died at sea and rumors soon spread that he had killed himself because his wife was unfaithful. Jackson advised Eaton to marry Peggy and make her an honest woman.

Senator Eaton did not require any arm-twisting. By the time Old Hickory was elected president, Peggy was Mrs. Eaton. But the whitewashing only accelerated the Washington gossip machine. "Eaton has married his mistress, and the mistress of eleven doz others," one politician wrote to a friend.

Andrew Jackson had met Peggy during his senatorial sojourn in the capital and thought well of her. It never occurred to him that she might prove to be a problem when he made John Henry Eaton his secretary of war. But the rest of Washington, D.C., was aghast. Because Jackson's wife had died a few months after his election, it seemed likely that he would follow the example of a previous widower president, Thomas Jefferson, and ask the wife of his closest friend in the cabinet to serve as his hostess. That friend, Secretary of State Martin Van Buren, was also a widower. And who was next on the list of friends? John Henry Eaton—which meant that the notorious Peggy O'Neale Timberlake Eaton would preside at the White House as the leader of Washington society!

The moment the newspapers reported Jackson's probable cabinet choices, a group of Washington insiders, led by Colonel Nathan Towson, a hero of the War of 1812, called on the president-elect to warn him that he was making a serious mistake. The resultant explosion almost blew out a few windows in Gadsby's Hotel where Jackson was staying. He had not been elected to "consult the ladies of Washington" about his cabinet appointments, Old Hickory roared.

Fueling the president-elect's temper was the memory of his campaign, in which John Quincy Adams's backers had tried to paint Rachel Jackson as an adulteress because she and Jackson had married before her divorce from her first husband was final. Jackson was convinced the slander had killed Rachel—and he may not have been entirely wrong.

Colonel Towson retreated from Gadsby's Hotel in disarray, but the ladies of Washington were unintimidated by the president's famous temper. At Jackson's inaugural ball, they launched the "Petticoat War." Ninety percent of them refused to speak to Peggy.

The leader of the boycott was Floride Calhoun, wife of vice president John C. Calhoun. Rather than return a social call from the secretary of war and Mrs. Eaton, Floride went home to South Carolina and stayed there for the next four years. Before she left, she persuaded Emily Donelson, wife of Jackson's nephew and secretary, to refuse to greet Mrs. Eaton in the White House. When Peggy called, Emily stayed in her room.

The agitated president spent more time fighting "Eaton malaria," as Washington wits called it, than he devoted to affairs of state. When a clergyman wrote him a letter detailing evidence of Peggy's previous sins, Jackson's reply was longer than his inaugural address. Entire cabinet meetings were devoted to the president lecturing his appointees on Peggy's spotless reputation. Old Hickory got nowhere. The hapless males all said they could not persuade their wives to change their minds.

The one cabinet member who was in a position to make hay of the mess was Martin Van Buren. With no wife to object, he was delighted to entertain Secretary and Mrs. Eaton. Simultaneously, the "Little Magician," as some called him, never missed a chance to remind the president that the instigator of the anti-Peggy campaign was Floride Calhoun. The president began to look with less and less enthusiasm on his vice president, who had joined his ticket with the understanding that Old Hickory would serve only a single term, keeping the chief executive's seat warm for President Calhoun.

The Petticoat War became a stalemate. The president would not budge and neither would the women of Washington. As a result, social life in the capital came to a stop. No one gave parties for fear of offending the president if they failed to invite Mrs. Eaton. A hundred congressmen, presumably pressured by their spouses, convened a secret meeting in which they threatened to vote against everything President Jackson proposed if he did not get rid of Peggy. One agitated Washingtonian told a friend: "For the first time, I believe the destiny of the country hangs on a woman's favor." (His underline, not mine.)

It would have been more accurate to say the destiny of John C. Calhoun. One newspaperman opined that the vice president had "doomed himself to oblivion by his refusal to rehabilitate Peggy Eaton." This soon proved to be the case. The canny Martin Van Buren convinced President Jackson that the best solution to the contretemps was the resignation of the entire cabinet. That would remove Eaton and his wife from contention and the government could begin to function. Van Buren led the way by resigning without further ado. Eaton followed suit and Jackson fired the three remaining secretaries when they did not take the hint.

The overnight disappearance of Jackson's cabinet created a national sensation. Peggy's name and reputation became the chief topic of conversation in cities and towns across the country. She was called the American Pompadour, Cleopatra, and Helen of Troy. Meanwhile, it was reported that John C. Calhoun was describing Mrs. Eaton as "the real president of the United States." This completely destroyed the vice president's standing in the White House. Soon Andrew Jackson was deciding to run for a second term and this time Martin Van Buren would be his vice president.

The embittered Calhoun became a foe of Jackson. When Old Hickory won reelection in a landslide, Calhoun's animosity extended to the entire federal government. Once an apostle of the

Union, the South Carolinian turned into a proponent of secession and civil war. As for Old Hickory, while he appeared to be a winner, he was actually the loser in the Petticoat War. As one historian summed it up recently, "the man who had defeated redcoats, Indians and Spaniards could not prevail over a handful of ladies."

Along with John C. Calhoun and his wife, Floride, who would have made a brilliant first lady, the other loser was Peggy Eaton. She went home to Tennessee with her husband and watched him flub an attempt to regain his seat in the Senate. In 1836, Jackson appointed Eaton ambassador to Spain, where he turned into a hopeless drunk. After he reeled back to Tennessee and finally died, Peggy took his money and returned to Washington where she lived quietly until she lost her heart to a dancing master who left town with a lot of her cash.

V

Peggy Eaton's story underscores the way the White House empowered women other than presidents' wives. Among the least recognized members of this group are the women who operated as substitute or stand-in first ladies for bachelor or widowed presidents or for chief executives whose wives were ill or simply not interested in serving as White House hostesses.

The first of these stand-in first ladies was Andrew Jackson's niece Emily Donelson, who was married to her cousin, the president's private secretary, Andrew Jackson Donelson. Although Emily was only twenty-one when she came to Washington, she had been born on a Tennessee plantation, and was unintimidated by either the size of the White House or its social responsibilities. Despite her affluent background, Emily was as unpretentious as her uncle. She told a friend she hoped to make the White House "a model American home." This sounds a little like campaign rhetoric, but Emily probably meant it.

Despite her busy family life—three of her four children were born at the White House—Emily did a good job as hostess and household manager. In addition to being a model of tact, she was one of the few people who was not afraid to stand up to the notoriously fierce-tempered Jackson. She even had the courage to oppose him in the Petticoat War, but after refusing to receive Peggy Eaton in the White House, she had the good sense to withdraw from the field by packing up her children and returning to Tennessee.

Jackson was lonesome without Emily and her little ones and he was happy to welcome them back when the controversial Mrs. Eaton departed, but Emily's stay was brief. She had always been frail, and by 1834 she was desperately ill with tuberculosis, one of the leading killers of women in that era. Once again, Emily Donelson returned to Tennessee, this time to die.

The next president, Martin Van Buren, was also a widower. He spent his first two years in the White House without a hostess, inflicting serious damage on his presidency. Then his son Abraham married a twenty-two-year-old South Carolina belle named Angelica Singleton, who soon took over the social side of the White House.

Angelica was a niece of Dolley Madison's—it was Dolley, in fact, who had masterminded her match with Abraham Van Buren—but in at least one respect Angelica lacked her aunt's political savvy. During her honeymoon in Europe, she picked up a somewhat dubious custom. Instead of standing in a receiving line, getting her pretty hand mashed, she adopted the tableau.

While the president continued to shake hands at the door, Angelica posed on a platform at the south end of the Elliptical Saloon with flowers in her arms and hair. She wore a gorgeous white dress and positioned a half dozen women friends around her, also in glowing white.

The youthful Queen Victoria was posing thus in London and the ladies of King Louis Philippe's family were doing likewise in France. But this was democratic America and the tableau was greeted with cries of political outrage, mingled with sarcastic yawps. Angelica finally got the message and started shaking hands.

Why the supposedly astute Van Buren tolerated his daughter-in-law's queenly behavior for so long is baffling. The only answer, I suppose, is the persuasive power of her pretty face. Angelica was indeed a beauty. If you ever tour the White House, be sure to look for her portrait. The last time I was there, it was hanging over the mantel in the Red Room. Painted by the noted New York artist Henry Inman, it is one of the finest portraits in the White House collection.

VI
***

My investigation into substitute first ladies revealed a somewhat surprising fact: Ronald Reagan was not the first actor to live in the White House. That honor belongs to Priscilla Cooper Tyler, wife of President John Tyler's oldest son, Robert.

The daughter of a famous nineteenth-century actor, Thomas A. Cooper, Priscilla had often performed with her father in Shakespearean dramas and other plays. She took over as the president's hostess after Mrs. Tyler, an invalid when she arrived in the White House, became bedridden.

Priscilla found her new role entrancing. "Here I am, actually living in and—what is more—presiding at the White House," she wrote to her sister. To her amazement, the part fit her perfectly. She felt as if "I had been living here always." She was astonished by the "facility" with which she greeted cabinet ministers, diplomats, generals, and admirals. "I am considered 'charmant' by the Frenchmen, 'lovely' by the Americans and 'really quite nice you know' by the English," she reported to this same sister.

Priscilla reveled in the wardrobe her father-in-law bought for her. One dress, she told her sister, was a "pearl-colored silk that would set you crazy." (By this time I was starting to feel sorry for the sister.) Priscilla needed all the dresses Tyler could afford. Scarcely a night passed without a dinner. As the first vice president to ascend to the White House, Tyler had enemies galore who sneeringly called him "His Accidency." He saw entertaining as his only hope of building a following in the capital.

The president also sent Priscilla and Robert to represent him at other capital parties. One night at Carusi's Ballroom, Priscilla overheard someone remark that "the great Cooper" had performed there in the building's former life as a theater. In a flash, Priscilla was catapulted back to her hard years as an actress. She "looked down at the velvet dress of Mrs. Tyler" and remembered the tawdry thing she had worn as Lady Macbeth. It had been "six nights of bad weather, bad houses, and bad spirits, for the little money we did earn was never paid."

For more than two years, Priscilla was, in President Tyler's words, "the presiding genius of the White House." Her schedule was daunting. One night she would have a formal dinner for forty congressmen and their wives, the next day might see a reception for a thousand people, with hours of handshaking. "Such big fists . . . some of the people have," she remarked. "And such hearty shakes they give my poor little hand. One great countryman gave me a clutch I almost expired under."

The pace finally got to Priscilla one evening. She was four months pregnant and her first child, still very young, demanded constant attention. Nevertheless Priscilla rushed around the White House all day getting the place ready for a formal dinner for the president's cabinet. That night, exhausted, she found herself sitting next to Secretary of State Daniel Webster, one of the more formidable examples of the capital's long history of larger than life characters. As the dessert was served, Mrs. Tyler fell back from the table, unconscious.

Consternation. "The God-like Daniel," as his fans called Webster, leaped to her assistance. He lifted her in his arms, intending to carry her to a sofa. Before he could find one, Priscilla's husband,

Robert, reached for a pitcher of ice water and dumped it on both of them. The ice water, Priscilla said, not only ruined her "lovely new dress" but also produced "a decided coolness between myself and the Secretary of State."

Priscilla came to and was taken to her room while a team of White House servants dried off the discomfited Webster. He soon forgave both Tylers and became Priscilla's favorite cabinet officer.

Unfortunately, Priscilla's run as mistress of the White House ended in disappointment. Her mother-in-law, Letitia Tyler, died and most White House entertaining was canceled for a year. In the interim, President Tyler met and married Julia Gardiner of New York, who was about the same age as Priscilla. The president sent Priscilla and Robert to Philadelphia, supposedly to drum up support for his run for a second term.

Julia Gardiner Tyler revived Angelica Van Buren's tableaus with smashing effect at her fabulous White House parties. Interestingly, no one said a word against them this time around. The political atmosphere was no longer democratic; the Whigs, forerunners of the Republicans, were in control. Julia Tyler's parties were part of a successful campaign to persuade Congress to admit Texas as the thirty-fifth state—another example of White House womanpower. Meanwhile, in distant Philadelphia, Priscilla Cooper Tyler read about her stepmother-in-law's dazzling performances and wrote mournfully to her father-in-law, "I fear I am already forgotten."

Alas, she was right. Only a few cranky old antiquarians like yours truly give Priscilla Tyler a thought these days. But for a while she was a White House star.

VII
★★★

The proxy first lady who may have enjoyed the job most was Harriet Lane, the vivacious niece of bachelor president James Buchanan. Ignoring the storm clouds of the oncoming Civil War, twenty-seven-year-old Harriet made the Buchanan White House a lively place. Her figure has been called "Junoesque," her hair was golden blond, her eyes violet, her mouth impish. Young men and not a few older ones swarmed from all directions to attend her parties. When "Nunc," as she called the president, objected to the rate at which she was spending his money, Harriet simply gave him one of her brilliant smiles and the subject was dropped.

The Buchanan era marked the high tide of the southern-dominated Democratic Party. Washington was awash in hospitality and Harriet was determined to have the White House lead the way. First, though, there were a few issues to be settled. The president disapproved of dancing; Harriet loved the waltz (still supposedly risqué) and the quadrille. The president disliked late-night parties; Harriet was a regular at the capital's cotillions, or "Germans," that lasted into the wee hours of the morning. The president preferred a plain sensible lifestyle. Harriet liked glitter, glamour, and splash. Guess who won?

Harriet Lane kept the White House lively right up to the eve of the Civil War. As things grew tense between the opposing sides, she banned political conversations at her parties and did not hesitate to show her temper when guests, usually southerners, disregarded her rule.

In 1860, the last year of her reign, Harriet presided at the great social event of James Buchanan's administration, the reception of Queen Victoria's handsome nineteen-year-old-son, Albert Edward, Prince of Wales. Harriet had met the prince when she acted as hostess during her uncle's years as ambassador to Great Britain. She planned a series of lavish social events, climaxed by a banquet on a coast guard cutter, appropriately named *Harriet Lane*.

The party-goers steamed down the Potomac to Mount Vernon, where Harriet and the great-grandson of George III paid a visit to George Washington's tomb. The solemnity of the occasion was underscored by the Marine Band playing a funeral dirge in the background. Lithographs of the event sold by the thousands.

Dinner was served on the return voyage with the Marine Band, in a more upbeat mode, providing music for dancing. Among their selections was the popular song "Listen to the Mockingbird," which the author Alice Hawthorne had dedicated to Harriet. For a final touch of mastery, Harriet challenged his royal highness to a bowling match—and beat him.

Did the prince have a good time? Four decades later, he personally invited Harriet Lane Johnston to London to attend his coronation as King Edward VII.

VIII
✯ ✯ ✯

The next stand-in first lady is even more forgotten than Priscilla Tyler. Like her, she ran a White House while the actual first lady lay dying upstairs. Her name was Martha Patterson. She was the thirty-eight-year-old daughter of Andrew Johnson, another accidental president, who faced a country torn by the chaos of the Civil War. Martha's mother (and Johnson's wife) was slowly expiring of tuberculosis. Among the other problems was the general assumption that Martha and the rest of the family were raw rubes from Tennessee, incapable of coping with social Washington.

The snobs soon found out how wrong they were. Martha knew more about the White House and the intricacies of Washington politics than nine-tenths of the congressmen and senators. For one thing, her husband was a senator from Tennessee. Perhaps more important, she had gone to school in Washington while her father was in the Senate. When he went home to Tennessee for the months when Congress recessed, young Martha spent most of her free time at the Polk White House, where she met every VIP in town. She took charge of the 1865 President's House with a savoir faire that soon had people saying "those who predicted Andrew Johnson's family would be a millstone about his neck forgot that Martha Patterson was his daughter."

Even the most die-hard skeptics became true believers in a matter of months. One rapturous social butterfly wrote in January 1866: "Society in Washington has gone through a complete transformation during the past year. It is seen at the receptions at the White House [which] remind a person of the gay scenes when Miss Lane did the honors at the Executive Mansion." This effusion was followed by palpitating descriptions of ladies in "rich silks, tarletons and velvets, with their diamonds and jewels" and gentlemen in "party attire." Clearly, Martha and her pretty blond sister, Marie Johnson Stover, knew how to throw a good party.

Martha reached her social zenith at the New Year's Day reception in 1867. Old Washington hand Ben Perley recalled it as one of his most memorable days at the White House. He told how Martha and Marie received a stream of visitors, starting with the diplomatic corps, in the drawing rooms where Dolley Madison had once presided. The rooms had been redecorated in their original colors and new furniture added to their splendor.

The president, dressed in meticulous black, stood at the door of the Blue Room. The two sisters received in the center of the room. They were dressed "with exceptional taste and elegance" in gowns of black corded silk, with tight-fitting basques. A vine of leaves was embroidered around the skirts a little below the waistline and descended to the bottom, where it formed a deep border. Each wore flowers in her hair, Martha a spray of mignonette, Marie a white japonica. No wonder a local newspaper declared: "The levees of President Johnson are especially brilliant, and frequenters of Washington society declare that under no former occupant of the White House has such good order and system reigned."

Three cheers for Martha Patterson, who proved that the ladies of the west can match the snobbish east in the elegance game. Moreover, Martha managed this coup while her father was under ferocious attack in Congress from Radical Republicans for opposing their desire for revenge on the defeated South. The three-year political brawl culminated in his impeachment and near conviction.

That turbulent background makes her triumph all the more remarkable.

IX
★★★

The last of the substitute first ladies, Rose Cleveland, proved that good looks were not a prerequisite for the job. Just under forty, Rose was the bachelor president's youngest sister. She was as plain as a fence post and did not try to disguise it. Nor did she make any effort to disguise her intelligence. A teacher in her native Buffalo, she had recently published a book, *George Eliot's Poetry and Other Studies*, which the amalgamated brains of the entire House and Senate would have had trouble finishing.

The tipoff to Miss Rose's purpose in life was in her subject. George Eliot was the premier woman writer in the world of that time. She was also a woman who was not afraid to defy convention. Miss Rose was something of a convention-defier herself. A feminist, she firmly believed that women should vote, hold jobs, and have opinions about everything, including politics. As the president's hostess, she did not hesitate to make this clear to his guests.

At first, Washington's reaction was pretty negative. They were not used to argumentative women or to those who were more interested in reading and writing than in the latest gossip. But gradually, among a select group, a different Rose emerged. Warm, often humorous, she established lifelong friendships with several members of Washington's elite.

It would be delicious to add that she changed the minds of enough politicians to win the vote for women. But it would take more than a White House hostess to move that mountain of nineteenth-century male prejudice in the right direction. Still, she may have pushed it a few centimeters down the road.

Miss Rose's reign ended when the president married Frances Folsom in 1886 and his sister went back to teaching and writing.

Thereafter womanpower in the White House became the exclusive property of first ladies.

X
★★★

Dolley Madison and Louisa Catherine Adams knew how to exercise political power. Abigail Adams was called a "compleat politician," but not as a compliment. Sarah Childress Polk came close to being co-president beside her workaholic husband. But Edith Bolling Galt put all these women in the shade when she married the widowed Woodrow Wilson in 1915.

Edith's love for Wilson was deep and sincere, and passionately reciprocated. She devoted herself to him totally. He liked to bicycle. She taught herself to ride in the White House corridors, risking not only life and limb but the walls, the furniture, and various works of art. Her golf game was atrocious but she played alongside Woodrow anyway. He didn't mind because he was not much better. It once took him twenty-six strokes to complete a single hole.

Edith also spent hours beside her husband at his desk in the Oval Office, reading secret dispatches from the leaders of Europe as they struggled to draw America into the appalling war they had launched in 1914. The second Mrs. Wilson and her husband became, in a word, inseparable. But the gods decreed that this remarkable burst of White House togetherness would come at a high price.

During his first term, Wilson had filled the White House with relatives; his brother, cousins, and nieces were all welcome. Evenings might be devoted to billiards or the private screening of a movie. On other evenings, they might take in a vaudeville show, Wilson's favorite entertainment. He knew many of the performers' comic songs by heart and sometimes sang them at family parties.

Edith gradually eliminated these pastimes from the president's life. She also discouraged visits from his relatives. Her love was so all-consuming, she could not bear to share him with anyone else.

This left Wilson exposed to the terrific pressures of fighting a war and making a peace without the family life he had enjoyed so much in the past. On top of all this, Edith invaded the president's relationships with his closest aides, rupturing and finally ruining them. The result was political as well as emotional isolation at a time when Wilson desperately needed advice and friendship.

Compounding the president's situation was his fragile health. Tension sent his blood pressure skyrocketing. Small strokes had already limited the use of his right hand and eye. His doctor, Cary Grayson, struggled to keep him from working more than four hours a day.

World War I inflicted terrible disappointments on this isolated man. Outmaneuvered by erstwhile political allies in Europe into backing a vengeful peace with Germany that contradicted everything he stood for, Wilson was also overwhelmed by political enemies at home, who repudiated the treaty he had negotiated. The exhausted president collapsed in mid-1919 and spent the rest of his term as a helpless invalid, protected by his adoring wife.

By controlling all access to the stricken president, Edith Galt Wilson in effect ran the country for nineteen months. I wish I could say the results of this loving protectiveness were positive. But as a Democrat, I can only wince at the outcome. The Republicans elected Warren Harding in a landslide that repudiated almost everything Wilson had fought to achieve.

Love is a precious ingredient in a White House marriage, as it is in every marriage. But if it eliminates political judgment, not to mention common sense, watch out.

XI
☆☆☆

The most famous representative of womanpower in the White House seems at first glance in a class by herself. Eleanor Roosevelt towers above the historical landscape these days as a force for tolerance, brotherhood, and human rights. She spoke out for these and other causes in her time, but the stature she achieved after she left the White House interferes with an accurate assessment of her years as first lady. A close look reveals she was not as powerful or influential as we all want to remember her.

Perhaps the clearest proof of the limitations of a first lady's womanpower is the story of Mrs. Roosevelt's brief career as second in command of the Office of Civilian Defense at the beginning of World War II. FDR warned her not to take the job but she ignored him. The head of the agency, Mayor Fiorello La Guardia of New York, was an old friend. But he and the first lady soon fell to quarreling because Mrs. Roosevelt had a bad habit of appealing to the president when she did not get her way.

FDR, up to his eyeballs in trying to organize a major war, had no time for minor ones. He solved the problem by putting the agency under the supervision of a New Dealer, who said yes to everything Mrs. Roosevelt wanted to do. La Guardia resigned with a farewell blast at the first lady.

Next, Congress began scrutinizing the Office of Civilian Defense. They discovered that Eleanor had put a pair of old friends on the public payroll who were drawing good salaries for very little work. Someone pointed out that the two were getting the same pay as General Douglas MacArthur, who was ducking Japanese bullets in the Philippines. A firestorm of negative publicity broke out in the media. The friends resigned and a humiliated Eleanor Roosevelt soon followed suit.

XII
***

Eleanor Roosevelt's experience illuminates the very tricky problems first ladies face when they try to move beyond the White House to the public arena. The next first lady to try it was Rosalynn Carter. She had a lot going for her. Like Louisa Catherine Adams, she had campaigned tirelessly to put her husband in the White House. She boldly set up an office and staff in the East Wing, sat in on cabinet meetings, and once a week had a "policy lunch" with the president to discuss the hot items on their political plates.

But Rosalynn, too, ran into trouble when she ventured into formal politics. A diplomatic tour of South America was a failure. The macho males south of the border were confused by her ambiguous status: Did she have the power to solve problems, or merely listen sympathetically to their tales of woe? The State Department was jealous and leaked damaging stories about the trip. The net result: The first lady never made another diplomatic tour.

Few if any first ladies worked harder than Mrs. Carter. She toured the country, she whizzed abroad on goodwill missions, she presided at White House receptions and somehow found time to learn Spanish. The *New York Times* called her "the most influential First Lady since Eleanor Roosevelt." But unlike nonpolitical first ladies, such as Pat Nixon and Mamie Eisenhower, Rosalynn never became the nation's most admired woman in the public opinion polls.

It may have had something to do with the nickname the press fastened on her: "the steel magnolia." It may have had even more to do with the way the voters view the first lady's role: as simply being there. The American people apparently do not like a woman who has not been elected to anything to start exercising political power. Running the White House, they seem to think, is more than enough responsibility. Going beyond it strikes them as excessive.

XIII
✷✷✷

This mind-set became excruciatingly apparent when Hillary Rodham Clinton tackled the very public job of overhauling the nation's health care system. She worked with Ira Magaziner, the president's senior adviser for policy development, and a task force that grew to more than 630 people. But Hillary was very definitely in charge. As one presidential aide put it, "Health care was her baby, a sweeping program that would save lives and prove to the world that a first lady could be a fully public presidential partner."

From the start, the venture had problems. In the chaotic Clinton White House, jealousies abounded. Many staffers felt health care might collide with an even more important priority, getting Congress to pass the president's budget. This may have been the reason for a major blunder—the total failure to draw Congress into the loop early in the game. Senior aide George Stephanopoulos described Hillary as feeling "like a single mother raising a problem child in a hostile neighborhood." Calling the operation the Intensive Care Unit did not help matters. Was the name chosen by a saboteur or a policy wonk with no sense of humor?

It took the better part of a year to get the plan in shape for the president to introduce in a speech. Eventually, Hillary testified on its behalf before five congressional committees, and gave bravura performances that made her, in the opinion of a *New York Times* reporter, "feminism's first mainstream icon, a powerful woman with mass market appeal." From there it was all downhill (no pun intended, I swear it!).

Nobody really liked Mrs. Clinton's health plan, including her husband's cabinet officers, but nobody wanted to criticize it either. Said one blunt male: "If you sleep with the president, nobody's going to tell you the truth." Congressmen and senators heaped unctuous public praise on the first lady and deplored the plan behind the scenes. One congressman wryly summed up the mounting fiasco. "Nobody's going to tell the president's wife, 'Ma'am, you don't have any clothes on.' "

After another sixty days of frantic work in the Intensive Care Unit, a 1,342-page bill was finally sent to Congress. Nine more months of argument in and out of the legislature did little but unite the opposition and splinter the first lady's forces. The bill was never even voted out of committee for consideration by the full Congress.

All in all, it was a humiliating experience for both the first lady and her husband.

George Stephanopoulos praised the first lady's efforts, but he dolefully concluded: "Her leadership was more than the political system could bear. It's difficult to escape the conclusion that having Hillary run health care was a mistake." That has to rank as one of the understatements of the decade. From Maine to California, Hillary's performance had people asking a tough but pertinent question: "Who elected her?"

XIV
***

Womanpower in the White House would seem to work best when it is subtle. It is interesting that Dolley Madison had the right idea two hundred years ago, and a very much with-it modern woman like Hillary Clinton had to learn this lesson the hard way.

From this vantage point, maybe the most influential first ladies are not the ones who do their politicking in public. My favorite example is someone I had the opportunity to watch in action from *very* close up—Bess Wallace Truman.

Coming into the White House in the wake of Eleanor Roosevelt, Mother made a decision that looks better and better as time goes by. She would not even try to imitate Mrs. Roosevelt's model of a first lady. Bess gave only one press conference—to announce she would not be holding any others. She never made a political statement if she could possibly avoid it. But behind the scenes, on the second floor of the White House, Bess Truman was as deeply involved in politics as any cabinet officer, congressman, or senator.

The president of the United States discussed his problems with her with a candor he would never dream of using with anyone else—and she didn't just listen. She gave him her unvarnished advice about the people in his administration and Congress. If the president and first lady did not agree, they had an unspoken, un-broken rule: The president had the last word.

The success with which Bess Truman pulled off this performance has never been satisfactorily praised, even by her daughter, when I wrote her biography, *Bess Wallace Truman*. Not until I saw Mother in the perspective of womanpower in the White House did I begin to appreciate her accomplishment. From Mother's point of view, the less people knew about her influence, the better. That was part of the game. Her covert political status gave her the freedom of thought and speech she wanted.

Only once, and it was before she got to the White House, did Mother drop her guard and reveal her role in Harry Truman's life. When Dad was nominated for vice president in 1944, reporters rushed to ask Mother what she had been up to while Senator Truman was reaching this pinnacle.

"I've been in politics for the last twenty-five years," Mother said.

That was the first and last time she flirted with admitting how the Trumans operated.

In her later years, when there were no prying reporters around, Mother was a bit freer with her political opinions. I remember one day in 1972 when I invited a historian who was doing research at the Truman library to drop by for cocktails. President Nixon had just mined Haiphong Harbor, in line with his policy of getting tough with the North Vietnamese. Mother asked the historian what he thought of this decision. He said somewhat hesitantly that he thought it was probably the right thing to do.

Mother gave the historian one of her coolest looks. "If he were president," she said, nodding toward Dad, "we would have done it six years ago."

I had the distinct feeling that "we" did not mean the government of the United States. It meant Bess and Harry Truman, operating as secret White House partners.

XV

★★★

Newswoman Sarah McClendon recently wrote an estimate of Bess Truman and the other first ladies she has known in her fifty years of covering the White House. Bess, she concluded, had "rejected the role of first lady." Citing one of Dad's favorite sayings, "If you can't stand the heat, get out of the kitchen," Sarah maintained that Bess Truman had adopted her own version of the saying, to wit: "If it's too hot for me, I'll get back to the kitchen."

When I read that, I laughed out loud. If there was one room Bess Truman stayed out of except in moments of dire necessity, it was the kitchen!

Somewhere, I suspect Mother was laughing, too. I can almost see her giving me an unladylike wink and saying, "See, I told you it would work." Without reporters or anyone else catching on, Bess Truman had White House womanpower down cold.

Harry S Truman and his appointments secretary, Matt Connelly. Matt always knew who should, or should not, be admitted to the Oval Office. Credit: Harry S Truman Library

7

★★★

The West Wing

From the start, people other than presidents and their families have played major roles in helping the chief executive run the country. During the twentieth century, the number of aides, advisers, directors, deputies, secretaries, and assorted other experts—collectively known as the White House staff—multiplied at an incredible rate. They now total some six thousand people working in over a hundred different offices. But the center of the power structure is still the West Wing.

Built in 1902, the West Wing contains the Oval Office, the Cabinet Room, a reception room—also known as the Appointments Lobby—and assorted meeting rooms and offices for secretaries and staff members who deal with the president on a day-to-day basis. The Cabinet Room faces the Rose Garden and has French doors that open onto the white-pillared colonnade that connects the West Wing to the residential part of the White House.

Proximity to presidential power gives a certain aura to anyone who works in, or has easy access to, the West Wing. Its denizens have become the subject of TV shows, movies, and novels. Tell-all books have portrayed them as combinations of Brutus and Machiavelli, with an occasional dash of P. T. Barnum's faith that there's a sucker born every minute and maybe one of them is their boss.

Most of these characterizations are pretty far from the mark. The best portrait of a compleat West Wing staffer was drawn by an old pro, United Press International reporter Merriman Smith, who offered a no-holds-barred description of what these jobs entail:

> **WANTED:** *Mature man, educated, witty, politically smart, pleasant personality, unlimited loyalty, to serve as senior secretary. Must be willing to work 12–15 hours daily, including nights. No days off or vacations. But travel constantly. Be prepared to take much blame, public criticism and ridicule. Should have patience capable of listening to thousands of complaints. Ability to say no absolutely necessary.*

"Smitty," as we Trumans called him, was only half kidding. When a new staffer went to work for Herbert Hoover, he asked a senior employee what the office hours were. "From seven A.M. until midnight, except the nights we work late," the bleary-eyed veteran growled.

II
★★★

It seems hard to believe now but our early chief executives had no staffs worth mentioning. Most of them made do with a single secretary, often a relative or close friend. Thomas Jefferson's man Friday, Meriwether Lewis, was not related to the president, but their families were old friends and Jefferson had taken an interest in the young man after his father's death.

Lewis lived and worked in a pair of rooms that had been constructed at the south end of the unfurnished East Room. His job was a snap compared to later presidential secretaries. He had so little to do, he often went hunting in the nearby woods and fields and brought back rabbits and grouse for the White House table. He also took three years off to explore the Louisiana Territory. Meanwhile, the workaholic Jefferson wrote all his own letters, hitting 25,000 by the end of his long life.

Jefferson's relationship with Meriwether Lewis was warmer than many other presidents and their secretaries. Long hours and close quarters often made subordinates a target for executive irritability. James Buchanan's nephew, James Buchanan ("Buck") Henry, had to put up with barked orders and frequent tongue-lashings. The breaking point came when Buchanan rebuked him for growing a mustache. Buck quit and headed for New York. His replacement was another namesake nephew, James Buchanan II.

Poor Buck Henry had reason to flee. He ran all aspects of the White House, scheduling appointments, paying bills, glad handing visitors. He also had to deliver all the president's communications to Congress, making a formal speech each time he did so. When evening came, there was still no letup: Buck was expected to attend all the social events his uncle didn't have time for. No wonder the poor fellow thought he had a right to grow a mustache!

Franklin Pierce's secretary was a lawyer in his early twenties named Sidney Webster. His chief qualification seems to have been his intense devotion to Pierce. Admittedly, this harried president needed all the emotional support he could get. His wife, Jane, had become a grief-stricken recluse after the death of their eleven-year-old son in a train wreck two months before her husband's inauguration. But Pierce also needed a secretary who had more experience in national politics and the energy and organizational ability to handle the enormous workload. Webster was not the man. It was to be another four years before a first-class staff went to work in the White House.

III

★★★

When Abraham Lincoln was nominated for president by the Republican Party in 1860, he invited a twenty-nine-year-old Illinois newspaperman, John George Nicolay, to be his secretary. Nine months later, with the southern states seceding and civil war looming, they prepared to leave Springfield for Washington, D.C. Foreseeing the immense workload ahead of him, Nicolay suggested engaging a twenty-three-year-old law student, John Hay, as his assistant.

"I can't take all Illinois with me," Lincoln told him. But eventually he agreed. Both men proved to be brilliant choices. Nicolay, tall and thin almost to emaciation, was a demon worker. He also possessed another trait that is essential to a presidential aide: He "never said anything worth quoting."

The short slim Hay was a witty man about town and a talented writer. Recently historians have tracked down pro-Lincoln stories he published anonymously in northern newspapers during the Civil War. They made a book of over three hundred pages.

The workload John George Nicolay had foreseen materialized all too soon. The day after the inauguration, he sat down to write a letter to his fiancée back in Illinois. After two sentences, the call bell in Lincoln's office rang. Nicolay did not finish the letter until midnight two days later.

John George Nicolay and John Hay soon acquired the cachet that goes with working in the White House. Outraged public officials and other VIPs sputtered that the two young men were blocking access to the president and not delivering their letters. Nicolay and Hay, in turn, often gazed with less than friendly eyes on cabinet members and congressmen. "I am utterly amazed to find so little real faith and courage under difficulties among public leaders and men of intelligence," Nicolay wrote in 1862. Hay wryly remarked that rather than pay another visit to short-tempered Secretary of

War Edwin Stanton, he would gladly "make a tour of a smallpox hospital."

Nicolay found himself not only running the president's office but most of the White House social functions. This put him on a collision course with Mary Lincoln, who had her own opinions about such things. Nicolay and Hay soon gave Mary a private nickname: "the hellcat." At one point she banned the two of them from state dinners, where they usually sat at opposite ends of the table and made sure the belles were not neglected. An appeal to the president quickly restored them to the guest list.

About Lincoln neither man had any doubts, no matter what anyone else said or thought about him—and he had plenty of critics in those days. Lincoln reciprocated their affection. The two men became semi-sons as well as employees. They slept in a bedroom across the hall from their second-floor White House office. On more than one midnight, the elongated chief executive appeared in their doorway in his nightshirt to read them a funny story from a newspaper or discuss a problem he had figured out how to solve when he should have been sleeping. When Lincoln's son Willie died in early 1862, the president stumbled into Nicolay's office about five P.M. and said: "My boy is gone—he is actually gone!" Bursting into tears, he retreated to his own office.

The White House was almost as unhealthy for Nicolay and Hay as it was for poor Willie. Hay compared summer odors from the swamps south of the mansion to "ten thousand dead cats." When one of them was laid low by the fetid air, the other worked twice as hard. Nicolay and Hay's contribution to the eventual victory of the Union was incalculable. Almost as important, they later wrote a ten-volume life of Lincoln that is a starting point for anyone who wants to understand his greatness.

IV
✫✫✫

For all their dedication and intelligence, Nicolay and Hay were still very young men. They never achieved the status of presidential advisers. The first aide to rise to this level was Grover Cleveland's secretary, Daniel Lamont.

This shrewd, genial man got to know Cleveland when he was hired to write his inaugural address as governor of New York. Cleveland took him to Washington after his election to the presidency and Lamont was soon the closest of companions. The bachelor president was so lonely in the White House that he sometimes invited Lamont and his wife and two small daughters to have breakfast, lunch, and dinner with him on a single day.

Lamont swiftly became Cleveland's political adviser as well as his man of all work. The secretary was a smoothie—the exact opposite of the man who was probably our grumpiest president. He talked Cleveland out of nurturing grudges against people who irritated or disagreed with him, which resulted in improved relations all around.

Lamont was also extremely astute in his handling of the press. Here Cleveland needed all the help he could get. He had come into the White House trailing the scandal of fathering an illegitimate son in his younger days. To get a glimpse of how this played in some papers, consider this from Charles A. Dana's *New York Sun*, the leading Democratic paper of the era: If Cleveland was elected, Dana wrote, he "would carry his harlots with him to Washington and lodge them in the White House."

Lamont got reporters on Cleveland's side with a combination of charm and a steady diet of information. One veteran newsman of the era described his approach: "He had tact, judgment, knew what to say and how to say it. . . . He let the 'boys' do most of the talking and guessing but never allowed them to leave the White House with a wrong impression, or without thinking they had got all there was in the story."

By the time Cleveland returned to Washington for his second administration, he thought so highly of Daniel Lamont he appointed him secretary of war.

V

★★★

In the White House of Cleveland's successor, William McKinley, a different kind of staffer emerged. George Cortelyou started out as a social secretary for Frances Folsom Cleveland and stayed on to become an assistant to McKinley's secretary, John Addison Porter.

Porter was a pompous character who changed his job title to "secretary" instead of the usual "private secretary" and insisted that the post was on a par with the cabinet. His staff consisted of two assistants, eight clerks, six ushers, and five messengers—quite a growth spurt since Nicolay and Hay's day—and he was rarely nice to any of them. Cortelyou confided to his diary that staying on good terms with Porter required "all my patience and diplomacy." Fortunately, he had a good supply of both.

McKinley was aware of Porter's failings but he was too kind-hearted to fire him. Eventually ill health forced him out, and by 1899, George Cortelyou was running the show. The most important assets he brought to the job were brainpower and an amazing ability to organize things. When McKinley embarked on a train trip under Cortelyou's supervision, the route involved thirty different railroads and five thousand miles. Cortelyou brought the whole thing off on schedule, except for one twenty-minute delay. No wonder he, too, ascended to a cabinet position—secretary of commerce and labor under McKinley's successor, Theodore Roosevelt.

VI

★★★

William Howard Taft was the first chief executive to work in the West Wing, setting up shop in the Oval Office that was built at his request. One of the most frequent visitors to the new office was Major Archie Butt, the engaging Georgia bachelor who had been Teddy Roosevelt's military aide and continued in the job for Taft. Butt adored Roosevelt and his family and at first was underwhelmed by the slow, phlegmatic Taft. But he gradually became devoted to this very different man, who had never aspired to the White House.

Two years before the end of his term as president, Roosevelt had chosen Taft, his secretary of war, as the best man to succeed him. As time went on, Roosevelt began cooling on Taft. Butt tried to bridge the gap between them. In this ugly contretemps, the miliary aide was caught between the good-natured Taft and First Lady Helen Herron Taft, who had been spoiling for a fight with the Roosevelts from the moment she entered the White House.

In one of his letters, Butt described the opening round—a discussion at a state dinner of a remark Teddy had made to a reporter in Europe, that he had put Taft in the White House to carry out his policies and if he faltered, he would run him out of the job. Butt defended Roosevelt, insisting that he must have been misquoted. Within earshot of a bevy of Washington gossips, Helen Taft remarked: "Oh I don't know. It sounded just like him."

A few days later, while the president and Butt were out riding, Taft said to his aide: "Archie, how can you make a woman discreet?"

"You can't, sir," Butt replied, "unless she is so by nature."

With a sigh, the president agreed.

When Roosevelt returned from his post-presidential travels, Taft asked Butt to deliver a confidential letter, inviting Teddy to the White House for a frank talk. Roosevelt declined with an ominously formal letter, in which he addressed Taft as "Dear Mr. President" instead of the usual "Dear Will." The two men finally met while Taft was vacationing in Massachusetts. Butt, who joined them, reported that the conversation was strained and nothing was resolved.

Meanwhile, Archie Butt slowly but steadily shifted his allegiance to Taft. It was a stressful time for the aide. Not only was he in charge of a full schedule of White House receptions and dinners, he was also William Howard Taft's sounding board as the president brooded over his former friend's threat to run him out of his job.

Finally came Teddy's announcement that he would be a candidate for the Republican nomination in 1912—the break Butt had struggled in vain to prevent. The exhausted aide had scheduled a trip to Europe to visit a friend, the artist Frank Millet, who was studying at the American Academy in Rome. Now he wondered if he should go.

"I lay awake for a long time last night, trying to make up my mind," he wrote to an aunt. "I really can't bear to leave him just now. I can see he hates to see me go, and I feel like a quitter in going."

The next morning, Butt canceled his reservations. When he told Taft, the president ordered him to reinstate them. A month's rest would restore Butt to fighting trim, Taft assured him, and he would be back in time for the election campaign. "He feels I will break down just when he needs me the most if I don't go now," Butt told his sister.

So the weary aide sailed to Italy, met Millet, and together they traveled across Europe to England. There they decided to return home on the maiden voyage of the new luxury liner, the S.S. *Titanic*. On the night of April 14, 1912, Archie Butt and Frank Millet were last seen on the slanting deck, calmly awaiting the final plunge. They had given their lifejackets to women passengers.

President Taft was devastated by the news that Butt was among the dead. "He was like a member of my own family," he said. "I feel as if he had been a younger brother."

VII
★★★

Under Woodrow Wilson, the presidential secretary added another responsibility to his chores: congressional liaison. Wilson was fortunate enough to find the ideal man for the job—thirty-three-year-old Joseph Tumulty of Jersey City, New Jersey, a town where politics came close to being the major industry.

Tumulty backed Wilson when he ran for governor of New Jersey in 1910, and gave the college professor a political education second to none. (Wilson later remarked that anyone who does not understand politics after playing the game for a year or two in the Garden State had better go into another line of work.) When Wilson headed for the White House in 1913, he took Tumulty with him and the genial Irish-American swiftly became one of the most powerful men in Washington.

Wilson trusted Tumulty's political judgment totally. He let him decide whom he should see and whom he should duck. He also depended on Tumulty to cajole leaders of Congress into looking with favor on the reform legislation Wilson sponsored, such as the Federal Reserve Act, which took control of the country's money away from Wall Street and put it in Washington where the people had some say in how it was used. Tumulty managed all this while making almost no enemies, thanks to his abundant charm.

Joe Tumulty was also a past master at getting visitors in and out of the Oval Office. The impatient president hated to spare more than five minutes for each appointment. When the allotted time ran out, Tumulty would appear in the office, ostensibly with some urgent and confidential message. Wilson would crisply assure the caller that the matter they had discussed would be given serious consideration—and the interview was over.

Alas, inside the White House, Tumulty found himself confronted by an unexpected enemy: Wilson's second wife, Edith Galt. She was jealous of Tumulty's influence with the president, and persuaded her husband to fire him at the beginning of his second term. A reporter friend of Tumulty's talked Wilson into changing his mind, but their relationship never regained its previous intimacy. The president's lingering distrust of his aide prompted him to ignore Tumulty's advice not to go to Europe to negotiate peace after World War I—a blunder that destroyed Wilson's presidency.

When Woodrow Wilson's health collapsed while on a speaking tour to persuade people to back the peace treaty he had negotiated, Tumulty became even more isolated. He sent the crippled president a stream of memorandums on the deteriorating political situation in Washington. Edith Wilson made sure not one reached the president.

Nevertheless, Tumulty remained devoted to Wilson to the sad end of the president's life in 1924. Few aides have left more emotional tributes to their departed chief. "Yes, Woodrow Wilson is dead," Tumulty wrote. "But his spirit still lives—the spirit that tried to wipe away the tears of the world, the spirit of justice, humanity and holy peace."

VIII

★★★

From Wilsonian tragedy to Warren Harding tragicomedy is quite a leap. American voters are unpredictable, to say the least. The man in the middle of this dolorous presidency was the Republican president's secretary, an earnest, hardworking man named George Christian.

The son of one of Harding's neighbors in Marion, Ohio, Christian was, of all things, a Democrat. He had run for the state legislature on the Democratic ticket and his father was the former editor and publisher of the town's Democratic paper. Harding, however, was more interested in friendship and loyalty than he was in party labels, so when he was elected to the U.S. Senate in 1914, he invited Christian to come to Washington as his private secretary. Christian held the job until Harding's death, becoming the president's close friend and trusted adviser, and defecting to the Republicans along the way.

George Christian had to do a lot of Warren's thinking for him, because the president was not highly qualified in this department. He was more interested in the shows at the Gayety Burlesque, where he had a special box that concealed him from the rest of the audience, than he was in affairs of state.

Harding thought so highly of Christian that he frequently invited him to join the poker games that were held in the second-floor oval room or at the homes of the president's friends. One of these friends was wealthy divorcée Louise Brooks, who later became General Douglas MacArthur's first wife. Harding challenged her to a two-person game with the winner naming the stakes. Mrs. Brooks won and exacted a set of White House dishes as her prize. The next day a barrel of china from the Benjamin Harrison administration was delivered to her door.

This looting of White House property was a minor scandal compared to some of the other presidential problems George Christian had to cope with. One day, Christian was confronted by the agitated boss of the White House mail room, Ira Smith. In Smith's hand was a letter from a woman named Nan Britton. In gooey prose, Nan reminded Warren of their passionate trysts in 1919, the year before he was elected president. She was now informing him that he was the father of her baby girl, whose photos she enclosed.

"My God!" Christian exclaimed. "If the president finds out we opened this, he'll fire both of us!"

While Smith quaked, Christian pondered the oddly slanted words for another moment, then abruptly tore the letter into shreds. In the course of the next few weeks, two more letters from Nan arrived. Smith disposed of them in the same way. Nothing more was heard from her, as far as Smith knew, although Nan later claimed that she had contacted the president through one of his Secret Servicemen.

After Harding died, Nan published a sensational book, *The President's Daughter,* which described trysts in the White House and elsewhere. Some historians suspect these sexual adventures never happened. Whether they did or not, Ira Smith and George Christian mutually congratulated each other for staving off any revelations while Harding was alive.

Christian's finest hour occurred after President Harding died of what may have been a cerebral hemorrhage, possibly brought on by acute embarrassment when he found out his friends were stealing everything from the nation's oil reserves to the Veterans Administration's medical supplies. Warren's bizarre wife, Florence, took charge and began burning all his papers. Yes, *all* of them. The appalled Christian discovered what was happening and managed to salvage enough official documents to leave historians with a modicum of information about Harding's presidency.

IX
✯✯✯

The White House staff kept growing—and growing specialized. Under Calvin Coolidge, Bascom Slemp functioned as a full-time appointments secretary. He became famous for his ability to dispose of callers briskly without making them angry. Slemp would assure some VIP, say a Republican bigwig who came to the White House to pin down a judgeship for a pal, that the deal was done, and there was no need to see the president.

As the VIP prepared to depart, Slemp would chirp: "Oh, say good morning to the president before you go." He would open Coolidge's door, the two men would exchange thirty seconds of pleasantries, and the man would go away satisfied.

Slemp was able to operate with more than the usual political smarts because he had spent sixteen years as a congressman from Virginia before joining Coolidge's staff. In those days, Virginia was solidly Democratic, but Slemp kept getting elected on the Republican ticket—a tribute to his dexterity all by itself. Being a millionaire (coal) did not hurt, of course.

Another Slemp tactic was suggesting that a caller put his request to the president in written form. If the man agreed, a White House stenographer would appear and the man would dictate and dictate. Meanwhile the president would have time to deal with four or five other callers. Slemp also arranged for Coolidge to be the first president to make a speech on the radio. Afterward, he wrote to some hillbilly friends in Tennessee to assess their reaction. "There wasn't no reaction," one man wrote back. "Everybody liked it."

X

Herbert Hoover expanded the White House staff from a secretary and a dozen or so office assistants to a "secretariat," as one historian put it. Their number (forty) seems positively minuscule by today's standards. Hoover's staff were anonymous, faceless men operating in the shadow of their boss. In contrast, Franklin D. Roosevelt's staff was twice the size of Hoover's and many of them rapidly became celebrities in their own right as they rampaged in and out of the Oval Office with ideas, some good and some godawful, on how to cure the Great Depression of the 1930s.

At the top of the list of Roosevelt aides was Harry Hopkins, a former social worker from Iowa. One newspaperman said he had the look of a dissipated bookie—not a bad description, considering Harry's fondness for the racetrack. FDR enjoyed his cynical humor and his ability to get things done. As head of the Works Progress Administration, better known as the WPA, Hopkins spent eleven billion dollars in five hyperkinetic years and created jobs for 8.5 million men and women.

On the downside, Harry was often too fast on the comeback for his own good. During a congressional hearing a Republican solon said to him: "I'm not trying to persecute you."

Hopkins's reply: "Oh hell, you're intellectually incapable of persecuting anybody."

When a reporter informed Hopkins that many congressmen said he was no politician, he sneered: "Tell 'em thanks for the compliment." At a WPA press conference, he declared that critics of the program were "too damn dumb" to understand it. Harry was also responsible for remarking (at a racetrack) that the New Dealers would "tax and tax, spend and spend and elect and elect." That wisecrack gave Republican orators more ammunition than the utterances of FDR and everyone else in his administration combined. Harry repeatedly denied it, but Arthur Krock, the *New York Times* Washington columnist, investigated it down to the last comma and proved "Harry the Hop," as FDR called him, unquestionably said it.

Many presidents would have jettisoned such a controversial adviser, but FDR was a stubborn man. He not only kept Hopkins around, he moved him into the White House when his health collapsed in the late 1930s. His illness, a rare form of stomach cancer, did not stop Hopkins from masterminding Roosevelt's bid for a third term in 1940. During World War II, Hopkins spent more time in the White House than anyone else except the president, inspiring not a few enemies to call him Roosevelt's "Rasputin." That was mild compared to what they called Hopkins at the State Department when FDR made him an unofficial secretary of state, sending him abroad as his "personal representative" to talk politics and military strategy with Winston Churchill and Joseph Stalin.

Another even more controversial aide was Rexford Tugwell, who leaned much too far to the left for his own and FDR's safety. Tugwell had no political sense whatsoever, and talked in professorese (Columbia University brand) most of the time. Democratic congressman Maury Maverick told of having a conversation in which

Tugwell predicted workers and farmers would soon form creative "nodules."

Maverick blew his stack. "Stop stop!" he shouted. "The word *nodule* is not understood by the American people. . . . It sounds like a sex perversion!"

Tugwell was also fond of praising "collectivism," convincing many people he was a Communist. He soon became target number one for the Republicans. One enterprising reporter, digging into Tugwell's past, found a bad imitation of Walt Whitman he had written in his youth. Republicans were soon joyously reciting it on the Senate floor.

> *I am strong.*
> *I am big and well-made*
> *I am muscled and lean and nervous*
> *I am frank and sure and incisive . . .*
> *I am sick of propertied czars*
> *I have dreamed my great dream of their passing*
> *I have gathered my tools and my charts.*
> *My plans are fashioned and practical*
> *I shall roll up my sleeves—and make America over!*

The Hearst papers began discussing the "Tugwell Bolsheviks" around Roosevelt. Once more displaying his stubbornness, FDR waited until he was reelected in 1936 before easing Tugwell back into private life. Tugwell took his dismissal with good grace. He summed up the White House insider's role admirably when he wrote in later years that everyone who plays that perilous part understands a president's aides are all "expendable."

One aide was not in that category, as far as FDR was concerned— Marguerite "Missy" LeHand. Attractive, with a vibrant laugh and a vivacious manner, Missy had large blue eyes, a pale oval face, and prematurely gray hair. One of Roosevelt's speechwriters noted:

"Missy is the one indispensable member of the secretarial entourage."

Missy had been with FDR since 1920, when she worked for him during his failed run for the vice presidency. She lived through his ordeal with polio and followed him to the governor's mansion in Albany. She was thirty-seven when she came to the White House and moved into a pair of rooms on the third floor.

Missy was often the hostess at small dinner parties for presidential insiders. She swam with FDR in the White House pool and traveled extensively with him. The same speechwriter who commented on her indispensability remarked somewhat ruefully that if Missy disapproved of a person or a policy, he, she, or it was as good as dead on arrival in the Oval Office.

Was she FDR's substitute wife as well as woman of all work? A lot of people, including his son Elliott, thought so, but few members of the inner circle ever admitted it. The evidence points strongly toward an affirmative answer. Missy acted far more like a wife than a secretary, boldly disagreeing with FDR in front of others, shopping for him, and making sure he took his cough medicine. "She was one of the very, very few people who was not a yes man," another aide said. When FDR made out his will, he left half of his estate to Eleanor and the other half to Missy.

In 1941, Missy's double life caught up with her. She collapsed from a stroke that left her partially paralyzed, and retreated to the home of a sister in Massachusetts. When FDR failed to call her one Christmas eve, she sobbed uncontrollably for hours. Missy died in a Boston hospital on July 31, 1944, nine months before the man she called "F.D." died in Warm Springs, Georgia.

XI

***

FDR started out with a staff of fewer than 100 people, but by 1945 the number had increased to 225. Some of the personalities who swirled through and around the Roosevelt Oval Office would make a book unto themselves. Virginian Steve Early was a brilliant press secretary in spite of a hot temper that exploded at least once a day. Ex–Tammany Hall pol Sam Rosenman combined political smarts and an aptitude for catchy phrases such as "a New Deal for the American people" that played well in FDR's speeches. The prize for most colorful character undoubtedly went to Major General Edwin "Pa" Watson, a rotund Alabamian who was the Roosevelt White House's court jester. FDR's day invariably started with a visit from "Pa," who always had a funny story for him.

Many people thought Watson was just a joker. But he was by no means politically stupid. As appointments secretary, he had a lot to do with who got to see the president. In 1944 he made sure no one who had a good word to say for Vice President Henry Wallace got anywhere near FDR for several months. That bit of infighting played no small part in making Senator Harry S Truman the Democratic nominee for the job. Watson joined this cabal (of which my father was totally unaware) because he knew FDR was dying and the vice president of 1944 was very likely to become president. He and others, including Harry Hopkins and Sam Rosenman, thought the ultraliberal Wallace would be a disaster.

Watson was an unlikely candidate for the select group of White House insiders who can say they helped change the course of American history. But proximity to the Oval Office almost guarantees such surprises. Ironically, "Pa" died of a cerebral hemorrhage on the way home from the Yalta summit conference in 1945, only a few weeks before FDR succumbed to the same malady.

XII

✬ ✬ ✬

The Truman White House also had a court jester who did his stuff in uniform—Major General Harry Vaughan. Not quite as fat as Pa Watson, but close, Harry wore his uniform so casually, one White House guest who spotted him waddling through the lobby said: "That man looks like yesterday's reveille."

"No," said one of Harry's friends. "When he got up this morning he just forgot to take off the covers."

Dad had a special problem with his aides—he inherited FDR's cadre plus his cabinet and had to decide who to keep and who should go. A lot of them—in his diary, Dad called them "The Palace Guard"—did not get the message he delivered to the cabinet the day FDR died: Harry Truman intended to be president "in my own right." The Palace Guard thought he was a temporary replacement they could manipulate for their own purposes. They were soon looking for new jobs.

The Truman aides who appeared in the West Wing underscored the growing maturity of the White House staff system. Dad was particularly careful about selecting his appointments secretary—no one sees more of the president or needs to be closer to what he is thinking. His choice for the post was Matt Connelly, who had worked for him on the World War II Truman committee, and had once been described by a White House reporter as a man who could walk a tightrope with chewing gum on one shoe—a neat way of saying he was one cool operator.

Matt quickly learned the most important lesson of a White House aide: Keep your eyes open and your mouth shut. He sat in on cabinet meetings and at all sorts of historic moments in the Truman Oval Office, such as the ferocious debate over whether to recognize Israel. No reporter ever heard a word about any of these sessions from him. He ate lunch each day, alone, in an obscure corner of the dining room at the Willard Hotel.

Matt did more than schedule appointments, of course. He was the "contact man," as he later put it, for politicians across the country when they came to Washington. Not all of them could get to see the president but they all saw Matt, and went home to tell their friends. "No, I didn't see the president but I talked to his secretary and he's going to get me some help."

In the matter of cabinet meetings, Matt intervened to save Dad from a problem that might have troubled his administration. Secretary of the Navy James Forrestal suggested that they keep a verbatim report of what was said by each cabinet member. Matt ferociously opposed the idea. "If you have [that kind of] record, they're not going to speak off the cuff," he argued. That meant the president would not be getting honest opinions. Dad instantly saw the point and at the cabinet meetings, Matt simply took longhand notes, stating "Forrestal took this position" and so forth. As a result, President Truman had down-to-earth cabinet discussions that were truly valuable.

That is an apt example of the myriad ways a trusted aide can influence things in the West Wing. Matt also "took the heat" (his term) when Catholic groups around the country were distressed because Dad appointed a Protestant to the so-called Catholic seat on the Supreme Court. Matt suggested appointing a Catholic as attorney general to squelch the complaints, thus neatly solving the problem. Best of all, Matt made a big difference in the 1948 campaign, when Dad, the underdog by umpteen points in every poll, whistle-stopped across the country giving the Republicans hell. Matt's role as presser of political flesh outside the Oval Office put him on a first-name basis with politicians all over the country. One reporter noted that on the Republican candidate's campaign train, "local politicians did not get the red carpet treatment they received from Truman's aide, Matt Connelly."

The other indispensable Truman aide was Charlie Ross, who literally worked himself to death as press secretary, as I described in the opening chapter. Charlie, who had covered Washington for decades as a reporter for the *St. Louis Post-Dispatch*, had enormous prestige with the press corps and was greatly loved by all the Trumans.

None of these Truman staff members sought or got the kind of publicity that Roosevelt's aides accumulated. Grandstanding was taboo in the Truman White House. There was only one exception to this rule—a big handsome Missourian named Clark Clifford. Some historians have called him "the Golden Boy" of the Truman White House.

There is no doubt that Clark was a smart lawyer and a polished writer. My father valued his services and his candid advice, particularly in the decision to recognize Israel. But after Clark left the White House to launch an extremely lucrative law practice in Washington, he began taking credit for almost everything the Truman administration did or undertook, from the Marshall Plan to rescue war-devastated Europe to the composition of the great state paper NSC-68, which laid out the policy of containment that led to the ultimate defeat of Soviet communism forty-some years later.

A distressing number of reporters and even a few historians believed Clark. They did not seem to realize that the phrase my father had on his desk—"The buck stops here"—was a description not only of presidential responsibility but of presidential leadership. No single White House aide or even all of them put together can claim credit for the big decisions. A president makes them in the lonely hours of his day (or night), after listening to dozens of people.

XIII

★★★

Clark Clifford's tendency to see himself at the center of every presidential accomplishment is another aspect of the White House's effect on staff members' psyches. I have already described the rise and fall of Sherman Adams, the glacially righteous Yankee whose official title in the Eisenhower White House was assistant to the president but who was regularly referred to as Ike's chief of staff.

This large-sounding appellation was a logical development as the West Wing bulged with layers of aides and assistants, and especially logical to a former general who was used to running an army with a real chief of staff serving as his right-hand man. But I must confess chief of staff bothers me somewhat. It does not fit the civilian nature of the White House as George Washington visualized it. Presumptuous as it sounds, I am ready to say I don't think the father of our country would like it any more than I do.

Despite his official—and less impressive—title, there was no doubt that Sherman Adams was a de facto chief of staff. Ike told him: "You [will] be associated with me more closely than anyone else in the government." In those words can be found the seeds of Mr. Adams's later delusions of grandeur.

Before you start feeling sorry for Sherman Adams, let me assure you that he was not a nice man. He had mastered one essential ability for White House aides—saying no on behalf of the president—but it was rarely a courteous no. Almost daily, Adams reduced at least one of his secretaries to tears. One morning he had all five sobbing in unison. He also went beyond his appointed duties, issuing ukases against "eccentric habits" and poor "deportment." One day he asked an aide who dressed well: "Where do you buy your suits? I hope you're working for them." With this Yankee Simon Legree to front for him, President Eisenhower could cultivate his image as a "beloved" president.

XIV

***

Succeeding presidents assembled new staffs, who soon displayed some of the tendencies that were already becoming apparent in the post–World War II White House. Infighting and vying for the president's attention were raised to fine arts and an enlarged ego became a predictable side effect of working in the West Wing.

In the all too brief Kennedy regime, another side effect developed. The president emanated such glamour and charisma that his aides could not help sharing the glow. As Dave Powers, JFK's old Boston pal, put it: "He made everybody around him look ten feet tall." After JFK died, Powers added: "Now he's gone and they're shrinking."

Kennedy's relationship to his staff was not nearly as cozy as it looked. He expected—and got—absolute loyalty. But he was never chummy with any of them. One man who served both Kennedy and his successor, Lyndon Johnson, characterized the two men as total opposites: JFK aloof, LBJ almost overwhelming in his insistence on intimacy.

Unlike Johnson, Kennedy never envied an aide his press clippings. When McGeorge Bundy, head of the National Security Council, was touted by the press as a one-man White House power center, JFK wryly remarked: "I will continue to have some residual functions."

The Kennedy staff was relentlessly male. But in their midst was an important woman whom most of them barely noticed: presidential secretary Evelyn Lincoln, whose desk was just outside the Oval Office. In appearance and demeanor, she was neither glamorous nor powerful, but she was capable and, equally important, loyal.

JFK remarked one day to his speechwriter Ted Sorenson: "If I said, 'Mrs. Lincoln, I have cut off Jackie's head. Would you please send over a box?' She would [reply] 'That's wonderful, Mr. President. I'll send it right away. Did you get your nap?' "

Mrs. Lincoln had far more power than most White House watchers suspected. People could get to see the president through her door when they were turned away by JFK's appointments secretary, Kenneth O'Donnell, who was known as "The Iceman" for his inclination to say no to any and all comers. But the biggest surprise to the ex-Cameloters came when Mrs. Lincoln published her book. She did not bother to tell any member of the Kennedy clan about it, so they had no opportunity to censor it, as they have done with numerous other books about the Kennedy White House.

While Mrs. Lincoln's portrait of JFK is affectionate on the whole, it revealed just how much this birdlike woman saw and remembered. She described a president who often deliberately pitted staffers against one another, FDR style. Her JFK did not always wear his famous smile. He often blew his stack and berated everyone in sight, including innocent bystanders. At the same time, the book is a touching story of a country girl from the plains of Nebraska who fulfilled a lifelong hunger for glamour and excitement by getting a job in the White House.

XV
★★★

In the LBJ White House, staff turnover was practically the order of the day. Not many people could deal with this explosive, unpredictable man without suffering burnout. An aide would be a favorite one day and ignored the next; the staff got so familiar with this turnaround they called it "the freeze-out." A man or woman never knew whether a summons to the Oval Office meant a warm bath of praise or a cold shower of vituperation, often delivered in front of other staffers who watched in appalled silence.

The list of people who fled the pressure is long. A mere sample includes George Reedy, who had served Johnson since 1951; he quit as press secretary in 1965. Jack Valenti, a Texas PR dynamo whom Johnson often displayed as the epitome of loyalty, abandoned ship in early 1966. Bill Moyers, a Johnson protégé since 1954, stuck it out until January 1967. Two of Jack Kennedy's best staffers, Richard Goodwin and McGeorge Bundy, tried to make the transition and gave up within a year or two.

As the man in charge of the president's public relations, Jack

Valenti was an unbelievable disaster. His problem was his total inability to attune his Texas-sized worship of Lyndon Johnson to the more low-keyed style of Washington, D.C. As one historian put it, he was "a Texas bull in a Georgetown china shop, a hard-sell huckster in soft-sell territory."

Valenti kept giving interviews that got him all but laughed out of town. He would compare LBJ to Abraham Lincoln, Winston Churchill, and other great men in world history. Johnson could do no wrong, even though it was common knowledge in Washington that a day seldom went by without the president furiously berating Valenti, cussing him out for, as one columnist put it, "everything from a malfunctioning doorknob to a slip-up of state."

This made it difficult for reporters to swallow Valenti's unadulterated praise of his boss. One newsman cracked: "If Johnson dropped the H-bomb, Valenti would call it an urban renewal program."

To his vast distress, poor Valenti became labeled "the valet." No one noticed that he had acquired a rather valuable niche as one of the president's best speechwriters. He was also handy in congressional relations because the Capitol Hill crowd knew he had LBJ's ear and might pass along their shouts and murmurs.

Eventually the beatings from the press and the beatings from Johnson got to him and Valenti left for the less stressful job of president of the Motion Picture Association of America.

Meanwhile, Bill Moyers was levitating himself to the very top of the White House pyramid. Only twenty-nine years old when he entered the West Wing on that mournful November 22, 1963, Moyers became, in the opinion of some people, the most powerful presidential aide of the twentieth century.

That estimate may suffer from Texas hyperbole. It is hard to picture anyone more powerful than Eisenhower's Sherman Adams in his five-year White House reign. Adams had the authority to hire and fire almost anyone in the executive branch of the government. Nor did Moyers speak for the president to the likes of Winston

Churchill and Joseph Stalin, in the manner of FDR's Harry Hopkins. But Bill Moyers is undoubtedly up there among the top movers and shakers.

In ten years, thanks to LBJ, this rather shy Baptist preacher from the Texas boondocks came a long way. A lot of it was a tribute to his ability. He ran Johnson's 1964 campaign for the presidency, which featured a devastating attack on Republican candidate Barry Goldwater. Later, he organized and ran the White House task forces that gave some coherence to Johnson's war on poverty. When Moyers became press secretary in 1965 in the wake of the burned-out George Reedy, he inherited a job with sudden death written all over it. For a while, however, he made it into a personal triumph, in spite of tidal waves of bad news from Vietnam.

Moyers inadvertently summed up his success when he remarked that the secret of working for a president was "to have an umbilical cord right to his character, nature and personality." Moyers created this cord in countless hours with Johnson, from midnight suppers in the Oval Office to weekends at Camp David, talking politics, politics, politics, Johnson's only real topic of conversation.

Unlike Valenti, who knew nothing about Washington, Moyers had worked there as Johnson's senate aide. The president valued his advice up to and including violent disagreement about one or another Johnson scheme. "I've seen them fighting like a couple of ten-year-olds," one fellow aide recalled. But that umbilical cord enabled Moyers to know just how far he could go. Also vital was Johnson's confidence in Moyers's ultimate loyalty: "That boy works like a dog for me and is just as faithful," the president said.

But Moyers found the press secretary's job went beyond knowing how far to go with Lyndon Johnson. Stepping out of the president's shadow into the limelight of daily appearances on television gave him more than a touch of Potomac fever. Soon he was schmoozing with top columnists and reporters at the best D.C. restaurants. Under their influence, he began hinting ever so slightly that he did not really agree with the president on the war in Vietnam. Soon, while Johnson was getting hammered for the seemingly endless war, glowing stories on Moyers as the best press secretary ever began appearing in *Time* and other magazines and newspapers. As one commentator put it, "if anything good happened in the government, it was Moyers, if anything bad happened, it was Johnson."

A new golden boy had been born, but he was in danger of outshining the man who had made it possible. The opening paragraph of a column by my friend Art Buchwald says it all:

> *Lyndon B. Johnson first came to Bill Moyers's attention about ten years ago, when Bill discovered the tall, smiling Texan tucked away in a Senate office on Capitol Hill. Bill was immensely impressed by Johnson's spirit and willingness to do anything asked of him. "Senator," said Moyers, "I think I can use you."*

Fellow staffers started calling Moyers "a good press secretary for Bill Moyers." One accused him of creating a "White House within the White House" composed of a personal staff more loyal to him than to the president. These gibes were mild compared to the epithets uttered in the Oval Office. LBJ began denouncing Moyers to reporters and other aides. Next Moyers got the "freeze-out" treatment. The president stopped inviting him to important policy meetings.

Moyers realized it was time to depart and headed for New York and a job as publisher of the Long Island newspaper *Newsday*. He later became a familiar face on public television.

XVI
★★★

Bill Moyers had tears in his eyes when he announced his resignation to the press. The same thing could not be said about another aide who got carried away by his own self-importance: Ronald Reagan's chief of staff Donald Regan. The son of a Boston cop, Regan had survived the battle of Iwo Jima and made his way through Harvard without Kennedy-esque cash or dash. On Wall Street he racked up enough millions to qualify as secretary of the treasury during Reagan's first term. He then switched to chief of staff, letting James Baker, the previous chief, succeed him as the administration's moneyman.

If Don Regan resembled anyone, it was the first White House chief of staff, Sherman Adams—a rather surprising convergence. Adams was a quintessential Yankee, descended from the founding Adamses. Yet Regan, a Johnny-come-lately Irish-American, had the same imperious temperament and fondness for macho power playing. Maybe there's something in the New England air.

Actually, Regan's Potomac fever made Adams's infection seem like a trifling case. In two years, Regan accumulated all the White House power that other once influential men, such as Attorney General Ed Meese, used to share. When people came into the Oval Office to ask questions, it was Regan, not the seventy-six-year-old president, who answered them. When First Lady Nancy Reagan urged him to keep Ronnie's schedule light after surgery for colon cancer, Regan ignored her. When she pestered him about it, he hung up on her.

Worse, Regan soon had the rest of the staff calling him "The Chief," which only a president as easygoing as Ronald Reagan would have tolerated. Can you imagine Franklin Roosevelt or Lyndon Johnson putting up with such arrogance? Before long one of the jokes circulating around the Washington cocktail circuit was that it was now okay to mispronounce the president's name as "Reegan."

Most reprehensible of all, Don Regan abandoned his boss in his hour of maximum need. When the Iran-Contra scandal exploded in Ronald Reagan's face, Regan should have taken some, even most, of the heat for this unwise attempt to free hostages by bribing their terrorist captors and illegally transferring some of the money to anti-Communist revolutionaries in Nicaragua. Instead, Regan let his president go ill-prepared into a disastrous press conference that sank his popularity rating below fifty percent for the first time.

Nancy Reagan began pressing her husband to fire "The Chief." In retaliation Regan started leaking stories to the press that made it sound as if Nancy were running the government. "That does it," the president wrote in his diary. "I guess Monday will be the showdown day."

The showdown was about as nasty as things can get in the White House. Regan resigned in what one writer has called "a paroxysm of fury," and exited snarling at the president and vice president. He then did the meanest thing an ex-aide can do to a president. He wrote a book, portraying President Reagan as an idiot and his wife as a monster.

Now do you see why I don't like the title chief of staff? It can make the person who holds it think he is more important than the president. I fear some future egomaniacal "chief" will inform the president he has been dismissed the way the Praetorian Guard used to make and unmake Rome's emperors.

XVII
★★★

In his memoir of his days in William Jefferson Clinton's administration, Secretary of Labor Robert Reich offers this glimpse of the White House staff.

> *The Secretary of Transportation phones to ask me how I discover what's going on at the White House. I have no clear answer. . . . The decision-making "loop" depends on physical proximity to B—who's whispering into his ear most regularly, whose office is closest to the Oval, who's sitting or standing next to him*

when a key issue arises. . . . In this administration you're either
in the loop or out of the loop, but more likely you don't know where
the loop is, or you don't even know there is a loop.

At least we didn't have to worry about a chief of staff seizing power in that White House. The Clinton regime was too chaotic to let anyone, even a Don Regan or a Sherman Adams, organize a coup.

George Stephanopoulos spent four years in the Clinton White House as the president's senior adviser, a job he describes as a combination "political troubleshooter, public relations adviser, policy expert, and crisis manager." Young, bright, and photogenic, Stephanopoulos was quickly singled out by the press as one of the stars of the White House staff. Eventually, however, he began to sour on life in the West Wing. Everywhere he looked, including the mirror, he saw vanity, ambition, and a love of power. Add in the long hours, the constant stress, and the ups and downs of presidential moods and Stephanopoulos decided to preserve his sanity by bailing out at the end of Clinton's first term.

XVIII
★★★

Some stars, such as Karl Rove and Condoleezza Rice, have emerged in George Bush's West Wing, but so far no one seems to have become a golden boy (or girl) or a grandstander. There have been rumors of intrigues and rivalries, backstabbing and betrayals—some of which may actually be true. Such things happen even—or perhaps especially—in the White House. But we will have to wait a few years for insider books to be written and historians to mull over diaries and letters and e-mails before we really know what's been happening. Meanwhile, I continue to believe that, whatever their political views or personal agendas, most of the small army of men and women who work in the West Wing have a genuine commitment to the country. They may never experience the close personal relationship that John George Nicolay and John Hay enjoyed with Abraham Lincoln, but there is a bond of mutual respect and affection. There is also the realization that grueling hours and constant crises are not a bad trade-off for the privilege of serving the president of the United States.

A 1982 photo of the residence staff in the State Dining Room. Do a head count and you'll
see why Nancy Reagan called the White House an eight-star hotel.
Credit: Courtesy Ronald Reagan Library

8

***

Frontstairs, Backstairs

Some of the most important people in the White House are all but invisible except to the families who live there. I'm talking about the household staff—the hundred or so men and women who prepare and serve the meals, vacuum the floors, polish the silver, repair the plumbing, check the wiring, and do whatever else is needed to keep the President's House in perfect condition.

Overseeing this large and varied assortment of workers is the chief usher, who is basically the general manager of 1600 Pennsylvania Avenue. He—so far they have all been men—works directly with the president and first lady and conveys their requests to the rest of the staff.

Every change in administration brings a spate of new requests. When President Dwight D. Eisenhower scheduled the first of what were to be many stag luncheons in the State Dining Room, Mamie went downstairs to inspect the arrangements. She took one look at the bentwood banquet chairs lined up on either side of the table and announced that they were much too small for a crowd of burly males. What was wrong with the high-backed Queen Anne chairs that were usually in the State Dining Room?

Chief Usher J. B. West had to explain that there were only twenty of them and they were mainly for show. The bentwood chairs were used at larger parties. "Have some more of the big ones made," Mamie ordered. The craftsmen in the White House carpenter's shop promptly went to work and duplicated enough of the heavy gold cut-velvet chairs to provide seating for future stag lunches.

The day after Lyndon Johnson moved into the White House, he demanded that Chief Usher West do something about his shower. "If you can't get it fixed," he snapped, "I'm going to have to move back to The Elms"—a reference to the house he and his family had lived in during his vice presidency.

West, with a couple of White House plumbers in tow, went up to inspect the offending shower. They found it in good working order, but it was not the superfancy model the president was used to. There was no way to regulate the direction and force of the spray.

Accompanied by the plumbers and the White House engineer, West went out to The Elms to study the shower. It was unlike any they had seen before, but they got in touch with the manufacturer and were able to order a duplicate. The new shower was no sooner installed than the president was on the warpath again. This one wasn't right either. West called the manufacturer again. This time they sent the company engineers to check out The Elms shower and make one that would be exactly the same.

The new shower still didn't satisfy the president so another one was ordered and when that one didn't work, it was replaced by yet another one. The engineer decided the problem was water pressure, so a special tank with its own pump was installed just for the president's shower. But it still wasn't strong enough. West and his staff kept designing and redesigning LBJ's shower, and spending thousands of dollars and untold man-hours in the process, trying to find one that would satisfy him. They ended up with a complicated fixture that had a half-dozen different nozzles and sprays, but by the time they finally achieved perfection, Johnson was on the verge of moving out.

When LBJ gave his successor, Richard Nixon, a tour of the White House, he made a point of extolling the wonders of his shower. After one encounter with LBJ's maximum force spray, the new president called the chief usher's office and said, "Please have the shower heads all changed back to normal pressure."

II
★★★

The job title, chief usher, dates back to Benjamin Harrison's administration. There are various explanations of why it was adopted, but the most plausible one is that in the old days, the top man at the President's House was the man who ushered people in to see the chief executive.

The most durable chief usher in White House history has to be Irwin Hood Hoover, who went by the nickname Ike. Hoover was a twenty-year-old employee of the Edison Company when he was sent to the White House in 1891 to install the first electric lights for Benjamin Harrison. The job took about four months, and Ike later recalled the satisfaction he felt when "the White House was illuminated with electric lights for the whole world to behold."

The next day he got a letter from the commissioner of public buildings, offering him a permanent job as the house electrician. Hoover accepted the offer and he soon figured out why it had been made. President Harrison and his family were afraid to touch the light switches for fear of being electrocuted!

Ike would turn on the lights in the downstairs rooms in the evening and turn them off when he came to work the next morning. It took the Harrisons the better part of a year to get up the nerve to use the electric lights in the living quarters. They were equally fearful of pushing the electric call buttons to summon the servants. "There was a family conference every time this had to be done," Hoover wryly recalled.

Ike was promoted to usher in 1904 and became chief usher during the Taft administration, a job he held for the next twenty-five years. In all that time, there was only one problem he was unable to solve. When Herbert Hoover became president in 1929, there were two Mr. Hoovers in the White House. To avoid any confusion, Mrs. Hoover insisted that Ike be referred to as "Mr. Usher."

III
***

In the early days of the President's House, some of the duties of the chief usher were performed by a steward. It was a much less complicated place back then. The steward's main job was overseeing the preparation and service of food and the arrangements for presidential entertaining.

The first White House steward was John Briesler, who had managed John and Abigail Adams's home in Massachusetts. He arrived in Washington with his wife, Esther, who became the housekeeper. Thomas Jefferson's steward was a Frenchman, Etienne Lemaire, and Dolley Madison followed suit with Jean-Pierre Sioussat, better known as French John.

Sioussat was not only responsible for Dolley's magnificent parties, he helped her pack the items she rescued from the White House before it was burned by the British. After she fled, he delivered her pet macaw to the French minister's residence for safekeeping until she returned.

John Quincy and Louisa Catherine Adams chose as their steward Antoine Michel Giusta, a deserter from Napoleon's army, whom Adams had hired as his valet while he was in Belgium negotiating the treaty of peace that ended the War of 1812. The ex-soldier married Louisa Catherine's maid and they emigrated to America to become the Adamses' steward and housekeeper during John Quincy's tenure as secretary of state and later in the White House.

Giusta swiftly became more than a steward. The lonely, morose president made him his favorite companion. The steward accompanied Adams on his walks and swims in the Potomac and the president allowed him to acquire a staff of more than twenty people.

Andrew Jackson kept the Giustas on his household staff but they remained friendly with the Adamses, who had stayed in the federal city after John Quincy left office. The Giustas used to visit the former first couple on Sundays, often bringing small gifts from the White House kitchen.

When President Jackson heard about their visits, he exploded. Adams was still high on Jackson's hate list for slandering his beloved wife, Rachel, in the dirty election campaign of 1828. The president issued a fiery veto on any further visits to his predecessor.

The Giustas encountered still more problems when Jackson decided to save money by firing most of the Adamses' staff and replacing them with slaves from his Tennessee estate, The Hermitage. This switch made the Giustas' lives miserable. Far from fitting the conventional image of craven obedience, these black men and women frequently ignored the steward's orders. In almost every clash, the president took their side. Only Emily Donelson, the president's niece and official White House hostess, could resolve their disputes.

When Emily retreated to Tennessee, mortally ill with tuberculosis, the Giustas also departed. They opened an oyster bar in the capital, which was so successful that they were able to retire within a few years and buy a farm not far from the home of the John Quincy Adamses.

IV
***

I'm sorry to say that slaves were not uncommon in the pre–Civil War White House. Abigail Adams, the first woman to examine the place with the eyes of a practiced hostess—she had been entertaining politicos for much of the previous twenty years—thought at least thirty servants were needed to run it. She was unquestionably right, but the early presidents tried to cope with far fewer than that number because Congress, already convinced the president was overpaid at $25,000 per year, declined to include the White House in their budgets.

Jefferson tried to economize by importing some of his slaves from Monticello, but he soon decided this was not a good idea. They did not get along with his French steward, who had a poor command of English and an autocratic style. By the end of his first term, Jefferson was telling his daughter back in Monticello that he preferred white servants. "When they misbehave, [they] can be exchanged," he wrote. He meant fired and replaced, of course.

Joseph Boulanger, who succeeded Antoine Michel Giusta as Andrew Jackson's steward, continued to run the President's House for the next twenty years. He was on hand to help President Tyler and his second wife, Julia, throw some spectacular parties, but he departed when another slave-owning president, James Polk, decided to staff his White House with blacks from his Tennessee plantation. Boulanger, too, found slaves difficult to deal with. Mrs. Polk, not averse to taking charge of things, replaced him with Henry Bowman, who set up shop in the porter's lodge next to the North Portico.

The new steward apparently had no expertise in the food or entertainment side of things. Basically, he functioned as a manager, hiring outsiders by the day to handle these tasks while Mrs. Polk issued orders to the slaves. The first lady also put Bowman in charge of contracting for such services as repairs and redecorating—the first step in the process of turning the steward into the chief usher.

The next president, Zachary Taylor, was also a slave owner. He, too, imported a number of blacks from his Louisiana plantation to reduce expenses. But a change in the American attitude toward slavery was beginning to take hold in many people's minds, particularly those in Taylor's Whig Party, which was on its way to evolving into the Republican Party, with its commitment to rid America of slavery.

Fearful of political repercussions, Taylor kept his slaves out of sight. They worked only in the second-floor family rooms and slept in the attic. Free blacks, who had previously comprised most of the household staff, were dismissed lest they be mistaken for slaves.

When the Thirteenth Amendment to the Constitution brought an end to slavery in 1865, blacks returned to the White House workforce but they were not always integrated. In President Ulysses S. Grant's administration, the inside servants were white and the outside ones black.

Grant's favorite servant was his coachman, a tall, brawny African-American named Albert Hawkins. The president spent hours at the White House stables, discussing his horses with Hawkins. The two men shared a passion for quality equines and a love of driving down country roads at a reckless pace.

In later administrations, white and black servants worked side by side and those who were entitled to meals ate together as well. This was the norm until 1909, when Helen Taft hired an arrogant house-keeper named Elizabeth Jaffray who decreed that henceforth white servants and black servants would eat in separate dining rooms.

When Calvin Coolidge discovered the whites were getting better food, he gave orders that the same meals be served to both groups, but it was not until Eleanor Roosevelt got to the White House that anyone addressed head-on the issue of segregation.

Mrs. Roosevelt's solution was to fire the whites on the household staff, except for the housekeeper, and hire only blacks, which solved the problem—up to a point. FDR was apparently indifferent to the matter. When black servants from the White House accompanied the first family to Hyde Park on weekends, they were not allowed to eat with the Roosevelts' white servants, who had their own din-ing room. The blacks had to eat in the kitchen.

Integration finally came to the White House during my father's administration. The man who banned segregation in the armed forces in 1948 could hardly tolerate it in his own household. The President's House has been an equal opportunity employer ever since.

V

★★★

It took many years and several presidents to finally convince Congress that the government should bear the expense of running the White House. Until federal funds were forthcoming, only the wealthiest chief executives could afford to hire an adequate staff and host a suitable number of social events. Even some of the wealthy ones balked at the cost. Claiming he was a poor man (he wasn't), Zachary Taylor kept entertaining to an absolute minimum and employed a measly three housemaids and a butler.

Congress had agreed early on to pay for the outside staff—the chief doorkeeper and his assistant, a day guard and night watchman, and a pair of gardeners and their assistants—but as far as the legislators were concerned, that was it. However, James Buchanan managed to sneak the steward onto the federal payroll by dismissing the chief doorkeeper and his assistant and using their combined salaries to pay him. But the bachelor president stubbornly resisted adding any servants he would have to pay for himself. He kept the staff around ten, still a long way from Abigail Adams's optimum number of thirty.

In 1866, Congress recognized the importance of the steward—by this time, he was responsible for disbursing public funds for the maintenance of the President's House—and made the job a federal post. Gradually, other employees were added to the federal payroll. Their salaries were modest but they no longer had to worry about getting fired when an incoming president started having anxiety attacks about the cost of running 1600 Pennsylvania Avenue.

With Congress keeping an eye on the White House budget, presidents became leery of appearing to live too high on the hog. To avoid criticism, they adopted James Buchanan's subterfuge of paying the help from other sources. President Grant had at least ten servants who were listed as "laborers" on the public buildings budget. Theodore Roosevelt gave his valet, Henry Pinkney, the title of steward, which had all but disappeared with the advent of the chief usher, but other than announcing "Dinner is served" at the Roosevelts' private parties, Pinkney's chief responsibility was seeing that the Roosevelt children got to school on time.

Congress's largesse in allotting funds to remodel the White House in 1902 was followed by a willingness to pay for a decent-sized staff. By the time Woodrow Wilson took office, Abigail Adams's ideal number of thirty had at last been attained. The Roaring Twenties brought even further congressional munificence. Calvin and Grace Coolidge were the first presidential couple to have the government pay for their official entertaining. Warren G. Harding had wangled the law through Congress but didn't live long enough to enjoy it. The Coolidges lived it up, although the term almost seems a misnomer when attached to the president's puritanical style. When he was vice president, Florence Harding called him "the cheap veep."

By the time the Trumans got there, Chief Usher Howell Crim presided over a staff of almost fifty people, including two assistant ushers, two electricians, five engineers, five carpenters, seven gardeners, two plumbers, a housekeeper, six cooks, three butlers and a maître d'hôtel, seven doormen, four housemen, five maids, and several typists and messengers. It seemed enormous at the time but now it is twice that size.

VI

★★★

The transition from one administration to the next is always difficult for the household staff. As of twelve o'clock on Inauguration

Day, they have a whole new family to deal with—a new set of personalities, different likes and dislikes, and more often than not, a complete change in routines.

The president's first dinner in the White House is an especially tense occasion. It's hard to be certain what his and his family's food preferences might be, especially on such a busy day. When the Nixons moved into 1600 Pennsylvania Avenue on January 20, 1969, Chef Henry Haller and the housekeeper, Mary Kaltman, stood by in the kitchen. They had been stocking up on groceries for the previous two weeks. They knew that steak was a Nixon favorite but, just to be on the safe side, they bought everything they could think of that might please the presidential palate.

That evening, Mrs. Nixon called down to the chef. The president and his daughters, Tricia and Julie, and Julie's husband, David, wanted steak for dinner. Mrs. Nixon would dine in her room and all she wanted was a bowl of cottage cheese.

The steak was a no-brainer but there wasn't an ounce of cottage cheese in the house. Although Chef Haller was sure that every grocery store in the District of Columbia would be closed at that hour, he called for a White House limousine. Minutes later, the head butler was speeding around Washington searching for cottage cheese. Luckily, he found some in a local deli. Mrs. Nixon's dinner was soon served and cottage cheese quickly became a White House staple.

William Howard Taft was a regular visitor to the White House during Theodore Roosevelt's administration. He seemed to be a genial man with a kind word or a joke for everyone on the staff. When he became president, the help could scarcely believe the change. "The smile was replaced by orders, not always given in a nice way," Ike Hoover reported.

Mrs. Taft was even more difficult. Among her many strange directives was an order that bald-headed butlers were not permitted in the dining room. Next she declared war on beards. One man, who had been on the staff for years, tried to get away with shortening his, but the first lady pursued him like a tigress and soon he, too, was clean-shaven.

Herbert Hoover and his wife complicated the staffs' lives when they insisted that, as far as possible, the servants should keep out of sight. "Heaven help you if you were caught in the hall when the president was coming," one maid recalled.

People dove into closets and empty bedrooms at the first hint that the president or first lady might be on their way. One particular closet on the second floor near the elevator would often be full of butlers, maids, and housemen as the president strode down the hall.

For the residence staff, the arrival of the Franklin D. Roosevelts was like the return of sunshine. When FDR saw people ducking into closets as he was wheeled toward them in the upstairs hall, he asked what in the world was going on. When the Hoovers' predilections were explained to him, he told everyone to relax. There was no reason to be afraid of him or the first lady.

With every change of administration, the maître d'hôtel, who is in charge of organizing and serving the food at White House social events, may be called on to issue new orders to his staff of butlers. During the Eisenhower years, Mamie Eisenhower told Eugene Allen, the maître d' at the time, not to let the butlers clear the plates after dinner until everyone had finished eating.

When Lyndon Johnson arrived, it was a different story. In the course of one of his first official dinners, the impatient president murmured to Allen, "Why don't you pick up?"

"Mr. President," Allen told him, "your guests haven't finished eating."

"Well, if you'd start picking up, they'd rush to get through!" was Johnson's response.

After Richard Nixon's first state dinner, he, too, complained of the slow pace. He suggested cutting the soup course. When his chief of staff, H. R. Haldeman, demurred, Nixon growled: "Men don't really like soup!" Haldeman retreated and called the president's valet, who told him Nixon had spilled soup all over his vest while trying to slurp and talk simultaneously. Haldeman fired off an "action memo" banning soup at future dinners.

The staff has long since learned to be philosophical. They are there to please the first family. They also know that no matter how outlandish the tenants' demands become, in four or, at most, eight years they'll be gone.

VII
★★★

There is often a lot of submerged tension between the staff and the first families. I suspect this is the origin of the tradition of the White House jinx. Staffers became convinced that certain first ladies or presidents (or both) were operating under an evil cloud. Helen Taft was the first target of this idea, which in her case grew into a firm conviction. So many things went wrong in her tenure, it is hard not to be convinced the staff was right. On Inauguration Day, for instance, one of the most tremendous blizzards of the century hit Washington. The first lady's inaugural ball dress was stranded on a train somewhere between New York and Washington. Within a few months of taking charge of things in her emphatic know-it-all way, she suffered a debilitating stroke.

Almost every time Mrs. Taft held a garden party, the staff was ready to bet it would rain—and they were almost always right. Cooks constantly quit on her, often a day or two before a big dinner. She did not help matters with her habit of constantly checking the contents of their pots and pans. The final blow, of course, was her husband's defeat in his 1912 run for reelection.

Backstairs considered the Hoovers another jinxed couple—and they, too, seemed to accumulate convincing evidence of bad luck as the Great Depression plunged the president and the White House into gloom. Occasionally the jinx was used to explain specific events, such as the tragic death of Calvin Coolidge's younger son. Sometimes a state dinner or an important reception could be, and apparently was, jinxed, with one of the dishes turning out badly, a guest fainting or becoming ill, or a dropped tray or other major spillage disrupting the smooth flow of the evening.

The Eisenhowers became still another jinxed couple when Mamie Eisenhower decreed that no one would be permitted to tip the staff. Tipping was a tradition inherited from the great houses of England, where visitors regularly left a little something for the help to express their appreciation for impeccable service. White House salaries were not high and previous first families had tolerated the custom— and even did some tipping themselves when a state dinner or a reception came off beautifully thanks to the staff's attention to detail. Sometimes my mother would inquire whether departing guests had tipped. If the answer was no, she made up the lapse out of her own pocketbook. The staff was dismayed by the abrupt end of this modest cash flow. Some of them had to moonlight to keep working in the White House.

Also dismaying was the president's behavior toward the staff. Reading the "I like Ike" slogans that had decorated his winning campaign, they had expected a warm and friendly man. Instead, they found a man who "hardly knew we were there," Lillian Rogers Parks told her mother. Maggie Rogers nodded and said: "Herbert Hoover." I know I shouldn't say it, but it does make you wonder about Republicans.

Mamie also banned all staff nicknames, again causing consternation backstairs. By this time nicknames had become part of the fun of working in the White House. They were also a release valve for the constant pressure. J. B. West, the chief usher at the time, was called "Perry Como" (there was a resemblance), diminutive houseman George Thompson was "Jockey," the chief electrician was called "Short Circuit." The carpenter was "Tojo" (suggesting he was sneaky, à la the Japanese at Pearl Harbor?). Maître d'hôtel Alonzo Fields was "Donald Duck" because he spluttered when he got mad.

I am quite certain these nicknames continued to be used. The staff just made sure they did not reach Mamie's ears. One nickname you can be sure Mamie never heard was hers: "Sleeping Beauty"— because she spent so much time in bed.

The White House jinx descended on the Eisenhowers when they kicked off the 1958–59 social season with a dinner for the Supreme Court. The opening gambit was a message from Chief Justice Earl Warren, about an hour before the first guests were due to arrive, reporting he was in bed with a virus. "Uh-oh," the staff said, instantly spotting the jinx.

When Mrs. Warren arrived without her husband, she tripped coming in the front door and ripped her coral chiffon evening dress. Halfway through the dinner, the wife of a railroad president had a heart attack and was rushed to the office of the White House doctor, who had to be summoned from his home to treat her. A few minutes later, another woman guest collapsed and was carried into the powder room, where cold towels were applied to revive her. During dessert, a third woman on the brink of passing out reeled into the powder room with a friend who gave her emergency assistance. Although most guests had no idea all these crises were transpiring, Mamie and Ike knew and must have looked back on that dinner as one of their worst nights in the White House.

VIII
★★★

White House doormen don't open doors. They welcome people to the President's House. At formal dinners, they take the guests' coats and present them with the escort cards that tell them which table they will sit at.

In the early days of the White House, there was only one doorman. He lived in a small room or lodge on the west side of the entrance hall and kept track of who went in and out. As more and more people started calling on the chief executive, the doorman began keeping a list, which was sent upstairs to the president or his secretary so they could decide who would be admitted.

The doorman's post seems to have been an Irish-American prerogative. For many years it was filled by Joseph Dougherty, who had started working at the White House as John Adams's groom and was promoted to doorman by Thomas Jefferson. Under Andrew Jackson, Dougherty was replaced by Jemmy O'Neil, who kept the president entertained with his jokes and good humor. O'Neil in turn was succeeded by Martin Renehan.

Like most Irish-Americans of the day, Renehan was a passionate Democrat. After Jackson's unlucky heir, Martin Van Buren, was voted out in 1840, Renehan became a political mole, reporting back to the party leaders that the new powers-that-be, the Whigs, were in the White House twelve hours a day, arguing with President William Henry Harrison over who got what in the spoils of victory.

When Harrison died after only a month in office and John Tyler took over the White House, Renehan could not conceal his delight. Tyler's loyalty to the Whigs was only skin-deep; he started to veto every bill the Whig majority passed in Congress. This switch produced a violent reaction among party loyalists. Political abuse, including numerous death threats, cascaded into the White House.

The uproar inspired the feisty Renehan to take charge of a large, ominous-looking wooden box that arrived at the White House one day. The staff feared, with some justice, that it was a bomb sent by irate Whigs to remove Tyler from the White House in the most literal fashion. While the president and everyone else took cover, Renehan attacked the box with a meat cleaver. " 'Tis better for me to die than that the president should be killed by such a divil of a machine," he roared.

Eventually the doorman smashed the thing open and discovered that it contained a model of a new iron stove the inventor hoped the president would help him promote.

The continuing animosity toward Tyler prompted "His Accidency" to request a security force for the White House. The doorman got several new assistants who were, in effect, plainclothes policemen. They continued to receive callers, however, and they were still called doormen lest their true job, "guard" or "sentry," make the White House sound like an armed camp. On the side, the doormen also performed a variety of other services, such as carrying confidential messages and meeting guests at the stagecoach or train station.

Perhaps because they were given so much authority, the doormen were an independent lot. When Julia Grant became first lady, she was horrified at the way they loitered in the entrance hall and used the doorman's lodge as a clubhouse where they and their friends smoked their pipes and ate their lunches.

Julia laid down the law: No more White House meals, no more lounging around the front door, no smoking except in the basement or outdoors. From now on, the doormen would have to wear black dress suits and white gloves and assume a more formal demeanor when they greeted White House visitors.

The threat of instant dismissal brought order to the ranks but there was evidently some backsliding, because in 1902, President Theodore Roosevelt's secretary, George Cortelyou, issued a booklet entitled *Special Instructions to the Chief Doorkeeper and Those Under His Immediate Supervision*. It spelled out the rules of conduct and dress and the appropriate way of receiving visitors, and reminded the doormen that they were there for security purposes and were not to abandon their posts to run errands or help with household chores. By this time, however, their security duties had been diluted. The doormen no longer carried firearms, and after President William McKinley's assassination in 1901, the job of protecting the president was assigned to the Secret Service.

These days, White House doormen are no longer called upon to risk their lives as Martin Renehan did when he attacked that suspicious box with a meat cleaver. Some historians have played this incident for comedy and it does have its amusing side. But to me it was a significant step toward White House staffers, whatever their jobs, thinking of themselves as special people, committed to working for a very special person, the president of the United States.

IX
☆☆☆

If there were a prize for the doorman who witnessed the most history, it would probably go to Thomas Pendel, who became a doorkeeper in Abraham Lincoln's White House. A big, gaunt, quiet man, Pendel worked at the White House for over forty years. Even in his old age, he retained vivid memories of the night Lincoln was shot. He could bring tears to the eyes of listeners as he told of hugging a distraught Tad Lincoln when the news of his father's death reached the White House.

When Ira Smith, another man who would become a White House fixture, went to work in the McKinley mail room in 1897, he encountered a graying Tommy Pendel.

"I'm the man who let him out," Pendel told him.

"How's that?" young Smith asked.

"The way it was that night," Pendel said. "He come down to the front door where the others was waiting for him. I remember it clear. The carriage was waiting and ready to take them to the theater where some famous lady was performing in a stage show. They was all ready to go and they come over to the door where I was standin' because I was an usher then like I am now. He was walkin' tall and straight and he smiled pleasant-like at me and I opened the door for him to go down to Ford's Theater. I'm the man who let him out."

It dawned on Smith that Pendel was talking about Lincoln on the last night of his life.

X
★★★

If the White House doorkeepers had a reputation for being an independent lot, a couple of the housekeepers could give them a run for their money. One of the most difficult was Elizabeth Jaffray, who arrived with the Tafts. She had been forced to go into domestic service when she was widowed early in her marriage, but she considered herself a lady and she expected to be treated as one.

Helen Taft was determined to spend as little time as possible on household management, so she was happy to find someone to relieve her of the responsibility. When the Tafts moved into the White House, Mrs. Jaffray was given a two-room suite on the second floor. She maintained an office there for seventeen years, ruling with such a firm hand that she managed to alienate everyone on the staff.

Helen Taft may have been imperious but her housekeeper was a veritable despot. She would not allow her subordinates to sit down in her presence and they could not speak to her unless she spoke first. As I've mentioned, she issued orders that black servants and white servants could no longer sit together during meals. The decree produced protests on both sides of the color line, but after being threatened with dismissal, everyone knuckled under.

Mrs. Jaffray also disapproved of automobiles, which were rapidly becoming popular. She dismissed them as "vulgar contrivances" that would never last, without mentioning the fact that she was scared to death to ride in one. When the White House acquired a fleet of cars, Mrs. Jaffray took over President Taft's discarded horse-drawn brougham. It would pull up to the North Portico each morning and the housekeeper would appear wearing a large hat with a veil and toting a parasol, to be driven off to do the marketing.

With the election of a Democrat, Woodrow Wilson, in 1912, there was apprehension among the staff. Those who had been hired by his Republican predecessors were fearful of losing their jobs. Mrs. Jaffray had no intention of giving up her fiefdom. She contacted the president-elect and was invited to call on Mrs. Wilson at her home in Princeton, New Jersey.

The housekeeper arrived with an uncharacteristic smile on her face and a floor plan of the White House in her hand. In the sweet and gentle tone she assumed when talking to the president and his family, she proceeded to deliver a lengthy monologue about the amount of expertise it took to run the mansion.

"My! What a difficult house," Mrs. Wilson said when the monologue ended. "We certainly want you to stay on and take care of things. . . . You will, won't you?"

Mrs. Jaffray cemented her position on Inauguration Day. When Woodrow Wilson stepped off the elevator on the second floor, she was there to greet him. "Welcome to your new home, Mr. President," she said sweetly, holding out her hand.

Wilson took her hand and bowed. "Oh! You are Mrs. Jaffray, aren't you?" he said. "I am so happy to meet you."

Elizabeth Jaffray's reign of terror continued through the Wilson and Harding administrations. One of Harding's favorite meals was breakfast. Because his wife slept late, he began inviting men friends to join him for a stag meal. Among the things he wanted on the table were toothpicks. The butler who got the request went to Jaffray, who said: "Surely you're mistaken!"

When the butler insisted he was not hard of hearing, Jaffray said: "Forget it."

The next day, the butler returned. "The President asked real forceful like for those toothpicks," he said.

Harding eventually got his toothpicks. But Mrs. Jaffray undoubtedly let him know he had failed to live up to her lofty standards of etiquette.

The tyrant met her match in Calvin Coolidge. Cal started calling her "Queenie" behind her back—a direct hit on her overbearing style. He refused to treat her with the deference she felt she deserved and, unlike previous presidents, he took an interest in what was going on in the kitchen. He revised the menus for state dinners and demanded to know what happened to the leftovers.

On a visit to the servants' dining room one morning, Coolidge noticed that the staff was dining on pancakes that were twice the size of the ones he got upstairs. The next time pancakes were on the presidential menu, Cal appeared in Jaffray's office with one of them in his hand. "Why can't I have big ones like they have downstairs?" he demanded.

After a couple of years of Cal's needling, Queen Elizabeth decided to retire. The rest of the staff silently cheered. As Grace Coolidge said later, the housekeeper "had come to consider herself the permanent resident and the President and his family transients."

Coolidge replaced Queenie with a genial dietician from Boston named Ellen Riley. He liked her so much he invited her to join his guests at White House musicales and movie screenings and gave her the combination to the vault where the gold and silver services were stored. He also gave her a wacky title: Custodian of the Plate, Furniture, and Public Property of the Executive Mansion. Despite his public image as a dour New Englander, Coolidge was a master of deadpan humor. Only a few people have noted that at his Amherst College graduation he was chosen by his classmates to deliver the Grove Oration, which gave the college and the professors a farewell horselaugh.

XI

★★★

Another tyrannical housekeeper, Henrietta Nesbitt, arrived at the White House with Franklin and Eleanor Roosevelt. She had worked as a cook at the Roosevelt home in Hyde Park, and Eleanor, impressed by her frugality, brought her along to Washington. The Roosevelts not only had a large family, they often invited friends for lunch or dinner. Since the president has to pay for his personal entertaining, Eleanor was counting on Mrs. Nesbitt to keep the expenses from getting out of hand.

Franklin D. Roosevelt had always loved good food; quail and pheasant were among his favorites. Fluffy, as the staff referred to the new housekeeper when she was out of earshot, disapproved of such delicacies. "Plain foods, plainly prepared" was her motto. Her meals were not only plain, they were totally predictable. She served the same food week after week and it was usually overcooked in the bargain.

FDR had announced more than once that he disliked broccoli. "Fix it anyhow," Fluffy told the cooks. "He *should* like it." At one dinner, when the president and his guests requested hot coffee, Fluffy sent them iced tea instead. Her explanation: "It was better for them."

Mrs. Nesbitt also had her own ideas about what the president should eat for breakfast—oatmeal. After one too many bowls of the stuff, FDR exclaimed to his secretary, Grace Tully, "My God! Doesn't Mrs. Nesbitt know there are breakfast foods besides oatmeal? It's been served to me morning in and morning out for months and months now and I'm sick and tired of it!"

Later that day, the president ripped out a newspaper ad for several other cereals including Corn Flakes and Cream of Wheat and had Grace Tully take it to Mrs. Nesbitt as a "gentle reminder."

Henrietta Nesbitt was so bent on having her own way that she would not even grant the president's request to serve chicken à la king at the luncheon after his inauguration for a fourth term. "We aren't going to have that because it's hot and you can't keep it hot for all those people," she said flatly, and served chicken salad instead.

Roosevelt was so displeased with Mrs. Nesbitt's menus that after his mother died, he brought her cook, Mary Campbell, to the White House and had her prepare meals in a small kitchen he had installed on the third floor. The president and his guests ate in the second-floor oval room while Eleanor and her friends dined on Mrs. Nesbitt's fare in the family dining room below.

Unfortunately, the Trumans inherited Mrs. Nesbitt. There was some improvement after Mother took over the meal planning, but when she had to go out of town and left me in charge, Dad and I found ourselves on a steady diet of Brussels sprouts. Dad detested the things, but did Mrs. Nesbitt care? Of course not.

I got the impression Mrs. Nesbitt enjoyed ignoring my father's preferences and disregarding the menus I planned. I was ready to evict her on the spot but Mother told me to hold off; she would speak to her when she got back. By that time, Mrs. Nesbitt informed us that she was planning to retire, which saved Mother the trouble of firing her and guaranteed that we would finally get some decent food.

XII
★ ★ ★

Out of the thousands of people who have worked at 1600 Pennsylvania Avenue over the years, two lemons—Queenie and Fluffy—are not a bad average. In the Trumans' experience and that of other first families I've talked to, the staff gets universally high marks for going out of their way to be helpful.

During the grim days of the Vietnam War, Lyndon Johnson had his hands full. The enemy refused to quit and protesters filled his days and nights with abuse. As the president toiled long hours in the Oval Office, the Johnsons' family dinners became later and later.

An embarrassed Lady Bird Johnson told John Ficklin, the head butler, that there was no need for anyone to stay on duty to serve them. The staffers could all depart at their usual time, eight P.M., and leave something she could warm up. Ficklin slowly but emphatically shook his head. "We've served the presidents and first ladies every meal in formal service since I can remember," he said. "Even if it's a cheese sandwich and a bowl of chili and a boiled egg. That's tradition!"

Ronald and Nancy Reagan called the mansion "an eight-star hotel," and with good reason. "Every evening, when I took a bath, one of the maids would come in and remove my clothes for laundering and cleaning," Nancy said. "Five minutes after Ronnie came home and hung up his suit, it would disappear from the closet to be pressed, cleaned, or brushed."

Barbara Bush was amazed when she arrived in 1988. "By this time I had lived [in] or visited many places but never had seen a household where every living human's only concern was to make us, our children, and our guests happy," she said.

One of my favorite memories of the White House staff underscores Barbara's comment. It involves Alonzo Fields, the tall, personable maître d'hôtel during our seven-year-and-eight-month sojourn. I loved the bread pudding the house chefs prepared to accompany the pheasant they generally served at state dinners. (Now you couldn't pay me to touch anything so fattening—oh, to be twenty-something again!)

At these sumptuous affairs, with everyone in white tie and tails and evening gowns galore, I was seated so far below the salt, I was practically in the kitchen. Seating at these fetes was (and still is) done by rank, and a president's daughter has none worth mentioning.

With pheasant and bread pudding on the menu, there was high anxiety for yours truly. Were they going to run out before they got to me? The stuff was so popular, it was all too possible. But I soon learned that Fields had stored in his capacious head some precious information about me. One evening, I watched the bread pudding supply dwindle as the butler who was serving it got closer to my place. My hopes sank until I heard Fields call softly into the kitchen: "More bread pudding for Miss Margaret!"

XIII
★★★

The White House staffers have some interesting memories of their own. I particularly like a couple of stories involving my father. Dad was in the habit of doing some work in his private study on the second floor while waiting for lunch to be served. When he left, houseman George Thomas would go in and make sure the room was tidied up.

One day Thomas yielded to temptation and sat down in Dad's big leather chair. Who should appear in the doorway but the chief executive himself, returning to pick up some papers he'd forgotten. "George," Dad said to the paralyzed Thomas, "I'll tell you one thing. You're in a mighty hot seat!"

With that, Dad picked up his papers and returned to the Oval Office and George Thomas breathed an enormous sigh of relief.

Another houseman, Herman Thompson, handled the dozens of phone calls that came into the kitchen from various people both inside and outside the White House. One day Herman answered the phone and a voice he didn't recognize said: "I'd like to order lunch for Mrs. Wallace [my grandmother] and me."

"Who is me?" Herman jauntily asked.

"I happen to be the president of the United States," the voice replied.

The rest of the staff told Herman to clean out his locker. He was definitely out of there. But, of course, he wasn't. Instead of reprimanding him, Dad got a good laugh out of the episode.

XIV
★★★

Working at the White House has become a way of life, not only for individuals but for families. Johnny Muffler was hired as an electrician in 1945 and celebrated his fiftieth year on the job by making sure every clock in the place was ticking and telling the same time. Johnny's father-in-law had been a chauffeur, and his son Rick worked in the calligraphy office, where the invitations to the state dinners and receptions are penned by a professional staff.

In recent years there have been three butlers named Ficklin: Charles, who later took Fields's job as maître d'hôtel; John; and Samuel. Samuel Ficklin recalled the training he received from his brother, Charles, and Fields before he got the job. He was told to take some bricks and use them to strengthen his hands and arm muscles by hefting them until he could hold a heavy tray without the slightest tremor. He was also trained to set the table with each plate exactly the same distance from the edge.

No one summed up this pride of performance better than Fields. Looking back on his twenty-one years as chief butler and maître d'hôtel, he said: "When I was directing a dinner, I'd seat the president and step back and give a nod to the men to start the service. From then on I was directing an orchestra. I had my strings here and my wind instruments in the back and I was directing. And people would watch and marvel at it, they really did."

It is a wonderful analogy and not at all surprising. As a young man, Fields attended the New England Conservatory of Music. He became a butler only because his funds ran out.

The tradition of impeccable service and the determination to keep first families contented and comfortable has been exhibited in hundreds of ways. Plumber Howard Arrington was proud of using his metal-working skills to build the elaborate stand for Tricia Nixon's wedding cake. Preston Bruce, who was a doorman from the Eisenhower through the Ford administrations, liked to say that people had only to visit once before he could greet them by name the second time around.

All these men and women are imbued with the same dedication that my favorite among them, Alonzo Fields, epitomized when he said in an interview at the age of ninety-two: "I never felt like a servant to a man. I felt I was a servant to my government, to my country."

There it is again, backstairs as well as frontstairs: glory.

FDR looks underdressed beside his royal houseguest, King George VI of England. The king and his wife, Queen Elizabeth, stayed at the White House in 1939.
Credit: AP/WIDE WORLD PHOTOS

9

***

Bed, Breakfast and Beyond

The White House has no shortage of guest rooms. I've stayed in a couple of them and I can assure you they're the equal of anything you'll find in the world's best hotels. More to the point, every one of them is steeped in history. Spend a night at the White House and you could find yourself sleeping in a room that in a previous life was Caroline Kennedy's nursery, Andrew Johnson's family parlor, or the suite that belonged to Franklin Roosevelt's personal secretary and good friend Missy LeHand.

The most famous of the White House guest rooms, the Lincoln Bedroom, is on the southeast side of the second floor. Lincoln never slept in his eponymous bedchamber. In those pre–West Wing days, when the executive offices were on the second floor of the residence, presidents used the space as either an office or a cabinet room. During the Lincoln administration, it was Abe's office.

It is highly unlikely that Lincoln ever sought repose in the elaborately carved rosewood bed that is the centerpiece of the room, although it was bought during his administration. Mary Lincoln originally put it in the northwest bedroom (where the Prince of Wales stayed when he visited the White House in 1860). Theodore Roosevelt, with his strong sense of history, had it moved into his own bedroom. Calvin Coolidge also slept in it, but after the Coolidges departed Lou Hoover moved it back to the Prince of Wales Room. She added a suite of parlor furniture that was supposedly owned by Lincoln and rechristened the room the Lincoln Bedroom.

That first Lincoln Bedroom remained in the northwest corner during President Franklin D. Roosevelt's administration. One of its longtime tenants was FDR's close friend and adviser Louis Howe, who stayed there when he was gravely ill with emphysema. Some years earlier it had been the room where Esther Cleveland was born and where Alice Roosevelt Longworth was operated on for appendicitis. Some years later it became my sitting room after another history-minded president, Harry S Truman, aided and abetted by his wife, Bess, moved the furniture to its present location and installed other pieces of Victoriana from the White House storerooms to create what is essentially a shrine to our sixteenth president. At least that's the official story.

The truth of the matter is I started the whole thing. Before we moved into the White House, Mother and I made an inspection tour. We had no trouble selecting the pair of rooms on the second floor that would be my bailiwick. The space was perfect, but the decor left a lot to be desired. (I don't think I used the word *hideous*, but I may have. You have to remember I was only twenty-one.)

In any case, I made it clear that the dark, clunky furniture that was cluttering up my future sitting room had to go. Preferably as far away as possible. Happily, Mother agreed with me. She took up the matter with Dad and the result was the present, and now famous, Lincoln Bedroom at the opposite end of the White House.

Traditionally, the Lincoln Bedroom is reserved for VIP—usually male—guests, but during the Clinton administration a virtual "for sale" sign was hung on the door and the room became the most overworked guest room in the White House. Hollywood stars like Barbra Streisand connived for a sleepover there and more than one big-bucks Democratic donor snoozed in the large, and as I recall rather lumpy, bed. I hope they had a better night's sleep than I had the night I stayed there. Then again, maybe I don't.

II
★★★

The second most famous White House guest room is also one of the prettiest: the Queens' Bedroom, which is on the northeast side of the second floor just across the hall from the Lincoln Bedroom. This was the president's secretary's bedroom when the job was a live-in post. During the Lincoln administration it was shared by John Hay and John George Nicolay—and I'll bet any amount of money it would never have been called pretty. When President James A. Garfield was brought back to the White House after being gunned down by an assassin, the space became an emergency tele-graph office from which bulletins about the president's health were flashed around the country.

The room was converted into a guest room after the White House renovation of 1902. It was, and still is, furnished with a Sheraton-style canopied four-poster bed that is said to have be-longed to Andrew Jackson, but probably didn't. It became known as the Rose Room because the curtains and bed hangings were in shades of red, rose, and white—colors selected by Edith Roosevelt over the vehement objections of Charles McKim, who didn't think they were stylish enough. Edith was very fond of the room and put her sister, Emily Carow, there whenever she came to visit.

Queen Elizabeth of England, the late and much beloved Queen Mother, slept in the Rose Room when she and her husband, King George VI, visited the White House in 1939. The king slumbered across the hall in what is now the Lincoln Bedroom. The Queen Mother was not the first queen to stay at the White House. That honor belongs to Queen Emma of the Sandwich Islands (now

Hawaii), who was a visitor during Andrew Johnson's administration. Given her choice of bedrooms, Emma chose a small one next to the Prince of Wales Room.

The Rose Room was rechristened in 1942 after a parade of royal refugees bedded down there. One of them, Crown Princess Martha of Norway, was a particular favorite of FDR's. The crown princess stayed at the White House for several weeks before moving to an estate in Bethesda, Maryland. Even then, she still returned for occasional overnight visits. Among the other crowned heads that have rested on the pillows in the Queens' Bedroom are Queens Wilhelmina and Juliana of the Netherlands, Queen Frederika of Greece, Queen Sonya of Norway, Queen Elizabeth II of Great Britain, and her daughter, Princess Anne.

Queen Elizabeth II made her first visit to the White House during the Eisenhower administration in 1957. (She had previously visited Washington as Princess Elizabeth and stayed with Mother and Dad at Blair House.) During Elizabeth II's visit, Prince Philip was given the Lincoln Bedroom that had been used by his father-in-law in 1939, and the couple's retinue of ladies- and gentlemen-in-waiting was scattered among the other guest rooms on the second and third floors.

The highlight of Elizabeth II's visit was a state dinner followed by a concert in the East Room with a champagne reception afterward—all of which made for a very late evening. The next day, the backstairs White House must have exchanged some wry comments when they compared notes on the post-party behavior of the first lady and her royal guest of honor. Mrs. Eisenhower's maid, Rose Woods, waited up to help her undress, hang up her gown, and lock her jewelry in the bedroom safe. The queen ordered her personal maids to retire at a reasonable hour. She undressed on her own, laid her evening clothes neatly on a chair, and left her diamond tiara and necklace and the sash with her bejeweled medals lying casually on the dresser.

For Mrs. Eisenhower, the queen's visit was the high point of her husband's presidency and the Queens' Bedroom became almost sacred territory. When Jack Kennedy was elected to the presidency, Jackie made a study of the White House floor plan to see which rooms they could use while the family quarters were being redecorated. "Please put me in the Queens' Room," she told Chief Usher J. B. West, "and my husband will stay in the Lincoln Bedroom."

West passed the word along to the White House staff but when Inauguration Day dawned and the departing first lady read in the papers that her successor would sleep in the Queens' Bedrooom, she was quite perturbed. Mrs. Eisenhower thought the Queens' Bedroom should be reserved solely for queens. Jackie didn't qualify.

III
★★★

The visit of King George VI and Queen Elizabeth of England in June of 1939 was a momentous occasion. It was the first time a British monarch had set foot in the former colonies. The royal couple came at President Franklin Roosevelt's invitation—an effort on FDR's part to send a signal to Adolf Hitler that the two countries had a special relationship that could lead to trouble if the Führer decided to declare war on England.

The imminent arrival of these ultimate royals touched off a frenzy of activity in the White House. Eleanor Roosevelt's interest in decorating was minimal and the place badly needed an overhaul. Rugs and wallpaper were replaced or dry-cleaned and the staff waxed floors and dusted furniture until everything gleamed to Housekeeper Henrietta Nesbitt's satisfaction.

With the king and queen scheduled to spend a night in the mansion, there were all sorts of questions about dealing with them on an intimate basis. Should the White House maids and butlers curtsy and bow when they approached their majesties? How do you say good morning to a king when he shows up for breakfast?

The president and first lady met the king and queen at Union Station when they arrived by train from Canada. In two limousines, they headed a military parade that wound its way along the avenues and around the circles to the White House. Ignoring an early summer heat wave, more than half a million people cheered while U.S. Army Air Force bombers flew overhead.

In the White House, the capital's diplomatic corps waited in full regalia. After the British ambassador presented the king and queen to the assembled circle, they retreated upstairs to recuperate from the blazing heat. They lunched privately with the Roosevelts and were guests of honor at a magnificent state dinner that night. Other lunches, teas, and receptions followed in swift succession. The royal couple endured them all with amazing savoir faire, considering the cooler temperatures they were used to at home.

The king and queen spent a mere forty-four hours in the White House and, as you might expect, they behaved like proper houseguests. Their servants, however, were a different story. They ensconced themselves on the third floor and proceeded to treat the staff as if they were *their* servants. They demanded menus so they could order their meals as if they were in a hotel and haughtily explained that in Buckingham Palace they had their own servants to tend to their needs, so why should things be any different in the White House? Needless to say, this did not sit well with their counterparts in the former colonies. Chief Usher Howell Crim had to use all the diplomacy he could muster to avert a second American revolution.

The press coverage of the monarchs' visit was awash in headlines from start to finish. Sad to admit, this show of solidarity between Great Britain and the United States was a bust as far as stopping Germany from going to war with England was concerned. Less than three months later, on September 1, 1939, they were at each other's throats.

IV

★★★

When Winston Churchill came to visit Franklin D. Roosevelt in 1941, shortly after the United States entered World War II, he stayed in the Rose Bedroom and his top aides stayed in the room across the hall in what is now the Lincoln Bedroom. Churchill, who could easily qualify as the houseguest from hell, tried a couple of other rooms before consenting to sleep in the one that had been assigned to him.

The British prime minister's visit was shrouded in secrecy. A few days after Pearl Harbor, President Roosevelt asked his wife for a list of the people who were coming to the White House over Christmas but gave no indication of why he wanted to know. Not until December 22 did Eleanor discover the reason for the president's query. That day, FDR casually announced that Churchill would arrive around nightfall. The secrecy had been necessary to guarantee Mr. Churchill's safety.

"Everyone scurried around to get ready," Mrs. Roosevelt recalled. When the British leader arrived, complete with cigar, he found the Roosevelts ready to offer him and his entourage tea in the West Hall on the second floor. "But they preferred more stimulating refreshments," Mrs. Roosevelt noted.

Churchill's preferences continued to be at odds with his host's and hostess's. FDR was inclined to go to bed early and rise at a reasonable hour. Churchill was used to working until three A.M. and sleeping late. Eleanor Roosevelt reported that it took "Franklin several days to catch up on his sleep after Mr. Churchill left."

The prime minister made several visits to the White House, often staying as long as two or three weeks. He was an unpredictable and demanding guest. A team of White House staffers had to be assigned to get him the food and drink—especially the drink—that he might ask for at any time. He also tended to take baths at odd hours and to rush up and down the corridors in his dressing gown.

In his memoirs, Churchill claimed that his and FDR's "work patterns coincided." They both were in the habit of doing "much of our work in bed," so they frequently visited each other's bedrooms to discuss outstanding problems. One of these visits produced a memorable scene. FDR unceremoniously pushed open Churchill's door and wheeled himself into the room to find the prime minister in the all-together. Churchill gave him a cheerful grin and said: "You see, Mr. President, I have nothing to hide!"

On another evening, Churchill decided his room was overheated and tried to open one of the White House windows. The window, which probably hadn't been opened in decades, resisted. The prime minister kept at it with mighty grunts—and suddenly felt an excruciating pain in his chest. He summoned an aide, who in turn summoned a doctor, who told the great man he had strained his heart, and if he wasn't more careful, he could become the war's best-known casualty. Thereafter, when a window needed opening, the PM called on the White House staff.

The English leader's 1941 visit added a profoundly touching dimension to that first Christmas of World War II. To protect the president, the Secret Service insisted that the traditional community Christmas tree be set up on the south lawn rather than in Lafayette Park. That way the general public—and any potential assassins—could be kept outside the grounds.

An enormous crowd gathered behind the iron fence and cheered when the tree came aglow. Both leaders gave brief speeches from the South Portico. Churchill's talk summed up the struggle against Hitler in a few unforgettable words:

> Let the children have their night of fun and laughter. Let the gifts of Father Christmas delight their play. Let us grown-ups share to the full in their unstinted pleasures before we turn again to the stern task and the formidable years that lie before us, resolved that by our sacrifice and daring, these same children shall

*not be robbed of their inheritance or denied their right to live in a
free and decent world.*

Deeply moved, the crowd began singing Christmas carols. Those
who were there remembered the scene as one of the most unforgettable moments of their lives. It remains an imperishable part of
the White House's glory—and more than made up for Churchill's
deficiencies as a houseguest.

V

★★★

If there had been a Lincoln Bedroom back in 1824, one of its
denizens definitely would have been the Marquis de Lafayette.
President James Monroe had invited the Revolutionary War hero
to cross the Atlantic to help the country celebrate the fiftieth anniversary of the American Revolution. What a welcome he received! By this time the Revolutionary era was engulfed in a golden
haze of sentiment. Lafayette's presence evoked long-dead heroes
and the struggle for nationhood. At the tender age of nineteen, he
had spent his own money (he was worth millions) to buy a ship, sail
to the colonies, and join the fight against British tyranny.

Lafayette spent the year after his arrival traveling through all
twenty-four states and being feted at Lafayette dinners and balls
in almost every town he passed through. By the time the old
warrior returned to Washington in the summer of 1825, James
Monroe was no longer in office. The marquis, dressed in his Con-
tinental Army uniform, was greeted at the White House by President John Quincy Adams, and invited to stay for as long as he
pleased.

First Lady Louisa Catherine Adams was appalled. It meant she
had to turn most of her family out of their beds to accommodate
Lafayette and his party. She also had to find room for the stagger-

ing amount of luggage they brought with them, much of it gifts collected on their grand tour.

One item that added to Louisa's consternation was a live alligator. The creature and the rest of the booty were stored in the East Room while the marquis enjoyed the final phase of his triumphal tour. He became the first foreigner to address Congress, and paid an emotional visit to Mount Vernon, where he entered Washington's tomb alone and emerged with tears on his cheeks.

On September 6, 1825, Lafayette's sixty-eighth birthday, President Adams gave a farewell dinner to the nation's guest in the State Dining Room. The table was as splendid as White House steward Antoine Michel Giusta could make it. The speeches rang with patriotic fervor. At one point, the two men were so carried away, they burst into tears and embraced. The president summed up the meaning of the grand occasion in his closing words:

"We shall always look upon you as belonging to us. . . . You are ours . . . by that tie of love, stronger than death, which has linked your name for the endless ages of time with the name of Washington."

VI
✯✯✯

Not every Revolutionary War hero received as warm a welcome as Lafayette. In 1802, Thomas Paine, the author of the famous pamphlet *Common Sense*, which did much to swing the colonies behind the movement to independence in 1776, returned to America after an absence of fifteen years. For most of the country, this was not a cause for celebration. In the intervening years, Paine had been kicked out of England for trying to incite a revolution and had been imprisoned and almost guillotined in France for backing the wrong faction in their sanguinary upheaval.

On this side of the Atlantic, the pamphleteer's stock had declined after he wrote a public letter calling George Washington a lowlife and an ingrate and accusing him of conspiring with the French to keep him in prison. His popularity did not improve when he published the book *The Age of Reason,* which scoffed at Christianity.

Thomas Jefferson, tolerant of freethinkers and mindful of Paine's contributions to the American Revolution, was among the minority who were not averse to seeing him return to the United States. Before he left France, Paine leaked to more than one reporter that President Jefferson had offered him passage on a U.S. Navy ship and was looking forward to shaking his hand. Both stories happened to be true and the opposition Federalist Party, led by Alexander Hamilton, had a field day with the news.

A fondness for brandy had left Paine with a bright red nose, which made a perfect target for his enemies and led to verses like the following:

> *Tom is come from afar . . .*
> *His coming bodes disastrous times*
> *His nose is a blazing star!*

Paine's invitation to the White House was not immediately forthcoming. Jefferson's two daughters, who were visiting at the time, made it clear to their father that this tippling atheist was not welcome in their company. The president let Paine loiter in a Washington hotel until the young women went back to Virginia and then invited him to dinner along with several members of Congress.

One of the guests, Federalist senator William Plumer of New Hampshire, registered shock and outrage at the sight of Tom Paine sitting beside Jefferson at the table and treating him "with the familiarity of an intimate and equal." The senator wondered aloud if the public virtue could be protected by a chief executive who befriended such a man.

This was political hot air, of course, but the sheer volume of it got to Jefferson and no further dinner invitations were issued to Paine. Over the next few weeks, the president saw as little as possible of

Paine and the old revolutionary eventually left the capital in a sour mood, accusing Jefferson in a farewell letter of ignoring him.

By this time, the president must have been wondering: What have I done to deserve this? Tom Paine retreated to New York where he died in obscurity in 1809.

VII
★★★

A little less than a hundred years after Tom Paine's visit to Thomas Jefferson, there was another heated controversy over the White House guest list. I'm sorry to say that this one was racial rather than political.

In 1901, Theodore Roosevelt's secretary released the following statement to the press: "Booker T. Washington of Tuskegee, Alabama, dined with the president last evening." Washington was a distinguished educator and author of the popular book *Up From Slavery*.

Across the country, especially in the South, headlines erupted in dozens of newspapers. With them came angry editorials, denouncing Roosevelt for daring to cross the "color line." Georgia's *Macon Telegraph* declared: "God set the barrier between the races. No president of this or any other country can break it down." Another paper claimed that no self-respecting southern woman would ever visit the White House again.

The incident was a dismaying example of American racism in full, ugly bloom. Roosevelt, proud of his ability to deal with the press, was stunned. He had no large agenda in mind when he issued the invitation. He had simply heard Washington was in town and invited him to dinner, as he invited many other celebrities he wanted to meet. He also wanted to "show some respect to a man whom I cordially esteem as a good citizen and a good American." Roosevelt was finding out very early in his presidency how outspoken about certain issues the public could be. He never invited Washington or any other black American again.

Almost thirty years later, a courageous first lady, Lou Hoover, made another attempt to bring racial equality to the White House and found herself in similar hot water. She invited Mrs. Oscar De-Priest, wife of an African-American congressman from Chicago, to the White House for tea. Congressman DePriest announced the invitation to the press and an uproar immediately erupted in all directions.

Southern newspapers accused the first lady of "desecrating" the White House. The Texas legislature passed a resolution denouncing her. Sulfurous letters cascaded into the White House mail room. But Lou Hoover stood her ground. After carefully screening the other guests she had invited to the tea, she decided to split the group in half. The women who said they would be pleased to meet Mrs. DePriest were invited to one party, the naysayers to the second.

Years later, Herbert Hoover recalled that the incident had left his wife feeling wounded and appalled. But the president showed that he, too, had the right stuff. He coolly invited Dr. Robert R. Moton, Booker T. Washington's successor as president of the Tuskegee Institute, to have lunch with him a few months later.

VIII
✫✫✫

I don't have any exact figures but I'm willing to bet that World War II produced the greatest number of VIP White House sleepovers of all time. Security concerns made it advisable for FDR to confer with world leaders at the mansion and their conferences were more easily arranged, and less subject to scrutiny by the press, if the leaders stayed there, too.

The White House logbooks of the era list, among others, the king of Greece, the king of Yugoslavia, the president of the Philippines, the president of Peru, and the prime contender for Winston Churchill's title of houseguest from hell: Madame Chiang Kai-shek. The imperious and temperamental wife of China's embattled Nationalist leader, General Chiang Kai-shek, Madame Chiang was a Wellesley graduate who spoke excellent English and was her husband's partner in political and diplomatic affairs. She was also as willful as any blueblood in her expectations and demands.

Madame Chiang refused to sleep twice on the same sheets. Even when she retired for a brief nap, which she did several times a day, she wanted the entire bed changed. She brought along her own silk sheets, which had to be washed by hand and stitched into the heavy quilted bag she had also brought with her. Howell Crim, the chief usher, gave Madame Chiang a secret nickname: the China Doll. Other members of the staff called her Mrs. Generalissimo, because of the way she ordered them around.

Madame Chiang's visit began badly. Mrs. Roosevelt had scoured Washington, D.C., to procure some special Chinese tea for her guest. It was reportedly a hundred years old. As they sat in the West Hall sitting room sipping this brew, the first lady proudly informed Madame Chiang of the tea's long pedigree.

"In my country, tea kept so long is used only for medicinal purposes," Madame Chiang replied sweetly.

Madame traveled with an entourage of forty. Some of them were given rooms on the third floor, others slept at the Chinese embassy. On the second floor, beds were found for Madame's personal maid; her nephew and bodyguard, Mr. Kung; and a second nephew also named Kung.

As it turned out, the second Mr. Kung's clothes and haircut were deceptive. A valet who was sent upstairs to help him unpack came flying back to Chief Usher Crim's office to report in horror: "Your Mr. Kung is a girl!"

Miss Kung proved to be as much of a pain as her famous aunt. She not only made demands, she delivered them directly to the first lady. An exasperated Eleanor Roosevelt finally called the chief usher's office: "Mr. Crim," she said, "will you please explain to Miss Kung that she is to call you if she needs anything? She pops into my room a dozen times a day!"

Apparently the chief usher was not high enough in rank for Miss Kung. She transferred her complaints to the State Department, who solved the problem by moving her to a suite at the Mayflower Hotel.

Madame Chiang stayed at the White House more than once. She got along well with the president and made a favorable impression on Congress when she addressed them in a joint session. There is no question that she was an effective spokesperson for her country, but the only good thing the staff could say about her was that she was a very generous tipper.

IX
★★★

On May 29, 1942, a Mr. Brown was expected at the White House for a visit of several days. Mr. Brown turned out to be Vyacheslav Molotov, the dour foreign minister of Soviet Russia. If Molotov ever smiled, it has gone unrecorded by history. The staff was nervous about going anywhere near him. You can imagine the reaction of Caesar, the same valet who had discovered Mr. Kung was Miss Kung, when he unpacked Mr. Molotov's suitcase and discovered a gleaming pistol. Understandably agitated, Caesar rushed to report his discovery to Chief Usher Howell Crim.

What to do? Guns were not allowed in the White House. Although Crim notified the Secret Service, it was generally agreed that mentioning this fact to the foreign minister might upset the sensitive discussions that were going on in the president's office. An equally agitated Crim told Caesar: "Just hope he doesn't use it on you!"

Molotov's visit continued to create problems. He insisted on having a salad and soup for breakfast. This was a more or less standard Russian breakfast, but it was not on the White House's usual menu and it did not boost the Soviet foreign minister's standing with the kitchen staff. He and his aides also had a habit of staying up half the night. Equally disturbing was Molotov's incredibly suspicious attitude. Whenever the maids made his bed, one of his bodyguards stood by, evidently worried that someone might slip a bomb under his pillow.

Molotov returned for another visit in April of 1945, not long after President Roosevelt died. He had not acquired any additional charm. In fact, with victory over the Germans imminent, he was downright obnoxious. When my father learned from the State Department that Molotov was insisting on the installation of Communist puppet governments in Poland and other Eastern European countries, Dad summoned the foreign minister to the Oval Office and told him Soviet-American friendship could continue only by keeping both sides of an agreement and *not* by pretending diplomacy was a one-way street.

"I have never been talked to like that in my life," Molotov huffed.

"Carry out your agreements and you won't get talked to like that," Dad replied.

Charles Bohlen, one of the State Department's top Russian experts, and later ambassador to Moscow, was acting as interpreter in this confrontation. Mr. Bohlen recalled in his memoirs the pleasure he felt when he translated Dad's Missouri bluntness to the Soviet foreign minister. It was the first time anyone in the American government had stood up to the Russians since World War II began. As far as Bohlen was concerned, it was long overdue.

X
★★★

During Franklin D. Roosevelt's administration, the White House had a number of more or less permanent houseguests. In May 1940,

FDR was meeting with his closest adviser, Harry Hopkins, and invited him to stay for dinner. Hopkins became ill during the meal and FDR offered him a bed for the night. Three years later, Hopkins was still using it. His young daughter, Diana, whose mother had recently died, was given a bedroom on the third floor, adding another member to the household.

Harry Hopkins's room was one of the state guest rooms on the southeast side of the house, which later became the Lincoln Bedroom. It was only a few steps from the upstairs oval room that Roosevelt used as his study. When Hopkins remarried in 1942, a sitting room was created in an adjacent room so he and his wife could have their own suite. The suite is still there and the sitting room is now the Lincoln Sitting Room. When the Hopkinses moved to a house in Georgetown in 1943, the Roosevelts' daughter, Anna Boettiger, and her family took over their quarters.

Eleanor Roosevelt's favorite houseguests were Lorena Hickok, a former Associated Press reporter who worked for the Democratic National Committee, and Joseph Lash, a young man she had met through her work with the American Youth Congress. Wild rumors circulated about both these people. Hickok supposedly had a love affair with Eleanor, and Lash was also reputed to be sexually involved with the first lady—and was a Communist in the bargain! Someday I may do a separate book on White House gossip. The entry under Absurdities would be as long as the *Encyclopaedia Brittanica*.

A great many of Eleanor Roosevelt's houseguests were women she had met in the course of working on the various causes she supported. I'm sure the women were all very high-minded but at least one of them had a dark side. The guest, who shall remain nameless because the teller of the tale, Alonzo Fields, was too discreet to reveal it, was having trouble closing her suitcase and asked one of the maids to do it while she went down to breakfast.

The maid had to rearrange the woman's clothes, and in the course of repacking them she discovered a fourteen-inch silver tray that had been bought for the White House in 1898 and bore the inscription "The President's House."

The maid called Fields and asked him what she should do about it. "Maybe Mrs. Roosevelt gave the tray to her," the maid suggested. "Should I tell the chief usher?"

"Don't tell anyone," Fields advised. "Just give it to me and I'll take it back to the kitchen."

He knew that Mrs. Roosevelt could not possibly have given the woman the tray, because it didn't belong to her. It belonged to the White House.

The maid was still concerned. Suppose the woman discovered the tray was not in her bag and wanted to know what happened to it?

Fields laughed and said, "The lady will never question you about this, and if she ever returns as a guest she will be ashamed to look you in the eye."

I'm sure that's true, but I'm also sure that if the woman ever returned as a guest, Fields kept an extra sharp eye on the silver.

XI
★★★

Foreign dignitaries almost always have a political reason for visiting the White House. There are times when a president is eager to talk politics in return. Probably the topper in this department was Richard Nixon's 1969 sequence of meetings with no less than seventy-five world leaders who came to Washington, D.C., for former president Dwight Eisenhower's funeral. At ten A.M. on March 31, 1969, in the Yellow Oval Room on the second floor, Nixon started this political decathlon with President Charles De Gaulle of France. "Le Grand Charles" urged him to meet as soon as possible with Russia's leaders and settle the war with Vietnam at the same urgent rate of speed. The sooner Mr. Nixon made it clear that he was withdrawing from Vietnam, the sooner the South and North Vietnamese would compose their differences and make peace.

This advice turned out to be something less than grand. The Communists declined to make peace no matter how many soldiers Nixon withdrew. But Nixon not only flew to the Kremlin to talk détente with the rulers of Russia, he made an even more historic visit to the Communist rulers of China, proving he could play in De Gaulle's geopolitical league—and score touchdowns.

On the first day of the diplomatic marathon, Nixon absorbed advice from many world leaders. The president of Tunisia, the former prime minister of Japan, the prime minister of Turkey—the politicians did not stop streaming in and out of the Oval Office until 6:30 the following evening. By the time the last of them departed, Richard Nixon had gotten an inside look at the world's power structure without leaving 1600 Pennsylvania Avenue. It was a marvelous example of one of the least appreciated uses of the President's House.

XII
★★★

These days, when someone does something remarkable, he or she may be invited to the White House for a handshake and a photo op with the president, but that's usually about as far as it goes. The world moved at a slower pace back in 1931, which explains why a sixteen-year-old boy from Kiowa County, Colorado, was able to spend four full days at the White House as a guest of President and Mrs. Herbert Hoover.

The boy, Bryan Untiedt, had become a national hero for saving the lives of a group of younger children when they were trapped in a school bus during a blizzard. He had kept them awake and moving to prevent freezing to death until they were finally rescued thirty hours later.

Whoever made the arrangements for Bryan's visit to the White House had neglected to tell Mrs. Hoover. She was dismayed to discover that he was due to arrive on the same day as the king and queen of Siam. Not very convenient. On the other hand, the White House has coped with far worse crises.

A car was dispatched to Union Station and Bryan, with a Secret Serviceman for an escort, was driven to 1600 Pennsylvania Avenue. Instead of the mountain of luggage that most White House visitors bring, he carried only a cardboard suitcase tied with string and an inexpensive Brownie camera.

Bryan was taken up to the second floor where Mrs. Hoover waited to greet him. In spite of the royal visitors who were expected two hours later, she sat down and chatted with him for several minutes. After a while, Bryan was shown to one of the guest rooms and in keeping with White House custom, a valet was sent to help him unpack. It hardly seemed necessary. The suitcase contained only a few items of clothing and not much else.

Before long, one of the president's secretaries showed up and escorted Bryan to the Oval Office where he had a lengthy chat with the president. Hoover had two sons of his own and he and Bryan got along splendidly. The president listened with fascination to Brian's retelling of his wintry heroism and shared a few of his adventures as a mining engineer in distant lands.

Lou Hoover asked two women friends who were also staying at the White House to take Bryan for a ride around Washington. They were almost mobbed by photographers when they returned. Bryan was hot copy. But the Hoovers would not allow him to be interviewed. Can you imagine any recent president passing up a chance to get on the evening news with this appealing young hero? I find myself admiring the Hoovers' approach. They were not trying to exploit the boy. They only wanted to reward him for his courage.

The frustrated newshawks reported Bryan was hobnobbing with the king and queen of Siam. On the contrary, he never even saw them unless he peeked out the window of his room, which was just over the North Portico. The Hoovers made sure he did not read these embarrassing articles.

At lunch that day, Bryan sat at the president's right hand, the place of honor. He spent the next three days sightseeing and making good use of his camera. He played with the Hoovers' grandchildren, romped with their dogs, and shopped for souvenirs to take home to his family. He also had several more chats with Mr. Hoover, sitting in the big armchair in his study, feeling completely at home in the President's House.

XIII
★★★

I don't know about you, but I found Bryan Untiedt's story uniquely American—and deeply moving. It could have happened in no other country in the world but the United States of America. I like to think the President's House, where democracy and power so mysteriously blend, had a lot to do with making it possible.

President and Mrs. Theodore Roosevelt with their six rambunctious children (left to right):
Quentin, Theodore Jr., Archibald, Alice, Kermit, and Ethel.
Credit: Library of Congress

10

***

Growing Up Under Glass

There are plenty of perks to being the child of a president. One of my favorites was having my own car and driver. Another was the White House movie theater, where I could request any film I wanted. Also on the list: meeting, and being fussed over by, some of the greatest figures of the twentieth century; having the best seats in the house at the theater, opera, or ballet; traveling by private plane or train; and receiving an incredible number of fabulous gifts.

Was there a trade-off for all these perks? You bet there was. I couldn't go anywhere without a Secret Service agent in tow; I had to learn to say as little as possible when reporters were around; and, most annoying of all, I had to accept the fact that I was public property. Not only did everyone in the world feel entitled to know all the details of my life, but there were any number of people, both in and out of the media, who felt free to comment on my appearance. My nose was "crooked" and ought to be "fixed." I had "heavy" legs. I had no "taste" or "style." My hairdo was "messy." I was "immature." I was too "mature."

And so it went, on and on. A few of the comments gave me a good laugh. I learned to ignore the rest, especially the ones that came from people who would never, under any circumstances, say a good word about Harry S Truman or anyone connected to him.

From reading about, and talking to, other presidential progeny, I realize that although our experiences of living in the White House are similar in many ways, they are also quite different. Anyone who has spent any part of his or her growing up years at 1600 Pennsylvania Avenue has a highly personal set of memories, some good, some not so good, and, for an unfortunate few, some absolutely dreadful.

II
★★★

When John F. Kennedy moved into the White House at the beginning of 1961, America had its dream first family: a young and handsome president, with an even younger and strikingly attractive wife, an adorable three-year-old daughter, and an infant son born on November 25, 1960, less than two weeks after his father's election.

The Kennedy children, Caroline and John Jr., were the youngest occupants of the White House since Grover Cleveland's three children toddled the halls. They quickly became its star attractions. The media were so hungry for news of Caroline that one editor snapped at his Washington correspondent, "Never mind that stuff about Laos. What did Caroline do today?"

Being at an age where she was completely unself-conscious, Caroline provided more than a few newsworthy items. She once wandered into a press conference wearing her nightie and a pair of her mother's high heels. Another time, when a reporter asked where her father was, Caroline said, "He's upstairs with his shoes and socks off doing nothing."

Caroline often crept down the stairs to peer at her parents' dinner guests through the balusters. One evening she waved to some of the musicians in the Marine Band and their conductor responded by playing "Old MacDonald Had a Farm." Caroline was so delighted, she began clapping her hands. Jacqueline Kennedy heard her and invited her to come in and meet some of the guests. Although Caroline's visit was brief, it inspired the band to play several more children's songs, which added a unique touch to the evening and put the guests in a lighthearted (or -headed?) mood.

After that, whenever the Marine Band struck up "Old MacDonald," it was a sign that Caroline was in the vicinity. The tune made people stop and stare just as eagerly as when the musicians played "Hail to the Chief" for her father.

Jacqueline Kennedy set up a nursery school for Caroline and about a dozen other youngsters in the third-floor solarium. The parents shared the cost of hiring a teacher and purchasing blocks, paints, a sandbox, and other school supplies. Jackie also installed a small playground on the south lawn, which the president could see from his office. When he wanted to take a break from work, he would step outside and clap his hands and the children would come running over for a visit.

Not long after the playground was installed, Jackie realized that it was visible from the street. When the tour bus drivers started making it a stop on their schedule, she had a line of rhododendrons planted along the fence to block the view.

Jacqueline Kennedy was so determined to maintain her children's privacy that she requested her husband not to be photographed with them too often. Jack didn't always comply. Knowing how politicians love to get their pictures taken with children, as well as how cute these particular children were, I can understand why.

The Kennedy children were very much at home in the Oval Office. On a private visit to the White House, my father, who has always had a soft spot in his heart for little girls, was surprised and charmed when Caroline popped out from under her father's desk and said, "How are you? You used to live here."

When she met my father's old friend Sam Rayburn, the former Speaker of the House, she studied his bald head and asked, "Why won't hair grow for you?"

Once, during a visit to her father's office, Caroline left one of her toys behind. It was a large "talking" doll that had a tiny tape recorder concealed inside. The machine recorded whatever was said and played it back at the press of a button.

The doll was returned to the nursery later that day and the children's nannie, Maud Shaw, pressed the button to see what Caroline had been saying. Instead of the little girl's voice, Miss Shaw heard John F. Kennedy's unmistakable Boston accent delivering a tirade that included what Miss Shaw described as "a very naughty word."

The nannie tried, without success, to erase the tape. She enlisted the help of one of the children's Secret Servicemen, but he, too, was stymied. The only solution was to remove the tape completely and throw it away. Later that day, when Caroline wanted to play with the doll, she was told that it had temporarily lost its voice. Its laryngitis was miraculously cured after the Secret Service agent went out and bought another tape.

Like many little girls, and a few little boys, Caroline liked to talk on the phone. She was on the line with her father one day chatting about the gifts she was hoping to get for Christmas. In the course of their conversation, she told him how much she wished she could call up Santa Claus and tell him exactly what she wanted.

The president promised to see what he could do. He called the White House switchboard and asked one of the operators to take Caroline's call and pretend she was answering the phone at Santa Claus's workshop at the North Pole. Then the president put in a call to the nursery and told Caroline he had managed to get through to Santa Claus's workshop.

Caroline got on the line. Her face fell when she was told that Santa wasn't home but she brightened up when she discovered that she was talking to Mrs. Santa Claus, who offered to take a message for her husband. Caroline rattled off a long list of toys for herself and John and hung up thoroughly convinced that she had been connected to the North Pole.

In his early months at the White House, young John Kennedy—his mother disliked John-John, the nickname that got pinned on him by the press—spent many hours napping in his carriage on the Truman balcony. He was too young to get into mischief then, but he made up for it when he reached the toddler stage.

John was fascinated by the White House helicopter and loved to take it on family trips to Camp David or Glen Ora, the Kennedys' Virginia estate. He refused to accept the fact that his father sometimes used it for other purposes. John would be all smiles as he watched the helicopter land on the south lawn then burst into tears when his father climbed in and took off without him. Onlookers sometimes thought he was crying because his father was leaving, but it was really because John wasn't getting a ride.

The Truman balcony provided Caroline and John with a perfect vantage point from which to observe the arrival and departure of VIP visitors and the ceremonies to welcome heads of state. One day while the television crews were setting up their equipment to film the arrival of Marshal Josip Broz Tito of Yugoslavia, John dropped one of his toy guns. It fell through the railing on the balcony and landed in the tangle of wires below. A cameraman got a shot of the falling gun and it was later inserted into a newsclip of Tito's speech. One network reported that the gun had landed on Tito's head; another account had it beaning one of the soldiers in the presidential honor guard. Neither story was true, of course, but it made good copy and that's all the reporters cared about.

Caroline and John F. Kennedy, Jr.'s childhood days at 1600 Pennsylvania Avenue ended abruptly when their father was assassinated on November 22, 1963. Plans were already in the works for the children's birthday parties. John's third birthday was on November 25 and Caroline's sixth on November 27. The parties were canceled but the children had a combined celebration about a week later, the only happy event during those sad weeks when their mother was preparing to move out of the White House.

Isn't it ironic that John, who was so entranced with flying as a little boy, died in the summer of 1999 when the private plane he was piloting crashed into the sea off Cape Cod?

III
★★★

Over the years, there have been very few presidents' children as young as Caroline and John F. Kennedy, Jr. Most first offspring have had either one or both feet out of the nest for the simple reason that by the time most men get to the White House, they are fifty-something or more. Dad was a few weeks shy of sixty-one.

Grover Cleveland is the wild card in all this. A forty-seven-year-old bachelor when he was inaugurated for his first term in 1884, he surprised everyone by marrying his twenty-one-year-old ward, Frances Folsom, two years later. The Clevelands' first child, Ruth, was born in New York City, where her parents had moved after her father lost his bid for a second term. He was reelected the following year and returned to the White House on March 4, 1893, precisely four years after he left.

Two-year-old Ruth promptly became the nation's darling. She was so popular that the candy bar, the Baby Ruth, was named in her honor. The Clevelands took their daughter's fame in stride until the day Frances Folsom Cleveland looked out the window and saw a party of tourists on the White House lawn. They had spied Ruth, who had been taken out for some air, and wrested her from her nurse's arms so they could coo over her. On another occasion, a visitor had to be prevented by force from snipping a lock of the child's hair as she was carried through the White House in the arms of her nurse. After that, Ruth was carefully shielded from the public, which prompted rumors that she was either retarded or deformed. Her parents wisely ignored the gossip.

By the time Cleveland's second term ended in 1896, Ruth had two little sisters, Esther and Marion. Esther was the first, and only, child of a president to be born in the White House. Marion arrived while her parents were at their summer home on Cape Cod.

Grover Cleveland had always cherished his privacy and given short shrift to the press. Now that he had three young daughters, he became more determined than ever to keep his family out of the limelight. Somebody wrote a song called "Esther's Lullaby" that was quite popular for a while, and little Marion pressed a button in the White House that signaled the opening of a cotton fair in Atlanta. For the most part, however, the three little girls lived very private lives. Their parents bought a home, Woodley, in a rural section of Washington and the family spent as much time there as possible.

One of the few reports we have on the Cleveland children comes from White House usher Ike Hoover. Of all the presidential offspring he had the privilege of knowing in his forty-two-year tenure, Hoover maintained, "none have been so loved and admired by the White House household as these three little Clevelands."

Having met their mother, I can readily believe it. In June of 1947, I joined my parents in New Jersey to celebrate the two hundredth anniversary of the founding of Princeton University and had the opportunity to chat with a lovely woman in her eighties named Frances Preston. We discovered that we had something in common. She, too, had lived in the White House—as Frances Folsom Cleveland.

After leaving Washington, the Clevelands moved to Princeton where they had two more children, Richard and Francis. Grover Cleveland died in 1908 and in 1913, Mrs. Cleveland married Thomas J. Preston, Jr., a professor of archaeology at Princeton. I was always glad that I went to Princeton that day. Otherwise our paths might never have crossed. Mrs. Preston died the following October.

In 1962, a writer for the *New Yorker* talked to Esther Cleveland Bosanquet about her memories of the White House. She recalled several things: a huge Christmas tree with heaps of toys underneath, the Easter egg rollings on the lawn, and visiting her father in his study in the evenings "I remember very vividly that he once let me dip my fingers in his inkwell and make big blobs on his papers."

Mrs. Bosanquet also remembered sitting alone in the downstairs hall snapping and unsnapping the button on her brown leather gloves while her parents were getting ready to leave the White House.

"Then somebody came along and asked me why I was leaving. 'Because McKinley's coming,' I said, 'and there can't be two presidents.' I don't quite remember saying that, but I'm sure I did, because I remember Papa telling guests about it later."

In 1929, Marion Cleveland Amen was invited to the White House by Lou Henry Hoover. The visit triggered no memories until she visited the family quarters on the second floor. There she was struck by the strong, slightly musty scent of roses. Later, she asked her mother if there was anything unusual about the smell of the second floor. "Yes," Mrs. Preston replied, "that one floor had the smell of an old house by the sea, a musty scent, overlaid with roses."

Although the Clevelands' sons never lived in the White House, they sometimes had trouble convincing people of that fact. At a 1959 luncheon honoring presidential descendants, Richard Cleveland remarked, "It is disconcerting to be told, 'I remember seeing you and your brother playing on the White House lawn,' but one must try to understand the spirit in which it was said."

IV
☆☆☆

It took the public a long time to become curious about presidential children. John Tyler's family of seven was pretty much ignored when he became president after the death of William Henry Harrison in 1841. The two youngest, fourteen-year-old Alice and ten-year-old Tazewell, might have provided a few human interest stories, but if they did anything out of the ordinary, the tales have not survived. I suspect they have been eclipsed, like their sister-in-law Priscilla Cooper Tyler's hard work as stand-in first lady, by Julia Gardiner, the glamorous young New Yorker whom their father married in his last year in the White House.

When his term expired in 1845, John and Julia Tyler returned to his farm, Sherwood Forest, not far from Richmond, Virginia, where—are you ready for this?—they had another seven children. It's enough to make you think John Tyler deserves equal billing with George Washington, who was childless, as the father of his country.

V
★★★

Not until Abraham Lincoln became president in 1860 did the White House have honest-to-goodness kids in residence. The Lincolns' oldest son, Robert, was a dignified Harvard freshman, but his younger brothers, ten-year-old Willie and seven-year-old Tad (whose real name was Thomas), kept things hopping at 1600 Pennsylvania Avenue.

The boys were rarely disciplined, or as Mary Lincoln described it, they were growing up "free, happy and unrestrained by parental tyranny." I suspect this means they were brats, but they did provide some much-needed levity in the Civil War White House.

In the course of exploring their new home, Willie and Tad discovered the bell system that was used for summoning the White House servants. They also figured out how to make all the bells ring at once, which caused chaos when footmen and housemaids rushed to respond, only to discover that no one had called them.

Willie and Tad became friends with the sons of a Washington judge, Horatio Taft, who lived nearby. The boys—Horatio Jr., who was known as Bud; and Halsey, whose nickname was Holly—often visited the White House, and occasionally all four boys could be found wrestling with the president on the parlor floor.

Willie and Tad also organized their own cadet company, which they called Mrs. Lincoln's Zouaves. (The Zouaves were a volunteer regiment organized by a family friend, Oliver Ellsworth. They were named after an infantry unit in the French army, noted for their colorful uniforms.) Willie was the colonel, Bud and Holly were officers, and Tad was the drum major, all decked out in blue-and-red uniforms.

When Willie died of typhoid fever in February 1862, Tad was as downhearted as his parents. His father did everything he could think of to cheer him up, including buying him a pair of goats. The president knew Tad's high spirits had returned when he hitched the goats to an upside-down chair to make a chariot and went tearing through the East Room. The sight startled a group of women visitors and sent the president, who was watching from the hall outside, into a fit of laughter.

Tad's other misdeeds included locking his father in Lafayette Park, accosting White House callers on their way upstairs to see the president and demanding that they make a contribution to the Sanitary Commission that was set up to assist sick and wounded soldiers, and standing in front of the White House waving a Confederate flag while his father was reviewing Union troops.

I wish I could report that Tad developed into a charming and fun-loving adult but he died of pneumonia at the age of eighteen, adding still further to his widowed mother's enormous burden of grief.

VI
☆☆☆

By the time Ulysses S. Grant became president in 1869, the White House and its occupants found themselves in full view of the public eye. This new focus developed in tandem with the growth of the popular press. As more and more women became educated, newspapers and magazines started catering to their interests. Presidential receptions and dinners were written up in detail, with descriptions of the women's gowns often taking up several columns. Articles about the chief executive and his family became a staple in the women's magazines of the era.

The Grants did not object to all this attention. But they tried to keep it under control. At Julia Grant's insistence the White House windows were fitted with shutters so the public could not peer in. She also had the south grounds closed so the children could enjoy the White House backyard without being gawked at by strangers.

There were four children in the Grant family. The oldest, Fred, was at West Point. The second, Ulysses Jr., nicknamed Buck, went off to boarding school not long after his father's election. That left only thirteen-year-old Nellie and ten-year-old Jesse living at the White House full-time.

As the only girl, Nellie was her parents' pet and they could not resist spoiling her. Realizing that she was in need of more discipline than she was getting at home, they decided to send her to Miss Porter's School in Farmington, Connecticut. The president took her there himself lest "Julia cry and bring her back."

Grant had barely returned to the White House when a telegram arrived from Nellie demanding to come home. Her parents urged her to stay longer, assuring her that she would get used to the school, but Nellie was adamant. By Thanksgiving, she was back in Washington, where she spent most of her time going to parties and driving around town in her phaeton, a horse-drawn version of today's convertible.

Jesse gave his parents fewer headaches. He was one of those boys who are always involved in some kind of hobby. He had a microscope and a camera but his favorite instrument was a telescope that was a gift from one of Ulysses S. Grant's admirers. Jesse set it up on the White House roof and he and his father became amateur astronomers, studying the planets and constellations each night until Julia Grant had to send someone up to remind them that it was time for Jesse to go to bed.

Another of Jesse's hobbies was stamp collecting. Once he and one of his cousins, Baine Dent, saved up the astronomical sum of five dollars and sent away to a Boston company for some foreign stamps they had seen advertised in a newspaper. Weeks went by and the stamps never arrived. Finally, Jesse consulted his good friend Kelly, a member of the Washington police force assigned to the White House.

"In my eyes," Jesse wrote later, "Kelly, next to my father, was the greatest man in Washington."

Kelly advised young Jesse to speak to his father about the matter. Jesse did and the president responded by asking him what exactly his son expected him to do about it.

"I thought you might have the secretary of state or the secretary of war, or Kelly, write a letter," Jesse replied.

"A matter of this importance requires consideration," the president told him. "Suppose you come to the cabinet meeting tomorrow and we will take the matter up there."

When the problem was presented to the cabinet members, both the secretary of state, Hamilton Fish, and the secretary of war, William W. Belknap, offered to intervene, but after some discussion it was agreed that a warning from Officer Kelly would carry the most weight.

And so, "the sweat standing out on his forehead, his great fingers gripping the pen," Officer Kelly wrote the following letter on Executive Mansion stationery:

> *I am a Capitol Policeman. I can arrest anybody, anywhere, at any time for anything. I want you to send those stamps to Jesse Grant right at once.*
>
> *Kelly, Capitol policeman.*

Jesse and Baine got their stamps and then some. "As I remember," Jesse recalled, "that five-dollar assortment exceeded our expectations."

VII

★★★

The two presidents who came after Ulysses S. Grant—Rutherford B. Hayes and James A. Garfield—each had five children. The Hayes's three older sons were born before the Civil War and were pretty well grown by the time their father took office, but their two younger children, nine-year-old Frances, better known as Fanny, and six-year-old Scott, were very much in evidence during their father's presidency.

The children were tutored at home in a schoolroom set up in the White House and Scott also attended the private Emerson School. Both children were taught dancing, drawing, swimming, and horseback riding and Fanny took French and music lessons as well.

Fanny spent many hours arranging and rearranging the furniture in the two large dollhouses that stood in an upstairs hallway. One was an elaborate Victorian home that had been given to her mother at a Methodist fair in Baltimore. The other, a Christmas gift from her parents, was built by the White House carpenter.

The Hayeses celebrated their first Thanksgiving in the White House by inviting the secretaries, executive clerks, stenographers, and telegraph operator with their wives and families to dinner. After dinner, the children played blindman's buff in the State Rooms. Another game of blindman's buff was held in the East Room when thirty children, Scott and his guests, celebrated his seventh birthday. The president and three important callers—a general, a governor, and a bishop—took time out from their meeting to watch the fun.

In a letter to one of his other sons, the president reported, "Scott and his bicycle are fast friends." Another means of locomotion was the goat cart that hauled the boy around the White House grounds. There is no record of misdeeds on Scott's part, but that doesn't mean there weren't any. Colonel William H. Crook, the White House paymaster, wrote a memoir in which he described Scott as full of fun and getting into "a good deal of trouble." Unfortunately, he did not provide any details, possibly because they might have incriminated his own son, Harry, who was one of Scott's playmates.

Rutherford and Lucy Hayes often included their children in White House activities. One of Scott's biggest kicks was meeting a delegation of Native Americans who came to plead for their homelands. He was thrilled when the Sioux chief, Red Cloud, patted him on the head and called him a "young brave."

On Memorial Day, Fanny joined her mother and some friends at Arlington National Cemetery to decorate the graves of Civil War soldiers. At Christmas, the children helped their mother distribute gifts to the White House staff, and on Easter Monday they donned their Sunday best and presided over the annual Easter egg roll on the White House lawn.

For many years, this event had been held on Capitol Hill, but in 1878, Congress decided to prohibit public use of the grounds. Unaware of the ban, the children showed up on Easter Monday 1879 and were turned away by the Capitol police. Disappointed and angry, they proceeded down Pennsylvania Avenue to the White House, where President Hayes offered them the use of the south lawn and created a White House custom that endures to this day.

VIII
★★★

James and Lucretia Garfield arrived in the White House in 1881 with four boisterous sons—Harry, seventeen; Jim, fifteen; Irvin, ten; and Abram, eight—and a daughter, Mollie, who was fourteen.

Harry and Jim were studying with a private tutor who was preparing them to enter their father's alma mater, Williams College. Mollie was occupied with piano lessons and giving luncheons for her girlfriends. The two younger boys were also being tutored, but they were less interested in their studies than they were in having a good time.

High-wheeled bicycles were all the rage and each of the younger boys had one. Abram used to invite his friends over for races in the East Room, leaving more than a few gouges in the wainscotting. Irvin, the daredevil of the pair, would start at the top of the Grand Staircase and go barreling through the main hall into the East Room, shouting to anyone in his path to stand clear. It's a miracle no one ended up with a broken leg or fractured skull.

The Garfields moved into the White House in March. About two months later, Lucretia Garfield developed malaria and came close to dying. When she finally rallied, the doctor recommended sea air to hasten her recovery, so on June 18, the entire family set out for Long Branch, New Jersey. The president returned to Washington nine days later, taking Harry and Jim with him. They planned to be back in Long Branch in time to celebrate the Fourth of July.

On the morning of July 2, Garfield awoke in a lighthearted mood. After some roughhousing with his sons—a favorite Garfield pastime—he did a handspring to show them how agile he was. The three of them ate a hearty breakfast and set out in two carriages for the Baltimore & Potomac Railroad Station, five blocks away.

Although the president was unaware of it, a seriously disturbed man named Charles Julius Guiteau had been stalking him for almost a month. Guiteau chose that morning to strike. As Garfield entered the station, the madman pulled out a pistol and shot him in the back.

By the time Harry and Jim's carriage reached the station, their father was lying on the floor in agony. Jim burst into tears and Harry barely managed to control his sobs. The president was brought back to the White House and Lucretia Garfield returned from Long Branch that evening.

Garfield remained bedridden in the sweltering White House for the entire summer while various medical experts tried to locate the bullet. They had no way of knowing it had lodged in his back muscles and his body had manufactured a protective cyst around it. If the doctors had left him alone, he probably would have recovered.

As it was, their constant probing caused an infection that, coupled with weeks of inactivity, led to his death.

It must have been a long, dismal summer for the Garfield children. They spent most of their time in their rooms, venturing downstairs only to take their meals. The White House was no longer the home they had lived in so happily for the past few months. Now it stood dim and silent, the blinds closed against the sun, the furniture shrouded in muslin for the summer. Nurses and doctors seemed to be everywhere and the minister of the Vermont Avenue Christian Church, which the family attended, called every day to offer what consolation he could. The children were allowed to visit their father but it was dismaying to see the man who had always been so active lying helplessly in bed.

From time to time, Garfield would show signs of recovering, but they never lasted more than a few days. In his lucid moments, the president expressed a wish to go outdoors. The doctors finally agreed that he could be moved to a cottage at the Jersey shore. On September 6 he was taken by ambulance to the Baltimore & Potomac Railroad Station and carried onto a special train. He died in Elberon, New Jersey, thirteen days later.

The Garfield children had lived in the White House slightly more than six months, and about half that time had been devoted to their father's death watch. Surely their memories must be among the saddest of all presidential children.

IX
***

Of the many social events that have been held in the White House, the one that took place on March 1, 1891, has to be the most unusual. Fourteen guests assembled in the Blue Room where they were greeted by President Benjamin Harrison with the guest of honor at his side. From there they trooped into the family dining room, where fifteen high chairs were set up around the table. The menu included beaten biscuits in the shape of baby chicks, bouillon, cakes, and ice cream. Flags and flowers decorated the table, the Marine Band supplied music, and a bevy of mothers and nursemaids helped serve the guests. The occasion? The president's grandson's fourth birthday party.

The young man, Benjamin Harrison McKee, was the son of Harrison's daughter, Mary, who lived at the White House with her husband and a younger child, Mary. Harrison's son, Russell, and his wife and their daughter, Marthena, were frequent visitors. What is believed to be the first White House Christmas tree was set up for the president's grandchildren in December 1889.

As the first grandchild and the president's namesake, little Ben was his grandfather's pride and joy. The only time Harrison was known to lose patience with him was the day Ben was toddling around his office and a roll of important documents suddenly disappeared. The president's secretary instituted a frantic search and found Ben sitting quietly behind the draperies using the roll to stir the contents of the office spittoon.

"Baby" McKee became the darling of the press and his activities were reported as if they were earth-shaking news. When Mary McKee took him out on the lawn, she had no hesitation about bringing him over to the fence to shake hands with his adoring public. As White House doorkeeper Tommy Pendel described it, Ben was "one of the principal personages of the White House."

X

The largest and liveliest group of children to live at 1600 Pennsylvania Avenue was Theodore Roosevelt's family of six, which included sixteen-year-old Alice, his daughter by his first marriage to Alice Lee, who died in childbirth, and her half-brothers and sister, Theodore Jr., fourteen; Kermit, twelve; Ethel, nine; Archibald, seven; and Quentin, four.

The older children, Alice and Ted, might have been expected to be more sedate, but they were not above joining their younger siblings in such antics as sliding down staircases on tin trays borrowed from the kitchen, roller-skating in the East Room, or stilt-walking and bicycle riding through the upstairs halls. Quentin, who liked to go speeding through the house in his wagon, once crashed into a full-length portrait of Lucy Webb Hayes, leaving a hole in the canvas. On another occasion, Quentin and Archie livened up an otherwise ordinary afternoon by following the White House lamplighter around the grounds and turning off the lights as he turned them on.

The president could be as rambunctious as his offspring. He would often slip into the nursery before a dinner or reception and find himself engaged in a vigorous pillow fight. More than once the encounter left him so rumpled he had to return to his room to put on a fresh shirt.

With the Roosevelts in residence, White House visitors never knew what to expect. A woman who attended the annual army and navy reception couldn't help noticing that the president kept jiggling his foot as he stood in the receiving line. She later discovered that there were two small boys concealed under a sofa behind him, pulling at his trouser leg.

Another trick was hiding in the center of the circular seats in the East Room, where potted palms were usually displayed. "When the palms were removed," Alice recalled later, "a not-too-large child could crouch in the vacant space and pop out at passersby."

For the most part, the Roosevelts enjoyed their children's antics, but they were quick to enforce discipline when the occasion demanded. Ethel Roosevelt once marched into the executive offices swinging a large stick and demanded that James Smithers, the chief telegrapher and telephone operator, put up the net on the tennis courts for her. When Smithers told her he could not leave his post, she struck him across the shins with the stick, cutting his leg. The telegrapher responded by turning her over his knee and spanking her. As he delivered the final whacks, Smithers looked up and saw the president standing in the doorway. Roosevelt not only made no objection, he seized Ethel by the shoulder and escorted her bodily out of the offices.

The president was similarly stern when he caught Quentin and his friends—they called themselves the White House gang—engaging in serious devilment. One night, when Quentin had a sleepover for the gang, they sneaked downstairs and peppered a portrait of President Andrew Jackson with spitballs. They finished the job by climbing on chairs and arranging the soggy lumps in designs— three across his forehead, one on each of his coat buttons, blobs on both ears, and another blob on the tip of his nose.

The boys scampered back upstairs and were just drifting off to sleep when the president flung open the door, dragged Quentin from beneath the covers, and whisked him out of the room. The next morning, the gang learned that Q, as they called him, had been forced to remove the spitballs under his father's watchful eye. Nor did the rest of the gang escape. They were all summoned to the president's office for a stern lecture on respecting public property.

With the exception of Alice, all the Roosevelt children attended public grammar schools before going off to private secondary schools. During their White House years, Archie and Quentin attended the Force School on Massachusetts Avenue. They traveled back and forth on their own, either walking, roller-skating, or riding their ponies. (Back then, security for first families was much less stringent, which is enough to make some of us later White House residents wildly jealous.) On the way home, they usually stopped at the local firehouse for a few slides down the pole.

As his siblings went off to boarding school one by one, Quentin and his gang all but took over the White House. They spent hours exploring the mansion from attic to basement and once disrupted the Departments of War and Navy, in their adjacent building, by using mirrors to flash sunbeams into their office windows, almost blinding the staff.

Another project was collecting old watch crystals to use as monocles in imitation of some the diplomats who came calling at the White House. One day, an Italian diplomat was having tea with Edith Roosevelt in an upstairs sitting room when he looked up and saw four gang members, each with a monocle in his eye, peering down through a skylight and gibbering away in a not very good imitation of his language. The diplomat was so surprised that he dropped his own monocle into his teacup. As you can imagine, the boys loved it. They dissolved into peals of laughter, and the visitor not only joined in but turned to his hostess and said, "Mrs. Roosevelt, I beg of you to command those monkeys to come to tea, with those things in their eyes."

One spring the gang encountered two plumbers working on the fountain on the south lawn and started pestering them with questions about what they were doing. The men quickly tired of the cross-examination and shooed the boys away. Whereupon Quentin led them to a large iron door sunk into the ground behind a clump of evergreens. The boys managed to open the door and turn the key in the massive valve that controlled the flow of water to the fountain. A few minutes later, streams of water came gushing out of the pipes on which the men were sitting. One man was lifted straight off his perch; his coworker slid backward into the empty pool. They both lay sprawled on the bottom while the water from the fountain rose in a graceful arc and thoroughly doused them. The gang members beat a swift retreat and avoided the south lawn for the next couple of weeks.

Perhaps the gang's worst crime was rolling a giant snowball off the roof of the North Portico. It hit one of the White House policeman squarely on the head and knocked him out. The president, who was just stepping into his carriage, saw the prank and although he tried to control himself, he couldn't resist laughing. Fortunately, only the policeman's dignity was injured, but the gang got yet another presidential lecture along with orders to apologize.

Roosevelt's lectures usually persuaded his children to behave themselves, at least temporarily. The one exception was Alice, who defied her father's attempts at discipline and seemed to delight in finding ways to annoy him. He disapproved of women smoking and forbade her to do it under his roof. Alice made her way up the White House staircases and smoked *on* the roof. To liven up a particularly dull social event, she once pulled out a cap pistol and started shooting at the startled guests.

As Roosevelt famously said to his old friend, author Owen Wister, "I can do one of two things. I can be president of the United States or I can control Alice. I cannot possibly do both."

XI

★★★

Calvin Coolidge was sworn in as president of the United States after the sudden death of Warren G. Harding in the early morning hours of August 3, 1923. The new president's sons, John, almost seventeen, and Calvin Jr., fifteen, were not at home that summer and the laconic Coolidge let them find out on their own that they would be moving into the White House.

Reporters quickly tracked down John, who was enrolled in a military training program at Fort Devens, Massachusetts, and demanded to know how he felt about his father becoming president. "Just as I did when he was governor of Massachusetts," said John coolly.

Calvin Jr. had a summer job harvesting tobacco for which he was paid $3.50 a day. When one of his coworkers heard the news, he remarked that if his father were president, he wouldn't be harvesting tobacco. Calvin responded, "If my father were your father, you would."

The following summer, John, who had just graduated from Mercersburg Academy in Mercersburg, Pennsylvania, was back at Fort Devens, while Calvin Jr., who was on vacation from Mercersburg, remained at home. The 1924 Republican convention met in June and nominated Coolidge to run for president in his own right and he was spending the summer in the White House preparing for the campaign.

Calvin Jr. did not expect to be bored. He had plenty of friends to keep him company. The south lawn was large enough for a game of baseball and there was a tennis court where he and his friends could play. One day toward the end of June, young Calvin was playing tennis without any socks on. With his bare feet rubbing directly against his tennis shoes, he soon developed a blister on his right toe. He paid no attention to it until it started to hurt. When he mentioned the pain to his parents, they sent him to the White House doctor who saw that the blister had become infected and ordered the young man to bed.

By the Fourth of July, the infection had turned into blood poisoning. Calvin's temperature rose and he drifted in and out of consciousness. By July 6 the doctors were holding out little hope. On the slim chance that surgery might help, he was taken by ambulance to Walter Reed Hospital, where, in his feverish state, he tossed and turned and seemed to have the impression he was leading a charge of troops into battle. Suddenly he murmured "We surrender" and fell into a coma. He died the following evening.

Some weeks later a newsman who had known Coolidge when he was active in Massachusetts politics called at the White House to express his sympathy. "I am sorry," he said. "Calvin was a good boy."

Coolidge swiveled around in his chair and stared out the windows of the Oval Office for several minutes. "You know," he finally responded, "I sit here thinking of it, and I just can't believe it has happened." The president was in tears as he repeated the last sentence. "I just can't believe it has happened."

Later, writing in his autobiography about the loss of his son, Coolidge said, "When he went, the power and the glory of the Presidency went with him."

Calvin Coolidge won the 1924 election with fifty-four percent of the popular vote and was inaugurated on March 4, 1925. In typical Coolidge style, he forbade his older son, now a freshman at Amherst, to take more than a single day off for the ceremony. John arrived from Massachusetts early that morning and departed at seven o'clock that night.

On the train to Washington, however, he met Florence Trumbull, the daughter of Governor Robert H. Trumbull of Connecticut and a student at Mount Holyoke College, only a short distance from Amherst. They saw each other at least once a week when school was in session and wrote to each other when it wasn't.

Being an attractive and personable young man as well as a semi-celebrity, John received fan mail from dozens of young women. Some of their letters were amusing and John would occasionally answer one with a humorous note. One day, the president asked Ira Smith, who was in charge of the White House mail room, if John received much mail. When Smith told him there were usually a few letters addressed to John, Coolidge ordered him to direct them to him instead of to his son.

The next day, John stopped by Ira Smith's office and in the course of a casual conversation, inquired whether his father had issued any special orders about his mail. When Smith told him what had happened, John said, "Well, it doesn't matter except for one thing. You see, there's one that's different. I don't mind Dad getting the others, but this one . . . you know what I mean?"

Smith nodded.

"She's an old friend, and not like the crazy ones that just write in without knowing me. I wondered if maybe . . ."

Smith told him that he would like to be helpful but he had been given a direct order by the president. Perhaps John ought to talk to his father.

One look at John's face showed how little that idea appealed to him. "Of course, you know how we do things around here," Smith told him. "I sort out your letters each morning and put them in a

pile right there on the corner of my desk. Then I sort the other letters. Sometimes I have to go out of the room for some reason or
other. Then later, I send the letters over to your father."

John smiled and departed. The next morning, Smith sorted out
his letters, including one with Florence Trumbull's familiar hand-
writing, and left them in the usual place. Smith kept his eye on the
door and when he saw John approaching, he got up and left. When
he returned, both the letter and John were gone.

Ira Smith did a masterful job as Cupid's assistant in the White
House mail room. John Coolidge and Florence Trumbull were
married in the fall of 1929.

XII
✫✫✫

Chelsea Clinton was the second young woman in history to be the
only child of the president of the United States. I was the first. In
some ways, our experiences are not really comparable. I was twenty-
one when we moved to the White House, Chelsea was only twelve.
But there are a few parallels.

With no siblings to share the limelight, we both came in for an
inordinate amount of attention—good and bad. My parents made
sure I didn't let being a first daughter throw me, and from everything I've seen and heard, Bill and Hillary Clinton were just as careful not to let Chelsea get carried away by it either.

In spite of the myriad problems with which the Clintons had
to cope—scandals, investigations, impeachment—Chelsea's needs
were not neglected. Not only did she get through eight years in the
White House with a reasonable amount of privacy, she seems to
have had a very good time.

When my husband and I stayed overnight at 1600 Pennsylvania
Avenue in 1993, we had an opportunity to visit with Chelsea. She
had already settled in at Sidwell-Friends, the private school she attended in Washington, and was taking classes at the Washington

School of Ballet. She appeared to be seriously interested in dance and enjoyed hearing about the former prima ballerina of Britain's Royal Ballet, Dame Margot Fonteyn, who was an old friend of ours.

Chelsea had pizza parties in the State Dining Room and sleepovers on the third floor of the White House with her classmates. When she graduated, Bill Clinton was the speaker, joining two other presidents—Lyndon Johnson and Theodore Roosevelt—who delivered commencement addresses at their daughters' schools. Knowing her father's tendency to be long-winded, Chelsea warned him in advance to be brief.

As a student at Stanford University, Chelsea blended in with the crowd, and except for the Secret Service agents who were never far away, no one would have known that she was anything but an average kid.

Jenna and Barbara Bush, the latest presidential daughters to occupy the White House, are also the first set of twins. That's had the media panting for stories, but so far the Bushes have followed the policy the Clintons adopted with Chelsea: No comments, period. The Bushes' friends have been equally tight-lipped. "A really good friend is loyal," Laura Bush has said. "My friends are very loyal."

Not so loyal or even friendly have been the bar owners who turned in the girls for underage drinking in the spring of 2001. This reportedly led to a stern parental lecture at Camp David. Fortunately, First Lady Laura Bush is philosophic about such problems. She does not expect perfection from her daughters or anyone else. I am sure the twins learned a lesson about life under glass that made their parents' lecture almost superfluous.

The Bush daughters are both in college, just as I was when my father became president. Back then, the reporters were all over Dad's press secretary, Charlie Ross, begging him to let them interview me. Even if I had wanted to hold a press conference (which I didn't) and even if my parents would have let me (which they wouldn't), I didn't have anything to say.

Charlie, smart, wonderful man that he was, was as anxious as my parents were to protect my privacy, but having been a newspaper-man himself, he knew he couldn't hold the reporters at bay indefi-nitely, so he came up with a clever solution.

"We'll let them follow you around for one whole day," he said, "and they'll soon realize that there isn't anything to write about."

Charlie, as usual, was right. After clearing the matter with the university administration, he told the reporters they could follow me around the campus of George Washington University for a day and see how I spent my time.

If any of those journalists thought they were going to come away with a great story, they must have been pretty disappointed. They spent most of the day shuttling from one classroom to another and sitting through courses in history and government. It quickly dawned on them that I was leading a life that was much like that of any other college student and, as Charlie had foreseen, they decided to leave me alone—at least until I graduated and did something newsworthy on my own.

XIII
★★★

When I chatted with Chelsea Clinton during our visit to the White House, one of the key questions she asked me was "Did you enjoy living here?"

My answer was an unqualified yes. Living in the White House is a unique privilege, and for anyone who is as interested in American history as I am, it provides unbeatable insights into the workings of the government and the day-to-day lives of the men and women who shaped this country.

The biggest lesson I learned from the experience is that the White House is not the real world, and when you walk out the door and the next president and his family walk in, it's all over. No more household staff ready to press a skirt or sew on a button in an emer-gency, no more unending supplies of chocolate ice cream—my favorite—in the freezer, no more special treatment everywhere you go.

Unless you've learned to put the experience in perspective, it can be a terrible letdown. I have to confess that after a year or two in my role as first daughter, I got a little full of myself, which was against the rules in the Truman household. My father saw what was happening and after I had spent a weekend in Washington—by this time, I was living in New York—he sat down and wrote me a letter. The gist of his message was not to get carried away by the White House aura. "Keep your balance," he said. "Do not let the glamour get you."

If I were the advice-giving type, I'd pass that along to every young person who faces the challenge of living in the White House.

FRANK LESLIE'S ILLUSTRATED NEWSPAPER

Entered according to the Act of Congress, in the year 1871, by FRANK LESLIE, in the office of the Librarian of Congress, at Washington.

No. 975—VOL. XXXVIII.]   NEW YORK, JUNE 6, 1874.   [PRICE, 10 CENTS, $4 00 YEARLY, $1 WELLS, $2 00

THE WEDDING AT THE WHITE HOUSE

THE CEREMONY IN THE EAST ROOM—REV. DR. TIFFANY DECLARING MR. A. C. F. SARTORIS AND MISS NELLIE GRANT HUSBAND AND WIFE.
SKETCHED BY OUR SPECIAL ARTIST, MR. HARRY OGDEN, WHO WAS PRESENT.—SEE PAGE 199.

Nellie Grant was not the first White House bride, but her wedding was the first to attract public attention. Every detail was reported in the press. Credit: Library of Congress

11
✵ ✵ ✵

Here Come the Brides

During the seven and two-thirds years Dad was in the White House, there was never any shortage of news. Just for openers, we had the dropping of the atomic bomb, the end of World War II, the adoption of the Marshall Plan, and the beginning of the Korean War. But in the midst of all this, the media was always on the lookout for the really big story: When was I going to get married?

I'm afraid I disappointed them. I didn't get married until 1956—four years after Dad left office. It was another ten years before the reporters finally got the story of their dreams: a White House wedding. But perhaps to make up for the long wait, they got a doubleheader: Luci Johnson's in 1965 and her sister Lynda Bird's two years later.

The Johnsons weren't the first pair of presidential daughters to get married during their father's administration. Two of Woodrow Wilson's three daughters did the same thing. There have been other White House brides as well, but the wedding that occupies a truly unique place in the annals of 1600 Pennsylvania Avenue took place on June 2, 1886. The bride was a twenty-one-year-old beauty from upstate New York named Frances Folsom and the groom was none other than the president himself—corpulent, crotchety, forty-nine-year-old Grover Cleveland, a lifelong bachelor who supposedly worked so hard he didn't have time for a wife.

II
✯✯✯

Grover Cleveland had known Frances Folsom—her family and friends called her Frank—all her life. Her father, Oscar Folsom, had been Cleveland's partner in his Buffalo, New York, law office. When Oscar was killed in a carriage accident in 1875, Cleveland became Frank's legal guardian. She was eleven years old at the time.

It is not clear when he started thinking about a change in their relationship, but by the time Frances was a student at Wells College in Aurora, New York, Cleveland was regularly sending her flowers. After he became president in 1884, the flowers came from the White House conservatory.

Frances graduated from Wells in 1885 and embarked with her mother and her cousin Benjamin Folsom on a tour of Europe. She had already agreed to marry Cleveland. He proposed one night when they were walking together in the East Room during a visit she paid to the White House as the guest of his sister, Rose.

Sometime between that conversation and the time Frances sailed for Europe, the wedding date was set and they agreed to be married at the White House. As I mentioned earlier, Frances decided it was the only place they could be sure of having some privacy.

Shortly before the Folsoms were scheduled to return to the United States, rumors of the president's secret engagement began circulating, but because of the difference in the couple's ages, it was assumed that he was engaged not to Frances, but to her widowed mother.

Toward the end of May, the Folsoms' ship docked in New York. A crowd of reporters was on hand to interview the bride-to-be but there was no sign of her. The president's secretary, Daniel Lamont, had arranged to meet the ship in the harbor, take the Folsoms aboard a government revenue cutter, and whisk them off to their hotel.

By this time the identity of the bride was no longer a mystery. Cleveland had sent handwritten notes to slightly more than two dozen friends with the following message:

> *I am to be married on Wednesday evening at seven o'clock at the White House to Miss Folsom. It will be a very quiet affair and I will be extremely gratified at your attendance on the occasion.*

The bride arrived in Washington by overnight train on the morning of June 2. There was a breakfast with some family members and old friends and a meeting with the Reverend Dr. Byron Sunderland, the Presbyterian clergyman who was to perform the ceremony. Other than that, the hard-working president spent most of the day in his office.

Meanwhile, the press was using every imaginable form of pressure to be allowed to cover the proceedings, and a small army of would-be gate crashers were racking their brains for ways to get past the guards. One enterprising fellow offered band leader John Philip Sousa fifty dollars to let him don a uniform and pose as a triangle player in the Marine Band.

Frances wore a gown of ivory satin, heavy enough to stand up on its own, with a fifteen-foot train. Her veil was equally long and was held in place by a crown of myrtle and orange blossoms. Aside from the elaborate gown, it was a very simple wedding. The ceremony was held in the Blue Room, which was decorated with flowers and greenery, and the date was spelled out along the mantel in light-colored flowers set against a bank of dark purple pansies.

The president entered the room with his bride on his arm. The twenty-eight guests stood in a semicircle during the brief ceremony while outside cannon boomed in an official salute. Church bells rang out all over Washington and in many other cities as well.

Afterward the guests adjourned to the State Dining Room, which was decorated with more flowers. On the table, floating on a huge mirror was the good ship *Hymen* fashioned out of pansies and roses and decked with flags and the initials C-F. The wedding cake, which had the same initials in the center, was prepared by a fashionable New York caterer, John Pinard, and brought to Washington by overnight train. Pinard came with it and put its four layers together in the White House kitchen.

Shortly after nine o'clock the newlyweds appeared in their traveling clothes. A carriage was waiting for them at the South Portico and they drove off amid a shower of rice to board a private railroad car for a honeymoon at a resort in Deer Park, Maryland.

Frances and Grover Cleveland not only enjoyed an extremely happy marriage, but Frances turned out to be the most popular first lady since Dolley Madison. Having had the pleasure of meeting her sixty-one years later, I can understand why.

III
☆☆☆

Alice Roosevelt Longworth was one of my favorite Washingtonians. She had a sharp eye and an even sharper wit plus a gift for being delightfully outrageous. I always liked the inscription on the pillow she kept on her living room sofa: "If you haven't got anything nice to say about anybody, come sit next to me."

"The other Washington Monument," as Alice was sometimes called, was a commanding figure on the D.C. social scene long before the Trumans got to Washington and long after we left. She died in 1980 at the age of ninety-six, almost seventy-eight years after she swooped into the public eye by becoming the first presidential daughter to make her debut in the White House.

In those days, "coming out" was a signal, not unlike the sound of the starter's pistol in a race. If you didn't get married within the next two or three years, you were counted among the losers. So, of course, Alice's debut immediately started a wave of speculation about when, where, and, above all, whom she would marry.

Alice tantalized the gossipmongers for three years before she finally said yes to Congressman Nicholas Longworth of Cincinnati, Ohio, who was fifteen years her senior. Their engagement was announced in December 1905 and the wedding was to take place in the White House on February 17, 1906.

The always imperious "Princess Alice" had quite a bit to say about the arrangements, but her chief interest was in the gifts. As one White House aide remarked, she would accept anything but a red-hot stove "and will take that if it does not take too long to cool."

No red-hot stoves appeared, but the collection did include a packet of pins from an old lady, plus mousetraps, bales of hay, feather dusters, and a hogshead of popcorn—all sent by the companies that sold them in hopes of gaining some publicity for their products. To make up for what Alice called the "freak presents," there was a gold snuff box from King Edward VII of England with his miniature set in diamonds on the lid, a Gobelin tapestry from the French government, a $25,000 string of pearls from the people of Cuba, a diamond bracelet from Kaiser Wilhelm of Germany, and some bolts of brocade and silk from the dowager empress of China that provided Alice with evening wear for the next few decades.

A couple of days before the wedding, ten Ponca Indians from Oklahoma, in full ceremonial dress, arrived at the Capitol bearing a buffalo skin vest for Congressman Longworth. Their leader, Horse Chief, reportedly told the doorkeeper that he and his braves "were saddened by the news that came from the home of the Great White Father. In all the talks that reached us about the many presents for the young wife, there was no word of even a blanket for the young sachem. Can a man be boss of his own wigwam if all the ponies, the beads, the buffalo hides belong to his wife?"

Reluctant to deal with the issue, Nick Longworth hid in a cloakroom while Horse Chief and his braves did an about-face and marched down Pennsylvania Avenue to present their gift at the White House.

The wedding took place at noon. Although sketches of the event show the bride marching down the Grand Staircase on her father's arm, according to Alice they actually took the elevator down to the State Dining Room and walked through the main hall to the East Room. A platform had been set up in front of the wide center window along the east wall. On either side of the platform were two large Satsuma vases filled with Easter lilies. The rest of the room was decorated with banks of white and pink azaleas, American Beauty roses, and white rhododendrons.

The bride dispensed with attendants. Rumor had it that she didn't want to share the spotlight, but Alice said later that most of her friends were either married or pregnant at the time. In those days, married women were not asked to be bridesmaids and pregnant ones didn't go out in public. Alice's second cousin, Eleanor Roosevelt, happened to be pregnant with her first child and her husband, Franklin, attended the wedding on his own. According to Alice, he did a superb job of arranging her train when it was time for the photographs to be taken.

Alice walked down an aisle cordoned off by white satin ribbons and lined with eight ushers and twelve military aides, including Lieutenant Ulysses S. Grant III, grandson of the former president, and future five-star general Douglas MacArthur. Her gown of heavy white satin had diamonds on the yoke and was trimmed with rose-point lace from her mother's and grandmother's wedding dresses. She carried a bouquet of white orchids.

The ceremony was performed by the Episcopal bishop of Washington and the guests included Roosevelt family members and personal friends, ambassadors, cabinet members, senators, Supreme Court justices, and the president's favorite hunting guide wearing a frock coat and top hat for the first time in his life. When it was over, the guests adjourned to the State Dining Room, where they feasted on fresh fruits, salads, pâtés, sandwiches, ice cream, champagne, claret punch, and lemonade. There were several wedding cakes including one that was two and a half feet high and topped with a statue of Cupid ringing a silver wedding bell. Alice, who rarely did anything the usual way, cut it with a sword borrowed from Major Charles McCawley of the U.S. Marine Corps, one of the White House military aides.

By four that afternoon a large crowd had gathered outside the White House, hoping to catch a glimpse of the newlyweds as they left on their honeymoon. It was not clear which gate they would use and the crowd kept moving from one to another each time they caught sight of a waiting car. Eventually there were four different cars parked at various points on the White House grounds. While the crowd was trying to decide which one to keep their eyes on, Nick and Alice went into the Red Room, opened a window, stepped onto the South Portico, and scurried down the steps. They jumped into the car that belonged to millionaire John R. McLean, owner of the *Cincinnati Enquirer* and the *Washington Post.* The couple sped off to McLean's country estate, "Friendship," where they stayed for a few days before sailing to Cuba.

Hardly anyone in the crowd saw Alice in her going-away outfit, a plumed hat and a dress she later described as "depressingly, muddy-colored." Among those who missed the departure was a movie photographer who had been ordered by his boss to come back with some footage or else. Rather than risk the "or else," the man hired a car and enlisted a look-alike couple to reenact the scene. With the jerky, blurry film of the day, nobody knew the difference.

IV
★★★

Among the guests at Alice Roosevelt Longworth's wedding was fifty-year-old Ellen Wrenshall Grant Sartoris, better known as

Nellie, who had enjoyed an equally glittering White House wedding thirty-two years earlier.

Nellie was fifteen when her father was elected president. She was beautiful, headstrong, and alarmingly precocious. Instead of tying back her hair with a ribbon like most girls her age, she wore it in an elaborate Grecian twist. Her wardrobe was equally high style and she regularly appeared at late-night parties and dances that were frequented by an older crowd.

Nellie was determined to enjoy every bit of the attention she got from being the president's only daughter. A few years after she resisted her parents' attempt to get her out of the Washington whirl by sending her to boarding school, the Grants decided a vacation from the limelight was in order. In the summer of 1873, some old friends—a Mr. and Mrs. Borie—were planning a tour of Europe with their children, and at her parents' suggestion Nellie was invited to join them.

If the Grants had hoped the trip would get their darling out of the public eye, they could not have been more wrong. Nellie was treated like a princess everywhere she went. She was entertained by American ambassadors and ministers, and in England she was presented to Queen Victoria at Buckingham Palace, which gave her a chance to wear the one evening dress her mother had allowed her to pack, although it's hard to believe she didn't pick up a few more when they stopped in Paris. I know I would have.

Nellie's European tour turned out to be one long round of party-going—just what her parents had been hoping to get her away from. To top if off, on the return voyage, she met, and fell madly in love with, a young diplomat named Algernon Sartoris, who had just been posted to the British legation in Washington. Sartoris was rich, good-looking, well-educated, and the nephew of the famous actress Fanny Kemble.

In spite of these recommendations, the Grants were less than thrilled with the match. They would have preferred that Nellie marry an American. Moreover, she was only seventeen, and she and

Algernon had not known each other long enough to be sure they were making the right choice.

As usual Nellie got her way, although her parents achieved a victory of sorts by making the couple agree to wait a year before announcing their engagement. When the year was up, early in 1874, the announcement was made and preparations for what was later called "one of the most brilliant weddings ever given in the United States" got under way.

The date was set for Thursday, May 21, and the guest list was said to be small. Only 250 invitations were sent out. But the first order of business was selecting a wedding dress. Nellie and her mother went to New York by private railroad car to meet with the best dressmakers and chose a dress that was variously reported to have cost $1,500, $2,000, and $4,000. The expedition also resulted in the purchase of a trousseau that included dresses, shoes, hats, and accessories for every imaginable occasion.

Meanwhile, the wedding gifts came pouring in—silver punchbowls; tea and coffee services; gold knives, forks, and spoons; jewelry; rare laces; and silk fans. The most unusual gift was a poem, "A Kiss to the Bride," by Walt Whitman; the most touching, a silver fruit dish from Tiffany's, given to Nellie by the White House staff because of "the sweetness and amiability of her disposition."

The wedding was held in the East Room, which had been redecorated the previous summer. The new decor was in the heavily ornamented "steamboat palace" style of the era—gold-framed mirrors, massive gas chandeliers, a profusion of gilt on the mantels and ceiling, and carpeting in a pattern that can charitably be described as busy. It was dreadfully overdone but at the time was considered the height of good taste.

The White House steward, Valentino Melah, was in charge of the wedding arrangements. The East Room, and indeed the entire White House, overflowed with flowers. The platform in front of the great window where the ceremony was to take place was banked with roses and lilies. Above it a large wedding bell, made out of white flowers and tea rosebuds, was suspended from the ceiling by a rope of flowers. The bell was flanked by a pair of green wreaths, one with Nellie's initials and the other with Algernon's.

At eleven A.M. the Marine Band struck up the wedding march and the bridal party came down the Grand Staircase. Algernon and his best man, Nellie's brother Fred, led the way. Behind them came Julia Grant escorted by her younger sons, Buck and Ulysses, and Nellie's bridesmaids—eight young women in identical white satin dresses with filmy overskirts and wide sashes that cascaded down into trains.

The bridesmaids formed a semicircle in front of the dais, Algernon and Fred stood to the left of the Reverend Otis H. Tiffany, the pastor of Washington's Metropolitan Methodist Episcopal Church, who was to perform the ceremony. With everyone in place and the guests agog, Nellie and her father, who had been waiting in the Blue Room, finally appeared.

She wore a gown of white satin trimmed with Brussels point lace, and a white tulle veil held in place with a crown of orange blossoms and white orchids intertwined with green leaves. Her bouquet of tuberoses and orange blossoms had a cluster of pink rosebuds in the center along with a tiny flag with "Love" printed on it.

The ceremony was brief, and when it was over the bridal party formed a receiving line in front of the dais. Then everyone adjourned to the State Dining Room for a wedding breakfast that one guest described as being "as elaborate as money and thought could make it." The menu included lamb cutlets, woodcock and snipe on toast, broiled chicken, aspic of beef tongue, Maryland softshell crabs, strawberries and cream, ices, chocolate pudding, and chilled fruit. The pièce de résistance, of course, was the multi-tiered wedding cake, which stood in the center of the table with ropes of roses and white orchids extending across the tablecloth.

Interestingly, despite the spring sunshine outside, the curtains and shades in both the East Room and the State Dining Room were drawn. The only light came from the gas chandeliers overhead and the hundreds of candles that Valentino Melah had placed on the table and sideboards in the dining room.

As a souvenir of the occasion, each guest was given a copy of the menu printed in gold on white satin. The ladies also received tiny white boxes tied with a satin ribbon. Inside was a small piece of the wedding cake to eat or save, or for the single women to put under their pillows and dream of their future husbands.

Unlike Alice and Nick Longworth, Nellie and Algernon Sartoris made no secret of their departure. Mobs of well-wishers lined the streets as they drove to the railroad station. The bells of the Metropolitan Church serenaded them with Mendelssohn's "Wedding March," "God Save the Queen," and "Hail Columbia."

The couple took a Pullman palace car to New York, where Nellie's family joined them the next day. There was a second and somewhat sadder farewell as they sailed off to their new home in England.

I wish I could report that Nellie and Algernon lived happily ever after. Unfortunately, their marriage did not go well. Algernon developed a serious drinking problem and Nellie left him to return to the United States with their four children. Algernon died of pneumonia in 1893 at the age of forty-two. Eighteen years later, Nellie married one of her childhood sweethearts, but a few months after the wedding she became seriously ill and remained an invalid until her death in 1922.

V

Nellie Grant's was the first White House wedding to become a national sensation, but she was by no means the first presidential daughter to be married at the executive mansion. On March 9, 1820, President James Monroe's younger daughter, seventeen-year-old Maria Hester, married her first cousin and her father's secretary, twenty-one-year-old Samuel Lawrence Gouverneur.

The ceremony, which took place in the Blue Room, was a quiet affair. Maria Hester may have preferred a splashier wedding but she had little hope of getting one. Her mother, Elizabeth Monroe, had lived in France and England when her husband was ambassador to those countries, and she found Washington hopelessly provincial. She had no use for anyone who lived there and she made it clear that she would have as little as possible to do with them.

Elizabeth had further offended Washington society by having her older daughter, Eliza, take over most of her social responsibilities. No one should have been surprised when the two women announced that Maria Hester's wedding would be in the "New York style," by which they meant ultra-exclusive. The only people invited were family members and a few close friends. The Washington social set was infuriated and one can only imagine what scenes ensued behind closed doors on the second floor. In any event, Elizabeth Monroe relented to some extent and allowed the newlyweds to have a festive reception in the East Room when they returned from their honeymoon.

Twenty-two years later, John and Letitia Tyler's third daughter, Elizabeth, got married at the White House. The groom was William Nevison Waller, a fellow Virginian, and the ceremony took place in the East Room. The wedding was larger and more elaborate than Maria Hester Monroe's, but it was far from the lavish affairs later White House brides enjoyed.

For one thing, Lizzie's mother was gravely ill. The wedding was her first appearance at a public gathering since she moved to Washington. In addition, the East Room, along with the rest of the White House, had become dreadfully shabby. President Tyler's battles with Congress had resulted in a cutoff in appropriations for its upkeep.

The shabbiness did not deter the bride's sister-in-law, Priscilla Cooper Tyler, who was in charge of the arrangements, from pronouncing it a "grand wedding." Lizzie looked "lovely in her wedding dress and long lace veil, her face literally covered with blushes and dimples," Priscilla reported.

Lizzie Tyler's wedding may have marked the beginning of the bonds that continue to exist among White House brides. A previous bride, Maria Monroe Gouverneur, obviously reminded of her own nuptials, sent a poem entitled "To Miss Tyler on Her Wedding Day." Here is one of the verses:

> *To be a blest and happy wife*
> *Is what all women wish to prove;*
> *And may you know through all your life*
> *The dear delights of wedded love.*

VI
✶✶✶

I used to think my father was overprotective until I read about Woodrow Wilson. When Wilson and his first wife, Ellen, moved into the White House in 1913, his three daughters—Margaret, twenty-six; Jessie, twenty-five; and Eleanor, or Nellie, twenty-three—were all living at home. I have no problem with that. In those days most young women lived with their parents until they got married. But the president was so fond of being surrounded by his family that he would have been quite content if they never set up homes of their own.

His possessiveness reached the point where every time one of his daughters showed more than a passing interest in a young man, he would remark to his wife, "What on earth does she see in that fool?"

Before his election to the presidency in 1912, Wilson had been governor of New Jersey. The family lived in Princeton and Jessie, the middle daughter, an angelic-looking blond who had graduated Phi Beta Kappa from Goucher College in Baltimore, worked at a settlement house in Philadelphia during the week and returned to Princeton on weekends.

One weekend, a friend of the Wilsons, a somewhat eccentric sculptor, painter, and poet named Blanche Nevin, invited Jessie and Nellie to her country home in Pennsylvania. She also invited her nephew, Francis Bowes Sayre, a recent graduate of Harvard Law School, with an eye to promoting a romance between him and Jessie.

Blanche's matchmaking talents proved to be excellent. Frank and Jessie fell in love at first sight and before long Frank proposed. Since Jessie's father was in the final days of his campaign for the presidency, they agreed not to say anything until after the election.

Jessie's mother, Ellen Wilson, was pretty sure what was going on, but her husband was so preoccupied with the campaign that he didn't have a clue. As he was leaving home one day, he met a young man walking up the steps. The two men smiled and nodded and Wilson later asked his wife who "that nice-looking sandy-haired boy" might be.

"That's Frank Sayre," she replied. "And I think you're going to be his father-in-law."

It took a few weeks for Woodrow Wilson to get used to the idea of losing one of his daughters, but he finally conceded that he was growing to love his prospective son-in-law and that Frank was "almost good enough for Jessie."

By a happy coincidence, Sayre looked somewhat like Wilson, which was a big help in continuing his courtship after the Wilsons moved to the White House. When the reporters were on the prowl, he could easily pass himself off as a cousin, although just to be on the safe side, he did not attend the president's inauguration in March of 1913.

Frank and Jessie's engagement was announced the following July and it was agreed that the wedding would take place at the White House on Tuesday, November 25. (The couple insisted on a Tuesday because that was the day Jessie said yes.) Mrs. Wilson made the announcement through her social secretary, Belle—short for

Isabella—Hagner, who had been an arbiter of White House etiquette since the days of Edith Roosevelt.

Jessie's would be the first White House wedding since Alice Roosevelt Longworth's, so Mrs. Hagner consulted the bulging scrapbooks where information about social events in the Executive Mansion was stored. She also contacted former Major, now Colonel, Charles McCawley, a military aide during the Roosevelt administration, who had kept his notes on the arrangements for Alice's wedding.

Once again, the press and the public were denied details of the event, which, of course, drove them wild. The couple's personal Cupid, Blanche Nevin, wrote a poem in honor of their engagement and distributed it to the newspapers, but her verse wasn't the front-page story the press had in mind.

Since the wedding was a private affair, President Wilson let it be known that presents were not to be sent by anyone who wasn't a personal friend of the couple. Theodore Roosevelt had made the same announcement, to no avail. Jessie was inundated with gifts. In addition to the usual collection of "freak presents" as Alice Roosevelt Longworth called them—washtubs, boxes of soap, coal scuttles, and sacks of onions—the list included a set of silver plates from Mr. and Mrs. Andrew Carnegie, a pure white vicuña rug from the Peruvian minister and his wife, a fourteen-piece silver service from the Senate, and a diamond necklace and pendant from all but one of the members of the House of Representatives. That gentleman, Congressman Finley H. Gray of Indiana, claimed the gift was "in bad taste" and chose to make a contribution to the poor instead.

In contrast to previous White House brides who prided themselves on selecting imported fabrics, Jessie's gown was "all-American." The material, a soft satin, came from a textile mill in Paterson, New Jersey. The dress was made in the hobble-skirted style that was so popular at the time—very narrow at the ankles with a crinkled effect at the hips. It was slit at the back to make it easier to walk and the slits were concealed by a three-yard train. The veil was standard issue for White House brides—white tulle held in place by a wreath of orange blossoms.

The standing rule for White House weddings is that no one is admitted without a ticket. In this case, the one person who forgot his ticket was Frank Sayre. He arrived at the front gate a few hours before the wedding and the guard on duty refused to let him in. Frank identified himself as the groom but the guard was adamant. Anyone could claim to be the groom, he said. Finally, Frank suggested that the guard call his captain. The captain came marching out of his sentry box, listened sternly to Frank's explanation, and with a slight wink, let him in.

At six P.M. the Marine Band struck up the Bridal Chorus from *Lohengrin* and the wedding began. Margaret Wilson was the maid of honor and Nellie Wilson was one of the four bridesmaids. Their dresses were satin in four different shades of red, ranging from a very pale pink to a very deep rose.

The double-ring ceremony was performed in the usual place— before the wide window in the East Room—on a dais surrounded by flowers and covered with the Peruvian minister's vicuña rug. The Wilsons' Presbyterian pastor officiated, assisted by Frank's brother, the Reverend John Nevin Sayre, an Episcopal missionary who had recently returned from China. The ceremony was a combination of the Presbyterian and the Episcopalian services and at Jessie's request the word *obey*, not usually included in the Presbyterian service, was inserted.

The receiving line formed in the Blue Room. From there the guests proceeded to the State Dining Room where the usual elaborate refreshments were served. A few hours later, the newlyweds played the Longworths' game of musical cars so they could make their getaway without being spotted by the press. A reward of one thousand dollars had been offered to the newsman who could find out where they were honeymooning but it was never collected.

The couple stayed at the home of some friends in Baltimore and then returned to Washington for Thanksgiving dinner at the White House before sailing for a two-month honeymoon in Europe. Once again, the reporters were hot on their trail, but Frank and Jessie managed to elude them by traveling like ordinary citizens. Their ship departed from Hoboken, New Jersey, so they took the Hudson tube from New York and a taxi from the Hoboken terminal to the pier. They boarded the ship via the third-class gangplank with no one in the press the wiser.

VII
★★★

Just as one Wilson daughter's wedding was winding down, a second was starting up. After Jessie and her new husband left their wedding reception, the party kept going, thanks to her younger sister Nellie, who loved to dance and kept the Marine Band playing for several hours beyond their agreed-on quitting time.

Of the three Wilson daughters, Nellie was by far the most frivolous. Margaret was bent on becoming a professional singer—something I can certainly identify with—and Jessie was wrapped up in her social work, but Nellie's world was one long round of parties and flirtations.

On the evening of Jessie's wedding her most frequent dance partner was Secretary of the Treasury William Gibbs McAdoo, a widower with six children who was almost fifty years old and a grandfather to boot. McAdoo, whom Woodrow Wilson once described as "attractive and dynamic," was tall and handsome with courtly southern manners. His business successes had led to his appointment as vice chairman of the Democratic National Committee, and he and Wilson had become close friends during the 1912 presidential campaign.

One of McAdoo's successes was masterminding the building of a railroad tunnel under the Hudson River to connect New York City with neighboring New Jersey. The feat earned him the nickname "The Tunnel Man." He also created the Hudson tubes, the subway under the Hudson River that enabled Jessie and Frank Sayre to leave on their honeymoon without attracting the attention of the press.

By the time Jessie and Frank returned from their trip to Europe, Nellie and the secretary of the treasury were seeing quite a bit of each other. One evening when the family was together in the second-floor Oval Room, one of the servants announced the arrival of Secretary McAdoo. The president started to get up and then the servant added, "For Miss Eleanor."

Mac had already proposed once and Nellie had put him off. When he proposed a second time, she said yes. Their engagement was announced in March and the wedding was scheduled for May 7, 1914, at six o'clock in the evening. Nellie's nuptials were smaller and less glittering than Jessie's, partly because Mac had been married before and partly because Nellie's mother, Ellen, had not been feeling well.

The ceremony took place in the Blue Room and only about one hundred people were invited. The room was adorned with apple and cherry blossoms and flowering dogwood. Nellie's sisters were her only attendants. They wore matching organdy gowns, except that Margaret's was blue and Jessie's rose, and carried shepherd's crooks entwined with roses and lilies of the valley.

Nellie's gown was ivory satin trimmed with lace that supposedly had once belonged to the Empress Eugenie of France, and she carried an all-white bouquet of orchids, gardenias, and lilies of the valley. As the bride started down the Grand Staircase on her father's arm, she suddenly noticed that her train had flipped over, exposing the lining instead of the fabric. In the great tradition of White House ushers, who can handle just about any emergency, Ike Hoover flipped it back and the march proceeded.

The ceremony was performed by the Presbyterian minister who had officiated at Jessie's wedding, the Reverend Dr. Sylvester Beach.

★ ★ ★

*In the Grant era,
the East Room was
decorated in the
"steamboat palace"
style. I can't imagine
living with this
mishmash. Just
looking at it gives
me a headache.
Credit: Library of
Congress*

*The South Lawn has always been a popular spot for parties. This one was given by Theodore and Edith
Roosevelt, who were noted for being gracious hosts. Credit: Library of Congress*

Above: *Archie Roosevelt and his pony in front of the Executive Office Building, now the West Wing. At left is the current Eisenhower Executive Office Building.*
Credit: Library of Congress

Left: *Woodrow Wilson, his first wife, Ellen, and their daughters enjoyed a happy family life. The young women sometimes played practical jokes on White House tourists.*
Credit: Library of Congress

Grace Coolidge holding the Coolidges' pet raccoon, Rebecca. Her bad habits included unscrewing light-bulbs and shredding silk stockings with her claws.
Credit: Library of Congress

President Coolidge illuminated Washington's first community Christmas tree in 1923. The idea was suggested by a janitor in the city's school system.
Credit: Library of Congress

A team of pastry chefs puts the finishing touches on Tricia Nixon's wedding cake. The cake was so heavy a White House plumber had to build a special stand for it. Credit: Library of Congress

Caroline Harrison tried to enlarge the White House by adding wings in a style that was popular in Paris at the time. Thank goodness the plan was stillborn. Credit: Library of Congress

Above: *Here's history in the making—FDR giving one of his famous fireside chats. They made the president and the White House a living presence in American homes.*
Credit: Franklin D. Roosevelt Library

Left: *FDR with three longtime staff members. From left: the indispensable Missy LeHand, press secretary Steve Early, and secretary Grace Tully.*
Credit: Franklin D. Roosevelt Library

Missy LeHand was the only staffer who dared to say no to Franklin D. Roosevelt. She started working for him after his failed vice presidential race in 1920. Credit: Franklin D. Roosevelt Library

The entire Truman-Wallace clan gathered for Christmas dinner at the White House in 1947. That's me in the foreground sitting to the left of my father. Credit: Harry S. Truman Library

★ ★ ★

Despite the questions about my love life, I seem to be enjoying myself at this 1947 press conference—or perhaps I was just smiling at a few of those hats.
Credit: Harry S. Truman Library

Charlie Ross, Dad's classmate at Independence High, gave up a well-paid reporter's job to become his press secretary. When he died of a heart attack in 1950, Dad wept. Credit: Harry S. Truman Library

Left: *Abraham Lincoln with John George Nicolay (left) and John Hay, the first modern White House staffers. The men shared a bedroom across the hall from Lincoln's office. Credit: Library of Congress*

Below: *I find it hard to look at this picture. It's a diagram of the attempt to assassinate my father in 1950 while we were living in Blair House. Credit: Harry S. Truman Library*

Where President Viewed Gun Battle

Guard House

TORESOLA

Blair House Entrance

Collazo Crumples At Foot of Steps

Guard House

Floyd Boring

Path of Toresola, Slain Assassin

Path of Collazo, Wounded Gunman

Birdzell

★ ★ ★

My father took the oath of office in the Cabinet Room hours after Franklin D. Roosevelt's death. I'm invisible behind Chief Justice Harlan F. Stone. Credit: Harry S. Truman Library

This split beam, directly under my sitting room, caused my piano to break through the floor and left no doubt that the White House needed major repairs.
Credit: Harry S. Truman Library

★ ★ ★

It took two years to rebuild the White House. In this picture, bricks are being lowered into a wheelbarrow for storage during the reconstruction. Credit: Harry S. Truman Library

My parents returned to the restored White House in March 1952. The tall smiling man in the white tie and tails is Alonzo Fields, my favorite White House butler. Credit: Harry S. Truman Library

In 1961, the Kennedys gave a dinner in honor of my father. My husband, Clifton Daniel, and I are in the second row, flanked by a pair of military aides. Credit: Harry S. Truman Library

After dinner with the Kennedys, Dad played for one of his favorite pianists, Eugene List. They first met in Potsdam in 1945, when List was a sergeant in the army.
Credit: Cecil Stoughton, White House/John Fitzgerald Kennedy Library, Boston

Few presidents demanded more loyalty from their aides than Lyndon Johnson. Most of the time he got it, but many cracked under the pressure and left for other jobs.
Credit: LBJ Library, Photo by Yoichi Okamoto

The Situation Room is the White House crisis center. Here Ronald Reagan is briefed by members of the National Security Council on the 1986 bombing of Libya.
Credit: Courtesy Ronald Reagan Library

★ ★ ★

This 1848 daguerrotype shows (left to right) Secretary of State James Buchanan, Harriet Lane, Joanna Rucker, Postmaster General Cave Johnson, Sarah Polk, Senator Thomas Hart Benton, President James Polk, Dolley Madison, and an unidentified guest. Dolley was still a Washington celebrity, thirty years after her days of White House glory. Credit: Courtesy George Eastman House

Benjamin Harrison's grandson, "Baby" McKee, shown sitting in his goat cart, was the star of the White House. He often got more press attention than the president. Credit: President Benjamin Harrison Home

Fire! *The West Wing went up in smoke on Christmas Eve 1929. Fortunately no one was injured and President Herbert Hoover's most important papers were saved.*
Credit: Library of Congress

President and Mrs. Harding and their dog, Laddie Boy, on the South Portico. Those droopy awnings were among the reasons Dad wanted to build his balcony. Credit: Ohio Historical Society

Ellen Axson Wilson was a gifted painter and an enthusiastic gardener. The noted landscape architect Beatrix Farrand helped her design this rose garden. Credit: Library of Congress

Edith Roosevelt was opposed to removing the White House greenhouses. Architect Charles McKim talked her into it at a meeting he described as the battle of Oyster Bay. Credit: Library of Congress

During the Spanish-American War, President William McKinley set up a War Room where telegraph operators received up-to-the-minute reports on the fighting. Credit: Library of Congress

★ ★ ★

The body of our first assassinated president, Abraham Lincoln, lay in state in the East Room. His widow was so distraught she did not attend his funeral. Credit: Washingtoniana Division, D.C. Public Library

Above: *Grover Cleveland and Frances Folsom were married in the White House. Many years later, she told me why: It was the only place where they could have some privacy. Credit: Library of Congress*

Left: *Robert and John Kennedy confer outside the Oval Office during the Cuban missile crisis. Who could have dreamed they would both die at the hands of assassins? Credit: AP/Wide World Photos*

There was a supper in the State Dining Room afterward and then the guests returned to the Blue Room for dancing.

When it was time for the newlyweds to depart, Mac showed himself to be as adept at devising getaways as he was at building tunnels. He arranged to have his own car and three White House cars parked conspicuously around the White House grounds. Frank and Jessie climbed into one car, Margaret and her father's doctor, Cary Grayson, got into another, and two other couples took the third and fourth. As the photographers set off in hot pursuit of the caravan, Mac and Nellie slipped into a fifth car that was hidden behind some bushes and drove off without being noticed.

By the time Nellie returned from her honeymoon at the Wilsons' summer home in Cornish, New Hampshire, her mother's health had deteriorated. Ellen Wilson died in August 1914, leaving her daughters devastated and her husband deeply depressed.

A little more than six months later, Woodrow Wilson met an attractive widow named Edith Bolling Galt and his spirits began to lift. By the end of 1915, another member of the Wilson family got married. This time it was the president, but the wedding took place at Mrs. Galt's home, not at the White House.

William Gibbs McAdoo was among the many political advisers who was uneasy about the match. He feared that a remarriage a mere sixteen months after his first wife's death might ruin Wilson's chances of being reelected in 1916. It didn't and Mac continued to serve in his father-in-law's cabinet for another two years before resigning to return to private life. His abrupt departure was something of a public shock. He was widely considered a sure bet to become Wilson's successor in the White House.

A witty poet named Arthur Guiterman wrote Mac a wry farewell in *Life* magazine.

> *The Who preeminently Who,*
> *Is William Gibbs, the McAdoo*
> *(Whom I should like to hail, but daren't,*

As Royal Prince and Heir Apparent).
A Man of high Intrinsic Worth,
The Greatest Son-in-Law on Earth
With all his burdens thence accruing,
He's always up and McAdooing
From Sun to Star and Star to Sun—
His Work is never McAdone.
He regulates our Circumstances—
Our Buildings, Industries, Finances
And Railways, while their wires buzz
To tell us what he McAdoes,
He gave us (Heaven bless the Giver!)
The Tubes beneath the Hudson River.
I don't believe he ever hid
A single thing he McAdid.
His name appears on Scrip and Tissue,
On bonds of each successive issue,
On Coupons bright and Posters rare,
And every Pullman Bill-of-Fare.

POSTSCRIPT

But while with sympathetic Croodlings
I sing his varied McAdoodlings
And write these Eulogistic Lines
That thankless McAdoo resigns!

VIII

✫ ✫ ✫

After John F. Kennedy's assassination in 1963, Lyndon and Lady Bird Johnson arrived in the White House with two teenaged daughters. At sixteen, Luci was too young for any serious romance, but the gossip columnists quickly discovered that nineteen-year-old

Lynda Bird was dating a young navy lieutenant and supposedly wearing his ring. That started a buzz about an impending wedding, but the chatter ended abruptly when the couple broke up a few months later.

As it turned out, Luci beat Lynda Bird to the altar by more than two years. One of her friends, Beth Jenkins, attended Marquette University in Milwaukee, Wisconsin, and in the course of visiting Beth, Luci met a young man named Patrick J. Nugent. Before long, she and Pat were commuting back and forth between Milwaukee and Washington, but the press never caught on—possibly because they were preoccupied with Lynda Bird's love life or maybe it was because Luci's blond wig threw them off the scent.

In the fall of 1965, Luci and Pat made a trip to the LBJ ranch in Johnson City, Texas, to request the president's permission to marry. As soon as the media got wind of their plans, the White House press office was bombarded with questions and requests for details.

Eventually, all—or almost all—was revealed. The wedding was to take place at noon on Saturday, August 6, 1966. The reception would be held at the White House but the ceremony would be performed at the National Shrine of the Immaculate Conception in northeast Washington, a splendid blue-domed Byzantine-style building that is the largest Catholic church in the Western Hemisphere. Although it was not generally known, Luci had converted to Catholicism, the religion of her fiancé.

Luci insisted that the design of her wedding dress be kept secret until she walked down the aisle. This produced security precautions worthy of a summit conference. The designer, Priscilla of Boston, was met at the airport by the Secret Service, and the dress was hand-carried to the White House and locked in the Lincoln Bedroom. It was taken out, presumably under armed guard, so Luci could wear it for her bridal portrait, but during the photo session no one was allowed to use the elevators or walk through the White House halls until the all-clear was sounded.

There were innumerable prenuptial parties, several of which took place at the White House. A few days before the wedding, Luci gave a buffet supper for her bridesmaids in the third-floor solarium, which she had converted into her private retreat. Earlier that day, she gave another party for the entire White House staff—cooks, butlers, laundresses, doormen, secretaries, telephone operators, as well as the photographer and the kennel keeper.

Some weeks earlier, Lady Bird invited another White House bride, Alice Roosevelt Longworth, to tea. It was a private occasion. Only Luci, Lynda Bird, and Lady Bird were there. Mrs. Longworth was her usual entertaining self and she was happy to share some of her recollections of her own wedding. In those days, she told the Johnsons, no details were given to the press so they had to make them up. As a result, the newspapers were full of silly, often contradictory stories about the event. Alice had been trying to set them straight ever since.

Luci's wedding day dawned hot and humid—hardly a surprise in a city noted for its sweltering summers. Needless to say, the Shrine of the Immaculate Conception was not air-conditioned. During the ceremony, Lynda Bird, the maid of honor, and two of the bridesmaids almost fainted. Another bridesmaid and the matron of honor did pass out.

Even more noteworthy was the way the perennially impatient father of the bride sat still during the entire eighty-five-minute ceremony. Lady Bird's social secretary, Bess Abell, reported in amazement, "I do not remember him looking at his watch one single time during the service."

The White House reception included the usual sumptuous array of food in the State Dining Room, but the pièce de résistance was the wedding cake—seven tiers, separated by lacy Gothic arches and decorated with swans and white roses, with a bouquet of lilies of the valley at the top.

The only glitch of the day occurred when someone mistakenly packed Luci's going away outfit in one of the suitcases she planned to take on her honeymoon. The suitcase was already stowed in the

trunk of the getaway car, but Luci refused to leave until the outfit—
a deep pink suit with matching turban—was retrieved.

When it was finally found, she changed out of her wedding gown
and went down to the South Portico to throw her bouquet, which
landed squarely at Lynda Bird's feet. With this last ritual performed,
Luci slipped back upstairs, changed out of the pink suit and turban
and into an inconspicuous dark dress and a hairpiece that turned her
short hair into shoulder-length curls. At last she was ready to depart.

The newlyweds' getaway worked out as planned. Luci and Pat
went through the tunnel that connects the White House to the
Treasury Building next door. There, a nondescript black sedan was
waiting in the basement garage. The couple crouched on the floor
until they were out of sight of the White House and on their way
to New York.

IX

☆☆☆

With Luci married off, the press was free to devote their full attention to Lynda Bird. Her romances, rumored and otherwise, kept
them busy. At one point, she was dating a White House military
aide, but he was replaced by a medical student who in turn was replaced by the movie actor George Hamilton. At the end of 1965,
Hamilton flew in from London to spend New Year's Eve at the LBJ
ranch. A few months later, he gave a twenty-second birthday party
for Lynda Bird at his Beverly Hills mansion, and in June, he showed
up at her graduation from the University of Texas. The relationship
seemed to be thriving but there was still no sign of an engagement
ring.

Lynda Bird took a job as a magazine editor in New York while
Hamilton continued to jaunt around the world making movies.
They managed to see each other often enough to persuade the press
that marriage was a distinct possibility. Then early one morning in

1967, just about a year after Luci's wedding, Lynda Bird slipped into her parents' bedroom to announce that she was going to marry Charles Robb, a marine officer who was the captain of the White House color guard.

George Hamilton, not to mention most of the nation's working press, was totally surprised by the news. And what news it was. Lynda Bird Johnson's marriage—scheduled for four P.M. on Saturday, December 9, 1967—was going to be the first White House wedding in fifty-three years.

As with previous weddings, the ceremony took place in the East Room and was followed by a reception in the State Dining Room. To accommodate the almost seven hundred guests, a seventy- by thirty-foot electronically heated tent was erected on the roof of the west colonnade.

On the morning of the wedding, Lady Bird Johnson's hairdresser, Jean Louis, set up a salon in the East Hall on the second floor so the women in the wedding party could have their hair done. There were four bridesmaids plus a matron of honor, Luci, and a maid of honor, Warrie Lynn Smith, Lynda Bird's closest friend. Jean Louis must have had his hands full.

Lynda Bird's white silk-satin wedding gown, designed by Geoffrey Beene, was long-sleeved with a high collar and a front panel outlined in embroidered silk flowers studded with seed pearls. Her attendants wore red velvet. The ceremony was performed by Canon Gerald McAllister from St. Barnabas Church in Fredericksburg, Maryland, on an altar surmounted by a gold cross and decorated with ficus trees and masses of greens dotted with tiny white lights. The ceremony was over by 4:16 and Lynda and Chuck marched out of the East Room under an arch of swords held by his brother marine officers in their full dress uniforms.

No less an authority than Alice Roosevelt Longworth put her official stamp of approval on the event. "I've never seen a wedding as pretty as this," she declared. Another veteran of White House weddings was also present—Mrs. Benjamin King of Charlottesville, Virginia, who had been a bridesmaid at Jessie Wilson's wedding in 1913 and a guest at her sister Nellie's a year later.

In contrast to those earlier weddings, there was no hope of barring the press. Lady Bird had wanted to avoid television coverage but she was quickly overruled. As a small concession to family privacy, however, the cameras and lighting equipment were hidden behind poles draped in\white to match the walls of the East Room and the networks were allowed to shoot only during the wedding procession and at the beginning of the reception—twenty minutes of footage, all told.

X
✯✯✯

In 1971, President and Mrs. Richard M. Nixon's older daughter, Tricia, became the first, but surely not the last, White House bride to be married in the Rose Garden. Until a few weeks before her engagement was announced, the gossip columnists had failed to notice that Tricia was being seen more and more in the company of a young Harvard Law student from New York City named Edward Cox.

Apparently, the press can only concentrate on one presidential daughter at a time, so for a long while their attention was almost completely focused on Tricia's sister, Julie, who had married Dwight David Eisenhower II, the only grandson of President Eisenhower, about a month before her father was sworn in as president. Julie and David had met some eighteen years earlier when Richard Nixon served as Eisenhower's vice president. There were dozens of photos of the two of them together as children, not to mention their families' political prominence, so from the media's point of view, it was a marriage made in heaven.

I'm sure Tricia was more than happy to have her sister be the center of attention since it gave her a chance to conduct her own romance in private. She and her future husband had known each other since 1964 when Richard Nixon joined a New York law firm after his 1960 defeat for the presidency. They met at a school dance but the relationship took off after Cox, then a Princeton freshman, served as Tricia's escort at the International Debutante Ball at the Waldorf-Astoria.

Marriage was out of the question because the young people were still in school, but by the time Cox was in his second year of law school, it was a different story. By then, the press had finally begun to notice that Edward Cox was spending a significant number of holidays at the White House and Camp David, not to mention such other Nixon hangouts as San Clemente, California, and Key Biscayne, Florida.

For several weeks, rumors were rampant. They were finally confirmed on March 17, 1971, when President Nixon announced Tricia's engagement at a St. Patrick's Day reception honoring Prime Minister John M. Lynch of Ireland. It was also Mrs. Nixon's fifty-ninth birthday.

The wedding was set for four P.M. on Saturday, June 12. With anti–Vietnam War protesters liable to show up at the White House gates without warning, security was tight. Guests were not only required to produce their invitations, but the documents were studied under a fluoroscope to make sure they were authentic.

Outdoor weddings are always a gamble, even in the normally sunny month of June. Everything was set for a Rose Garden ceremony, but in case of rain, the plans called for moving it to the East Room. I hate to imagine the tension in the family quarters as the weather reports came in. The forecast indicated a fifty percent chance of showers, and as predicted, it began to drizzle about an hour before the ceremony.

President Nixon strolled down to the press tent that had been set up on the south lawn and informed the reporters that the Nixons had advised their daughter to play it safe and move indoors. Tricia had refused. "I want a Rose Garden wedding," she insisted.

According to the meteorologists, who must have been dreading the president's wrath if they got it wrong, the rain would not last very long. Based on that information, the ceremony was postponed to 4:30. Miraculously, the rain stopped and the wedding began.

The eight groomsmen marched in pairs from the Diplomatic Reception Room on the ground floor. They were followed by the bride and her party, who entered from the steps on the South Portico. Tricia, with her blond hair and tiny stature—she's only five-foot-three—was a fairy-tale bride. She wore a white organdy gown decorated with pearls and lace, and a pearl-encrusted Juliet cap with a veil that cascaded to the floor. Her attendants, including Julie Nixon Eisenhower, who was matron of honor, wore mint green and lilac organdy with wide-brimmed hats to match.

The Rose Garden is always lovely in June and I'm sure the White House gardeners worked extra hard to make it perfect for the wedding. The altar was a white wrought-iron pavilion decorated with flowers and greens. The ceremony was performed by the Reverend Edward G. Latch, chaplain of the House of Representatives, whom Tricia had known all her life.

Tricia and Ed had barely become Mr. and Mrs. Cox when the rain resumed. Everyone fled indoors where there were plenty of refreshments including three kinds of champagne, all domestic. Among the four hundred or so guests were two recent White House brides, Luci Johnson Nugent and Lynda Bird Johnson Robb, and a somewhat less recent one, Alice Roosevelt Longworth.

In addition to the weather, Tricia's wedding produced two other causes for anxiety. Her father was so nervous about dancing in public that he asked the press corps to send in some sympathetic reporters—"people who know nothing about dancing"—when it was time for the obligatory dances. Although he looked nervous, the president performed no worse than any other father of the bride, circling the floor in a carefully executed two-step with Tricia, and going on to dance with her mother-in-law and the first lady as well.

The second source of anxiety was the 355-pound 7-foot-high wedding cake. The recipe had been published in advance and several well-known food writers had tried to duplicate it without success. One attempt resulted in something that looked and tasted like baked sludge. The actual product proved to be edible as well as beautiful. The top tier had a miniature gazebo on it and the bottom one, which measured 5 feet across, was decorated with sugar lovebirds and cherry blossoms with the couple's initials intertwined.

Tricia threw her bouquet, as planned, to Ed's sister, Mary Ann Cox. Around seven o'clock, the couple, still in their wedding clothes, departed to the music of a small combo playing "Toot, Toot, Tootsie, Good-bye." Unlike previous White House newlyweds, there was no attempt at a stealthy exit. Their black limousine was parked at the North Portico and their destination was later revealed to be a private hideaway with security provided by the Secret Service—Camp David.

XI

★★★

There is no question that White House weddings are special. The setting is unique and the White House staff are experts at providing the very best in food, music, flowers, and gracious service. A White House bride is not only a star on her wedding day, she can claim a place in the history of the nation's most famous house.

Do I regret not having been married at 1600 Pennsylvania Avenue? Not in the least. I wasn't ready to get married when Dad was in the White House. For one thing, I was determined to have a career as a concert singer. For another, even more important, I hadn't met the right man. When I finally achieved both those goals, I was more than happy to be far away from Washington. My wedding took place at Trinity Episcopal Church in Independence, Missouri, where my parents had been married in 1919. The reception, too, was the same place theirs had been—219 North Delaware Street, my mother's, and later my own, childhood home. It suited me just fine.

There have been more dogs than presidents in the White House, but Fala, pictured here with his master, is without question the most famous.
Credit: Franklin D. Roosevelt Library

12

★★★

Talking Dogs and Other Unnatural Curiosities

President John F. Kennedy's press secretary, Pierre Salinger, was awakened one morning at three A.M. by a call from White House reporter Helen Thomas.

"I wouldn't call you at an ungodly hour like this, Pierre, if it weren't important," she said. "But we have a report that one of Caroline's hamsters has died. Would you check it out for me?"

The hamster was indeed dead—drowned in the president's bathtub—but the story wouldn't have merited even a single line in the press if the rodent hadn't succumbed in the White House.

White House pets are, and always have been, big news. Algonquin, the calico pony that belonged to Theodore Roosevelt's son Archie, was constantly being written up in the papers. Warren G. Harding's Airedale, Laddie Boy, had his picture taken almost as often as his master. When Lyndon Johnson mistreated one of his beagles by picking him up by the ears, the story made headlines around the world. Fortunately for Lyndon, the beagle was unable to call a press conference to tell the media how much it hurt.

In most cases, presidents don't mind being upstaged by their pets. If they did, you can be sure the creatures would be out of sight when the press showed up. Theodore Roosevelt was often photographed riding his favorite horse, Bleistein. The pictures reinforced his image as an outdoorsman and reminded the public of his bravery as a Rough Rider during the Spanish-American War.

John F. Kennedy gave orders for the White House kennel keeper to have one or two of the family dogs rush to greet him whenever he returned from a trip. Maybe it was a publicity stunt. Maybe he really missed them. Whatever the explanation, it provided great photo ops.

JFK was not the first president to note that a pet can do wonders for a politician's image. When Herbert Hoover was running for president in 1928, one of his campaign managers circulated a picture of Hoover smiling warmly as he held the front paws of his German shepherd, King Tut. The picture helped dispel Hoover's dour image and made him look more like the compassionate man he truly was.

A pet can also come in handy when a president wants to divert attention from sticky issues. Do you remember how many pictures of Bill Clinton's dog, Buddy, we saw during the impeachment proceedings? One can only wonder if Richard Nixon made a mistake in not being photographed more often with his Irish setter, King Timahoe, during the Watergate scandals. Earlier, his cocker spaniel, Checkers, played a major part in saving him from being dumped as Dwight Eisenhower's running mate in 1952. The dog sat at Nixon's feet when he appeared on national television to defend himself against charges of having a secret "slush fund."

Franklin D. Roosevelt, who hated personal confrontations, often used his Scottish terrier, Fala, to avoid them. Once, when FDR had an appointment with a government official who was planning to tell him something he didn't want to hear, the president made sure that Fala was ushered into the Oval Office at the same time.

Before the man could get down to business, FDR took a ball from his desk drawer and began showing him some of Fala's tricks. Then Fala had an accident on the rug and by the time the puddle was

mopped up, the president's next appointment was announced. The
man left without ever getting a chance to speak his piece.

II
★★★

Not long after Gerald Ford moved into the White House in 1974,
his daughter, Susan, and White House photographer David Kennerly, decided to surprise him with a gift of a golden retriever
puppy. Kennerly did some research and found that a prize retriever
had given birth to a litter at a kennel in Minneapolis. He called the
owner of the kennel and asked if he could buy one of the puppies
for a friend of his.

No problem, said the owner, what was the friend's name?

"I can't tell you," Kennerly replied. "It's a gift and we want it to
be a surprise."

"We don't sell dogs that way," the owner said sternly. "We have to
know if the dog is going to a good home."

"The couple is friendly," Kennerly told him. "They're middle-
aged, and they live in a white house with a big yard and a fence
around it. It's a lovely place."

"Do they own or rent?" the owner demanded.

Kennerly thought for a minute. "I guess you might call it public
housing."

More dubious than ever, the owner warned him that the dog was
going to eat a lot. Did his friend have a steady job?

After Kennerly assured him that his friend was a very important
person, the owner finally agreed to fly the dog to Washington. He
must have been vastly relieved, and perhaps slightly embarrassed,
when he discovered that Liberty, as the puppy was called, was being
given to the president of the United States.

As Kennerly had promised, Liberty's new home would indeed be
a white house with a big yard and a fence around it, but that was

only the beginning. Liberty was going to live the cushy life of a White House dog, with her own kennel and dog run, a kennel keeper to see to her personal care, a visit to the vet at the slightest sniffle or twinge, and eighteen acres full of trees, squirrels, and rabbits to romp around in. It certainly gave new meaning to the expression "a dog's life."

III

★★★

Dogs are not the only pets that have lived in the White House, but somehow they always get the most press coverage. Perhaps it's because they're more photogenic than the competition, which has included goats, birds, snakes, lizards, rats, and raccoons. I also think dogs have a talent for getting attention.

I'll never forget my one and only dog, an Irish setter puppy named Mike, that was given to me by one of my father's cabinet members not long after we moved into the White House. Talk about getting attention! One of Mike's favorite habits was bounding into my lap whenever I sat down. I simply could not convince him that long and lanky Irish setters were not cut out to be lap dogs.

Mike once leaped into a pool in the White House garden and my mother's secretary, Reathel Odum, jumped in to rescue him. Knowing very little about dogs, Reathel didn't realize that setters are good swimmers. She emerged from the pool dripping wet and hopping mad. Mike, of course, loved every minute of it.

Mike also had a habit of cadging candy from the White House policemen. He ate so much he developed rickets and had to be packed off to an animal hospital for treatment. I had graduated from college by this time, and was getting ready to move to New York and embark on a career as a singer. I knew Mike was too much of a free spirit to ever be happy as a city dog so I found him a good home in Virginia. I understand that he was quite content with his new owner and had no regrets about leaving 1600 Pennsylvania Avenue.

Mike was a model of good behavior compared to some of the dogs that have lived in the White House. Dwight Eisenhower's weimaraner, Heidi, left endless stains on the White House rugs and also had a bad habit of leaping up in front of Mamie whenever a photographer tried to take her picture.

I don't know what crimes Ulysses S. Grant's son Jesse's dogs committed, but several of them died suddenly and under mysterious circumstances. I suspect they were executed for some malfeasance by a member of the White House staff. President Grant thought so, too. After several unsuccessful attempts at dog-owning, Jesse was presented with a fine Newfoundland. His father promptly called the White House steward into his office. Without mentioning the string of unexplained deaths, Grant said, "Jesse has a new dog. You may have noticed that his former pets have been peculiarly unfortunate. When this dog dies, every employee in the White House will at once be discharged."

The dog, Faithful, lived to a ripe old age.

IV
★★★

Many presidential families already owned pets that they brought with them when they moved to the White House. But no matter how many pets they had, people inevitably gave them a few more.

Among the many gifts the Kennedys received were a pair of deer from President Eamon de Valera of Ireland, which were kept at their Virginia estate, Glen Ora, and eventually were sent to the Children's Zoo in New York's Central Park. A handsome horse named Sardar was presented to Jacqueline Kennedy by President Ayub Khan of Pakistan after she had ridden the animal on a visit to his country.

When President Kennedy attended a summit meeting in Vienna

with Russian premier Nikita Khrushchev, it was not a particularly cordial encounter. But Khrushchev was charmed by Jacqueline Kennedy and later sent her a large collection of gifts, including a fluffy white mongrel named Pushinka for Caroline. Despite her questionable bloodlines, Pushinka had an illustrious background. She was the daughter of Strelka, the dog the Russians had sent on one of their early space missions.

At that time, the United States and the Soviet Union were in the midst of the Cold War, so the Secret Service was understandably suspicious of Pushinka. For all anyone knew, she might have an electronic bug implanted in her tail. Before the dog could be admitted to the White House, she had to undergo a security check. Fortunately, she turned out to be clean.

President Kennedy got along much better with Pushinka than he did with Premier Khrushchev. The dog's only breach of propriety in the White House was biting the nose of one of the Kennedy cousins, Anthony Radziwill. Knowing small boys as I do, I wouldn't be surprised if she had good reason.

If the State Department had been paying attention, they might have noticed that Pushinka played a role in one of the first efforts at U.S.-Soviet détente. Caroline Kennedy's Welsh terrier, Charlie, fell madly in love with her. The inevitable happened and Pushinka and Charlie became the parents of four Russian-American puppies. JFK dubbed them the pupniks.

In 1855, Commodore Matthew C. Perry returned from his historic voyage to Japan, a trip that opened that country to trade with the West. Perry brought back several crates full of gifts for President Franklin Pierce, including Japanese silks, porcelains, fans, lacquered boxes, and swords. The gift that appealed to the president most was a collection of seven tiny canines that were known in Asia as "sleeve dogs."

Pierce kept one of the dogs at the White House. The others were given to friends, including Secretary of War Jefferson Davis, who was so delighted with the creature that he carried him around in his pocket.

Davis's wife, Varina, described the dog as having "eyes large and popped, and a body like a new-born puppy of the smallest kind." He was so tiny that "a coffee saucer made an ample scampering ground for him." Most probably the dogs were Japanese spaniels or chin chins, now known as Japanese chins. They lived in the Imperial Palace and were often given to important foreign visitors. The name "sleeve dog" comes from the fact that they could be carried in the sleeve of a kimono.

As soon as word got out that Calvin and Grace Coolidge were animal lovers, they were inundated with would-be pets. The list included an antelope, a bobcat, a cinnamon bear, a donkey, a pair of lion cubs, a pygmy hippo, and a wallaby, all of which were sent to the zoo.

One gift, a large white goose named Enoch, managed to escape. He was given to the president by the comedienne Marie Dressler to publicize her latest Broadway play, *The Goose Woman*. The Coolidges were vacationing in Swampscott, Massachusetts, at the time and someone forgot to close the door of their cottage. Enoch took off and was last seen flying high above the Atlantic Ocean.

V

There have been quite a few cats in the White House, but most of them have kept a low profile. Cats are much too cool to curry favor with the press. They are also experts at hiding under beds or curling up in closets to avoid being interviewed. But if they want attention, they know exactly how to get it.

Theodore Roosevelt's family had two cats, Slippers and Tom Quartz. Slippers had a habit of wandering off but the White House staff noticed that he invariably reappeared when an important dinner was scheduled. The dinners always included a fish course and he was probably thinking of the leftovers.

One evening, President Roosevelt, with the wife of a visiting dignitary on his arm, was leading his guests from a reception in the East Room to dinner in the State Dining Room. As they proceeded down the main hall, they came across Slippers stretched out on the carpet. Not only was he blocking their path but he was not the least bit interested in moving. The president gave an amused bow to his dinner partner and escorted her around the cat. All the other gentlemen and their partners followed suit.

Tom Quartz was not as laid-back as Slippers. One evening he seized the pompous, bewhiskered Speaker of the House "Uncle Joe" Cannon by the leg as he was walking down the stairs after an evening visit with the president. It was never clear whether the cat was making a political statement (Cannon was one of TR's perpetual problems) or just being playful.

Lucy Webb Hayes had a cat named Siam that was sent to her by the U.S. consul in Bangkok. It was reputed to be the first Siamese cat ever seen in the United States. Siam was a great favorite in the White House, although he was usually overshadowed by the other Hayes pets, which included two dogs, a goat, and a mockingbird.

Calvin Coolidge's pet collection included a pair of cats named Tiger and Blacky. Tiger was an alley cat who came wandering in from Pennsylvania Avenue one day and decided to stay. Blacky, whose ancestry was equally undistinguished, was sent to the president by a nurse in Massachusetts because she didn't have room for him.

Blacky was a hunter and was such a menace to the squirrels, birds, and rabbits that inhabit the President's Park that he had to be kept in the guardhouse by the front gate in the spring and summer when the wildlife was out in force.

When he was not playing serial killer on the south lawn, Blacky's favorite pastime was riding in the White House elevator. He would sit and wait for someone to open the door for him, then he would hop onto the seat and ride up and down for hours, obviously gathering his strength for another run at the wildlife.

The president liked Blacky well enough, but Tiger was his favorite. The two of them spent many an afternoon sitting on the South Portico conferring about the state of the union. One day, Tiger wandered off and the president was so upset he asked a local radio station to broadcast the cat's description with an appeal for his return.

Tiger was recaptured and after that escape both cats were provided with collars that said "White House" on them. Unfortunately, Tiger's didn't help. He developed another case of itchy feet and slipped past the White House guards again. This time he was gone for good, collar and all.

The White House did not have another first feline until 1961, when Caroline Kennedy was given a cat named Tom Kitten. The cat had only a brief taste of life at the top, however. President Kennedy was allergic to animal fur and although the Kennedys had several dogs, they slept in their own kennels and pretty much stayed out of the way. Tom Kitten, on the other hand, was a permanent resident in the family quarters. After JFK's allergies kicked up once too often, the cat was sent to live with Jackie Kennedy's personal secretary, although Caroline retained visiting rights.

When nine-year-old Amy Carter moved into the White House in 1977, she brought along her Siamese cat, Misty Malarky Ying Yang. The cat seemed to know her place. She stayed out of the Oval Office and had no interest in cabinet meetings. Aside from posing for a few photos, she tended to shun the limelight, but as it turned out, she was simply waiting for the right moment to dazzle the public with her charms.

The moment came when Amy's parents, Rosalynn and Jimmy Carter, held their first state dinner. Everything was proceeding according to plan. The Carters were upstairs dressed in their evening clothes when a military aide informed them that the guests of honor, President and Mrs. José López-Portillo of Mexico, were leaving Blair House, the White House guest quarters just across Pennsylvania Avenue.

When the López-Portillos arrived at the North Portico two minutes later, the Carters welcomed them and escorted them to the second floor for a private visit in the Yellow Oval Room. The visit lasted for half an hour or so before it was time to go downstairs and greet the other guests.

With the Color Team preceding them, the Marine Band playing, and their guests waiting expectantly at the bottom of the Grand Staircase, the Carters looked down and saw that Misty Malarky had appeared from nowhere and was padding down the stairs in front of them.

"I don't know who was more surprised," Rosalynn said later, "the guests, the press, me, or Misty. But immediately there was laughter in the great hallway, and a relaxed and comfortable, warm, elegant, and thrilling evening had begun."

The next White House cat of note was Socks Clinton, who arrived in 1993. Socks is a real rags to riches story. The Clintons picked him up as a stray in Arkansas and gave him a home in the Governor's Mansion in Little Rock. A few years later, he had taken another leap forward and was living in the White House.

For the first few years, it was a dream existence. Socks whiled away his days napping in the sunshine on the south lawn or poking through the papers on the president's secretary's desk. He also became an instant celebrity and was inundated with fan letters, all of which he dutifully answered, signing his responses with a paw print.

Then in 1997, Socks's carefree life was disrupted. The Clintons adopted a chocolate Labrador retriever named Buddy, after Bill Clinton's great uncle, Henry "Buddy" Graham. Not only did Socks drop to second place in the White House pet standings, but he had to put up with all sorts of barking and growling from his replacement.

Cat and dog fights can be contained in the White House, where there's plenty of room and more than enough help to keep them from getting out of hand. (After all, there are plenty of battles in the West Wing, too.) But the Clintons knew it would be impossible to deal with the situation after they left 1600 Pennsylvania Avenue. They decided to take Buddy with them and give Socks to Clinton's secretary, Betty Currie, whose White House desk had long been one of his favorite haunts.

If Socks was bitter about this arrangement, he's kept his mouth shut—at least so far. The inside story is that he actually preferred Betty Currie's company, especially after first daughter Chelsea went off to college. But you can't believe everything you hear about the White House. Perhaps Socks will write a book one of these days and we can find out how he really feels about it all.

The latest White House cat in residence, Willie, has been a member of the Bush family for over ten years, but she has never tried to capitalize on the relationship. On the contrary, she keeps such a low profile that most people don't even know she exists, which doesn't bother Willie in the slightest. Willie spends most of her time hiding from her owners, napping under one of their beds, or munching on tuna-flavored kitty treats. Her real name, incidentally, is India, after the former Texas Ranger baseball player Ruben Sierra, who was called "El Indio." The Bushes acquired her when George W. was managing partner of the team.

VI

★★★

During the Kennedy administration there were always at least a dozen exotic pets in residence, including lambs, guinea pigs, hamsters, birds, and rabbits. Their upkeep was rumored to cost about $1,500 a month. At one point, Jackie decided it would be fun to have a few ducks swimming in the pool on the south lawn. The ducks liked the pool well enough, but in between plunges, they snacked on the tulips and had to be given away.

Among the pets in the Kennedys' private menagerie was Caroline Kennedy's pony Macaroni, who divided his time between his stable at the White House and the Kennedy home in Virginia. When he was in Washington, he roamed freely around the White House grounds. One day Macaroni wandered over to the West Wing and stood staring into one of the tall windows in the Oval Office. President Kennedy stared back. After a few minutes, he went over, opened the door, and motioned to Macaroni to come in. The pony thought about it for a few minutes, then turned around and ambled off.

Macaroni missed his chance to become the first pony in history to visit the Oval Office. He may have considered this only a minor accomplishment in view of the fact that another pony had gotten as far as the second-floor living quarters.

When nine-year-old Archie Roosevelt was stricken with both measles and whooping cough, his younger brother, Quentin, decided that a visit from his pony, Algonquin, would cheer him up. Quentin persuaded one of the White House footmen to help him coax the 350-pound animal into the White House elevator. Algonquin was jittery about the venture until he became absorbed in studying himself in the elevator mirror and gave the footman a chance to press the button. The invalid was so happy to see Algonquin trotting into his bedroom that he immediately began to recover.

Abraham and Mary Lincoln's two younger sons, Willie and Tad, had their own ponies, which they rode around the grounds under the watchful eye of Tom Cross, a White House messenger. In 1862, when Willie died of typhoid fever, Tad lost all interest in his pony. To cheer him up, his parents bought him a pair of goats. Strange as it may seem today, goats were popular pets in the nineteenth and early twentieth centuries. They were known for being gentle and good-natured and they could be hitched to small carts to give children a safe ride.

The Lincoln goats, Nanny and Nanko, did yeoman service as cart pullers and they quickly won the affection of the entire family. When the Lincolns left the White House for the summer and moved to a house at the Soldiers' Home, an old-age home for army veterans on a wooded hill in northeast Washington, the goats went with them.

One of Lincoln's aides was horrified to see the animals riding in the carriage with the rest of the family. When he suggested that it was unseemly for goats to be traveling in the presidential carriage, Lincoln calmly responded, "Why not? There's plenty of room in here."

When they weren't busy pulling Tad around in his cart, Nanny and Nanko made a beeline for the White House flower beds, destroying the plants and driving the gardener into a frenzy. The only solution was to keep them in the stables. Nanko was the better behaved of the pair and when he was put in the stables, he stayed there. Nanny, however, always managed to get out and, of course, headed straight for the garden.

To keep the goat from causing too much destruction, the president had her brought into the White House, but instead of staying docilely in the basement, she wandered upstairs and curled up on Tad's bed. The housekeeper shooed her outside where she attacked the flower beds once again. That was her last foray. The next day Nanny disappeared. Somehow I don't think it was a coincidence.

There is a sad postscript to the story of Willy and Tad's ponies. One February night in 1864 there was a fire in the White House stables. Lincoln saw the flames from his window and rushed out to rescue the ponies. When he reached the stables he was told that most of the horses, including the ponies, had refused to leave the burning building. Although a number of prize horses were killed in the fire, it was the loss of Willie's pony that the president felt most keenly. It plunged him into a depression that lasted for days.

Among the other White House children who had goats to pull

them around were President Rutherford B. Hayes's youngest son, Scott, and Benjamin Harrison's grandson, Ben McKee. Ben's goat, His Whiskers, could often be seen on the front lawn of the White House with the little boy in tow.

One day, as President Harrison was standing on the North Portico, about to leave for an appointment, His Whiskers abruptly shifted into high gear and went tearing down Pennsylvania Avenue with Ben and his cart bouncing along behind him. The president, in his frock coat and high silk hat, took off after them, waving his cane and calling for His Whiskers to stop.

The goat finally slowed down and Harrison was able to grab him by his harness. Instead of finding his grandson screaming in fright, as the president had expected, Ben was fine. He told his grandfather that the ride had been great fun.

Unlike Tad Lincoln's goat Nanny, His Whiskers didn't get into the flower beds, but he did take a dislike to Willis, the White House coachman. Every time Willis entered the stable, His Whiskers would lower his horns and charge, and Willis would have to flee. After several encounters with the goat, Willis announced that he had had enough. Either His Whiskers went or he did. Faced with the prospect of losing his coachman or disappointing his grandson, the president came up with a compromise. His Whiskers was taken out of the stable and housed in a pen under the South Portico.

VII
***

Among the various animals that were sent to the White House during the Coolidge administration was a raccoon. It was intended to be the main course at Thanksgiving dinner, but Coolidge, a traditionalist, decided to stick with turkey. He took a liking to the raccoon and decided to keep her as a pet. He christened her Rebecca, installed her in a pen near the Oval Office, and gave her a steady diet of her favorite foods, shrimp and persimmons.

When Coolidge let Rebecca out of her pen, she would follow him around the White House, causing quite a stir among visitors, who thought there was a wild animal loose on the premises. They weren't entirely mistaken. Rebecca could be pretty wild when she wanted to be.

Since raccoons have forepaws shaped like tiny hands, they are amazingly dexterous and can get into all sorts of mischief. Rebecca could unscrew lightbulbs, open cabinet doors, and unpot palms. Grace Coolidge's social secretary was scared to death of her because she had a bad habit of destroying silk stockings and ripping holes in clothing. But the White House housekeeper, Ellen Riley, was one of her biggest fans. She would carry Rebecca into her bathroom and put her in the tub where the raccoon would have a high old time splashing around with a cake of soap.

Being a nocturnal animal, Rebecca was at her best after dark. On pleasant evenings, she and the president used to take long walks together. It must have been quite a sight to see Coolidge strolling along with Rebecca on her leash waddling beside him.

In an effort to give Rebecca some companionship, Coolidge had a male raccoon, Reuben, brought to the White House. He turned out to be a tough character and was so abusive to his would-be mate that he had to be put in a separate pen. It was built around a giant Norwegian spruce tree so Reuben could work off his aggressions by climbing up and down the trunk.

Reuben not only climbed on the trunk, he swung out on one of the branches, dropped to the ground, and made a break for freedom. He was spotted by one of the White House policemen who nabbed him and returned him to his pen. The branch was cut back to avert any further escapes, but Reuben was not so easily foiled. He made two more getaway attempts and the last one was a success. Since he and Rebecca didn't get along anyway, I don't think her heart was broken by his departure, and the White House police force was probably relieved. They had enough to keep them busy without having to be on the alert for a fugitive raccoon.

Theodore Roosevelt's children shared their father's love of wild creatures. As a boy in New York, Teddy once met a friend of his mother's on a streetcar. As he tipped his hat politely, several frogs jumped out and landed in the woman's lap.

During their years in the White House, the young Roosevelts had an assortment of exotic pets including a parrot named Loretta, a blue macaw named Eli Yale, and Kermit's kangaroo rat who liked to be fed lumps of sugar at the breakfast table. In 1903 the president made a trip across the country and returned with a collection of gifts for his family, including still another pet, a badger named Josiah.

Josiah adapted well to life in the White House and stayed out of trouble. His only bad habit was biting, but the Roosevelts did not regard this as a serious problem. As Archie explained, "He bites legs sometimes but he never bites faces."

Whatever you think of badgers, you'll probably agree that they are infinitely more appealing than snakes. The Roosevelt children had those, too. Quentin, the youngest of the Roosevelt sons, once went barreling into the Oval Office to show his father a pair of snakes he had found in the garden. The president, who was conferring with some of his cabinet members, directed him to wait outside.

Quentin retreated to the reception room and promptly struck up a conversation with a group of congressmen who had come to call on the president. The men displayed a great interest in the snakes until it dawned on them that they were real. By then, it was too late to retreat. When the president emerged from his meeting some minutes later, he found one of the congressmen gingerly helping Quentin retrieve a snake that had slithered up the man's coat sleeve.

The best known of the White House snakes (nonhuman variety) belonged to Roosevelt's teenaged daughter, Alice. She called it Emily Spinach "because it was as green as spinach and as thin as my aunt Emily." Aunt Emily was her stepmother Edith Roosevelt's unmarried sister, Emily Carow.

According to Alice, the snake was affectionate and completely harmless, but the press made such a fuss about it that, as Alice said later, "one would have thought that I was harboring a boa constrictor in the White House."

The newspaper stories frightened Alice's friends so much that they wouldn't allow her to visit them unless she promised not to bring Emily along in her handbag, which she often did. Emily's permanent home was a stocking box that Alice considered the perfect place for a garter snake.

Unfortunately, Emily Spinach met an untimely end. Alice came home one day and found it dead in its box. Worse yet, it was lying in such an unnatural position that she had no doubt it had been killed. Alice was furious and would have found some way to exact revenge on the murderer, if only she had known who it was.

At one point Jesse Grant expressed a desire to raise pigeons, "but it appeared that at an earlier time Tad Lincoln had been fired by the same ambition," Jesse later wrote, "and that the caretakers of the Treasury and other public buildings were still striving to exterminate the hardy survivors of Tad's breeding. For me, pigeons were taboo. . . ."

VIII

☆☆☆

Not all the animals that lived at the White House were kept as pets. In preautomobile days, there was always a stable full of horses, some for riding, others to pull presidential carriages. Andrew Jackson and Ulysses S. Grant also kept racehorses and Zachary Taylor brought along Old Whitey, the horse he had ridden during the Mexican War, although the poor steed was so ancient that he was good for very little except grazing on the White House lawn.

The only thing that could distract Old Whitey from his grazing was parade music. Every time he heard a brass band he would go looking for his place in the line of march. When the Marine Band appeared on the south lawn for their evening concerts, Old Whitey had to be sequestered in the stables. Otherwise, he would have been breathing down the musicians' necks trying to find out when the parade was going to start.

I can understand horses at the White House, even Old Whitey, but cows? I have to keep reminding myself that keeping livestock in the backyard wasn't so strange in the nineteenth century. In those days, there weren't any supermarkets or convenience stores where you could pick up a quart of milk whenever you needed it.

The cows used to graze in an area just beyond the south fence (now the Ellipse), but they were locked up at night because for many years cattle rustling was a serious problem in Washington. The cows were milked by a cow man and the milk was stored in crocks for use in the White House kitchen.

The last cow to graze on the White House lawn was Pauline Wayne. She was sent to another pasture during President William Howard Taft's administration when commercial dairies became common and milk no longer had to be obtained directly from its source.

During World War I, Woodrow Wilson, or more likely one of his advisers, decided that the White House should do its part in the war effort by acquiring a flock of sheep. The theory was that the sheep would eat the grass on the White House lawn, thus releasing the men who normally did the mowing for some type of war-related jobs.

A flock of thirteen ewes and a ram named Ike were brought to 1600 Pennsylvania Avenue and installed on the south lawn. It was a great public relations gesture but not as practical as it sounded. The sheep ate the grass all right, but they also devoured some very expensive shrubbery and entire beds of prize perennials.

The sheep did serve one purpose, however. They were sheared periodically and the wool was auctioned off for the benefit of the Red Cross. This raised quite a bit of money, but there are no reports of whether it was enough to pay for replacing the White House gardens.

IX
★★★

Other animals come and go but none of them have been able to edge dogs out of the White House spotlight. Almost every president has had at least one. Herbert Hoover had eight in addition to the famous King Tut. They ranged from a small black poodle called Tar Baby to a giant wolfhound named Shamrock.

Warren G. Harding's favorite dog was an Airedale named Laddie Boy that was one of the first gifts he received when he became president in 1921. In addition to sitting in on presidential appointments and attending cabinet meetings (where a special chair was provided for him), Laddie Boy made personal appearances. He was also the star of a "Be Kind to Animals" parade sponsored by Washington's Humane Education Society. Instead of risking sore paws by marching, he rode in style on a special float.

Laddie Boy became so prominent that a reporter from the *Washington Star* requested an interview with him. The first pet agreed and his comments took up almost an entire page in the Sunday *Star*. Predictably his main focus was on dog-related issues. Laddie Boy urged the attorney general to investigate the use of sled dogs to carry mail in Alaska, suggested that the secretary of agriculture check out the ingredients in dog biscuits, and pushed for an eight-hour day for watchdogs.

It was a well-known fact among the backstairs staff at the White House that Laddie Boy also played a key role in helping the

Hardings deal with their marital disputes. When the president and first lady were having one of their periodic spats and not on speaking terms, they would direct their questions and comments to Laddie Boy instead of to each other.

Calvin Coolidge had almost as many dogs as Herbert Hoover. One of them was named Paul Pry, presumably because he was a busybody. He was Laddie Boy's half-brother. The others included two chows named Timmy and Blackberry, and a pair of pure white collies named Prudence Prim and Rob Roy.

Rob Roy was far and away the president's favorite, and the collie made sure everyone knew it. He accompanied Coolidge to his office every morning, walking directly in front of him looking neither to the left nor the right in a canine imitation of the Presidential Color Team. When Coolidge took his afternoon nap, the collie would stretch out nearby and not make a sound until he got up.

My father, who collected stories about Calvin Coolidge, particularly liked the one about the time Coolidge invited Texas senator Morris Sheppard to breakfast at the White House. Rob Roy was in his usual position beside the president, but when the food was served, he went over to Sheppard and proceeded to stare at him as if he were trying to tell him something. The senator was puzzled and turned to the president for an explanation.

"He wants your bacon," Coolidge told him.

Sheppard obligingly gave his bacon to the dog, who gobbled it down in a flash. Then the senator waited for another serving. It never came.

Rob Roy was a model of good behavior with the first family, but he could be a hellion when the Coolidges were not around. One of his worst offenses was teaching the other dogs to tear through the upstairs halls and terrify the White House maids. When Rob Roy and his gang were on the loose, the frightened women would scurry into the nearest closet to get out of the way.

Rob Roy's greatest claim to fame was having his portrait painted with Mrs. Coolidge. In the picture he's looking up at her with what I used to think was adoration on his face. I've since learned that she got him to pose by feeding him candy during the sittings. He may just be looking for another handout.

The portrait, by Howard Chandler Christy, hangs in the White House and has probably produced an acute case of jealousy in every other first dog who has seen it. I must say it's a remarkable painting not only because Mrs. Coolidge is so attractive, but because of the striking color scheme. The artist painted her wearing a bright red dress, which stands in vivid contrast to the snow-white dog at her side.

Calvin Coolidge had wanted his wife to wear a white brocaded satin gown that was one of his favorites, but Howard Chandler Christy objected. He felt that the combination of the red dress and the white dog would make a more pleasing picture.

The president deferred to the artist's judgment but not before offering one last argument: "She could still wear the dress and we'd dye the dog."

I have a personal fondness for Mrs. Coolidge's portrait that has nothing to do with either her dress or Rob Roy. If you ever get the chance to view this work of art, look closely and you will see that the first lady is wearing the gold arrow pin of Pi Beta Phi, her sorority at the University of Vermont, the same one I joined at George Washington University. The portrait was commissioned by Pi Beta Phi and presented as a gift to the White House.

X
✩✩✩

Traphes Bryant, who was the White House kennel keeper during the Kennedy, Johnson, and Nixon administrations, rated Lyndon Johnson as the greatest pet lover of all our presidents. In his pre–White House days, LBJ had a dog named Old Beagle. When the dog died, he had it cremated and kept the ashes in a box over the refrigerator. When the family cook found out what was in the box, she blew her stack, and Old Beagle's remains were removed for burial on the Johnson ranch.

When the Johnsons moved into the White House, they brought along a pair of beagle puppies that had been given to their younger daughter, Luci. Their names were Him and Her and they were soon joined by another gift dog, a white collie named Blanco.

Lyndon was devoted to all three dogs. He often took time out from his busy schedule to play with them and when he stepped out of his office and gave a whistle, they would come bounding over to him, each trying to be the first to get a pat on the head.

Her died when she was a little over a year old after swallowing a small rock she found on the White House lawn. A couple of years later, Him followed Her to the grave. He was indulging in his favorite sport, chasing squirrels, when he was hit by a White House car.

LBJ was heartbroken. He was not consoled by the fact that Blanco remained. Although Blanco was a fine-looking dog, he had very little to offer in the way of brains or personality. Then Yuki appeared.

Luci and her husband, Patrick Nugent, found him at a gas station in Austin, Texas. Nobody knew whom he belonged to so they took him home and when he and LBJ met, it was love at first sight. Yuki went back to Washington with the president and had the run of the White House. He hung out in the Oval Office, sat under the table at cabinet meetings, and was introduced to statesmen and celebrities. One of the few important occasions from which he was excluded was Lynda Bird Johnson's wedding to Charles Robb in 1967. After the ceremony, the bridal party assembled in the upstairs Yellow Oval Room to be photographed. Traphes Bryant, the White House kennel keeper, had dressed Yuki in a red velvet sweater with "congratulations" spelled out in sequins on it. When the dog came wandering in unexpectedly, LBJ said: "We've got to get Yuki in the picture. We can't have a family portrait without him."

As former chief usher J. B. West tells it, "Lady Bird Johnson drew herself up to her full five feet three inches and backed off until she could look her husband in the eye.

" 'That dog is *not* going to be in the wedding picture,' she said.

"The president started to argue. But Mrs. Johnson whipped out a Lyndon-like command.

" 'Mr. Bryant, get that dog out of here right now! *He will not be photographed!*' "

According to West, Lynda breathed a huge sigh of relief and the picture-taking continued.

After the wedding, Yuki was restored to his most favored pet status. He continued to attend cabinet meetings and flew back to Texas with the Johnsons on Air Force One when LBJ's term was over.

What made Lyndon Johnson, whose dogs had always had impeccable pedigrees, become so attached to a homeless mutt? According to LBJ, there were two reasons: First, "He speaks with a Texas accent," and second, but even more important, "He likes me."

I've often thought how fitting it was that when Lyndon Johnson died suddenly of a heart attack in 1973, he was alone, except for Yuki.

XI

★★★

Warren Harding's dog, Laddie Boy, may have given an interview to the *Washington Star* in 1921, but since then dogs have gotten even smarter. In 1990, President George Bush's English springer spaniel, Mildred Kerr Bush, actually wrote a book. She freely admitted that she didn't do it entirely on her own; she dictated it to First Lady Barbara Bush. The book became a best-seller and raised almost a million dollars for the Barbara Bush Foundation for Family Literacy.

Millie was very much in the news during the Bush administration, particularly after she gave birth to six puppies at the White House in 1989. The Bushes got so many letters welcoming her brood that they had a thank-you card made up with their signatures and Millie and her offsprings' paw prints.

One of Millie's puppies went to George and Barbara Bush's granddaughters, Jenna and Barbara, in Texas. The girls named her Spot Fletcher after one of their heroes, Scott Fletcher, who played baseball for the Texas Rangers. When Fletcher was traded to another team, they dropped the dog's last name and now she is known simply as Spot.

In 2001, Spot followed in her mother's footsteps by moving into the White House, giving her the distinction of being the only second-generation presidential pet in White House history, and enabling her to feel quite superior to the first family's other dog, a Scottish terrier puppy named Barney. He is no slouch when it comes to family connections. His mother belonged to Bush cabinet member and former New Jersey governor Christine Todd Whitman. But compared to the White House pedigree, that's pretty far down on the power scale.

XII
★★★

Speaking of Scottish terriers, no discussion of White House pets would be complete without some observations on the most famous one of all: Franklin D. Roosevelt's Scottie, Fala.

Fala was not the first of FDR's dogs. He had previously owned several German shepherds including one, Major, who bit Senator Hattie Caraway of Arkansas and ripped the trousers of British Prime Minister Ramsey MacDonald. Another Scottie, Meggie, who belonged to Eleanor Roosevelt, was no better behaved. She bit two of the Roosevelt grandchildren and also gnawed on White House reporter Bess Furman.

Then there was Winks, a mischievous little Llewellyn setter, who slipped into the kitchen staff's dining room one morning when no one was around and devoured all nineteen plates of bacon and eggs that had been prepared for their breakfast. Winks died (from overeating?) when he was still a puppy and Major and Meggie were given away. There were several other Roosevelt dogs but they all faded into the background when Fala came along in the spring of 1940.

He was given to FDR as a puppy by his cousin Margaret Daisy Suckley and his original name was Big Boy. The president changed it to Fala, with the explanation that he was honoring an obscure Scottish ancestor, Murray the Outlaw of Fala Hill.

Fala and the president became all but inseparable. The Scottie would sleep on a blanket in Roosevelt's bedroom and play on the grass outside the Oval Office. When the president went for a car ride, Fala was usually perched beside him on the seat. The Secret Service gave him the code name "The Informer," because when Roosevelt traveled by train, the dog had to be walked, alerting everyone to the fact that the president was on board.

Fala was at home in the White House, in FDR's home at Hyde Park, and in Warm Springs, Georgia, where Roosevelt went to be treated for the polio that had paralyzed his legs in 1921. When FDR and Prime Minister Winston Churchill of Great Britain met at Placentia Bay, Newfoundland, in 1941, Fala went along and had his photograph taken with the two world leaders.

The dog also accompanied the president to Hawaii on a navy warship for another high-level meeting. Because of quarantine restrictions, Fala was not allowed to go ashore. The warship's crew took good care of him in every respect but one. The sailors started snipping off locks of his hair as souvenirs, and before long, Fala was sporting a large bald spot. Their commander in chief chewed them out for disfiguring his dog, but Fala's hair grew back so the damage wasn't permanent.

Perhaps the biggest news story about Fala concerned the time he accompanied Roosevelt on a voyage to Alaska. When they returned, one of FDR's political enemies circulated a rumor that Fala had been inadvertently left behind and a destroyer had been deployed to fetch him, costing the American taxpayers several million dollars.

Roosevelt's Republican opponents seized on the story as just one more example of the president's proclivity for taking advantage of the American people. But Roosevelt got back at them in his most famous speech of the 1944 election campaign.

"These Republican leaders have not been content with attacks on me, or my wife, or on my sons," he said with marvelous sarcasm. "No, not content with that, they now include my little dog, Fala.

"Well, of course, I don't resent attacks, and my family doesn't resent attacks, but Fala *does* resent them.

"You know, Fala is Scotch, and being a Scottie, as soon as he learned that the Republican fiction writers in Congress and out had concocted a story that I left him behind on the Aleutian Islands and sent a destroyer back to find him—at a cost to the taxpayers of two or three, or eight or twenty million dollars—his Scotch soul was furious. He has not been the same dog since.

"I am accustomed to hearing malicious falsehoods about myself, such as that old, worm-eaten chestnut that I have represented myself as indispensable. But I think I have a right to resent, to object to libelous statements about my dog."

The Republican candidate, Thomas E. Dewey, claimed to be angered and dismayed by such levity. One Democrat cracked that the campaign had become a contest between Roosevelt's dog and Dewey's goat.

Fala was with Roosevelt in Warm Springs, Georgia, when the president was stricken with, and died almost instantly from, a cerebral hemorrhage. The dog returned to the White House with the body of his master and was eventually taken to live with Eleanor Roosevelt. He died in the spring of 1952 and lies buried beside Franklin D. Roosevelt in the Hyde Park Rose Garden. He has also been immortalized in bronze at the Franklin D. Roosevelt Memorial in Washington, where he can be seen sitting at Roosevelt's feet just as he did in life.

Here is a shot of President Ronald Reagan talking to reporters in the Oval Office. Their relationship appears to be a whole lot warmer than it really was.
Credit: Courtesy Ronald Reagan Library

13

✮ ✮ ✮

Minding the Media

There's one section of the north lawn of the White House that is covered with gravel rather than grass. This particular part of the President's Park, which is known to insiders as Pebble Beach, is the place where television reporters stand when they're delivering the latest news from the Oval Office. TV watchers never see the gravel, but they get a fine view of the North Portico of the White House and, although it probably never occurs to them, a chance to observe freedom of the press in action.

The Founding Fathers included freedom of the press in the Bill of Rights because they believed that an informed citizenry was essential to the survival of a democracy. As James Madison, one of those founders, noted, "A popular government without popular information or the means of acquiring it is but a prologue to a farce or a tragedy, or perhaps both."

I'm quite sure no president of the United States would disagree with James Madison or with the Bill of Rights he helped to frame. In principle, every chief executive believes in the First Amendment guarantee of a free press. In practice, however, almost all of them have been wary of, if not downright hostile to, the men and women who represent it.

II

⋆⋆⋆

Contrary to popular belief, the war between the presidents and the press didn't start with Vietnam or Watergate; it has been going on ever since the country began. President George Washington accused the journalists of his era of abusing him as if he were a "common pickpocket." John Adams was certain the tribe of "scribblers" had deprived him of a second term.

Then came Thomas Jefferson, one of the shrewdest politicians ever to preside over the nation's destiny. To outwit his enemies in the press, Jefferson made one Washington newspaper, the *National Intelligencer*, the unofficial White House organ. Its editor or editors frequently dined with the president, then rushed back to the printing presses to peddle the latest party line.

Andrew Jackson went Jefferson one better. He not only brought Kentuckian Francis Preston Blair to Washington to found the *Globe*, he made him a member of his "kitchen cabinet," the group of unofficial advisers who met with the president at all hours of the night.

The *Globe* quickly became must reading around the nation. President Jackson boosted its circulation by informing everyone on the government payroll making more than $1,000 a year (over $19,000 in today's dollars) that they had better subscribe or start looking for other jobs. He also made sure the paper got every federal printing contract in existence.

Francis Preston Blair gave his name to Blair House, which he purchased around 1830, giving him easy access to his patron and prime source of news. Blair's friendship with Jackson grew even more intense during the 1832 reelection campaign. Surviving letters in Jackson's scrawl reveal the president telling Blair "you could get a message tonight if you would come up" to the White House.

Can you imagine what a modern reporter would do to achieve such intimacy with a president? Murder would not be out of the question. Needless to say, the *Globe*'s loyalty to Jackson was total. Blair's stories and editorials scalded the president's numerous enemies and exalted his friends. When a cholera epidemic ravaged Washington, D.C., the *Globe* barely mentioned it. Blair was too busy filling his columns with pro-Jackson stories and endorsements.

III
***

Women were practically nonexistent in this dawn of White House journalism. For years I nurtured an admiration for one of the pioneers, a feisty female named Anne Royall, who published a newspaper called *Paul Pry* that was a forerunner of today's supermarket tabloids. (She lifted the title from a hit London comedy about a character who specialized in sticking his nose into other people's business.) Not a little of my admiration for Anne was based on the story that in the late 1820s she caught that ultimate presidential sourpuss, John Quincy Adams, swimming in the Potomac without a stitch on (something he did regularly). Anne supposedly sat on his clothes and refused to depart until he gave her an interview. Unfortunately, in the course of researching this book, I concluded the story (sigh) is not true.

Anne Royall nevertheless deserves a salute for her perseverance. Although her paper's circulation was never very high, she was a fixture on the Washington scene for forty years. In 1854, at the age of eighty-five, she interviewed Franklin Pierce and bestowed on this luckless president, caught in the growing animosity between North and South, the sort of praise he rarely found in other newspapers.

IV
***

Long before that sentimental moment, things had begun happening in the newspaper world that made insider journalism passé.

Steam-driven presses replaced the laborious handpresses on which apprentices broke their backs, turning out one or two sheets at a time. Soon a mordant genius named James Gordon Bennett decided he could sell papers for as little as a penny a copy and still make money. That startling idea led Bennett to conclude he did not need a president's favor, or the backing of his enemies, to prosper. The era of the president as fair game for any and all reporters dawned.

Bennett went from being Washington correspondent for the *New-York Enquirer* to being owner and editor of the hugely successful New York *Herald* and a man almost as famous as the president, whoever he happened to be. His style of no-holds-barred reporting is evident in his account of an 1839 White House visit to Martin Van Buren. The president had been a prime target of Bennett's sarcasm since his election in 1836. Here are the opening lines of the newspaperman's report on his visit.

> *His Excellency . . . held out his hand. It was soft and oily. I took hold of it, gently, by the very hand, too, which has quizzed [abused] him so unmercifully during the past four years.*
>
> *"How do you do, Mr. Bennett?" said Mr. Van Buren with a half smile.*
>
> *"Pretty well, thank you," I responded with another half smile.*
>
> *I was almost ready to burst into a horse laugh . . . but being in the presence of the Chief of the Democratic Party, I restrained myself.*
>
> *I sat down on the couch, crossed my legs, and looked very knowingly into the hickory fire blazing on high.*

How is that for effrontery?

Soon Bennett escalated his attack, announcing: "Martin Van Buren and his atrocious associates form one of the original causes of the terrible moral, political and commercial desolation that spreads over the country." Yet Bennett claimed to be a Democrat! Poor Van Buren must have muttered that with friends like this guy, he did not need enemies.

The disciples of James Gordon Bennett did similar numbers on succeeding presidents. James Polk, for instance, was called "Jim Thumb," an uncomplimentary comparison to Tom Thumb, P. T. Barnum's famous midget. A reporter from the influential New York *Evening Post* described Franklin Pierce as a "parlor knight—pale and soft looking. But not what I would call elegant." The reporter finished Pierce off by noting that he was talking about running for a second term. "Could fond self-conceit go further?" he asked.

Almost as startling as this casual abuse by the press is the access these scribes had to the president. The *Evening Post* man described how he strolled into the White House "unheralded" and thrust himself into a reception President Pierce was giving for "a bevy of ladies." The president greeted him "politely" and even introduced him to Mrs. Pierce. That did not stop the newshawk from launching into a diatribe against his host in the very next sentence.

V

★★★

In the crisis of the Civil War, the press acquired even more power. Thanks to the country's hunger for news, newspaper circulation soared and, with the invention of the telegraph and the rise of the railroads, stories could be quickly disseminated throughout the country.

That realistic man, Abraham Lincoln, saw newspapers as crucial to maintaining public support for the war. Lincoln seldom if ever turned away a reporter's request for information. Sometimes the newsmen were not above interrupting him in a cabinet meeting. Often he came out to talk to them, or wrote out an answer on a card. "The press has no greater friend than I am," Lincoln insisted.

Like many presidents, Lincoln soon found that this protestation did not make friendship a two-way street. Among his most vicious critics was James Gordon Bennett's New York *Herald*. The paper published a stream of reports, most of them hostile to the president, from generals and cabinet members who seemed willing to tell everything. The stories were written by a con-man-turned-journalist, Malcolm Ives, and most of them were fiction.

On the plus side, Lincoln found one reporter he could trust—Noah Brooks, a correspondent for the *Daily Union* in Sacramento, California. A Maine Yankee who covered the Railsplitter when he ran for the Senate in Illinois in 1858 and followed him to Washington, Brooks became a fixture in the White House, and often accompanied Lincoln on his trips to the front. His dispatches, signed "Castine" (his Maine birthplace), eventually became a book, *Washington in Lincoln's Time*, which is still consulted by historians.

While Lincoln was never reluctant to meet with reporters, he sometimes dispensed with charm and talked to them in language that curled their hair. Joseph Medill, the lordly editor of the powerful Chicago *Tribune*, came to the White House in 1864 with a delegation from the Windy City protesting their draft quota of six thousand men.

Lincoln led the group down the street to the office of Secretary of War Edwin Stanton and the two men listened to the arguments from both sides. Then the president turned to Medill and his fellow Chicagoans and said:

> *Gentleman, after Boston, Chicago has been the chief instrument in bringing this war on the country. . . . You called for war until we had it. You called for emancipation [of the slaves] and I have given it to you. . . . Now you come here begging to be let off from the call for men which I have made to carry out the war which you have demanded. You ought to be ashamed of yourselves. . . . You, Medill, are acting like a coward. You and your*

Tribune have had more influence than any paper in the North-
west in making this war. . . . Go home and send us those men.

As the flabbergasted Medill later recalled it, "I couldn't say anything. It was the first time I ever was whipped. . . . We all got up and
went out and . . . one of my colleagues said: 'Gentlemen, that old
man is right. We ought to be ashamed of ourselves.' "

Lincoln got his six thousand men.

VI

***

By the time the Civil War ended, newspapers had become so popular that succeeding presidents regarded them the way kings in the
Middle Ages viewed dukes and barons—potential rivals for power,
to be propitiated or outwitted or defied, depending on the circumstances. No less than 150 reporters were now permanently based in
Washington, D.C., sending back news to their home papers.

Andrew Johnson, Lincoln's harried successor, gave long interviews to individual reporters, which did not save him from impeachment, though it may have rescued him from conviction.
Ulysses Grant, secretive by nature, decided to tell reporters as little
as possible. His wife, Julia, filled the gap and became the first presidential spouse to be interviewed by the press.

When President James Garfield was shot in 1881, reporters were
allowed to set up a press office on the second floor of the White
House and transmit their stories from the telegraph room. Frederick Hathaway Trusdell, chief of the Washington bureau of the National Associated Press, filed updates on the president's condition by
visiting his sickroom and listening to him breathe.

The steadily increasing power of the press was one of several reasons why Grover Cleveland appointed a former newspaper editor,
Daniel Lamont, as his secretary. Lamont performed many of the

duties that would later be taken over by the White House press secretary. Essentially he served as a buffer between the president and reporters, whom Cleveland lumped into a single epithet: "the dirty gang."

Cleveland's antipathy to "the gang" was intensified after a dozen reporters descended on the Deer Park, Maryland, resort where he was spending his honeymoon. He hired a squad of Baltimore & Ohio Railroad detectives to make sure they kept their distance, forcing the newshounds to peer at the newlyweds' cottage through telescopes and snoop around the hotel kitchen to find out what they were having for dinner.

In the course of five and a half days, the reporters filed 400,000 words about such momentous matters as what time the couple got up in the morning and went to bed at night. An irate president accused the reporters of using "the enormous power of the modern newspaper to perpetuate and disseminate a colossal impertinence" and predicted that American journalism would soon become "contemptible in the estimation of people of good breeding."

The *New York Times* responded with a defense of the journalists, insisting they were "a self-respecting set of men, who had gone to Deer Park in the line of their business in response to a good-natured unobtrusive popular demand, and they found means through callers and in ways perfectly legitimate and inoffensive to get enough information for truthful and entertaining reality."

The president's rage may have been overdone and the *Times*'s defense a bit too pious, but both sides were convinced they had a legitimate argument. In one form or another, the debate has been going on ever since.

VII
★★★

Grover Cleveland must have been appalled when a reporter appeared, quite literally, on his doorstep in 1896. William Price had come to the capital from a small town in South Carolina hoping to get a job on the *Washington Evening Star*. Looking for a way to get rid of him, the city editor sent him to the White House with orders to come back with a story. If he got one, the job was his.

As the editor well knew, the chances of a tyro getting any news from the Cleveland White House were almost nil. But Price was unfazed by the challenge. As the editor of a small-town weekly, he had gotten his news by hanging around the local train station and interviewing the people who arrived each day. Deciding to use the same strategy at the White House, he stood outside the North Portico and talked to the visitors who went in and out. "Fatty" Price—he weighed three hundred pounds—soon had a job at the *Evening Star*.

Cleveland's second term was already winding down, which probably saved "Fatty" from being evicted from his beat. He continued to collect news outside at the North Portico until someone in President William McKinley's administration took pity on him and invited him inside. It was at best a marginal improvement; he still had to write his copy leaning against a wall.

With the outbreak of the Spanish-American War in the spring of 1898, the press finally managed to win working space in the White House. Price and other reporters were allowed to gather in the east hall on the second floor. There they could write their stories, interview visitors going in and out of the president's office, and badger his secretary for scraps of news. If the president happened to walk by, there was an unwritten rule that the reporters would not ask him any questions.

McKinley's successor, Theodore Roosevelt, ordered Charles McKim to include a pressroom in the new executive office building—today's West Wing. The room was next to the office of the president's secretary and the scribes were even provided with telephones, eliminating the need for them to send their copy to Western Union by bicycle. There was something in all this for the president, of course. The press was instantly accessible anytime he wanted to barrage an opponent with hostile headlines.

VIII

★★★

With Teddy Roosevelt, the country got a president who showed future Oval Office occupants how to handle the press and set the style for making the White House the red-hot center of the nation's politics. We have often heard about the way Theodore Roosevelt turned the presidency into a "bully pulpit," but not many people realize how much manipulation of news and newsmen this involved.

Also forgotten is what a formidable character Theodore Roosevelt was. Few presidents before or since have come close to matching his brainpower. He wrote books that wowed historians. He could also read Italian and French, had made a special study of Romanian literature, and was honorary president of the Gaelic Literature Association. Throw in his status as a Spanish-American War hero and you have a president who reduced most journalists to stuttering awe.

Teddy (he hated the name) set his large brain to work on these more or less willing targets. Soon he had produced a gallery of presidential tricks still in use today. Bad news was released at the end of the day on Friday because many people slept late on Saturday and skipped reading the papers. Middling news was released in time for the Sunday papers, when hard-up editors were likely to put it on the front page for lack of anything more interesting. TR was the master of the trial balloon, an idea or proposal that he floated through some willing reporter and then might deny or even denounce if the public disliked it.

He was also adept at playing reporters off against each other. He divided them into two groups, the Paradise Club, for his favorites, and the Ananias Club, for those who wrote critical stories, which he usually dismissed as lies. (Ananias was the name of the high priest who condemned Jesus before Pontius Pilate.) Teddy was also not above calling an overly critical reporter's paper to get him fired.

Nothing illustrates Roosevelt's artful use of the press better than the day in 1903 when he summoned a group of reporters to his office to demolish John D. Rockefeller. After making them promise not to reveal him as the source of the story, Teddy told them that Rockefeller, the nation's richest man, had sent telegrams to six senators who were arguing against antitrust legislation that was pending in Congress.

The reporters made no attempt to find out what Rockefeller had said in the telegrams, or even if they existed. The stories were filed and the resultant explosion of headlines sent the antitrust bill rocketing through the House of Representatives by a 251–10 margin.

Even my father, who had mixed feelings about Teddy Roosevelt (he was a Republican after all) would have to admit that kind of power over the press enabled a president to have few worries about his coverage.

IX
★★★

Woodrow Wilson's opinion of the press was on a par with Grover Cleveland's. "Those contemptible spies, the newspaper men," he called them on one occasion. Nevertheless, Wilson became the first chief executive to hold regularly scheduled press conferences. Unfortunately, they were not very successful. The president, with his college professor background, lectured the reporters as if they were not-too-bright freshmen, and when their stories failed to get passing grades, he stopped seeing them almost entirely.

Wilson could never understand why the press insisted on commenting on his statements and speculating about his decisions instead of simply passing them along to the public. He would have preferred to see the White House have its own news service and issue stories directly to the papers. When World War I began, he created the Committee on Public Information, which proceeded to do just that. The White House reporters hated it and Wilson's popularity took a steep dive.

Although Wilson considered his press conferences a waste of time—and the reporters were inclined to agree with him—the fact that they had been established was an important step in the relationship between the White House and the press. The relationship was further formalized in 1914 when the newsmen organized the White House Correspondents Association. The move led to stricter rules about who could, and could not, attend presidential press conferences and created a forum where complaints by and against reporters could be heard.

X
★★★

Although you would never guess it from all the stories about his taciturnity, Calvin Coolidge supplied more wordage to the press during his tenure than Theodore Roosevelt and Woodrow Wilson combined. He was not only the first president to make radio addresses, he made them at the rate of one a month. He also met with the press twice a week, chalking up a total of 520 press conferences, a higher monthly average than Franklin D. Roosevelt's.

Coolidge followed the presidential custom of accepting only written questions submitted to him in advance. That precedent was broken by Franklin D. Roosevelt, who let the reporters fire away. FDR also revived regular press conferences, which had all but disappeared during the Hoover administration. Roosevelt turned them into a Washington institution—and an ongoing nightmare for succeeding presidents whose verbal skills were not as well-honed as his.

Once or twice a week, FDR would invite about twenty newspaper and radio reporters into the Oval Office and let them pelt him with questions that he sometimes answered and more often ducked, dodged, or joked away with his marvelous combination of charm and wit. His first conference was such a tour de force, the reporters gave him a standing ovation when it ended.

FDR also introduced a new brand of press mastery, based to a large extent on the techniques of his distant cousin, Teddy, including manufactured headlines, trial balloons, and carefully timed announcements.

As time went on, the Roosevelt magic began to fade. The newsmen realized that they were getting more style than substance. As author John Gunther put it, "I never met anyone who showed greater capacity for avoiding a direct answer while giving the questioner a feeling he *had* been answered."

Nevertheless, there were few reporters who could resist falling under FDR's spell, even when they caught him telling whoppers. During World War II, when rising prices and shortages of civilian goods were major problems on the home front, Roosevelt would say almost anything to get his message across to the public. One day he told about a mechanic who had stopped him as he drove around his hometown of Hyde Park, New York, and complained about the high price of strawberries. The president replied that the man shouldn't be so worried about prices on the home front while soldiers were fighting and dying for freedom overseas.

A few months later, FDR told another story about a Hyde Park mechanic who had complained to him about the high price of lettuce. "Mr. President," asked Merriman Smith, the United Press reporter who became something of an institution at White House press conferences, "is that the same mechanic who complained about the price of strawberries?"

Smith's fellow reporters erupted into roars of laughter. FDR turned "a little pink," Smith recalled, and shouted over the guffaws: "By God Merriman, it's true, it *is* true. It was the same man." He could hardly finish the sentence, Smith recalled, "because he was laughing too hard himself."

FDR's amicable relations with the press did not last. Some journalists grew disillusioned when he failed to cure the Great Depression. Others became skeptical after the outbreak of World War II when he barred them from covering such major stories as his 1941 meeting with Winston Churchill at Placentia Bay, Newfoundland,

and the 1943 Teheran conference with Churchill and Joseph Stalin. In both instances, British reporters broke the stories.

Among the disillusioned fraternity, Roosevelt was particularly unhappy with short, dour Arthur Krock of the *New York Times.* The president claimed Krock "never loved anybody or anything. He never patted a dog, never had a real friend, man, woman or beast."

Krock repaid these compliments by claiming that FDR's administration was guilty of "more ruthlessness . . . in trying to suppress legitimate unfavorable opinion than any other I have ever known."

Sometimes I think politics should be classified as a blood sport.

XI
☆☆☆

Meanwhile, First Lady Eleanor Roosevelt was changing White House coverage in a very important way. She started holding press conferences—for women reporters only. The Washington bureau chiefs, male to the last grizzled whisker, were thunderstruck. It meant they might have to let women start writing about something more important than the first lady's taste in china. The assorted scribes of the White House Correspondents Association were almost as undone at the thought of letting women into their all-male clubhouse.

Mrs. Roosevelt's conferences were not replays of FDR's free-for-alls. The women reporters all wore hats and gloves—and that dreadful topic, politics, was forbidden. Mrs. R. sat among the women, often knitting while they chatted. Only gradually did the topics change from cooking, interior decorating, and White House entertaining to Mrs. Roosevelt's concern for the poor and neglected.

Though Eleanor Roosevelt often spoke up on behalf of black Americans, she never managed to reverse her husband's exclusion of black reporters from the White House, in spite of their frequent petitions. The president's press secretary, Steve Early, offered the not very convincing argument that the blacks represented weeklies, and White House correspondents were supposed to be from daily papers.

The blacks, good reporters, discovered that Early was letting in journalists from weekly trade papers and testily asked: How come? In 1944, after twelve frustrating years, black journalists finally joined the throng in the Oval Office.

By that time, alas, the flamboyant combination of vaudeville and politics that characterized the president's press performances was gone. He was a mere ghost of the vital effervescent politician whom reporters applauded in 1933. His heart congested to the brink of imminent failure, his blood pressure out of control, his brain damaged by repeated strokes, FDR was a dying man.

When reporters asked about his health, he grew petulant. Toward the end of a press conference, his voice would dwindle until it could barely be heard. Merriman Smith sadly recalled FDR's fight for re-election in 1944 when "he should have been sitting quietly on the banks of the Hudson River . . . hoarding his last few months of life."

XII

★★★

FDR's death after only eighty-two days of his fourth term catapulted Harry S Truman into the White House. Dad tackled the unwanted, unsought job with all the energy and determination he could muster. Although he was often taken to task in the press, historians seem to agree his performance was pretty creditable. But he, too, had more than his share of troubles with reporters, beginning with the very fundamental question of where they were going to meet.

Membership in the White House Correspondents Association had grown substantially since FDR started jousting with the press in the Oval Office. By 1945, some two hundred people were likely to show up at a press conference, and the office often would be so packed that the reporters in the back had trouble hearing. In addition, the pressroom that had been set up in Theodore Roosevelt's day was outdated and overcrowded, with the result that reporters tended to camp out in the West Wing lobby.

The West Wing was already bursting at the seams, and one of Dad's first orders of business was to find a way to enlarge it. Plans were drawn up for a 15,000-square-foot expansion that would provide more office space, a staff cafeteria, a new pressroom, and a 375-seat auditorium where press conferences could be held. In December 1945, Congress approved an appropriation that would cover the cost of the added space plus a number of other renovations, including the installation of a new heating system.

Inevitably, a sketch of the proposed addition to the West Wing appeared in the newspapers and as one of Dad's advisers put it, "all hell broke loose." The project became a preview of the balcony battle but with less felicitous results. The public was convinced that the White House itself was going to be changed and no amount of explanation could persuade them otherwise. Always sensitive to the voice of the voters, Congress amended the appropriation bill and the precise amount allotted for enlarging the West Wing disappeared.

Ironically, it was the president perhaps with the strongest antipathy to the media who finally managed to get them decent facilities. Annoyed at the noisy, messy pressroom adjoining the lobby where his visitors entered, Richard Nixon started looking for new space. He found it in the basement of the West Wing, where Franklin D. Roosevelt had installed the swimming pool he used as therapy for his polio-damaged legs.

The swimming pool and some adjacent utility areas were torn out and the space was reconfigured to accommodate a press center with forty writing desks and twelve broadcast cubicles, plus a briefing room where the White House press secretary could fill reporters in on the latest news from the Oval Office. Formally opened in 1973, the pressroom is currently due for another expansion.

Plans are in the works for a new headquarters to be built under the West Wing drive. In addition to a larger press center and briefing room, it will have audiovisual rooms, and space for interviews, camera operations, and storage.

When—and if—it is built, the new facility will spell the end of Pebble Beach, but it seems unlikely that its disappearance will provoke an uproar. No one will miss the crush of lights and cameras on the White House lawn, least of all the TV reporters who have to endure all kinds of bad weather in the course of doing their jobs.

XIII

★★★

Every president has had at least one member of the media on his permanent hate list. In my father's case it was Washington columnist Drew Pearson, who had also driven Presidents Hoover and Roosevelt into paroxysms of rage. FDR wanted to lift Pearson's press pass, and only strenuous objections from press secretary Steve Early dissuaded him.

Bob Hannegan, the chairman of the Democratic Party and one of Dad's closest friends, was horrified when Pearson accused him of trying to dump Harry S Truman from the ticket as the 1948 election loomed. Bob rushed a letter to the White House denying Pearson's canard. Dad's opinion of this so-called reporter whose column ran in over four hundred newspapers is evidenced in his reply:

I appreciated your note of the 9th but you didn't have to write it.

Whenever I get my information from Drew Pearson, I hope somebody will have my head examined—I'll need it.

Any time Pearson ever told the truth, Dad added, it was by accident and not intentional.

The columnist's attitude toward the White House became downright malevolent after Dad's victory in 1948. Pearson had published a column just before the election, ponderously discussing the Republican candidate Thomas E. Dewey's cabinet choices. Infuriated at his own gaffe, Drew devoted column after column to sniping at everything and everyone in the Truman White House.

One of his favorite targets was Dad's military aide, General Harry Vaughan. Pearson accused General Vaughan of taking a huge bribe to fix a tax case. Dad ordered the FBI to probe the matter but after several years of questioning and record checking, they found nothing. In the interim, Pearson was able to report that one of the president's closest friends was "under investigation." Meanwhile, the columnist's legmen were racing around the country, offering bribes to other Democrats to swear that General Vaughan had helped fix a tax case for them.

The Trumanites had their revenge when Pearson announced that General Vaughan was to receive a medal from the "fascistic" Argentine government, then in the hands of dictator Juan Perón. The columnist conveniently ignored the fact that General Omar Bradley, the army's chief of staff, and a half dozen other top generals had received the same medal with no opprobrium.

Pearson announced that he was going to station himself outside the Argentine embassy the day the medal was presented and take down the names of everyone who dared to attend the event. No one paid the slightest attention to him as he ran up and down peering in car windows, furiously writing down VIP names.

The climax came when General Hoyt Vandenberg, commander of the air force, tapped Drew on the shoulder and gave him his card. "I want to make sure you don't miss me," he said. Pearson's nastiness hit a new low the next day; he claimed the general had sneaked into the embassy through a rear entrance to avoid being seen.

Like presidents before him and since, Dad acquired a low opinion of newspapermen during his White House years. Always mindful of history, he dug into the press relations of previous presidents and was comforted to discover he was not alone.

"It seems that every man in the White House was tortured and bedeviled by the so-called free press," he wrote to his sister. "They were lied about, misrepresented and actually libeled, and they have to take it."

With this as background, you can easily imagine why I administered one of the worst shocks of Dad's post-presidential life when I called him from New York to tell him I had fallen in love and was planning to marry a man named Clifton Daniel.

"What does he do for a living?" Dad asked.

"He's a newspaperman."

There was a moment of thunderstruck silence on the Missouri end of the phone. Finally, gamely, Dad said: "Well, if you love him, that's good enough for me."

(P.S. They got along beautifully.)

XIV
★★★

In 1954, Dwight Eisenhower became the first president to hold televised news conferences. They were broadcast from the Indian Treaty Room in the Executive Office Building. Ike was coached in advance by actor Robert Montgomery and the telecasts were carefully stage-managed by Ike's press secretary, former *New York Times*man James Hagerty, who reserved the right to edit the tapes before they were released to the public. But Hagerty, with Ike's approval, permitted verbatim transcripts of the presidential remarks to be released to the press. This made for more truth in journalism, but also led to Ike being lampooned for his often tangled syntax.

Both televised press conferences and stage-managing were raised to high arts by Ike's successor, John F. Kennedy. JFK's first press conference was broadcast live from the East Room, beginning what one weekly newsmagazine called "a new era in political communication."

The president, who was not only young and handsome but had a quick wit and an engaging manner, apparently had no difficulty pulling whatever facts he needed from his agile brain on demand. Not many people knew that his astute press secretary, Pierre Salinger, gave him a thorough briefing on the probable questions as Jim Hagerty had done with Ike. Salinger also briefed the press twice a day, creating a sort of semiclosed circuit from their heads to the president's head and vice versa.

When it came to charming the press, Jack was well on his way to outclassing Franklin D. Roosevelt. He had the added advantage of a stylish wife, two small and very cute children, and a huge cast of photogenic family members, all of whom made excellent copy.

Jack also mastered the Rooseveltian art of manipulation. He leaked stories, planted news, gave exclusives to favored journalists, and played reporters off against each other. Like FDR, he was not above withholding news from the media when it suited his interests. As he remarked to one of his staff members, "Always remember that their interests and ours ultimately conflict."

Kennedy has to bear at least some of the blame for the adversarial relationship that developed between the White House and the media over the war in Vietnam. By attempting to restrict the amount of information correspondents were getting about the American involvement in southeast Asia, JFK helped foster the distrust and cynicism that became the trademarks of journalism during the Johnson and Nixon administrations and beyond.

XV
✵✵✵

The undeclared war between the press and the president saw the media's greatest triumph in that seeming Waterloo of presidential prestige and power: Watergate. But while the press was busy congratulating itself on the victory, the White House was gearing up to fight back.

Under Gerald Ford, Richard Nixon's successor, 1600 Pennsylvania Avenue started to become a media powerhouse in its own right. The press office staff was increased to forty-five people, most of them hired by Nixon, about seven times more than there were in John F. Kennedy's day.

The trend continued under President Jimmy Carter. In 1978, the Carter press office, now called the Office of Media Liaison, sent out 35,551 press releases, audiotapes, and films each month to 6,500 news organizations. The output grew even larger under Presidents Reagan, Bush, and Clinton.

In a further effort on the communications front, President George H. W. Bush decided snaking cables in and out of the Oval Office at periodic intervals was too much trouble and set up a White House TV studio in the nearby Executive Office Building (now named the Eisenhower Executive Office Building).

In this blizzard of information and images, press conferences lost much of their importance. No longer were they vehicles for telling the American people what a president was thinking. More and more they became forums in which the president was out to sell some idea or program. The conferences dwindled in number until, in Ronald Reagan's administration, reporters were often reduced to screaming questions at the president as he boarded his helicopter on the White House lawn. Most of the time all they got in response was a friendly wave.

With the scarcity of press conferences came a lurch toward presidential image-building that was more than a little scary. Apparently determined to give each appearance maximum impact, the Reagan White House redesigned the briefing room as a theater, with permanent seats. Television reporters were put in the front row, which guaranteed them on-screen appearances and ninety percent of the president's attention.

Presidential entrances and departures became pure Hollywood.

The doors behind the briefing room podium were guarded by a marine in full dress uniform. At the appointed time, they opened to reveal the president. When the conference ended, the doors swung open again and the cameras followed the president as he strode down the long corridor leading to the executive offices. It was a fade-out worthy of Mr. Reagan's favorite movie director, John Ford.

Nothing summed up the growing sense of presidential dominance more than Reagan's press conference after he won reelection in 1984 in the greatest landslide in American history. He had carried every state in the Union except his Democratic opponent's Minnesota. Every age group in the country had given him a majority. A reporter asked him if he was going to make himself more accessible to newspeople. Reagan looked at the man with a combination of amazement and benign contempt. "Look," he said. "I won. I don't have to subject myself to—" He stopped just in time, and managed to restore his cheerful smile. The correspondents laughed nervously.

President Bill and First Lady Hillary Clinton, leaping from scandal to scandal like a pair of Little Evas getting from ice floe to ice floe in *Uncle Tom's Cabin*, had an even more negative attitude toward the media. Press conferences sank to the vanishing point during their tenure. The Clinton White House preferred to rely on its own awesome ability to communicate directly to the American people.

Most previous presidents gave thirty or forty speeches a year. Bill gave over five hundred, leaving his speechwriters spavined. The Clinton White House beamed programs from the TV studio in the Old Executive Office Building to public and commercial television stations at the rate of one a day, often with the president participating for as long as two hours by satellite to Arizona, California, or other points west or south.

Meanwhile the White House website (www.whitehouse.gov) was bundling transcripts of the president's speeches and remarks over the Internet and "streaming" live interviews with the president, creating a virtual theater in which fifteen thousand people could fire e-mail questions at the Oval Office. It was all part of Mr. Clinton's "permanent campaign." The ultimate goal, not reached under Bill and Hill but articulated by one of their media managers, was a White House TV channel that would "broadcast White House events around the clock: BC [Bill Clinton]-TV." Somewhere, Woodrow Wilson may be applauding that dangerous idea.

Has the president become an eight-hundred-pound media gorilla who can talk his way out of anything? There were times during the Clinton years when it looked as if that might be true. One of my favorite reporters, David Broder, gloomily opined that the "White House propaganda machine has . . . clearly been winning the battle" for control of public opinion.

Before panic sets in, it might be helpful to recall that people were worrying about this possibility in 1908. That year, a pundit named George W. Alger fretted in the *Atlantic Monthly* about "the enormous increase in the power of the executive" after watching Teddy Roosevelt manipulate reporters for seven years.

I have too much faith in the people who write and edit and broadcast the news to believe that presidential overpowerment will become the status quo. Not long after I wrote that line, I read that White House spokesman Ari Fleischer had warned the media not to expect President George W. Bush to hold formal press conferences in the East Room, like many of his predecessors. Instead, he would hold them in the White House briefing room, supplement them with informal chats with reporters, and answer a few questions during photo ops.

At first I thought the elimination of the East Room cross-examinations was just another presidential ploy to get the upper hand with the media. Then I read an interview with my old friend Helen Thomas, the Hearst newspaper columnist and former UPI correspondent who has been covering the White House since John

F. Kennedy took office in 1961. Helen has made more than one president squirm at a press conference.

Was Helen concerned about Bush's approach? "I don't think it matters when or where the press conference is held," she said, "just so we really get a crack at him."

She went on to point out that press conferences are the only real chance Americans have to question their president. With Helen and her colleagues around, we are unlikely to lose that chance. That means sooner or later at least some of the truth about what's happening in the White House is going to reach the American people, whether the president likes it or not.

The man on the left of President Calvin Coolidge is Secret Service agent Edmund Star-
ling. Of the five presidents he protected, Coolidge was his favorite.
Credit: U.S. Secret Service

14

☆☆☆

Keeping Killers and Kooks at Bay

My parents had to move to Blair House while the White House was undergoing its historic foundation-to-roof reconstruction, but the West Wing was perfectly sound so there was no reason why my father couldn't continue to work in the Oval Office. The only question was: How would he get there?

The West Wing is only a few steps across Pennsylvania Avenue, but Jim Rowley, the Secret Service agent in charge of the White House detail, wanted him to go by car. Dad was not too happy about the idea. "Can you imagine being *driven* across the street?" he said. But he took Jim's advice.

A couple of years later, Dad had reason to be glad the Secret Service was on the job. On November 1, 1950, around two P.M., two armed Puerto Rican nationalists, Oscar Collazo and Griselio Torresola, approached Blair House. My father and mother were upstairs dressing to go to Arlington National Cemetery to preside at a dedication of a statue honoring British Field Marshall Sir John Dill, who had died in Washington during World War II. I was far away, preparing to give a concert in Portland, Oregon.

The two gunmen planned to assassinate the president on behalf of Puerto Rican independence. Collazo, who had never fired a pistol before in his life, approached from the east, Torresola from the west. They planned to meet on the front steps of Blair House and charge inside together.

The house was guarded by White House policemen in booths at either end of the building. Another policeman, Donald T. Birdzell, was on duty at the front door, which was open to the mild fall weather. Only a lightly latched screen door prevented access from the street.

Collazo mingled with some tourists as he passed the east booth. When he was within three or four feet of the front door, he whipped out his pistol, aimed it at Birdzell, and pulled the trigger. Nothing happened.

If that pistol had gone off, the plot might well have succeeded. With Birdzell dead, Collazo planned to whirl and shoot the guards in the east booth while his partner took care of the men in the west booth. After that the only person between them and the president would have been the Secret Serviceman stationed at the head of the stairs to the second floor. The assassins might have shot him, too, leaving the president and first lady unprotected.

Hearing the click of Collazo's gun, Birdzell turned to find him pounding on the jammed pistol. It suddenly went off, striking the policeman in the knee. Not wanting to fire with pedestrians in the area, Birdzell stumbled down the steps to the street before drawing his gun. A Secret Service agent who was with the policeman in the east booth opened fire. Meanwhile, Torresola reached the west booth and quickly pumped two bullets into Policeman Leslie Coffelt and another slug into Joseph Downs, the other policeman in the booth. Whirling, he took a second shot at Birdzell and another policeman coming out a basement door. As Torresola paused to reload his gun, the dying Coffelt tottered to the doorway of the west booth and put a bullet in his brain. By this time, three shots fired by other policemen and Secret Service agents had hit Collazo, flattening him. In less than two minutes twenty-seven shots had been fired.

The bark of the guns drew my mother to the window. She looked disbelievingly at the sprawled bodies of the two would-be assassins and the fallen policemen. "Harry!" she gasped. "Someone's shooting at our policemen!" My father rushed to the window. One of the Secret Service agents in the street shouted "Get back, get back!" President Truman quickly obeyed.

My parents left for the dedication ceremony on schedule. "A president has to expect these things," Dad said. The next day, at a press conference, one of the reporters asked him if he would give them his version of the nightmarish incident. He shook his head and said: "There's no story as far as I am concerned. I was never in any danger. The thing I hate about it is what happened to these young men—one of them killed [Coffelt] and two of them [Downs and Birdzell] badly wounded."

II
★★★

There are any number of people who gravitate to Washington from all parts of the country to tell the president their troubles, or to give him advice on his troubles—or to do him serious bodily harm. The Secret Service has been trying to keep them at bay for over one hundred years, with varying degrees of success.

If you have any doubts about the need for the Secret Service, consider these statistics. One in every three presidents has been shot at or otherwise attacked. Four have been killed by assassin's bullets. In the past few decades, Gerald Ford survived two blasts of gunfire and Ronald Reagan came within a hair's breadth of being killed by a seriously disturbed man who thought shooting a president would impress screen star Jodie Foster.

During Herbert Hoover's administration, a tall, blond, rather imperious-looking woman appeared in the entrance hall of the White House. Her eyes were blue and bold and she was wearing a stylish pink dress with shoes to match. "Please tell the president I'm here," she said to the doorman.

The man parked her in a corner and called the head of the White House Secret Service detail, Edmund Starling. A few minutes later, Starling appeared. He greeted the woman cordially and asked why she wanted to see the president. "Because I'm carrying his child," she said, in a voice that could be heard out on Pennsylvania Avenue.

Starling urged her to speak in lower tones. "Why should I?" she shouted. "I'm proud of it. I don't care who knows it!"

It took three hours for Starling to calm the visitor down and persuade her to leave. Another Secret Service agent followed her to a nearby hotel, where he obtained her name and an address in Kansas City, Missouri, from the register. Before long an agent in Kansas City was trying to find out who she was.

The next day Starling received a hair-raising phone call. The agent in Kansas City had discovered that the woman was dangerously insane. The daughter of a prominent family, she had recently escaped from a mental institution. When Secret Service agents arrested her at her hotel and dragged her to their car, she kicked out two windows and dislodged the front seat as they drove to St. Elizabeth's, Washington's chief psychiatric hospital.

III
★★★

In the beginning, the president had no protectors. Thomas Jefferson included guardhouses in his plans to complete the White House but no one, including him, implemented the idea. The Democratic-Republicans never stopped trying to prove they were presidents of all the people. They were uncomfortable with the idea that a few of the people could be dangerous. Luckily, Jefferson, Madison, and Monroe escaped unscathed and unthreatened, except for Madison's encounter with those red-coated pyromaniacs in 1814.

Monroe, however, had the distinction of coming close to being killed by one of his own cabinet members. One day, the president and his secretary of the treasury, William Crawford, had a heated argument over which of them had control of the political patronage in the Treasury Department.

When Monroe insisted it was the president's prerogative, Crawford gave him a sharp reply. Monroe answered in kind and Crawford responded by lunging at the president with his cane, shouting he was "a damned infernal old scoundrel!" When Monroe grabbed some tongs from the fireplace to defend himself, Crawford decided a quick exit was the best solution.

John Quincy Adams and Andrew Jackson displayed no interest in employing bodyguards, although they both could have used them. Adams incurred the wrath of an army doctor named George P. Todson, who had been court-martialed and booted out of the service. When the president declined to review his case, Todson threatened to shoot him dead.

Todson's lawyer took the threat seriously and warned Adams not to see him. Undeterred, the president invited Todson to the White House and refused his plea for clemency face-to-face. No shots were fired, possibly because Adams mollified his would-be killer by offering to get him a job on the frontier, which he did, perhaps hoping the Indians would solve the problem for him.

On January 30, 1835, President Andrew Jackson was striding through the rotunda of the Capitol on his way back to the White House when an assassin stepped out of the crowd and aimed a pistol at his heart from a distance of about three feet. The gun barked but only the cap exploded, not the charge that fired the bullet. Cursing, the would-be killer whipped another pistol from beneath his coat and pulled *that* trigger. The same thing happened.

The infuriated Jackson bashed his attacker with his cane and seven or eight congressmen piled on top of the man, who shouted that Jackson was preventing him from becoming king of England.

The two guns were taken to an armory where experts tested them.

They were in perfect working order and fired bullets the first time someone pulled their triggers. The experts estimated the odds against both guns failing to work were about 1 in 125,000.

If there is any conclusion that can be drawn from this incident, it may be that some presidents lead charmed lives and others are just unlucky.

IV

★★★

In the decades before the Civil War, passions swirled through American politics and lawmakers began to attack each other with canes and fists on the floor of Congress. During John Tyler's embattled administration, he was repeatedly burned in effigy by irate Whigs who considered him a traitor to their party. One midnight in the summer of 1841, a drunken mob gathered outside the White House shouting insults and denunciations of the president and firing guns in the air. One version of the story has them equipped with a cannon.

Inside, President Tyler, who was entertaining some friends including several Democratic senators, grew alarmed. Like most cities of the era, Washington, D.C., lacked a police force. Guns were hastily distributed to the guests and they waited at the windows for an assault. Fortunately, the mob backed off and settled for another cremation of a dummy president.

In the wake of this episode, a jittery Tyler asked Congress to pay for a four-man cadre of White House guards. Some senators sneered at the idea of the president of a free country needing a guard, but the Senate voted to give Tyler his four men.

The new protectors were called doormen, which made them sound more innocuous than they really were. They had the authority to act as policemen and frequently did. At public receptions they never hesitated to muscle suspicious-looking or -acting guests out of the White House, sometimes to jail. When Washington, D.C., organized a police force, the doormen were its first members.

Franklin Pierce was the first president to have a personal bodyguard. He had been in the Capitol when Andrew Jackson was almost assassinated, so he knew all too well that the presidency was a dangerous job. For his protector, Pierce chose former army sergeant Thomas O'Neil, who had saved his life when he was wounded during the Mexican War, in which Pierce served as a brigadier general.

O'Neil escorted Pierce whenever he left the White House and manned a chair just outside his second-floor study so he could rush to the rescue if a caller turned ugly. To everyone's relief, especially Pierce's, the ex-sergeant never had to draw his gun.

V

★ ★ ★

Abraham Lincoln began receiving death threats almost from the day he was elected. He had won with only forty percent of the popular vote, which left a lot of the country angry. By the time the new president set out for Washington, D.C., in February 1861, most of the South had seceded and the atmosphere was even more rancid. Lincoln's former law partner, a physically imposing man named Ward Lamon, and a professional detective, Allan Pinkerton, made the journey with him, armed with knives and pistols.

As the war between the North and the South escalated, so did Lincoln's death threats. There were more than enough to make him acutely conscious of his safety. Although he insisted on making access to the White House appear open and easy, he saw to it that the doormen and many of the inside servants were armed. A contingent of plainclothesmen from the Washington, D.C., Metropolitan Police was hired with instructions to conceal their guns by wearing suits that were a size too big for them. Additional pistols and rifles

were stashed away in the doorkeeper's lodge in case of a more organized attack.

White House callers quickly discovered that President Lincoln
was anything but accessible. Visitors were allowed upstairs only by
appointment and the president seldom appeared on the front staircase. Instead, he used the servants' stairs, which were not only concealed but were guarded by a well-armed doorkeeper. Lincoln also
had a partition built on the second floor that enabled him to move
unseen between his office and the family quarters.

In this tense atmosphere, First Lady Mary Lincoln became the
victim of an apparent assassination attempt. In July of 1863, she was
again staying in a house at the Soldiers' Home, where the Lincolns
spent their summers. Confederate and Union armies were locked in
a death struggle near the town of Gettysburg, Pennsylvania. Desperate to hear some news, the first lady climbed into her carriage
and ordered the driver to head for the White House at top speed.

As they hurtled down the road, the carriage suddenly disinte-
grated. Mrs. Lincoln and the coachman were flung headfirst into
the dirt. By a miracle, they both escaped serious injury but Mary
Lincoln was a battered wreck and had to be put under a nurse's care
for the next two weeks. Many people concluded that the carriage
had been tampered with in the hope of killing the president.

Another time, when Lincoln was riding out to spend the night at
the Soldiers' Home, a gunshot startled his horse. The president
thought it was an accidental discharge, until someone inspected his
hat and found a bullet hole. Thereafter, he never rode anywhere
without a cavalry escort.

Despite his precautions, Lincoln still fell victim to an assassin's
bullet. He died because he and his guards wrongly assumed that
with the surrender of Robert E. Lee at Appomattox, the Civil War
was over and there was no longer any need for vigilance. The moral
of the tragic story of Lincoln's decision to go to Ford's Theater on
Good Friday night is one that the modern Secret Service never for-
gets. A president is never safe, anytime, anywhere.

VI

★★★

En route to that grim conclusion, two other presidents had extremely narrow escapes. Lincoln's successor, Andrew Johnson, stepped out of his office on the second floor one day to find a madman with a loaded gun rampaging down the hall. Johnson shouted for help and several servants and aides leaped on the man, who for some unknown reason did not pull the trigger.

Next on the close call list was Benjamin Harrison. One evening in 1891, shouts and the sounds of a struggle drew him to the Red Room. He found two doorkeepers wrestling with a deranged man wielding a knife. The doughty president helped the doormen pin the intruder down and cut a length of window cord to tie him up.

These incidents were quickly forgotten, but the deaths of two other presidents could not be so easily overlooked. We have already seen James Garfield struck down by the bullets of a crazed job seeker as he walked through the Baltimore & Potomac Railroad Station in July of 1881. Next to die was William McKinley, in a scene that no modern Secret Serviceman can read about without wincing.

The president was in Buffalo, New York, to open an exposition. On September 5, 1901, he arrived at the exposition grounds for a public reception that was supposed to last only ten minutes. Twice McKinley's perspicacious secretary, George Cortelyou, had scrubbed this event, arguing that it was dangerous. Twice the president had written it back into the schedule, saying: "No one would wish to hurt me."

Although Cortelyou dropped the subject, he made sure there was plenty of security. Eighteen exposition policemen and eleven well-armed soldiers formed a lane through which people passed to greet the president. Three Secret Service agents were also on hand. Two of them were stationed directly opposite the president and the third was about ten feet away.

The Secret Service had been organized by the Treasury Department in 1865 to investigate and prevent counterfeiting. It was not responsible for protecting the president but its agents helped with security on an informal basis. Unfortunately, the arrangements were so informal that no one was really in charge. Nor did the agency have any system to detect potential killers before they struck. One of these, a man named Leon Czolgosz (pronounced chol-gosh) entered the line of handshakers without the slightest difficulty.

Czolgosz, a native of Cleveland, had suffered a mental breakdown some years earlier. He drifted into anarchism, a philosophy that considered all rulers evil and capitalism even worse, and became obsessed with the assassination of the king of Italy in 1900 by an American-born anarchist, Gaetano Brescia. Czolgosz had been talking about killing McKinley ever since.

Incredibly, not one of the supposedly alert guards noticed when Czolgosz, while standing in the receiving line, drew a pistol from his pocket and wrapped a handkerchief around it, making it look as if he were wearing a bandage on his right hand. By awful coincidence, the man just ahead of him had an authentic bandage on his right hand. When the man reached the president, he said: "Excuse my left hand, Mr. President." McKinley smiled and shook his left hand.

When Czolgosz approached the president, he, too, extended his left hand. As McKinley reached for it, the anarchist fired two shots through the handkerchief at such point-blank range there were powder burns on McKinley's waistcoat. The president toppled backward into the arms of those around him. Fatally wounded, he died eight days later.

The sad story almost speaks for itself. Today, the Secret Service would very likely have heard of Czolgosz before he even got to Buffalo. Assuming the killer made it that far, they never would have let him get away with his gun-wrapped-in-a-handkerchief ruse. Even the innocent man who preceded him would have been hustled off before he got anywhere near the president.

VII
⋆⋆⋆

After the McKinley assassination, the Secret Service was put in charge of protecting the president and two agents were assigned full-time to the White House detail. Even then there were lapses.

Theodore Roosevelt often had evening appointments. Most of his callers were known in advance, but occasionally there were people whom the president had asked to stop by without bothering to add their names to his schedule.

One evening a man appeared in full evening dress, complete with top hat, and informed the usher on duty at the front door that he had an appointment with the president. The man was invited to step into the Red Room and another usher went upstairs to tell the president that Mr. John Smith was there to see him. Roosevelt could not recall making an appointment with Mr. Smith but he decided to see him anyway.

The president went downstairs and within minutes pressed the call bell that summoned Chief Usher Ike Hoover to the Red Room. When Hoover entered, Roosevelt walked over to him and said quietly, "Take this crank out of here."

The president quickly left the room by another door while the chief usher signaled for help. When the visitor was searched, he was found to be carrying a large-caliber pistol. The incident led to the suspension of the usher who had let him in and a heightened awareness of the need for security.

A similar episode occurred about a week after Herbert Hoover moved into the White House. The president was having dinner with several guests when a strange man suddenly appeared in the dining room.

"What do you want?" the president said.

"I want to see you," the man replied.

"I have no appointment with you," the president told him.

"You better have an appointment with me," the man said menacingly.

Mrs. Hoover turned to the only butler in the room at the time. "Get the Secret Service man," she ordered.

With that, four other butlers who were within earshot rushed into the dining room and dragged the man into the hall outside. A Secret Service agent arrived within seconds and took him into custody. As it turned out, he was unarmed and harmless, although emotionally unbalanced.

Inattention to duty was the primary explanation for how the intruder had managed to get past the police officer at the gate, a second police officer and a doorman at the front entrance, and a Secret Service agent and an usher not far away. However, the weather was a contributing factor. The temperature was balmy and the man arrived without a hat and coat. The doorman and the police officer, obviously distracted, didn't notice him until he was halfway down the hall. When they finally saw him, his back was turned and they assumed he was one of the Secret Servicemen.

With the onset of the Great Depression in 1929, the White House became a magnet for people who blamed the president for the collapse of the nation's economy. Herbert Hoover was inundated with death threats, crank letters, and bizarre visitors.

As a result, forty to fifty men were assigned to the White House Police Force and two Secret Servicemen accompanied the president whenever he went out. When he traveled, the number of agents was increased to eight or ten and additional men were recruited from Secret Service field offices in the areas he was visiting. In addition, White House visitors were subjected to greater scrutiny. Briefcases, cameras, and women's purses had to be inspected before their owners were admitted and anyone carrying a package was forbidden to approach the president.

In spite of this extra effort, slipups still occurred. Franklin D. Roosevelt's oldest son, Jimmy, tells a story that the Secret Service would rather forget. One night during World War II, he was home on leave and joined his parents at the White House for dinner. Afterward they watched a movie. When the lights came on, a neatly dressed young man, a complete stranger, was standing next to FDR.

Instead of brandishing a weapon, however, the interloper asked for the president's autograph. Somehow, apparently for a lark, he had gotten past the doormen and the Secret Service to penetrate the heart of the house. FDR gave him the autograph and the embarrassed Secret Servicemen escorted him to the door. You can be sure this breach of White House security never happened again.

VIII
✯✯✯

These days, there are an estimated two hundred agents assigned to the White House, although they are not all on duty at the same time. Other Secret Service agents protect such potential targets as the vice president, presidential and vice presidential candidates and nominees, former presidents and their spouses, and visiting heads of state. In addition, the Secret Service continues to investigate counterfeiting and other types of financial fraud.

The Secret Service agents assigned to the White House detail wear civilian clothes and operate from a command post under the Oval Office. Agents are stationed near the second-floor living area and at one of the doors leading to the Oval Office. At least one agent accompanies the president whenever he leaves the family quarters.

The Secret Service also has a Uniformed Division. It grew out of the White House Police Force that was created by President Warren G. Harding in 1922 and which Herbert Hoover placed under the supervision of the Secret Service in 1930. Officers of the Uniformed Division are posted at strategic areas around the White

House. One unit, wearing black combat gear and silver helmets, cruises the President's Park on multigear mountain bikes. Another, the Secret Service Counter-sniper Team, is stationed on the White House roof whenever protectees are entering or leaving the building or are anywhere on the grounds. Its officers are equipped with specially built rifles and other sophisticated weapons to counter any long-range attacks.

Secret Service agents and officers carry .357-caliber pistols but they are also trained to use shotguns, submachine guns, and automatic weapons. Their training begins with a nine-week stint at the Federal Law Enforcement Training Center in Glencoe, Georgia, where they learn basic police skills. After that, they spend twelve weeks at the James J. Rowley Training Center in Beltsville, Maryland, where they are taught skills that are basic to the Secret Service, from how to deal with the emotionally disturbed people who show up at the White House gates to how to respond to a rocket-propelled grenade attack on a motorcade. They also receive additional training throughout their careers.

IX
★★★

Thanks to the Secret Service, the history of presidential security in the twentieth century has been concerned more with near-misses and close calls rather than with tragic deaths, except for the inexplicable fate-ridden assassination of John F. Kennedy in Dallas, Texas, in 1963.

Not a little of the service's commitment to presidential safety emanates from tall, strong-jawed Edmund Starling. His personal story is almost as fascinating as the White House history in which he participated for thirty years. When Starling was four years old, his father was assassinated by a political enemy while running for sheriff of Christian County, Kentucky. Isn't it interesting that as a grown man, Starling spent most of his life making sure the country's presidents did not meet the same fate?

Ed Starling started his job at the White House in 1914. In the course of his career, he worked for, or with, Presidents Wilson, Harding, Coolidge, Hoover, and Roosevelt. In those days the government paid for practically nothing except the Secret Service man's gun. Starling and his fellow agents had to buy their own evening clothes so they could participate in White House receptions. Starling's position was along the receiving line, a few feet from the president, where, as he put it in his memoir, he could look for "bulging pockets, handkerchiefs that might have something concealed in them, and eyes with a fanatical gleam."

Probably because he looked so physically impressive, Starling was often mistaken for the president. One day, Starling and Calvin Coolidge were out for a walk near the White House not long after Warren Harding died and Coolidge had became yet another accidental president.

As they passed a gang of laborers digging a ditch, the Irish foreman spotted them and said to a Secret Service man a few feet ahead of them: "What a fine-looking fellow the new president is. So tall and straight! Who's the little fellow with him?"

Sotto voce, the agent informed the foreman that the little fellow was the president. "Glory be to God!" the Irishman said. "Now ain't it a grand country when a wee man like that can get to be the grandest of them all?"

Like many presidents, Calvin Coolidge at first declined to take the Secret Service seriously, and was always trying to sneak out of the White House without them. Starling converted this habit into a game, which he invariably won. He asked the staff to let him know when the president was planning to leave the mansion and what exit he would take.

One day Coolidge was sure he had won. He had descended to the White House basement and slipped out a side door at the east entrance. As he passed the sentry box, Starling stepped out and said: "Good morning, Mr. President." Cal did not speak to him for the entire walk.

X
★★★

Edmund Starling initiated the Secret Service tradition of exercising authority over a chief executive's travel plans and public appearances to minimize the chances of the worst happening. At times he could become quite vehement. Not even a president with an ego as strong as Franklin Roosevelt's could stand up to him.

On a western trip in 1935, FDR violated Starling's carefully thought out travel plan and came within a whisker of getting himself killed. Starling had left the president in Las Vegas with a half-dozen other agents while he went ahead to get things ready at the next stop on the trip, Los Angeles. As Roosevelt was about to depart, a Nevada senator urged him to take a quick trip up nearby Mount Charleston to visit a Civilian Conservation Corps camp.

The next thing the appalled Secret Servicemen knew, they were driving up a gravel road barely wide enough for a single car, with a drop of several thousand feet only inches from their hubcaps. The tires constantly slipped in the gravel and the radiators started to boil over. The Secret Service agents, who were in the lead car, stopped and begged the president to turn back. FDR agreed—and found himself sitting in the rear of the car while the driver tried to turn on the narrow road, backing to within inches of the precipice. The story was picked up by some reporters and a steamed Starling went to see Roosevelt when he arrived in Los Angeles the next day.

"I don't think it was fair to me or to the Secret Service or to the country to go up that mountain last night," Starling said. "You took an unnecessary chance. I know it is hard to realize that you have no right to endanger yourself, but you haven't. Your life isn't your own to give or take now. It belongs to the people of the United States.

That's why I am paid to look out for you. If anything had happened last night, my whole life would have been ruined, not to mention what would have happened to the country."

At that point, Eleanor Roosevelt entered the fray. She told FDR she agreed with everything Starling had just said. She wanted him to promise right then and there to stick to the Secret Service's schedule without any deviations. "Apparently the majority is against me," a humbled FDR said. "Very well. I'll promise."

The Roosevelt years also provide a tale that illustrates how cold-blooded the Secret Service can be when it comes to protecting the president. One day FDR decided to go to a popular play. The Secret Service amazed the White House press corps by inviting a dozen or so reporters to accompany him. They had great seats, in a semicircle behind and to one side of the president's box.

As they were leaving the theater, the scribes thanked the agent in charge of the detail for inviting them along. "Oh, think nothing of it, fellows," he said. "If you'll notice, it would have been impossible for anybody to shoot the President without hitting one or two of you guys first—and by that time we'd have him."

XI
★★★

One of the largest units of the Secret Service's Washington office is its Technical Security Division, which provides security devices for the White House. The division has installed such low-tech protection as the fat concrete stanchions, called bollards, that line the sidewalks around the mansion, as well as such high-tech apparatus as the electronic locator boxes that indicate where their protectees are every minute of the day and night.

Among the other devices the division can take credit for are the hydraulic gates at the vehicular entrances, the video and alarm systems along the perimeter and the radioactivity detectors in the areas adjacent to the Oval Office to indicate the presence of any nuclear devices. As an added precaution, after the bombing of a federal building in Oklahoma City in 1995, the division closed off a three-block stretch of Pennsylvania Avenue to eliminate the possibility of having the White House destroyed by a car or truck bomb.

The Technical Security Division also handles packages and letters addressed to the White House that might contain lethal substances. In the summer of 1947, the Stern Gang, proponents of the not-yet-created state of Israel, sent my father a number of cream-colored envelopes full of powdered gelignite, rigged to explode when opened. The Secret Service was on the job, screening our mail, and these murderous billet-doux wound up dismantled in a Dumpster.

When John Tyler's doorkeeper attacked a mysterious wooden box with a meat cleaver, the first White House bomb scare turned out to be more comic than tragic. Today, the Secret Service would have taken the box to their examining room several blocks away from the White House. There packages can be X-rayed and tested for timing devices. If the thing ticks, it is immediately soaked in oil to gum up the machinery—a good reason not to send any president a watch or clock as a gift.

If the Secret Service has reason to suspect a package is deadly, it is placed in a special egg-shaped bomb carrier mounted on a truck. The bomb carrier is constructed of interwoven one-inch cable and can withstand the blast of fifty sticks of dynamite. The package is then driven to a deserted area where a specially trained agent opens it with grappling hooks operated from outside the truck.

XII
★★★

Each year, several hundred guns are detected at the White House gates. Thankfully, almost all of them are carried by people who have permits. Surprisingly enough, it was a long time before the Technical Security Division could install the magnetometers that detect such weapons. Officials in the Carter administration deemed them "not politically acceptable." The officials changed their minds the day a man walked in with a gun and said, "Take me to the president!"

The absence of metal detectors may explain how one well-armed visitor was able to walk into the West Wing without being spotted. One day in 1970, a dude in a flashy suit and a haircut that Richard Nixon would never tolerate for ten seconds breezed into the White House.

Before you could say Elvis Presley, the king was in the Oval Office, shaking the president's hand. Elvis had shown up earlier in the day, saying he wanted to meet Nixon. A shrewd aide saw good publicity and talked the president into making time for the singer.

"I'm on your side!" Elvis told Nixon, who was fighting off hordes of anti–Vietnam War protestors at the time. Then came a moment that left the Secret Service gasping: from his inside coat pocket Elvis drew a gold plated .45-caliber pistol! He had somehow managed to carry it past the White House police without anyone spotting it. Worse, he had bullets for it in another pocket. Fortunately, it was only a gift—and arresting Elvis would have spoiled the point of the visit.

XIII
★★★

Although airspace over downtown Washington is off-limits to planes flying below eighteen thousand feet, airborne assaults on the White House remain a threat. There is a strong probability that the United Airlines flight that crashed in Pennsylvania on September 11, 2001, may have been headed for either the White House or the Capitol.

Thanks to a group of heroic passengers, the plane never reached Washington. If it had been aiming for the White House, the Secret

Service might have been forced to use the antiaircraft weapons and ground-to-air missiles that are rumored to be in place for such contingencies.

Actually, the mansion has already been attacked by air, but the consequences were worse for the pilots than they were for the president. One night in September 1994, a man named Frank Corder, who had a history of alcohol addiction and depression, stole a Cessna and aimed it at the White House. It clipped some branches off Andrew Jackson's magnolia tree and slammed into the south wall beneath Bill Clinton's bedroom. The runaway pilot was killed. The president, who was staying at Blair House while the White House air-conditioning was being repaired, took an apologetic call from his chief of staff, Leon Panetta, and went back to sleep.

Twenty years earlier, during the Nixon administration, Private First Class Robert Preston stole an army helicopter from Fort Meade, Maryland, and landed on the lawn at 9:30 one night. Before the White House police could do anything, he flew away.

Fifty minutes later, Preston returned and the White House police riddled the chopper. Private Preston survived by diving under the aircraft. He got a year in jail and a dishonorable discharge.

XIV
★★★

The White House seems to have a special attraction for the mentally ill. Disturbed people regularly appear at the gates demanding to see the president. About 250 of these unwanted visitors are packed off to St. Elizabeth's Hospital each year for observation.

Before the bollards were put in place, a fair number of people would attempt to penetrate the White House grounds by ramming a car through the gates. One seventy-seven-year-old woman tried to get at Gerald Ford by assaulting the northwest gate in her car. The Secret Service put her in St. Elizabeth's, where the psychiatrists decreed that she was not a danger to herself or others and let her go.

The woman got another car and attacked the gate again. This time she went to the hospital for a much longer stay.

One summer late in President Roosevelt's second term, when World War II was beginning to loom, a White House policeman stared down Pennsylvania Avenue and said: "The heat is getting to me. I'd swear that guy coming there was wearing wings."

He was. A tall, athletic-looking man in a white robe was skipping toward the White House gate, flapping large, shimmery white wings and carrying an ornate scroll under his arm. He beamed at the policeman and announced: "I have a message from the Lord, a message of peace for the president."

The officer let the angel cool his wings while he called the Secret Service. The agent on duty, who had been handling cases like this since Teddy Roosevelt's day, decided the heavenly messenger was harmless. He told him the president was too busy to see him personally, but his message would be delivered. The disappointed angel trudged off, his big white wings drooping.

Less amusing was a man who showed up around the same time, insisting he had a message for "the big guy." The Secret Service agent who interviewed him instantly spotted a large bulge under his left armpit. "You better let me have that gun," the agent said.

The man chuckled and handed over a Colt .45. "Think you're pretty smart, don't you? You think you've got all my guns?" the visitor sneered.

"Hand over what's left," the agent said, no doubt loosening his own weapon in its holster.

The man pulled a .38 from inside his coat and two more guns from his hip pockets. He was soon on his way to St. Elizabeth's, where the diagnosis was psychosis.

These days, the Secret Service lists about fifty thousand Americans as potential threats to the president. Of this number, only about a hundred are in Category Three, considered seriously dangerous. At any point, the Service is usually investigating about twenty-five active cases. It is a crime to threaten the president's life—something many would-be killers do not know, thank goodness. It makes arresting them much easier.

XV
★★★

Federal law provides Secret Service protection for presidential families. In a world rife with instability and tension, this protective mandate is sorely needed, but it has involved the agents in some unlikely assignments for brawny males trained to do battle with killers. When I graduated from college in 1946 and launched my singing career, seven agents were assigned to keep me out of harm's way.

Here I have a bone to pick with the Secret Service—the only one, I should add. In a semi-official history, they claim I later complained that these seven gentlemen made it impossible for me to find a husband. I never said any such thing, nor was I looking for a husband in those years. I was a career woman and I might have stayed one if I had not met the right man, long after my Secret Service protectors were guarding other presidential families.

One of these family assignments still makes me chuckle every time I think of it. Two agents were ordered to protect Barbara Ann Eisenhower, President Eisenhower's twelve-year-old granddaughter, while she attended an all-girls camp in West Virginia. The agents lived in a tent next to Barbara Ann's and were soon participating in cookouts, campfires, and Indian dances. The twelve-year-olds were entranced to have these two proto-heroes in their midst. At the end of the summer they made them members of their sacred campers' club—the only males ever so honored.

The agents assigned to guard Lyndon Johnson's older daughter, Lynda Bird, encountered even more complications. She belonged to Zeta Tau Alpha at the University of Texas in Austin. The sorority house was in a large white colonial mansion near the campus. After some no doubt delicate negotiations, the Secret Service persuaded the Zeta Taus to allow two Secret Service agents into their all-female ménage. The guys operated out of a small first-floor room equipped with a closed-circuit TV system that enabled them to see everyone who entered the house. The room also contained a two-way radio and enough guns to hold off a small army.

Nowadays, the Secret Service is an equal opportunity employer. With women agents, the job of guarding presidential daughters and granddaughters is a lot less sticky. But it doesn't have nearly as much potential for amusement.

XVI
★★★

In their efforts to keep the residents of the White House safe, the Secret Service is determined to leave nothing to chance. The thought of a president being attacked on home turf appalls them, which undoubtedly explains a story told to me by a recent visitor to the West Wing. While using the men's room, he noticed that the neatly folded paper hand towels were imprinted with "The President's House" and blithely pocketed a couple of them as souvenirs.

When he emerged, a Secret Service agent fell in step beside him and asked him to return the towels. There would be no charge, the agent added with a smile. It seems that the men's room is monitored by a two-way mirror to make sure no one decides to load a pistol or set the fuse of a bomb in there.

Some people may think this is carrying security a bit too far. But in and around the White House, eternal vigilance is the price of safety. At seven A.M. on December 6, 2001, the Secret Service arrested a twenty-six-year-old man loitering near the southwest gate, "acting suspiciously." He was armed with a foot-long knife. After some tense questioning, he led them to his pickup truck, parked several blocks away. In the cab they found an assault rifle, another rifle with a scope that snipers use to kill people at a distance, and a loaded handgun. Also in the haul was a bulletproof vest and a Kevlar helmet. The man had no fixed address. He was jailed on weapons charges.

Such incidents, which barely get a paragraph in the newspapers, only underscore that being president of the United States is dangerous work. I am sure every member of a presidential family pauses now and then to thank God that the Secret Service is on the job. I do it regularly.

Look at the line waiting to get into President William Howard Taft's 1911 New Year's re-
ception. I'm glad I didn't have to shake hands with them all.
Credit: Library of Congress

15

★★★

The People's White House

One evening President Franklin Pierce was strolling the White House grounds, enjoying music from the Marine Band and nodding cordially to hundreds of tourists and local Washingtonians. A man nervously approached him and said: "Mr. President, can't I go through your fine house? I've heard so much about it that I'd give a great deal to see it."

Pierce replied: "Why, my dear sir, that is not my house. It is the people's house! You shall certainly go through it if you wish." Summoning a doorman, he ordered the visitor to be given a thorough tour of the first-floor rooms.

That touching tale sums up one side of the story of tourists in the White House, a very important side. But the whole story is a lot more complicated. The first uninvited visitors appeared in the president's house in 1800, even before the place was finished. Paperhangers and plasterers were still hard at work and furniture was being uncrated. These unwanted callers became so numerous and so nosy, the commissioners in charge of the new capital's public buildings ordered them barred unless they had a written pass justifying their presence.

This rule did not discourage numerous local ladies, who conned written passes out of friendly bureaucrats and were soon sashaying all over the house, including the second floor, where Secretary of State John Marshall had set up housekeeping until he found decent rooms elsewhere in the federal city.

A tradition had been launched that future residents of the White House would sometimes cheer and sometimes lament. Whose house was it, anyway? The American people apparently thought it belonged to them. This was poignant and encouraging in its way. But presidential families would occasionally exclaim: "What about us? Don't we have a vote on that question?" Most of the time, the answer was no.

II
★★★

President Thomas Jefferson ordered the White House doors kept open every day, so visitors could inspect the State Rooms on the first floor. They were more interested in Jefferson's basement kitchen, which had a fireplace equipped with an iron range—very rare at the time. Jefferson, however, made sure no one saw his wine cellar, which would have put a dent in his claim to personify Democratic-Republican "simplicity." During his two terms, Tom spent around $10,000, about five percent of his presidential earnings in those years, on wine. No wonder the ladies of Washington were infuriated when he tried to exclude them!

Jefferson also added what we would call tourist attractions. Lewis and Clark shipped skins of hitherto unknown beasts and birds from the west. Zebulon Pike also sent his share, and General James Wilkinson, commander of the U.S. Army, was not above currying favor with the president by sending dinosaur bones and Indian artifacts from Texas and other unmapped portions of the southwest. Jefferson displayed these curios in one of the downstairs rooms.

Pike's biggest contribution to the displays were two grizzly bear cubs. Jefferson put them in a ten-foot-square cage in the middle of the circular driveway on the north side of the White House. People came from miles around to get a look at these creatures, who were very friendly because, as Jefferson said, "they know no benefactors but man." Eventually he had to ship them to Baltimore where presidential portrait painter Charles Willson Peale maintained a natural history museum, a forerunner of the modern zoo.

Some of Jefferson's tourists were even more exotic than the cubs. They arrived wearing feathered headdresses, deerskin moccasins, cloth leggings, and streaks of paint on their faces. The president had told Lewis and Clark to extend invitations to visit the "Great Chief" of the white men in Washington to any and all tribes they met along their route west. Jefferson probably did not realize that Indians were prodigious travelers, who loved an excuse for a journey. Soon chiefs from the Osages, Pawnees, Miamis, and other western tribes were camping on the White House lawn, along with their squaws and their uncles and their cousins and their aunts.

Margaret Bayard Smith, that tireless chronicler of the early White House, thought these visitors were "noble specimens of the human race." They were "tall, erect and finely proportioned." The chiefs exchanged gifts with the president, who usually gave them a silver medal with his likeness in profile, which could be worn around their necks. They also exchanged orations, in which they pledged friendship and mutual respect. President Jefferson told them that his "grandfather" President Washington had been a good friend of the Indians. (Then why, I wonder at this point, did the Indians nickname him "Townburner"?) Occasionally the tribesmen would respond with a war dance.

III
***

The first president to curtail access to the White House was James Monroe. The few people who succeeded in getting in did not have much of a tour. The State Rooms were off-limits and the Monroes' gilded French furniture, the talk of Washington, remained under slipcovers. The East Room may have impressed visitors by its size but it had little else going for it. There was no furniture and the chandeliers were drab metal.

Monroe's successor, John Quincy Adams, tried to overcome his lack of appeal to the voters by keeping the White House wide open all day, every day. Anyone could come in and wander around. If he wanted to shake the president's hand, all he had to do was join the line of callers waiting on the stairs. This led to some strange encounters, which Adams recorded in his diary.

One day a down-at-the-heels character presented himself to the president as St. Peter the Apostle. He had a message for the nation from God. Adams, declining to be flustered—his self-control was monumental—curtly asked the man what his name was before he became St. Peter. "Peter McDermott," he muttered, collapsing like a pricked balloon. In his diary, Adams added with obvious, if unstated, contempt, "an Irishman." John Quincy was a classic icicle of Yankeeland, as the Irish called the proper Bostonians.

On another occasion, Adams was the beneficiary of his open house policy. The president was conferring in his oval study with Secretary of State Henry Clay when one Eleazar Parraly strolled into the room. Parraly was mainly interested in shaking the president's hand, but in the course of introducing himself, he mentioned that he was a dentist. The president instantly dismissed the secretary of state and invited Parraly to remove a tooth that was aching ominously. There was no resident dentist in the national capital. Parraly not only did the job, he refused to take money for it. Life was simpler when the United States of America was an undeveloped country.

IV
★★★

When President Andrew Jackson had the good fortune to receive a $50,000 appropriation from Congress to refurbish the White House, he spent a large chunk of it on finishing the magnificent cavern called the East Room. On the floor went a fawn, blue, and yellow Brussels carpet with a red border, while blue and yellow draperies framed the windows. Three cut-glass chandeliers were suspended from the ceiling, each with eighteen oil lamps to set the room aglow. New furniture was purchased and twenty spittoons were placed at strategic points around the room.

No one, including Jackson, had yet figured out how to heat this vast space. "Hell itself couldn't warm that corner," Old Hickory groused. But tourists did not consider the chill a problem. The room remained the chief attraction during his administration and the single term of his successor, Martin Van Buren.

The rest of the house was not accessible to uninvited visitors. The White House grounds, however, were open from eight A.M. to sundown to anyone in the mood for a stroll. Enjoying the President's Park became popular, not just for the flora and fauna. First families grew more than a little discomfited when they glanced out the window and found twenty or thirty people staring up at them.

V
★★★

The White House was at war with Mexico for most of President Polk's sojourn but this did not prevent tourists from invading any and all parts of it. Visitors with appointments to see the president often transmogrified into tourists after they left his second-floor office. One day, Mrs. Polk's niece, Joanna Rucker, was sitting in the oval parlor on the second floor when a stranger barged into the room. "He pretended to miss his way in going from the President's office," she told her mother in a letter. "The house belongs to the government and everyone feels at home. . . . They sometimes stalk into our bedroom and say they are looking at the house."

Polk's successor, General Zachary Taylor, continued the custom, begun by John Tyler, of having the Marine Band play on the South Portico on summer evenings, attracting hundreds of visitors. "Old Zach" seemed determined to be on a first-name basis with everyone who wandered across the grounds or into the White House. He regularly appeared among the strollers with his hand out, eager to introduce himself.

In the White House, Taylor operated from a second-floor office that was open to anyone who felt like dropping in. He usually sat with his legs up on a table, chomping on a quid of tobacco. The only thing a visitor had to remember was never to get between Zach and the spittoon.

VI
★★★

By the time Franklin Pierce arrived in 1852, the White House grounds had acquired a reputation as a beauty spot. In addition to graveled walks and carefully tended flower beds, the President's Park provided a vista to the south that extended over open country all the way to the Potomac. The base of what would become the Washington Monument was beginning to rise on the mall. Slowly but surely, the whole federal city was turning into a tourist attraction and the White House and the resident president were the centerpieces of the show.

Pierce could not go out on the street without being mobbed. Nor with strollers swarming could he count on finding privacy on the White House grounds. To give him and his family access to some fresh air, Pierce set up a sentry box beside the entrance to the east garden and stationed a doorkeeper there full-time to keep the tourists away while he and his family enjoyed a few rays of sunshine.

VII
★★★

The Civil War made the White House even more fascinating to the American people. A good many of the tourists of those years were transported to Washington at government expense. They were wearing army blue, and the White House was only a way stop on their journey to fight and possibly die in Virginia. Lincoln gave orders to admit soldiers freely to the first floor, where they gaped at the East Room and occasionally stretched out on one of the sofas for a nap.

Only a few visitors with some knowledge of the house's history asked to see "Ogle's Elliptical Saloon"—the oval room that President Martin Van Buren had decorated in blue, giving it its permanent name. The room, with its supposedly lavish furnishings, was one of the targets of Congressman Charles Ogle's long-ago denunciation of Van Buren's alleged extravagances.

The answer to the visitor's request was usually no. The rest of the first-floor rooms were also closed to visitors. Concern for Lincoln's safety was one of several reasons for not encouraging wanderers. Another reason was the visitors' tendency to carve souvenirs out of the rugs, draperies, and upholstery.

After Lincoln's assassination, the White House collapsed into near chaos. Mary Lincoln spent the next few weeks weeping and brooding in her upstairs bedroom, forcing the new president, Andrew Johnson, to set up his office in the Treasury Building next door. This left the President's House with no one in charge. It remained open to visitors and the public came pouring in. For most of each day, they swarmed through the State Rooms, collecting mementoes of the martyred president and wreaking havoc in the process.

The East Room was still decorated with the flags, crape, and flowers from Lincoln's funeral. These were soon picked to pieces. After the remains were removed, the souvenir hunters went to work on everything else that was portable. Vases, lamps, and small statues vanished and still the pillagers were not satisfied. They proceeded to carve yard-long chunks out of the draperies and carpets and cut the filigreed medallions from the lace curtains. After they discovered the chest where the silver and china were stored, these items, too, disappeared at a dismaying rate.

The New York *Herald*, persecuting Lincoln's widow as it had hounded the president, reported that Mary Lincoln, not the great American public, was responsible for this wholesale plundering of the White House. It ran a story claiming she had taken everything not nailed down back to Illinois. Ain't politics wonderful?

VIII
★★★

That orgy of misbehavior made everyone connected to the White House a lot more wary of tourists. It was generally recognized that some sort of supervision was needed. The Civil War had made Americans history-minded. The number of Washington sightseers kept growing each year. The President's House was a place where they could glimpse the early days of the republic.

The mansion was redecorated after Andrew Johnson moved in and all evidence of vandalism was erased. Sightseers were again welcome to visit the East Room, but there were detectives on hand to make sure nothing was removed. Theoretically at least, the state parlors were still restricted. Those who wanted to view them needed a letter from their congressman or senator, a favor easily procured.

If the doorkeepers were not busy, one of them would double as a tour guide and spice up the visit with tidbits of White House history. Sightseers heard about Abigail Adams's wash hanging in the

East Room, Andrew Jackson's chaotic inaugural reception, and the rebuilding of the White House after the British burned it down during the War of 1812.

One of the most interesting sights was a gallery of presidential portraits created by Andrew Johnson. Congress had commissioned most of these paintings in 1857, but with the onset of the Civil War, they had never been framed, much less hung. The Stuart portrait of George Washington, rescued from British torches by Dolley Madison, was the premier attraction, followed by William Cogswell's portrait of Lincoln that was commissioned by Ulysses S. Grant in 1869.

The White House had achieved reverential status but that did not eliminate the souvenir hunters. On the contrary, it may even have stimulated them. The East Room was open to the public three days a week, and despite the presence of plainclothes detectives, there were always a few things missing when visiting hours ended. Even the select group of tourists who had special passes to visit the state parlors regularly indulged in petty thievery. According to Rutherford B. Hayes's son, Birch, "After every public reception a man had to go the rounds with a basket of crystal pendants to replace those taken from the chandeliers. They cut pieces off the bottoms of curtains and carried off everything in sight."

IX

★★★

In 1889, Benjamin and Caroline Harrison ran afoul of the tourists in their attempts to find more White House living space. The Harrisons had six adults and two children in residence. With half of the second floor devoted to offices for the president and his staff, they were hard put to find room for them all.

In desperation, Caroline Harrison converted the upstairs hall into a living room. There are three pretty sitting rooms along the hall now. In the Harrisons' day the space was too long and narrow to allow for much sociability, and it was dim and drafty besides. The first lady decided to close off the state parlors so they could be used by the family. From now on, even VIP visitors could view only the entrance hall and the East Room.

Wow, the uproar was terrific. After Chester A. Arthur had spent a small fortune redecorating these rooms, they had become extremely popular with tourists, also known as voters. The president read about their wrath in the newspapers. To soothe their feelings, he started popping downstairs in the afternoon to shake hands. Sometimes he threw in a lecture on the history of the White House.

The president as tour guide was a ridiculous idea and it did not last. Neither did Mrs. Harrison's attempt to use the state parlors as family sitting rooms. There was no real privacy from the stares of the tourists in the East Room and the president's appearances did not atone for the offense of giving visitors a truncated tour. After a few months, the Harrisons retreated upstairs and the first lady started looking, without success, for a way to expand the White House.

X

Meanwhile, the grounds were still pretty much open to all comers. President Hayes had tried to foil would-be assassins by creating a separate park for the public, the Ellipse, but his successors were reluctant to turn the President's Park into their private preserve. Tourists still strolled the south lawn throughout the day and continued to stream through the White House at a steady pace.

When Theodore Roosevelt launched his vast redecoration and building program, public interest was intense. Pictures of the East Room, resplendent with ivory and gilt, filled the magazines and thousands came to see it with their own eyes. That was about all they saw. Roosevelt was not very enthusiastic about tourists. His successor, William Howard Taft, was very much the opposite. During his administration, visitors were actually admitted to the Oval Office, and when the president was out of town they could bounce in Big Bill's chair.

Woodrow Wilson shared Theodore Roosevelt's attitude toward tourists but his daughters Margaret, Jessie, and Nellie found them a good source of laughs. Every once in a while they would join the crowd waiting to get into the White House and walk through the downstairs rooms, making catty remarks about themselves. "I wonder where that stuck-up creature Margaret Wilson is hiding today," Jessie would say.

"Yes," Nellie would reply. "I'd like to see her, just to give her hair a good yank. I hear she wears a wig."

The tourists around them would be horrified. Any minute they expected the White House police to arrest the entire crowd.

Another time, the sisters boarded a tour bus and pretended to be three country bumpkins. They yakked on and on about how they were dying to see "the whole White House." Before the ride was over, the driver was grandly promising to take them through "every room." They returned home, howling with laughter.

XI
★★★

The flow of tourists ceased when Woodrow Wilson declared war in 1917, and did not resume until Warren Harding became president in 1921. Harding, having nothing better to do all day—his administration was run mainly by his cabinet and staff—began coming downstairs around lunchtime to greet the tourists. People liked it and soon crowds gathered to exchange a few words with the supposedly great man. Harding's gray hair and handsome features made him look like the ideal president. Few knew there was nothing upstairs but cobwebs.

Florence Harding did her share to make people regard the mansion as the people's house. During the summer after her husband's inauguration, she gave a series of garden parties that were a huge success. One awed reporter wrote: "Mrs. Harding has literally shaken hands with tens of thousands of persons in a steady streaming line through the White House gates. No President's wife in the memory of the Capital has displayed such endurance."

Calvin Coolidge felt no need to greet the tourists or anyone else, if he could help it. He shortened the visiting hours and let the ushers deal with the crowds. Herbert Hoover might have done the same thing if the stock market had not collapsed early in his presidency. With the country sinking into the Great Depression, Hoover decided visiting the White House might boost public morale. He ordered the mansion opened to visitors from ten A.M. to four P.M. every day except Sunday.

The president's sense that the people's house could serve as a beacon of hope during the dark days of the Depression was on target. People were eager to visit the mansion and the number of tourists doubled to 900,000 a year. To give them further inspiration, Mrs. Hoover had the portraits of Martha and George Washington removed from the Red Room and hung in a more prominent position in the East Room.

The flood of visitors continued when Franklin D. Roosevelt became president, and the White House grounds remained popular with tourists and Washingtonians out for a stroll. The north grounds were open eight or ten hours a day and the south lawn, while often restricted, was usually open in the spring when the trees and flowers were at their best.

This free and easy access to the President's Park ended with the declaration of war against Japan on December 8, 1941, and it has never resumed. The White House, and the country, had lost its innocence.

XII

★★★

A lovely leftover from those bygone days is the annual lighting of the White House Christmas tree, which now takes place on the Ellipse. In December 2001, after much internal debate, the Secret Service reversed its decision to bar everyone without a ticket to the ceremony because of their fear of a terrorist attack. The White House had been closed to tourists since the September 11 assaults, leading some people to complain about Uncle Sam's Scrooge-like behavior. As a professional worrier about a president's safety, I must add I was not one of these carpers.

Nevertheless, it was heartening to know that the Secret Service had decided President George W. Bush could undertake this ceremony, which goes back to 1923. That year, Calvin Coolidge had gotten a letter from a Washington, D.C., public school janitor, suggesting it would be a nice idea to start the holiday season by lighting a tree on the south lawn. Coolidge imported a balsam fir from his native Vermont and presidents have been performing this pleasant chore ever since. The ceremony was moved to the Ellipse in 1954.

At five P.M. on December 6, 2001, President Bush pushed a switch and ignited red, white, and blue lights on a forty-foot Colorado blue spruce. Soprano Audra McDonald and country singer Travis Tritt performed, starting a month-long pageant in which Washington-area dance groups and choirs performed nightly. The symbolic blend of patriotism and the ancient feast of Christmas was hailed by everyone as a stirring reminder of what our soldiers were defending in the war against terrorism. "I get a lump in my throat every time I think about it," said Ron Hudler, a North Carolina tree farmer who sends small firs to Washington for display around the national tree.

What can you add to that besides "Amen"?

XIII
★★★

Another festive event that adds a unique dimension to the people's house is the annual Easter Monday egg rolling festival. This celebration attracts as many as thirty thousand kids under six. To handle the crowd, the event has been extended from the White House's south lawn to the Ellipse. The Marine Band is on hand to serenade the youngsters, and there are folksingers, jugglers, and clowns in traditional regalia and in bunny costumes. One year, a petting zoo included rabbits, a horse, and a large bald eagle, who did not get petted.

The first lady is the official hostess of the event. The president blows a whistle and the kids, armed with spoons, start trying to persuade their hard-boiled eggs to roll across the sloping grass. Cries of excitement and frustration fill the sunny air. In the end, the first lady declares everyone a winner and the children each get a wooden egg to take home as a souvenir. During the Clinton years, kids also hunted in piles of straw for eggs that bore celebrity signatures, including the pawprint of Socks, the first cat. Not surprisingly, the Easter egg roll has become the largest public event of the White House year. If you and your kids are in the vicinity on Easter Monday, go for it by all means. It is an experience they will remember all their lives.

XIV
★★★

Visitors to the contemporary White House are unlikely to get a glimpse of the president, much less shake his hand and give him their thoughts about the economy. Yet that does not stop them from getting in touch with him in other ways. Faxes and e-mail have become increasingly popular, but letters remain the medium of choice for Mr. and Mrs. John Q. Citizen.

In the months after Bill Clinton's 1993 announcement that Hillary would head a task force on health care, 700,000 letters poured into the White House. The average number of letters received that year was eight million, but the number tends to decline once a president settles in. Ronald Reagan and the first George Bush averaged about six million a year.

The American people have been sending letters to the White House since 1800. Some of our early presidents tried to read and answer these missives personally, but as the numbers increased, the chore was passed to a secretary. By the end of the nineteenth century, when even two secretaries were not enough to keep up with the flow, the mail room was created.

The most prominent name in this segment of the White House saga is Ira Smith, a thin, unflappable Ohioan who presided over the mail room for forty years, covering the terms of six Republican and three Democratic presidents, ending with Harry S Truman. His office staff grew from one man—Smith all by himself, handling about a hundred letters a day in 1897—to twenty-two in the Truman era. Another fifty or so people were on Smith's standby list for emergency days when for various reasons, the letters and parcels leaped from an average of 8,000 a day to an avalanche of 150,000.

The current White House mail room, now called the Correspondence Office, has a staff of almost ninety people plus a couple of dozen interns and a pool of over seven hundred volunteers. Most correspondents receive some kind of reply, usually a printed card rather than a regular letter.

Letters that might be of special interest to the president are extracted from the pile and brought to his attention. President George H. W. Bush's staff secretary once sent a memo to the Correspondence Office stressing the importance of being on the lookout for such letters. Attached was a letter addressed to President Franklin D. Roosevelt telling him about a theory the writer had that could create an unbelievably powerful bomb. The letter was badly typed and full of misspellings and crossed-out words but an alert mail handler had rescued it from the "nut file" and sent it on to the president. It was signed: *Albert Einstein*.

XV
★★★

Another avenue to the president is the telephone. As more and more citizens became aware of this option, the White House switchboard was besieged with callers. By the 1970s, the lines were so overloaded that a new system had to be devised. A Comment Line was set up with a separate phone number and volunteers were recruited to handle the phone calls that can number as many as several thousand a day.

The Comment Line office is in a building not far from the White House. Over one hundred volunteers handle the phones. Additional help is called in when the president makes a speech or holds a press conference, two events that really make the lines light up.

The volunteers contribute an average of one or two days a week. Records are kept of the calls, noting which state the caller came from, what issue he or she was concerned about, and whether the caller agreed or disagreed with the president's position on it. Daily and weekly reports of the calls are sent to the president and senior members of the White House staff.

Many of the callers have questions, such as how to apply for veterans' benefits or what their Medicare coverage includes. The operators cannot answer such queries but they provide the callers with the phone numbers of the government agencies that can give them the information they need.

The line also attracts a fair number of mentally ill callers. "When the moon is full, they come out of the woodwork," says one volunteer. Although their comments often make very little sense, these callers are treated with the same courtesy as everyone else. For threatening calls, there is a buzzer that connects the call to the Secret Service and they take it from there.

Comment Line volunteers will not stay on the line forever, even though many people, both sane and insane, would like them to. They are instructed to limit the conversations to two minutes so other callers can get through.

Until recently, the only reward the volunteers could expect for their efforts was admission to the south grounds to view the welcoming ceremonies for visiting heads of state. In 2001, however, First Lady Laura Bush began inviting them to a pre-Christmas tea, a gesture that could well become a White House tradition.

XVI
★★★

The Gift Office has been set up to deal with the approximately fifteen thousand gifts that arrive at the White House each year. A staff of about a half-dozen highly experienced employees registers the gifts, sees that they are acknowledged, and decides what should be done with them. Many are gifts from foreign governments and are quite valuable. They are considered gifts to the nation rather than to the president and they are usually sent to the Smithsonian Institution or the Library of Congress or kept for use in a presidential library. The president is allowed to keep only those that have minimal value, which is currently defined as less than $260.

A high percentage of the gifts that arrive at the White House are sent by private citizens. Some of the senders are trying to make a point. An Iowa farmer once shipped my father a live hog weighing seven hundred pounds. (This charming fellow was protesting the high price of feed.) Other wiseguys sent crates of chickens when Dad suggested "chickenless Thursdays" to help feed starving Europe at the end of World War II. The birds were donated to Walter Reed Hospital.

The Gift Office tries to find a suitable home for every present but it isn't always easy. In my father's day, the questionable ones were relegated to a storage area in the West Wing underneath the Cabinet Room. By the time Dad left the White House, the room was so crammed it became known as the Black Hole of Calcutta.

If a president or a first lady has a special hobby or a fondness for a particular type of clothing, he or she is likely to get buried in the stuff. Bill Clinton received tons of golf-related gifts; Ronald Reagan and Lyndon Johnson were inundated with cowboy boots.

Shortly after he took office, Dad dropped in on his old haberdashery partner, Eddie Jacobson, to buy a half-dozen white shirts, size 15½, 33. He was trying to get his pal Eddie some free publicity—and he also needed the shirts, which had been hard to buy during the war years. Eddie was embarrassed to discover that he did not have Dad's size in stock. The story got into the papers and soon the White House was deluged by almost two thousand shirts in every imaginable color, including red, white, and blue.

Another time, Dad was seen pitching horseshoes on the White House lawn. Horseshoes by the hundreds descended on us. A similar glut occurred when a reporter wrote a story about Caroline Kennedy's love of chocolate. The White House Gift Office logged in everything from Hershey bars to a 6-foot, 190-pound chocolate rabbit from Switzerland.

Gerry Ford once received—and kept—a hand-knitted ski hat that had been sent to him by a retired nun. After she spied him wearing it on a television news clip, she decided it looked too tight. She immediately sent him a letter with instructions on how to care for it: Wet it and let it sit on your head until it dries.

XVII
★★★

I am always delighted to find evidence that when it comes to the White House, political differences tend to fall by the wayside and the public's admiration and respect for the President's House extends to its resident family. In her memoir, First Lady Barbara Bush recorded her astonishment at the public reaction when she and her husband opened the White House to the public at eight A.M. the day after George's inauguration.

Some people had waited in line all night for the chance to take the by now standard tour. "We saw you come in last night!" they yelled when they caught sight of Barbara gazing out the window at them. They were referring to the Bushes' return from the inaugural balls.

George's mother, Dorothy Walker Bush, had a wonderful time, sitting in her wheelchair, waving to the crowds from her bedroom window. When the crowd called: "Come on out!" Barbara just smiled but Grandma Bush regarded it as an invitation. A few hours later, Barbara looked out the window again and saw her mother-in-law on the lawn in her wheelchair, shaking hands with all comers. She in turn inspired several Bush grandchildren (there were ten of them at the time) to join her.

Barbara decided to go downstairs and shake hands with some of the visitors inside the White House. Alas, the line came to a dead stop as people bombarded her with questions and requests for autographs. As the frantic White House police begged the first lady to disappear, about eighty-five tourists on the North Portico started singing "God Bless America." Barbara retreated with tears in her eyes.

XVIII
★★★

The White House is the only residence of a head of state in the entire world that can be visited by the public free of charge. Before the terrorist attacks of September 11, 2001, it was open Tuesday through Saturday from ten A.M. to 12 noon. This wonderful privilege was one of the many casualties of that dire day. Since then, the Secret Service has decreed that only limited public tours are permissible, and even these may be suspended in the event of a serious security threat. The tours are restricted to school and youth groups and military and veterans organizations. They can be arranged by contacting a senator or representative, and participants can expect to be screened in advance to reduce the threat of terrorism.

Still open, and well worth a stop, is the White House Visitor Center on East Executive Avenue. It features exhibits about the mansion and its occupants plus a half-hour video on the storied subject.

A tour of the White House begins in the East Wing. Visitors pass through the Ground Floor Corridor before ascending the staircase to view the historic rooms on the main floor. The corridor was a grubby work area until Charles McKim got his hands on it in 1902. He restored the vaulted ceiling and covered the walls and floors with marble. It is now a red-carpeted entrance worthy of welcoming the most exalted VIPs. Among the displays is a gallery of presidential busts and other sculptures and a Sheraton-style breakfront displaying pieces of White House china and glass.

I have a special fondness for the rooms that open off the ground-floor corridor because their wood paneling was made from the timber that was removed from the White House during the Truman renovations. The Vermeil Room on the south side of the corridor features an exhibit of some rare pieces of vermeil—gilded silver. They are part of a collection bequeathed to the White House in 1958 by Mrs. Margaret Thompson Biddle. The room, which is used as a ladies' sitting room at formal events, also contains portraits of several first ladies, including two I especially like: Douglas Chandor's painting of Eleanor Roosevelt that captures her humanitarian spirit, and Elizabeth Shoumatoff's lovely likeness of Lady Bird Johnson.

Next door to the Vermeil Room is the China Room, where items from the White House china collection are displayed and Howard Chandler Christy's stunning portrait of Grace Coolidge dominates one wall. On the north side of the corridor is the library, with a large collection of books, continuing the White House tradition started by First Lady Abigail Fillmore in 1851. For formal events it serves as a male counterpart to the ladies' sitting room across the hall. It's always a shock for me to realize that prior to the 1902 renovation, this beautiful space was a laundry room.

Upstairs, visitors explore the State Rooms I have described in earlier pages. The East Room still features the Stuart portrait of George Washington that Dolley Madison rescued from British torches so long ago. On the mantels of the west wall are exquisite golden bronze candelabra bought in France by Elizabeth Monroe in 1817. She may have been a snob but she had superb taste.

The Green Room, completely redone by First Lady Pat Nixon in 1971, is still a treasure trove of Federal period furniture; many of the pieces were designed by the great New York cabinetmaker Duncan Phyfe. Don't miss Gilbert Stuart's wonderful portraits of President John Quincy Adams and First Lady Louisa Catherine Adams. These paintings remained in the Adams family until a descendant donated them in 1971. (His name: John Quincy Adams!) My favorite painting in this room is the famous "thumb portrait" of the mature Benjamin Franklin at the summit of his scientific fame in 1767.

The Blue Room, refurbished by Hillary Clinton in 1995, has seven of the gilded chairs Elizabeth Monroe purchased from one of Paris's foremost cabinetmakers. The rest of the furniture is in the same elegant Empire style. Here hangs a wonderful portrait of Thomas Jefferson in his vice presidential days by Rembrandt Peale. Over the sofa is a fine portrait of "His Accidency," John Tyler, looking as combative in oil as he was in life. The mahogany marble-top table is one of the oldest pieces of furniture in continuous residence; it was bought by the Monroes in 1817 and has never left the mansion.

The Red Room is also in the Empire style, one of my favorite modes. I love the hints of ancient Egypt, Greece, and Rome in its lines. This room's crowning glory, as I've noted on an earlier page, is the portrait of beautiful Angelica Singleton Van Buren in a stunning white dress, possibly one she wore in her White House tableaus. The lady—and the dress—deserve a second notice. During the 1840s, this was called the Washington Room because Stuart's portrait of the ultimate Founding Father resided here. Also not to be missed is Gilbert Stuart's portrait of the Firstest with the Mostest Lady of them all, Dolley Madison. She still emanates the marvelous good cheer that made her supreme.

The State Dining Room is almost as impressive as the East Room. Enlarged over the years, it can now seat 140 people comfortably. The Queen Anne–style chairs around the table go back to the Monroes. Above the mantel hangs George P. A. Healy's contemplative portrait of Abraham Lincoln, gazing down at the nation he preserved. He's all by himself on these walls—a lonely splendor that no one will ever contest.

That's a small sample of what you'll see in the President's House when you visit during the hours when it is also the people's house.

The entrance hall at the North Portico has witnessed over two hundred years of history.
Let's hope there are hundreds more to come.
Credit: White House Historical Association

16

★★★

The White House Forever

Ahundred years from now, if another presidential daughter walks by the White House in the twilight, what will she see and think? I am prepared to bet a large sum that it will be the same glowing vision, igniting different memories but invoking essentially the same experience. She will wonder how she survived it—and at the same time feel a wry mingling of gratitude.

By that time, the walls of the old house may be lined with titanium to withstand terrorist attacks, and the Secret Service may have equipment that enables them to do everything but read the minds of visitors. But the staff will still be smiling and undaunted by any and all presidential requests. Children will still play in the upstairs halls and pets will romp on the south lawn. The West Wing will be as full of devoted, energetic staffers as it is today and the media will still be tormenting presidents and press secretaries with nosy questions. Diplomats and VIPs will mingle at receptions and state dinners. The first lady will preside in the East Wing, continuing the White House tradition of graciousness and good taste and perhaps exerting some womanpower along the way—that is, unless there is a first man, trying to carve out a new role for presidential spouses. The president will prowl the halls at night, studying the faces of his—or her—predecessors on the walls.

Most important, the American people will remain fascinated by the President's House. It will continue to be not only the most beautiful public building in Washington, but a living museum of the nation's history. The mansion's story will recall the triumphs and tragedies of the United States of America and its chosen leaders. At the heart of the story will be the underlying idea everyone who lives or works there senses: glory. I still feel it every time I walk into 1600 Pennsylvania Avenue. I hope this book has brought some of it alive for you.

★★★

Presidents and Their Wives

★ **George Washington**
Martha Dandridge Custis Washington
April 30, 1789–March 3, 1796

★ **John Adams**
Abigail Smith Adams
March 4, 1797–March 3, 1801

★ **Thomas Jefferson**
Martha Wayles Skelton Jefferson
March 4, 1801–March 3, 1809

★ **James Madison**
Dolley Payne Todd Madison
March 4, 1809–March 3, 1817

★ **James Monroe**
Elizabeth Kortright Monroe
March 4, 1817–March 3, 1825

★ **John Quincy Adams**
Louisa Catherine Johnson Adams
March 4, 1825–March 3, 1829

★ **Andrew Jackson**
Rachel Donelson Robards Jackson
March 4, 1829–March 3, 1837

★ **Martin Van Buren**
Hannah Hoes Van Buren
March 4, 1837–March 3, 1841

★ **William Henry Harrison**
Anna Symmes Harrison
March 4, 1841–April 4, 1841

★ **John Tyler**
Letitia Christian Tyler
Julia Gardiner Tyler
April 6, 1841–March 3, 1845

★ **James Knox Polk**
Sarah Childress Polk
March 4, 1845–March 3, 1849

★ **Zachary Taylor**
Margaret Smith Taylor
March 4, 1849–July 9, 1850

☆ **Millard Fillmore**
Abigail Powers Fillmore
Caroline Carmichael McIntosh
  Fillmore
July 10, 1850–March 3, 1853

☆ **Franklin Pierce**
Jane Appleton Pierce
March 4, 1853–March 3, 1857

☆ **James Buchanan**
March 4, 1857–March 3, 1861

☆ **Abraham Lincoln**
Mary Todd Lincoln
March 4, 1861–April 15, 1865

☆ **Andrew Johnson**
Eliza McCardle Johnson
April 15, 1865–March 3, 1869

☆ **Ulysses S. Grant**
Julia Dent Grant
March 4, 1869–March 3, 1877

☆ **Rutherford B. Hayes**
Lucy Webb Hayes
March 4, 1877–March 3, 1881

☆ **James A. Garfield**
Lucretia Rudolph Garfield
March 4, 1881–September 19, 1881

☆ **Chester A. Arthur**
Ellen Herndon Arthur
September 20, 1881–March 3, 1885

☆ **Grover Cleveland**
Frances Folsom Cleveland
March 4, 1885–March 3, 1889

☆ **Benjamin Harrison**
Caroline Scott Harrison
Mary Lord Dimmick Harrison
March 4, 1889–March 3, 1893

☆ **Grover Cleveland**
Frances Folsom Cleveland
March 4, 1893–March 3, 1897

☆ **William McKinley**
Ida Saxton McKinley
March 4, 1897–September 14, 1901

☆ **Theodore Roosevelt**
Alice Lee Roosevelt
Edith Carow Roosevelt
September 14, 1901–March 3, 1909

☆ **William Howard Taft**
Helen Herron Taft
March 4, 1909–March 3, 1913

☆ **Woodrow Wilson**
Ellen Axson Wilson
Edith Bolling Galt Wilson
March 4, 1913–March 3, 1921

☆ **Warren G. Harding**
Florence Kling De Wolfe Harding
March 4, 1921–August 2, 1923

☆ **Calvin Coolidge**
Grace Goodhue Coolidge
August 3, 1923–March 3, 1929

☆ **Herbert Hoover**
Lou Henry Hoover
March 4, 1929–March 3, 1933

☆ **Franklin D. Roosevelt**
Anna Eleanor Roosevelt Roosevelt
March 4, 1933–April 12, 1945

☆ **Harry S Truman**
Elizabeth Wallace Truman
April 12, 1945–January 20, 1953

✷ **Dwight D. Eisenhower**
Mamie Doud Eisenhower
January 20, 1953–January 20, 1961

✷ **John F. Kennedy**
Jacqueline Bouvier Kennedy
January 20, 1961–November 22, 1963

✷ **Lyndon B. Johnson**
Claudia (Lady Bird) Taylor Johnson
November 22, 1963–January 20, 1969

✷ **Richard M. Nixon**
Patricia Ryan Nixon
January 20, 1969–August 9, 1974

✷ **Gerald Ford**
Elizabeth Bloomer Warren Ford
August 9, 1974–January 20,1977

✷ **Jimmy Carter**
Rosalynn Smith Carter
January 20, 1977–January 20, 1981

✷ **Ronald Reagan**
Jane Wyman Reagan
Nancy Davis Reagan
January 20, 1981–January 20, 1989

✷ **George H. W. Bush**
Barbara Pierce Bush
January 20, 1989–January 20, 1993

✷ **William J. Clinton**
Hillary Rodham Clinton
January 20, 1993–January 20, 2001

✷ **George W. Bush**
Laura Welch Bush
January 20, 2001–

Index

Page numbers in *italics* refer to illustrations.

Adams, Abigail, 12–13, 24, 25, 93, 142, 186, 187–88, 190, 378
Adams, John, 24, 48, 67, 93–94, 103, 186, 197, 320
Adams, John Quincy, 7–8, 32, 48–49, 64, 126–29, 131, 186–87, 219–20, 321, 349, 374, 391
Adams, Louisa Catherine, 126–29, 142, 144, 186–87, 219–20, 391
Adams, Sherman, 16–17, 171–72, 175, 178
aides, 151–81
airborne attacks, 363–64
Amen, Marion Cleveland, 238, 239, 240
Appointments Lobby, 151
Arlington National Cemetery, 246, 345
Army, U.S., 107–8, 113, 336
Arthur, Chester A., 15, 28–29, 30, 105, 380

Baker, James, 178
Bennett, James Gordon, 322–23, 324
Biddle, Mrs. Margaret Thompson, 390
Bill of Rights, 319
Birdzell, Donald T., 346, 347
Bizet, Charles, 48–49
Blair, Francis Preston, 320–21
Blair, Tony, 120
Blair House, 42, 320, 345–47
Blue Room, 26, 35, 44, 94, 125, 140, 248, 263, 270, 276, 278, 279, 391
bodyguards, 351
Boettiger, Anna, 227
Booth, John Wilkes, 80–81
Bosanquet, Esther Cleveland, 212, 238–40
Boulanger, Joseph, 188
Bowman, Henry, 188
brides, *260*, 261–89
Briesler, John, 186
Broder, David, 341
Brooks, Noah, 324
Bruce, Preston, 207–8
Bryant, Traphes, 311, 312
Buchanan, James, 15, 55, 81, 105, 137–39, 153, 190, 191
Buchwald, Art, 177
Bundy, McGeorge, 85, 173, 174

Bush, Barbara, 67, 97, 205, 313–14, 388–89
Bush, Dorothy Walker, 389
Bush, George H. W., 65, 67, 313–14, 339, 385, 389
Bush, George W., 36, 74–75, 120, 180, 257, 301, 314, 341, 342, 383
Bush, Jenna and Barbara, 257–58, 314
Bush, Laura, 120, 257, 387
butlers, 117, 192–93, 207, 356
Butt, Archie, 158–60

Cabinet Room, 75–76, 86–87, 151
Calhoun, Floride, 131–33
Calhoun, John C., 131–33
Camp David, 176, 257, 286, 288
Cannon, Joseph "Uncle Joe," 108, 298
Capitol, 23–24, 31
Carnegie, Andrew, 275
Carter, Amy, 299–300
Carter, Jimmy, 64, 67, 96–97, 120, 144–45, 299–300, 339, 363
Carter, Rosalyn, 96–97, 144–45, 299–300
Casals, Pablo, 6
Castro, Fidel, 86
Central Intelligence Agency (CIA), 88
Chiang Kai-shek, Madame, 224–25
chief of staff, 177–79
chief usher, 183–86, 191, 224, 355
children, *232*, 233–59, 395
  Clinton, 256–57, 258
  Coolidge, 253–56
  Garfield, 246–48
  Grant, 242–44
  Kennedy, 234–38
  Lincoln, 241–42
  Roosevelt, *232*, 249–53
  Secret Service and, 236, 257, 366–67
Children's Garden, *46*, 67–68
China, 90, 120, 224, 229, 265
China Room, 390
Christian, George, 161–63
Christmas, 218–19, 236, 383
Christy, Howard Chandler, 311
Churchill, Winston, 6, 165, 217–19, 315, 331–32

Civil War, 13, 18, 28, 29, 58, 77–80, 137, 138, 139, 155, 246, 323, 325, 351–52, 377
Clay, Henry, 129, 374
Cleveland, Frances Folsom, 2, 60, 141, 157, 238–40, 261–64
Cleveland, Grover, 2, 11, 15, 30, 59–60, 116, 156–57, 234, 238–40, 261–64
  children of, 238–40
  media and, 325–27
  wedding of, 261–64
Cleveland, Richard, 239, 240
Cleveland, Rose, 141–42
Cleveland, Ruth, 238
Clifford, Clark, 171
Clinton, Bill, 9–10, 15, 17, 36, 64, 104, 115, 117, 145–47, 212, 256–58, 300–301, 364, 384, 385, 388
  media and, 340–41
  pets of, 292, 300–301
  staff, 179–80
Clinton, Chelsea, 256–57, 258, 301
Clinton, Hillary Rodham, 5, 9–10, 64, 104, 117, 145–47, 256–58, 300, 341, 385, 391
  health care plan, 145–47
Cockburn, Admiral Sir George, 73–74
coffees and teas, 93, 115, 117–19
Collazo, Oscar, 345–47
Color Team, 97–98, 300, 310
Comment Line office, 386–87
Commission of Fine Arts, 38, 40
Communism, 86–87, 90, 171, 226, 229
Congress, 4, 8–9, 23–24, 30, 44, 51, 88, 93, 94, 108, 127, 129, 144, 146, 188, 190–91, 246, 329, 334, 350
Connelly, Matt, *150*, 169–70
Constitution, 11, 107, 189, 319
Coolidge, Calvin, 36–37, 41, 116, 163–64, 189, 191, 195, 201–2, 212, 253–56, 297–99, 304–5, 330, *344*, 359–60, 382, 383
  children of, 253–56
  pets of, 305–6, 310–11
Coolidge, Calvin, Jr., 253–54
Coolidge, Florence Trumbell, 255–56

Coolidge, Grace, 8, 12, 191, 202, 253–56, 297, 305, 311, 390
Coolidge, John, 253–56
Corder, Frank, 364
Correspondence Office, 385
Cortelyou, George, 157, 198, 353–54
Cox, Edward, 285–88
Cox, Tricia Nixon, 89, 192, 207, 285–88
Crawford, William, 349
Crim, Howell, 224–25
Cuban missile crisis, 85–87
Currie, Betty, 301
Curtis, Charles, 108, 109
Czolgosz, Leon, 354

Daniel, Clifton, 98, 337
Davis, Jefferson, 296–97
death threats and assassination attempts, 345–57, 362–67
Declaration of Independence, 73
De Gaulle, Charles, 228–29
Democratic Party, 22, 53, 55, 138
Democratic-Republicans, 22–26, 348, 372
DePriest, Mrs. Oscar, 223
Dewey, George, 107–8
Dewey, Thomas E., 316, 336
dinners, see receptions and dinners
Diplomatic Reception Room, 84, 90
Donelson, Emily, 133–34, 187
doormen, 196–200, 207, 350–51, 378
Dougherty, Joseph, 197
Downing, Andrew Jackson, 53–54, 59, 63

Early, Steve, 168, 333
Easter egg roll, 246, 384
East Room, 33, 39, 42, 81, 96, 100, 101, 111, 152, 214, 242, 247, 250, 269, 270, 272, 276, 284, 286, 298, 337, 341, 374, 375, 378, 379, 380, 382, 391
East Wing, 123, 145, 390, 395
Eaton, John Henry, 130, 133
Eaton, Peggy, 129–33, 134
Edward VII, King of England, 81, 138–39, 265
Einstein, Albert, 386
Eisenhower, Barbara Ann, 366
Eisenhower, David, 192, 285
Eisenhower, Dwight D., 3, 16–17, 44, 171–72, 175, 183, 195–96, 228, 285, 292, 295, 337, 366

Eisenhower, Julie Nixon, 70, 89, 90, 192, 285, 287
Eisenhower, Mamie, 145, 183–84, 193, 195–96, 214–15, 295
Elizabeth, Queen of England, 110, 210, 213–14, 215–16
Elizabeth II, Queen of England, 214
Ellipse, 59, 308, 380, 384
Elliptical Saloon, 26, 125, 134, 377
Emancipation Proclamation, 77–79
England, 9, 11, 24, 48, 49, 55, 110, 120, 138, 195, 215–16, 219, 220, 265, 268, 315
War of 1812, 71–74
Evarts, William, 112–13
Executive Office Building, 34, 35–36, 337, 339

families, see children; first ladies
Federal Bureau of Investigation (FBI), 88
Federal City, 21–23
Federalists, 22, 24, 221
Ficklin, Charles, 207
Ficklin, Samuel, 207
Fields, Alonzo, 117–20, 205–8, 227–28
Fillmore, Abigail, 44
Fillmore, Millard, 8, 44, 53–54, 104
fires, 10
of 1814, 26–27, 74
of 1929, 37
first ladies, 2–3, 6, 18–19, 123–49
as campaigners, 126–29, 144–45
power of, 123–49
substitute, 129–42
see also specific first ladies
First Ladies (Truman), 5
Fleischer, Ari, 341
Folsom, Oscar, 262
Ford, Betty, 90
Ford, Gerald, 5, 12, 65, 90–91, 293–94, 339, 347, 364, 388
Ford, Susan, 293
Forrestal, James, 170
Fourth of July, 82–83, 115–17
Fox, Vicente, 120
France, 11, 24, 44, 123–24, 220, 228–29
Furman, Bess, 315
furnishings, 8–10, 34, 43–45, 95–96, 212, 374, 375, 378, 390–91
Kennedy, 43–44

Gann, Dolly, 108–10
gardens and grounds, 8, 21, 34, 47–69, 190
Children's Garden, 46, 67–68
Fillmore, 53–54
Jackson, 49–51
Johnson, 66–68
Kennedy, 65–67
Olmstead, 63–64
Roosevelt, 60–62
Rose Garden, 38, 62–63, 65–66
Wilson, 62–63, 66, 67
Garfield, Harry, 246–48
Garfield, James A., 28, 59, 213, 245, 246–48, 325
children of, 246–48
death of, 247–48, 353
Garfield, Jim, 246–48
Garfield, Lucretia, 246–48
George VI, King of England, 210, 213–14, 215–16
Germany, 110, 143, 215, 216, 218, 265
ghosts, 13–14
Gift Office, 387–88
gifts, 99, 387–88
wedding, 265, 269, 275
Giusta, Antoine Michel, 186–87, 188, 220
Globe, 320–21
Goldwater, Barry, 176
Goodwin, Richard, 174
Gouverneur, Maria Monroe, 271–72, 273
Gouverneur, Samuel Lawrence, 271–72
Grand Staircase, 43, 98, 266, 270, 278
Grant, Buck, 243, 270
Grant, Fred, 243, 270
Grant, Jesse, 243, 244, 295, 307
Grant, Julia, 18, 58, 198, 242–44, 269, 270, 325
Grant, Ulysses S., 18, 28, 58, 81, 189, 191, 242–44, 295, 307, 325, 379
children of, 242–44, 267–71
Great Depression, 37, 84, 116, 164, 194, 331, 356, 382
greenhouses, 33–34, 51, 55–56, 60–61
Green Room, 41, 391
guests and guest rooms, 210, 211–31
of FDR, 210, 212, 215–19, 223–28
royalty, 210, 213–16, 223–24, 229–30

Gugler, Eric, 38
Guiteau, Charles Julius, 247

Hagerty, James, 337, 338
Hagner, Belle, 274–75
Haig, Alexander, 89
"Hail to the Chief," 98, 104, 105
Haldeman, H. R., 88, 193–94
Hamilton, Alexander, 22, 221
Hamilton, George, 283–84
handshaking, 114–15, 116, 370
Hannegan, Bob, 335
Harding, Florence, 163, 191, 310, 381–82
Harding, Warren G., 15, 143, 161–63, 191, 201, 253, 291, 309–10, 357, 359, 381–82
Harrison, Benjamin, 30, 59, 162, 185, 248–49, 304, 353, 379–80
Harrison, Caroline, 30, 379–80
Harrison, William Henry, 9, 51, 197
Havel, Václav, 104
Hay, John, 78, 154–55, 181, 213
Hayes, Fanny, 245–46
Hayes, Lucy Webb, 18, 59, 111–13, 245–46, 250, 298
Hayes, Rutherford B., 58–59, 64, 95, 103, 111–13, 245–46, 304, 379, 380
Hayes, Scott, 245–46
Hayes, Webb, 103
Henderson, Mrs. John B., 32
Henry, Buck, 153
Henry, Prince of Russia, 110–11
Hickok, Lorena, 227
history, 11–13, 71–91
Hoban, James, 22–23, 25, 26, 27, 32, 35, 42, 45
Hoover, Herbert, 15, 37, 64–65, 85, 108, 109, 116, 152, 164, 186, 193–95, 223, 229–31, 292, 309, 310, 335, 347, 355–56, 357, 359, 382
Hoover, Ike, 185–86, 192, 239, 355
Hoover, Lou, 13, 75, 118, 186, 193, 223, 229–31, 240, 356, 382
Hopkins, Harry, 164–65, 168, 176, 227
Horton, John, 102
household staff, *182*, 183–208, 215, 282
    slaves as, 187–89

tipping, 195
transition from one administration to the next, 191–94
White House jinx and, 194–96
housekeepers, 200–204
Howe, Louis, 212

Inauguration Day, 191–92, 194
Internet, 340–41
Iran-Contra scandal, 178–79
Israel, 169, 171, 362
Italy, 120, 354

Jackson, Andrew, 8, 14, 15, 27, 42, 49–51, 54, 55, 74, 100–102, 107, 128, 129–34, 187, 188, 213, 251, 307, 320–21, 349, 375, 379
Jackson, Rachel, 131, 187
Jackson magnolia, 47, 50, 65, 364
Jaffray, Elizabeth, 200–202
Japan, 97, 296
Jefferson, Thomas, 12, 15, 22, 24–25, 33, 48, 58, 82–83, 93–94, 103–4, 106–7, 116, 123, 130, 152–53, 186, 188, 197, 220–21, 320, 348, 391
    attitude towards women, 123–25
    tourism and, 372–73
Jiang Zemin, 120
jinx, White House, 194–96
Johnson, Andrew, 75, 139–41, 325, 353, 377, 378, 379
Johnson, Lady Bird, 18, 46, 66–68, 94, 204, 280–85, 313, 390
Johnson, Lyndon B., 16, 17, 36, 94, 102, 117, 173, 184–85, 193, 204, 257, 280–85, 388
    children of, 280–85
    pets of, 291, 311–13
    staff, 174–78

Kennedy, Caroline, 211, 234–38, 291, 296, 299, 302, 388
Kennedy, Jacqueline, 8, 43–44, 67, 87, 95, 295–96, 301, 338
    children of, 234–38
    redecorating and entertaining, 43–44, 95, 98, 215
Kennedy, John F., 6, 36, 43–44, 65–67, 75, 85–87, 173–74, 215

assassination of, 94, 237, 280, 358
    children of, 234–38
    Cuban missile crisis, 85–87
    media and, 337–38
    pets of, 291, 292, 295–96, 299, 301–2
    staff, 85, 173–74
Kennedy, John F., Jr., 234–38
Kennerly, David, 293
Key, Francis Scott, 74
Khrushchev, Nikita, 86–87, 296
Kissinger, Henry, 89, 90
kitchen, 97, 192
Knox, Philander C., 76, 77
Krock, Arthur, 332

Lafayette, Marquis de, 219–20
Lafayette Square, 54–55
La Guardia, Fiorello, 144
Lamon, Ward, 351
Lamont, Daniel, 156–57, 325–26
Lane, Harriet, 55, 137–39
Lash, Joseph, 227
League of Nations, 4
Lee, Robert E., 42, 78, 80, 352
Lee House, 42
LeHand, Marguerite "Missy," 166–67
L'Enfant, Pierre Charles, 21–22, 31
letters to the president, 384–86
Lewis, Meriwether, 83, 152–53
Lewis and Clark, 83, 372, 373
library, 390
Lincoln, Abraham, 12, 13, 14, 56, 57, 75, 77–82, 154–55, 181, 199–200, 211–13, 302–3, 377, 379, 392
    assassination of, 80–81, 199, 352–53, 377–78
    children of, 241–42
    death threats, 351–52
    media and, 323–25
Lincoln, Evelyn, 173–74
Lincoln, Mary, 56–57, 79, 81–82, 155, 211, 241–42, 352, 377–78
Lincoln, Tad, 199, 241–42, 302–3, 307
Lincoln, Willie, 155, 241–42, 302
Lincoln Bedroom, 34, 77–78, 88, 90, 211–13, 217, 219, 227
Lincoln Sitting Room, 88–89, 227
Long, Ava, 118–19

Longworth, Alice Roosevelt, 109–10, 111, 212, *232*, 249–53, 275, 282, 284, 287, 307
wedding of, 264–67
Longworth, Nick, 110, 265–67
López-Portillo, José, 299–300
Louisiana Purchase, 82–83
luncheons, 93, 117, 118, 183

Madison, Dolley, 18, 25–26, 72–74, 106, *122*, 125–28, 134, 142, 147, 186, 379, 391, 392
Madison, James, 25–26, 72–74, 83, 106, 125–26, 319, 348
Maher, Jemmy, 49–51, 64
Marine Band, U.S., 6, 90, 95, 98, 100, 103–5, 112, 138, 139, 234–35, 263, 270, 276, 300, 371, 376, 384
Marshall, John, 372
Maverick, Maury, 165–66
McAdoo, Nellie Wilson, 273, 276, 277–80
McAdoo, William Gibbs, 277–80
McKee, Benjamin Harrison, 249, 304
McKim, Charles, 31, 33–35, 38, 42, 60–61, 84, 111, 213, 327, 390
McKim, Eddie, 15–16
McKinley, Ida, 60
McKinley, William, 32, 60, 75, 76, 107–8, 157, 327
assassination of, 198, 353–55
McLean, John R., 267
McMillan Plan, 31–32, 38
media, 5, 8, 84, 148, 149, 156, 170–71, 174–77, 233, 257, 285, 294, *318*, 319–42
Cleveland and, 325–27
Clinton and, 340–41
Kennedy and, 337–38
Lincoln and, 323–25
pressroom renovations, 334–35, 339
Reagan and, *318*, 339–40
Roosevelts and, 327–29, 330–35, 338, 341
Truman and, 333, 335–37
see also radio addresses; *specific publications;* television
Medill, Joseph, 324–25
Meese, Ed, 178
Mellon, Rachel Lambert, 66, 67
Merry, Anthony and Elizabeth, 124–25
Mesnier, Roland, 120–21

Mexico, 120, 299, 375
Meyer, Mrs. Eugene, 109–10
military aides, 102–3, 267
Molotov, Vyacheslav, 225–26
Monroe, Elizabeth, 27, 96, 130, 272, 391
Monroe, James, 26–27, 34, 49, 75, 96, 116, 126, 127, 219, 271–72, 348–49, 373–74
Monroe plateau, 95–96
Morgan, J. P., 76–77
Moton, Dr. Robert R., 223
Moyers, Bill, 174, 175–77
Muffler, Johnny, 207

Napoleon Bonaparte, 82, 83
National Intelligencer, 320
Native Americans, 6, 246, 265, 372, 373
Navy, U.S., 107–8, 113
Nesbitt, Henrietta, 202–4, 215
Nevin, Blanche, 274, 275
New Deal, 164–65
New Year's Day, 115–16, 140, *370*
New York *Evening Post,* 323
New York *Herald,* 322, 324, 378
New York Times, 145, 146, 165, 326, 332, 337
Nicolay, John George, 154–55, 181, 213
Nixon, Pat, 44, 89, 90, 145, 192, 285–88, 391
Nixon, Richard M., 15, 44, 88–91, 148, 185, 192, 193–94, 228–29, 285–88, 334, 338–39, 363
pets of, 292
resignation, *70*, 88–91
Norman, Jessye, 6
North Portico, 25, 27, 33, 43, 65, 200, 252, 300, 304, 319, 327, *394*
Nugent, Luci Johnson, 261, 280–83, 287, 312
Nugent, Patrick, 281–83, 312

O'Donnell, Kenneth, 173–74
Office of Civilian Defense, 144
Ogle, Charles, 8–9, 377
Olmstead, Frederick Law, Jr., 31, 63–64
O'Neil, Jemmy, 197
O'Neil, Thomas, 351
Ousley, John, 49, 51–54
Oval Office, 38, 62, 68, 86, 87, 88, 142, 151, 158, 168, 173, 174, 179, 229, 230, 292, 302, 306, *318*, 333, 345, 357, 361, 381

Paine, Thomas, 220–22
paintings, 73, 135, 379, 382, 390–92
Panetta, Leon, 364
Parks, Lillian Rogers, 3, 14, 195
Patterson, Martha, 139–41
Pearson, Drew, 335–37
Pebble Beach, 319, 335
pell-mell etiquette, 106–7, 124
Pendel, Thomas, 199–200, 249
Pentagon, 71, 74
Perry, Commodore Matthew C., 296
pets, 242, *290*, 291–317
Clinton, 292, 300–301, 384
Coolidge, 305–6, 310–11
Johnson, 291, 311–13
Kennedy, 291, 292, 295–96, 299, 301–2
Lincoln, 302–3
Roosevelt, *290*, 291–93, 297–98, 302, 306–7, 314–17
Petticoat War, 131–34
Pfister, Henry, 58, 60–61
phone calls, 386–87
Pierce, Franklin, 55, 104, 116, 153, 296–97, 321, 323, 351, 371, 376–77
Pierce, Jane, 104, 153
Pinkerton, Allan, 351
policemen, 345–47, 351–52, 356
Polk, James, 53, 98, 104, 115, 139, 188, 323, 375–76
Polk, Sarah, 12, 98, 142, 375
Porter, John Addison, 157
power, 15–17
women, 123–49
Presley, Elvis, 363
press conferences, 329–42
press secretaries, 4, 168, 170–71, 174–77
Preston, Robert, 364
Price, William, 326–27
Prince of Wales Room, 81, 211, 212, 214
Prohibition, 119
protocol and etiquette, 96–97, 105–12

Queens' Bedroom, 213–15

racism, 187–90, 222–23, 332–33
radio addresses, 84–85, 90, 330
Rayburn, Sam, 235
Reagan, Nancy, 97, 178, 179, 182, 205

Reagan, Ronald, 12, 205, 318, 347, 385, 388
  media and, *318*, 339–40
  staff, 177–79
  receptions and dinners, 6, 7, 24, 26, 39, *92*, 93–121, 125, 167, 193, 196, 205, 214, 216, 242, 298, 299, 395
Red Room, 26, 41, 135, 267, 353, 355, 382, 391–92
Reedy, George, 176
Regan, Don, 177–79
Reich, Robert, 17, 179
religion, 86–87, 170
Renehan, Martin, 197, 199
renovation and redecoration, 8, 27–45, 95–96, 375, 380
  Arthur, 28–30, 34
  Coolidge, 36–37, 38, 41
  Harrison, 30, 31
  Kennedy, 43–44, 95, 98, 215
  McKim (1902), 33–35, 42, 60, 123, 192, 213, 327, 380, 390
  post-War of 1812, 262–67, 36, 42, 379
  Truman, 38–43, 45, 65, 95, 334, 345, 390
Republican Party, 22, 77, 137, 170, 189, 316
Revolutionary War, 219, 220, 221
Riley, Ellen, 202, 305
Robb, Charles, 102, 284–85, 312
Robb, Lynda Bird Johnson, 102, 261, 280, 282, 283–85, 287, 312, 366–67
Rockefeller, John D., 329
Rogers, Maggie, 3, 195
Roosevelt, Archie, *232*, 249–53, 291, 302
Roosevelt, Edith, 10, 33–35, 60–62, 115, 213, *232*, 249–53, 307
Roosevelt, Eleanor, 5, 117–18, 143–44, 147, 167, 189, 193, 202–4, 215–17, 224–28, 266, 315, 317, 361, 390
  media and, 332–33
Roosevelt, Ethel, *232*, 249–53
Roosevelt, Franklin D., 9, 15, 44, 47, 63, 65, 84–85, 117–18, 120, 123, 143–44, 189, 193, 202–4, *210*, 266, *290*, 357, 359, 380, 382, 385
  death of, 316–17, 333
  fireside chats, 84–85, 90

  guests of, *210*, 212, 215–19, 223–28
  media and, 330–33, 335, 338
  pets of, *290*, 292–93, 314–17
  Secret Service and, 360–61, 365
  staff, 164–69
Roosevelt, Kermit, *232*, 249–53, 306
Roosevelt, Quentin, *232*, 249–53, 302, 306
Roosevelt, Theodore, 6, 10, 33–35, 60, 75–77, 95, 102, 108, 110–11, 157–59, 191, 211, 222, *232*, 249–53, 257, 275, 355
  children of, *232*, 249–53, 264–67
  media and, 327–29, 331, 334, 341
  pets of, 292–93, 297–98, 301, 306–7
Roosevelt, Theodore, Jr., *232*, 249–53
Root, Elihu, 107–8
Rose Bedroom, 213–14, 217
Rose Garden, 38, 62–63, 65–66, 151, 285–87
Rosenman, Sam, 168
Ross, Charlie, 4, 170–71, 257–58
Rove, Karl, 180
Royall, Anne, 321
royal visits, 81, 110–12, 138–39, 213–16, 223–24, 229–30
Russia, 85–87, 112, 171, 225–26, 229, 296

Salinger, Pierre, 291, 338
Sartoris, Algernon, 267–71
Sartoris, Nellie Grant, 243, *260*, 267–71
Sayre, Jessie Wilson, 274–78
Sayre, Frank, 274–78
secretaries, 152–81
Secret Service, 3–4, 39, 71, 198, 233, *344*, 345–68, 383, 386
  beginnings of, 354
  death threats and assassination attempts, 345–57, 362–67
  protection for presidential families, 366–67
  Technical Security Division, 361–63
  training, 358
  Uniformed Division, 357–58
segregation, 187–90, 332–33
September 11 terrorist attacks, 7, 71, 74, 363–64, 383

Seward, William, 78, 79
Sinatra, Frank, 6
Sioussat, Jean-Pierre, 186
Situation Room, 21
slaves, 3, 77–79
  as White House staff, 187–89
Slemp, Bascom, 163–64
Smith, Ira, *255–56*, 385
Smith, Margaret Bayard, 127, 373
Smith, Merriman, 152, 331, 333
social events, 6–7, 24, 26, 39, *92*, 93–121, 125–28, 132
  Buchanan, 138–39
  handshaking, 114–15, 116
  Hayes, 111–13
  Jackson, 100–102, 107, 131–34
  Kennedy, 95, 98
  Marine Band at, 103–5
  protocol and etiquette, 96–97, 105–12
  Roosevelt, 102, 108–11, 115, 117–18
  royal visits, 81, 110–12, 138–39, 213–16, 223–24, 229–30
  Taft, 99–100
  Tyler, 135–37
  weddings, 260–89
Sorenson, Ted, 173
Sousa, John Philip, 105
South Portico, *xii*, 25, 27, 59, 65, 100, 104, 218, 287, 299, 304
  Truman balcony, 8, 39–41
Soviet Union, 225–26; *see also* Russia
Spanish-American War, 75, 107, 292, 327, 328
staff, 151–208
  household, *182*, 183–208, 215, 282
  West Wing, *150*, 151–81
Stalin, Joseph, 165, 332
Stanton, Edwin, 155, 324
Starling, Edmund, *344*, 348, 358–61
"The Star-Spangled Banner," 74
State Department, 35, 36, 107, 165, 226
State Dining Room, 26, 33, 41, *92*, 95–96, 98, 100, 111, 115, 118, 125, *182*, 183, 220, 264, 266, 270, 276, 279, 282, 284, 298, 392
State Rooms, 43–44; *see also specific rooms*

Stephanopoulos, George, 146, 147, 180
stewards, 186–88, 190
Stimson, Henry L., 109
stock market crash (1929), 37
Streisand, Barbra, 6, 212
Stuart, Gilbert, 391, 392
Supreme Court, U.S., 23, 77, 88, 107, 108, 127, 170, 196

Taft, Helen, 18, 62, 158, 189, 192–93, 194, 200
Taft, William Howard, 3, 62, 99–100, 158–60, 186, 192–93, 194, 200, 308, 370, 380–81
Taylor, Zachary, 53, 104, 188–89, 190, 307–8, 376
telegraph, invention of, 323
television, 337–39, 340–41
temperance, 59, 111–13
Thomas, George, 206
Thomas, Helen, 5, 291, 341–42
Thompson, Herman, 206
Tiffany, Louis Comfort, 29, 34, 269
Time, 177
Titanic, 159–60
Tito, Josip Broz, 237
Todson, George P., 349
Torresola, Griselio, 345–47
tourism, *370*, 371–92
  Christmas, 383
  curtailed, 373–74, 377–81, 382, 383, 389
  early, 371–79
  Easter, 384
  gifts, 387–88
  letters, 384–86
  phone calls, 386–87
  souvenir hunters, 378, 379
  tours, 389–92
Towson, Colonel Nathan, 130, 131
Treaty Room, 74–77
trial balloons, 328, 331
Truman, Bess Wallace, 2–3, 5, 16, 18–19, 39–43, 114, 147–49, 204, 212, 289, 345–47
Truman, Harry S, 2–3, 4, 10, 13–16, 35, 38–43, 44, 45, 47, 65, 75, 91, 96, 110, 114, 147–49, *150*, 168, 189–90, 204, 206, 212, 226, 234, 259, 261, 288–89, 294, 385, 388
  assassination attempts against, 345–47, 362
  media and, 333, 335–37
  staff, 169–71

Truman balcony, 8, 39–41, 237
Tugwell, Rexford, 165–66
Tumulty, Joseph, 160–61
Tyler, John, 15, 51, 75, 104, 135–37, 188, 197–98, 240–41, 272–73, 350, 362, 376, 391
Tyler, Julia, 15, 75, 137, 188, 241
Tyler, Letitia, 135, 137, 272
Tyler, Priscilla Cooper, 135–37, 241

United Press, 331
Untiedt, Bryan, 229–31

Valenti, Jack, 174–76
Van Buren, Angelica, 134–35, 137, 391–92
Van Buren, Martin, 8–9, 15, 116–17, 130, 131, 132, 134–35, 197, 322, 323, 375, 377
Vardaman, Jake, 16
Vaughan, General Harry, 169, 336
Vermeil Room, 390
Victoria, Queen of England, 268
Vietnam War, 148, 176, 204, 228, 286, 338, 363

Wallace, Henry, 168
Waller, Lizzie Tyler, 272–73
Waller, William Nevison, 272
Wall Street Journal, 85
War of 1812, 26, 48, 49, 71–74, 186, 378
Warren, Earl, 196
Washington, Booker T., 222–23
Washington, George, 11, 22–23, 45, 51, 73, 138, 220, 320, 373, 379, 382, 391
Washington, Martha, 382
Washington Evening Star, 327
Watergate, 88, 338–39
Watson, Pa, 168, 169
Watt, John, 54, 55–58
Webster, Daniel, 136–37
weddings, *260*, 261–89
West, J. B., 183–84, 195, 215, 313
West Wing, 5, 6, 34, 35, 37, 75, 86, 151–82, 345, 387
  fire (1929), 37
  renovations, 37–38, 63, 327, 334–35
  staff, 151–82
Whigs, 8–9, 51, 53, 137, 188, 197

White House:
  brides and weddings, 260–89
  children, 232–59
  early design and building, *20*, 21–28
  first ladies, 123–49
  gardens and grounds, 47–69
  guests, 210–31
  history, 71–91
  household staff, 182–208
  media, 318–42
  pets, 291–317
  renovations and reconstructions, 27–45
  Secret Service, 344–68
  social events, 83–121
  tourism, 370–92
  West Wing staff, 150–81
  see also specific rooms
White House Correspondents Association, 330–34
Whitman, Christine Todd, 314
Wikoff, Henry, 57
Wilson, Edith Galt, 142–43, 161, 279
Wilson, Ellen, 38, 62–63, 66, 67, 201, 273, 274, 279
Wilson, Margaret, 273, 276, 278, 279, 381
Wilson, Woodrow, 3–4, 38, 62, 114–15, 142–43, 160–61, 191, 201, 261, 308–9, 359, 381
  children of, 273–80, 381
  media and, 329–30
Works Progress Administration (WPA), 164–65
World War I, 143, 161, 308, 329, 381
World War II, 66, 91, 116, 123, 144, 165, 215–16, 218, 223, 226, 331, 357, 382

Yellow Oval Room, 44, 300, 312

★★★

About the Author

MARGARET TRUMAN has won faithful readers with her works of biography and fiction, including her ongoing series of Capital Crimes mysteries. Her previous bestselling biographies are *Harry S Truman, Bess W. Truman,* and *First Ladies.* She lives in Manhattan.